DOUBLE AGENTS

DOUBLE AGENTS

ESPIONAGE, LITERATURE, AND LIMINAL CITIZENS

Erin G. Carlston

COLUMBIA UNIVERSITY PRESS   NEW YORK

Columbia University Press
Publishers Since 1893
New York   Chichester, West Sussex
cup.columbia.edu

Library of Congress Cataloging-in-Publication Data
Carlston, Erin G., 1962–
Double agents : espionage, literature, and liminal citizens / Erin G. Carlston.
p. cm.
Includes bibliographical references and index.
ISBN 978-0-231-13672-3 (cloth : alk. paper) —
ISBN 978 -0-231-13673-0 (pbk. : alk. paper)—ISBN 978-0-231-51009-7 (ebook)
1. Literature and society. 2. Treason in literature. 3. Espionage—History.
4. Liminality in literature. 5. Homosexuality and literature. 6. Jews in literature.
7. Communists in literature.   I. Title.

PN51.C337 2013
809′.93358—dc23   2012039622

Columbia University Press books are printed on permanent and durable acid-free paper.
This book is printed on paper with recycled content.
Printed in the United States of America

c 10 9 8 7 6 5 4 3 2 1
p 10 9 8 7 6 5 4 3 2 1

References to Internet Web sites (URLs) were accurate at the time of writing. Neither the author nor Columbia University Press is responsible for URLs that may have expired or changed since the manuscript was prepared.

"August for the people," from *On This Island* by W. H. Auden, copyright © 1937 and renewed 1962 by Random House, Inc. Used by permission of Random House, Inc., and Curtis Brown, Ltd.

"Letter to Lord Byron," copyright © 1937 and renewed 1962 by W. H. Auden; "The Secret Agent," copyright © 1934 and renewed 1962 by W. H. Auden; "On Sunday Walks," from *Collected Poems of W. H. Auden* by W. H. Auden, copyright © 1976 Edward Mendelson, William Meredith, and Monroe K. Spears, Executors of the Estate of W. H. Auden. Used by permission of Random House, Inc., and Curtis Brown, Ltd.

The Orators: An English Study, by W. H. Auden, copyright © 1967 W. H. Auden. Used by permission of Random House, Inc., and Curtis Brown, Ltd.

Quotations from the unpublished letters of W. H. Auden used by permission of Edward Mendelson. Copyright © The Estate of W. H. Auden.

Quotations from the unpublished letters of Christopher Isherwood used by permission of Don Bachardy.

Some of this material appeared previously in *Modern Fiction Studies* 48.4 (December 2002).

Some of this material appeared previously in, and is reprinted with permission from, the *Romanic Review* 100.3 (May 2009). Copyright © the Trustees of Columbia University in the City of New York.

For Charles and Alice Carlston
and for
Carisa R. Showden

CONTENTS

ILLUSTRATIONS

ACKNOWLEDGMENTS

It is a tradition of acknowledgments that, like awards shows, they reserve the major prizes for last. But since my parents claim that at their age they don't even buy green bananas, I see no reason to dally in offering them my thanks for their incalculable generosity throughout my career. Carisa Showden, best and most patient of spouses, has also lived with this book too long to have to wait another minute for the expression of my gratitude for all her support. Nancy Ranno Carlston midwifed the project at a point when the labor threatened to prove fatal. I am indebted beyond words to all of them.

Particular thanks are due to Jessica Berman, Kathryn Burns, Pamela Cheek, Maura Lafferty, Eric Muller, Shantanu Phukan, Paul Saint-Amour, David Schmid, and Jonathan Weiler for reading, commenting on, and greatly improving parts of the manuscript. Jonathan Boyarin, Jonathan Freedman, and two readers who remain unknown to me wrote staggeringly detailed, thoughtful readers' reports of the kind every writer hopes for and few are lucky enough to get. Julia Kristeva introduced me to Proust and supervised my earliest work on the Dreyfus Affair, planting the seed that became chapters 2 and 3. Many others in and out of the academy offered ideas, helped with translations, sent me documents I needed, corrected errors, and answered questions; for these and other kindnesses I thank Bruce Baird, Richard Bozorth, Paul Breines, Marlene Briggs, Adam Cohen, Shirin Deylami, Nick Dobelbower, Ian Down, Linda Garber, David Halperin, David Johnson, Steve Johnstone, Joshua Landy and all the participants in the "Getting Through Proust" seminar,

Laura Leibman, Pericles Lewis, Stephanie Lysyk, Lucy McDiarmid, Edward Mendelson, Tyrus Miller, David Nirenberg, Marjorie Rauen, Naoko Shibusawa, Rashmi Varma, Phiroze Vasunia, Joseph Weissman, Michael Wood, and Gregory Woods. For questions and comments that sharpened and enriched my thinking I am also grateful to audiences of lectures, workshops, and papers I've given on this material for the ACLA, the ASA, the B'nai Brith Wildacres Institute for Judaism, the Durham–Chapel Hill Jewish Federation, the IAH, Judea Reform Aleynu of Durham, the MSA, the UNC Program in the Humanities and Human Values, the Raleigh Jewish Community Center, Stanford University, SUNY Buffalo, Temple Beth Israel in Fayetteville, the Triangle French Studies Seminar, the Triangle Jewish Studies Seminar, the University of Maryland–Baltimore County, UC Berkeley, and UC Santa Cruz.

Many others helped with my research. Don Bachardy and Tony Kushner were gracious hosts and generous interview subjects. Seth and Lisa Tucker's hospitality and unflagging patience in answering questions about legal matters made research trips to D.C. much more enjoyable. The project was supported by fellowships and grants from the Fred A. and Gail M. Fearing Faculty Enrichment Fund, the Huntington Library, the Institute for the Arts and Humanities, the Spray-Randleigh Fellowship program, and the University Research Council. The College of Arts and Sciences at UNC–Chapel Hill and especially my own Department of English and Comparative Literature, which has been blessed with a series of remarkably humane and beneficent chairs, allowed me several vital research and medical leaves during the writing of this book. Research assistance was provided by Nathan Anderson, Lynn Badia, Allison Bigelow, Elise Harris, Christin Mulligan, and April Munroe. Finally, I am beholden to all the librarians, administrators, and archivists who facilitated my work at the Archives nationales de France; the Bibliothèque nationale; the Federal Bureau of Investigation; the Service historique de la Défense, département de l'armée de Terre; the National Archives and Records Administration (with special thanks to Steven D. Tilley); Davis Library, UNC–Chapel Hill; Green Library, Stanford University; Houghton Library, Harvard University; the Library of Congress; Lilly Library, Duke University; and, last but certainly not least, Miller Library, Colby College, where so much of this book was written.

DOUBLE AGENTS

INTRODUCTION

In the fall of 2007, a small group of evangelical protesters arrived on the campus of the University of North Carolina at Chapel Hill to preach. Most of the slogans on their placards were familiar variations on themes of sexual and cultural corruption, but one banner, which announced that "Homo Sex Is a Threat to National Security," seemed to puzzle many who saw it. The protesters were, like the perplexed UNC students, too young to remember the 1950s, when that equation was evoked regularly by government officials and the media. And probably none of them knew that in claiming a connection between sexual conduct and the integrity of the nation-state, these evangelicals were drawing on a discursive tradition reaching back centuries that links sexual deviance[a] to religious heresy, cultural difference, and political subversion.

This book investigates the associations drawn between male homosexuals, Jews, and Communists as iconic threats to national security, particularly in the late nineteenth and twentieth centuries. By looking at three espionage scandals in three Western countries—the Dreyfus Affair in France, the defections of Guy Burgess and Donald Maclean from Great

a. A note on usage: In discussing same-sex sexuality I have tried to use the vocabulary appropriate to the relevant time period, while retaining the modern and slightly less value-laden *homosexuality* as a convenient shorthand; thus male homosexuality and lesbianism are variously termed, in the pages that follow, *sodomy, buggery, inversion, perversion*, and so on. I often use the term *deviance*, not as a pejorative judgment but in order to group phenomena that, while varying over time and in different countries, have all been forcefully designated as aberrant.

Britain, and the Rosenberg trial in the United States—I elucidate how conceptions of Communism and male homosexuality have been shaped by representations of Jewishness as potentially incompatible with citizenship in the modern Western nation-state. Reading these cases against literary works by Marcel Proust, W. H. Auden, and Tony Kushner, I find that Jewishness, homosexuality, and Communism are comparably and conjointly figured in these texts as liminal, alien, occulted, and disruptive to the nation— and, at times, as potential sources of the nation's transformative renewal.

Dreyfus, Burgess, Maclean, and the Rosenbergs were certainly not the only Jews, homosexuals, or Communists involved in espionage scandals in the modern West. Numerous other examples spring to mind: Roger Casement, a homosexual Irish revolutionary hanged for treason in 1916; Whittaker Chambers and Alger Hiss, whose alleged espionage was made public in the late 1940s; John Vassall, a homosexual British naval attaché blackmailed into espionage by the Soviets and convicted in 1962; Jonathan Pollard, still serving a life sentence in the United States for spying for Israel. But I am a scholar of literature, and so I have chosen to focus on cases that have found reflection in literary texts, texts that both generate political discourses and are inflected by them. Tracing the imaginative and expressive forms in which ideas about, for example, citizenship and difference have been posed enables me to recover the imprints of concepts that have otherwise largely disappeared from public discourse. It allows me to claim that homophobia and anti-Semitism are integrally related, that the conception of homosexuality as a political/politicized identity retains the mark of its origins in the anti-Semitic European climate of Proust's time, and that Communism has served as an axis connecting the two in the Anglo-American political context.

MAPPING THE TERRAIN:
DEFINITIONS AND BOUNDARIES

At the outset of this discussion I want to clarify how I am defining treason and espionage, and their relationship. Legally speaking, the crime of treason is defined very differently in different countries and particularly narrowly in America, where the founders, anxious not to recreate the sweeping statutes that made a great range of offenses against the British monarch treasonable in the eighteenth century, constitutionally restricted the definition of the crime to "levying War against" the United States or "adhering to their Enemies, giving them Aid and Comfort."[1] There are also significant evidentiary requirements for proving treason; thus only a handful of people have ever been convicted of the crime in the United States. In fact, in the cases I examine in this book, only Alfred Dreyfus was actually convicted of treason. Julius and Ethel Rosenberg were convicted of conspiracy to commit espionage; we will never know what Guy Burgess and Donald Maclean might have been charged with, since they defected to the Soviet Union before being arrested, but in all probability they would have been prosecuted for espionage or "treachery," a slightly different offense in Britain from treason.

If treason has only limited application within the strict definitions of the law, however, it is a vitally potent and charged concept emotionally and ideologically, long considered the most fundamental violation of any social contract; Dante, after all, consigns traitors to the lowest circle of his inferno, along with the archtraitor, Satan himself. In *The Meaning of Treason* (1947) Rebecca West defines treason broadly as "the betrayal of familiars to strangers," assuming that all members of one tribe, fiefdom, empire, or nation-state are "familiars," and that they are bound together by what West calls "real interests" against untrustworthy outsiders.[2] This is undoubtedly much closer to the popular or commonsense understanding of treason than the legal definition. It is, arguably, the real crime for which the Rosenbergs were executed, regardless of the legal charges against them; it still carries enough emotive force to be a dramatically effective, and remunerative, rallying cry for pundits on the political Right.

In the United States during the 1950s loyalty tests were established in many areas of government, education, and business in an attempt to distinguish between treasonous and loyal Americans. Voicing skepticism about these tests, legal scholar Ralph S. Brown neatly glosses the distinction between the judicial and popular understandings of terms like *treason, disloyalty,* and *loyalty* and adds the critical point that these terms actually refer to affective states without objective correlatives. Brown writes about loyalty that

> loyalty to a government or a country originally had etymological associations of lawful obligation; in this sense it is akin to allegiance, which in earlier times meant fealty to the monarch or other overlord. A citizen still owes allegiance to the United States; reciprocal rights and duties flow between him and the government. He must obey its lawful commands; government must give him its protection.

> But for most people loyalty has no such narrow legal bounds.
> It is something one *feels*, a generous emotion, personal and free.[3]

Brown notes the long-standing tradition in legal thought that loyalty "cannot be coerced."[4] In the age of the nation-state, loyalty is meant to coincide with the country of one's birth or naturalization, but there can be no concrete, objective proof that it does so. In an article on treason another legal scholar, referring to loyalty as "an inherently subjective and highly elusive condition," has written ruefully that "just as poets have struggled in vain to define romantic love, courts will probably never define that sort of political love."[5] Thus, any test of loyalty must be imperfect if not entirely quixotic, and any attempt to compel it bound to fail.

In the case of spies, who by definition pass as something other than what they are, questions about loyalty become especially fraught with anxiety. Naturally, not all spies are traitors to their own nations, but in one sense all are treacherous; they are supposed to lie and deceive, to perform loyalties that they do not actually feel. So a spy's capacity for dissimulation, which makes him useful, also makes him irremediably dangerous, since his employer—his country, usually—can never be sure that even the most apparently patriotic and dependable spy is not really a double agent, working in the interests of a foreign power. Thus, while treason can take many forms besides spying, spies are particularly liable to fall under suspicion of treason.

In addition to these definitions, I wish to issue two caveats about the nature and scope of this book. The first is an admission of deliberate oversight in my failure to address freemasonry, which has for centuries been as consistently imbricated with Jewishness, sexual deviance, and espionage as they have been with one another. Masons have been characterized as the original agents of the Crucifixion, purveyors of perversion, and the unseen power behind both world Jewry and international Communism; within the framework of some conspiracy theories, indeed, they are the progenitors of the entire genealogy of treason that I trace here. My reason for excluding freemasonry is simply that it constitutes a topic so vast that treating it adequately would have required greatly broadening the scope and length of an already expansive investigation. It is my hope that others will find in these pages tools that will allow them to fill in a picture I have thus purposefully left incomplete.

The second caution I want to offer is that the discussion that follows will be almost entirely confined to male subjects, except in the case of Ethel Rosenberg. This should not be taken as a token of indifference to the ways gender intersects with race, sexuality, culture, and politics; on the contrary. Men and women have such different relations to the nation that a single project of this nature could not coherently contain a discussion of both. In particular, I am primarily interested here in the question of citizenship, and women have not been citizens of most nations on equal terms with men. Jewish and homosexual men—but only rarely lesbians or Jewish women—have consistently been associated both literally and figuratively with themes of treason and espionage, first in the European cultural imagination and then in that of Americans. Furthermore, and probably consequently, treason and espionage seem to have fascinated a noteworthy number of prominent men writers, while these tropes apparently have less purchase on the imaginations of women writers. Thus, this book takes as its point of departure the following questions: What was it about Jews and sexually deviant men that made them appear, in different countries and over a considerable period of time, such obvious candidates as traitors to the state? Why should these specific groups be so often considered incapable of national loyalty? How did differences in religion, culture, and sexual expression come to be so closely identified with a specific political ideology—Communism? And why have male homosexual writers found treason and espionage such compelling vehicles for literary explorations of identity?

I propose that the answers to these questions have to do with the ability of certain exotic Others to "pass" across normative, visible boundaries of racial and sexual classification. The secrecy and treacherousness identified with Jewish and homosexual ontology may be attributable to the potentially *invisible* alterity of the Jew and the homosexual, which, at least as early as the Renaissance, had begun to provoke fears that the nation could be surreptitiously undermined by "moles" whose true loyalties might turn out to lie with their clan, race, or biological type rather than with their country. As double agents, invisible Others passing as the Same, they could act like, and on behalf of, both the "us" within the nation and the "them" outside it. By the end of the nineteenth century Jewishness and homosexuality had become densely imbricated sites of contestation about the meanings of citizenship and the nation. Subsequently, the Communist entered this discursive nexus, identified with both the Jew and the sexual deviant as a figure of duplicity. Discussions of Jews, homosexuals, and Communists press relentlessly on the apparently contradictory—yet almost invariably conjoined—beliefs that they are essentially different yet virtually indistinguishable from "normal" citizens. This anxiety is distinct from (though often related to) the stereotypes of race, gender, and class applied to visually legible otherness. Unlike racially marked colonial subjects, for example, Jews and homosexuals have typically been described as inclined to treason—and specifically to espionage—rather than, say, armed rebellion.

Because of this ideological history, it would seem that for men writers—and especially for white, middle-class men writers who have enjoyed in most regards an exceptional degree of social privilege—images of espionage and treason have offered themselves as aesthetically effective and emotionally resonant ways of registering a sense of decisive, yet imperceptible, difference. The spy who appears to be just like everyone else—that is, just like all other adult white heterosexual male citizens—but is secretly really something else, dangerous, threatening, perhaps reviled or hunted but also intriguing, attractive, even glamorous: is this figure not an admirable representation of the precarious, liminal position of the writer, or the fictional protagonist, who departs from the norms of his society only by some occulted anomaly of sexual taste, political or religious belief, ethnic descent, or cultural affiliation? And the trope of treason, I will argue, is a way of registering a genuine and profound sense of alienation, skepticism, or even outrage on the part of writers who are nonetheless far too assimilated to their social worlds and too embedded in their national identities simply to reject them.

LITERATURE AND THE NATIONAL IMAGINARY

In the first chapter I offer an overview of historical constructions of Jewishness and sexual deviance as Other to national identities in the West. I trace the interlacing of racial and sexual difference that by the nineteenth century drew ever more tightly together representations of the Jew with newly emerging concepts of sexual perversion and fears of left-wing radicalism. Political beliefs that aimed at radical revision of a nation's economy, like religious or sexual practices that conflicted with national norms, challenged the limits of national inclusivity in liberal nation-states, disclosing the profound tension between the ideals of liberal pluralism and the requirements of civic unity. Chapter 2 investigates how that stress led to national rupture in France when, in 1894, a Jewish army officer was accused of selling France's military secrets to the Germans. This chapter looks at the imbricated discourses of race and sexuality that informed the Dreyfus Affair and the way conceptual associations between Germans, Jews, illicit sexualities, and treason were used strategically to further the legal case against Captain Dreyfus.

The third chapter considers Proust's use of the Affair in *À la recherche du temps perdu*, whose volumes began appearing a decade after the case had fizzled to an end. At a time when authoritative discourses about homosexuality were almost exclusively medical and juridical, the novel offers the most thorough theorization of homosexuality that had yet been undertaken in fictional form. *À la recherche* gives us not only an immensely, indeed hilariously, complex taxonomy of sexualities but also a subtle and original analysis of the relationship between homosexualities and citizenship—one in which, as has often been noted in Proust scholarship, male homosexuality in particular is insistently analogized to Jewishness. Morris Kaplan has written that "Proust dramatized the 'racial' conceptions of 'Jewishness' and 'homosexuality' that emerged from complex negotiations between demands for conformity and assertions of difference" in France.[6] But the analogy's ramifications for republican concepts of political identity are ultimately even farther-reaching: for in examining the relationship of Jews and homosexuals to citizenship, Proust proposes a notion of identity that undermines the stability of the very concept of the nation as a culturally unified contract among publicly identical individuals.

The Dreyfus Affair and Proust's response to it provide the imaginative map for my analysis of how particular identities become ever more closely identified with espionage in the course of the twentieth century. In the second part of the book I look at the way W. H. Auden and his literary contemporaries in the interwar period fashioned themselves as secret agents, developing and adapting Proust's narrative to focus on the ambiguous social positioning of ruling-class homosexuals rather than that of Jews. The trope of espionage enabled writers in Auden's circle to articulate the status of the upper-middle-class, left-wing British homosexual as both emblem of, and traitor to, an empire he was bred to rule. The writers thus helped construct the framework within which the treason of the so-called Cambridge spies—Burgess, Maclean, Kim Philbess, and Anthony Blunt— would eventually be received and understood. Chapter 4 examines Auden's reliance in his early poetry on tropes of conspiracy, frontiers, wars, and espionage as a means of dramatizing the internal and external forces bearing on the bourgeois homosexual, whose sexual desires and gender position so complicate his relationship to institutional and cultural power. While Auden eventually abandoned the figure of the spy and turned to an exploration of the homosexual man's claim to citizenship, the early poetry registers an entrenched suspicion of the establishment and characterizes homosexuals as socially alienated and psychologically conflicted. As I show in chapter 5, when Burgess and Maclean defected to the Soviet Union in 1951, this sexual and political typology seemed confirmed, and the stereotype of the furtive Jewish conspirator was recast, in both Britain and America, as paranoia about a homosexual fifth column working in conjunction with international Communism, motivating McCarthyite witch hunts for sexual deviants and political subversives in both countries. In the United States in particular, the containment policies of the Cold War established an equation between national integrity and the impenetrable body of the normatively sexed man, partly in reaction to the heterodox sexualities and cosmopolitan transnationalism of both the British spies and European modernists like Proust and Auden.

The approach and aims of these later chapters are necessarily different from my treatment of Proust, who wrote directly and explicitly about the Dreyfus Affair after it took place. Auden never wrote poems about his friends Guy Burgess and Anthony Blunt or their coconspirators. Indeed, by the midfifties, when Moscow officially admitted that Burgess and Maclean had defected, the themes of conspiracy and espionage had largely disappeared from Auden's work. Instead, the poet's preoccupation with spying developed in the late 1920s and flourished in the early 1930s, roughly the same period during which the Cambridge spies became Communists and then were launched on their careers as double agents. So rather than investigating a historical event that surfaces as theme and metaphor in a work of fiction, as I do in chapters 2 and 3, in chapters 4 and 5 I look at a historical period and cultural climate that produced a number of notorious spies and a curious quantity of literature about spying—and at the connections between those two things.

In the book's sixth chapter I consider both the Rosenberg case and Tony Kushner's 1992 attempt in *Angels in America* to restage the meanings of McCarthyism. By midcentury red-baiters had easy access to familiar tropes equating Communists, Jews, homosexuals, and treason.

Anti-Communists were thus able to mobilize popular fear of and antagonism to the Red Menace quickly and decisively, using a shorthand that referred the public immediately to well-established assumptions about the nature of internal enemies. At the same time, however, a range of factors converged to encourage Jewish integration into the American polity, resulting in a strenuous conflict within American Jewry between those who advocated radical social and economic change, on the one hand, and those who espoused assimilation to a national ethic of patriotism, gender conformity, and religious piety, on the other.

I read the Rosenbergs' trial and Kushner's play as interventions into that struggle over Jewish American identity. The outcome of the Rosenberg case was the firm suppression of Jewish American Communism and the imposition of a conservative consensus represented, in *Angels*, by Roy Cohn and vigorously contested by the play's queer politics. Explicitly highlighting the longstanding ideological relations between Jewishness, homosexuality, Communism, and treason, Kushner allows Cohn's prosecution of the Rosenbergs to conjure all the knotty issues of loyalty and betrayal at the dramatic heart of both the trial and his own text. He also introduces Ethel Rosenberg's ghost into the play, in what we might assume is an attempt to restore a consensus of the Left, recalling Jewish Americans to the radical tradition of the 1920s and 1930s and thus valorizing Jewish political subversion as well as sexual deviance. I will argue, however, that the play fails to enact such a consensus, instead drawing its characters and, ultimately, its audience into an ongoing dialectic between modes of queer and Jewish citizenship.

The public discourses generated by the Dreyfus Affair, the Burgess-Maclean scandal, and the trial of Julius and Ethel Rosenberg reveal that regardless of the innocence or guilt of the accused, in each case Jews, homosexuals, or Communists *signified* more readily as traitors because they problematized sacrosanct tenets about national identity while "passing" as citizens. Cases of treason—a profound affront to a national community—bring to light the substantial religious, cultural, and ideological requirements for full citizenship, which far exceed the limited criteria of formal enfranchisement. Alfred Dreyfus, Guy Burgess, Donald Maclean, and the Rosenbergs were charged with betraying national secrets. Yet the discourses surrounding them suggest that they also stood accused of betraying a more fundamental secret about the modern nation-state: that national self-understandings are always unstable, what James Joyce called "a necessary fiction."

It is for that reason that deliberate fictions, in the form of literary texts, can be such a useful record of and response to the rhetorical investments of nationalism, prodding at inconsistencies in nationalist narratives and calling them to account for their blind spots. It is also why I have felt licensed to approach this project by producing close readings of such different kinds of cultural artifacts, from poems to trial transcripts. This is not to suggest that all texts have the same function or that all can be similarly read as manifestations of a vaguely defined zeitgeist. Rather, I attempt in the following chapters to offer site-specific exegeses of an ideational complex that both persisted in the nation-state over a sustained period and erupted forcefully into public consciousness and textual expression at particular historical moments. The archival materials and historical documents I draw on register instances in which instabilities in national self-conceptions in France, Britain, and the United States became especially visible; the literary works do the same thing deliberately and productively, using these moments to interrogate the relationship of subalterns to particular nations and to citizenship more generally. From that interrogation arises, for each of the three authors I treat in this study, a richly generative tension between their acknowledgment of the seductions of national belonging and national identity and their interest in resisting that pull, rewriting the terms of citizenship and enlarging or unsettling the concept of the nation. In 1939 Auden wrote, "Loyalty and intelligence are mutually hostile. The intelligence is always disloyal. There must always be a conflict between the loyalty necessary for society to be, and the intelligence necessary for society to become."[7] Paradoxically, I will claim, that intelligent, productive disloyalty is precisely what Auden, Proust, and Kushner contribute to the polity, helping it not only to be but also to become.

1

CITIZENS, ALIENS, AND TRAITORS

Judaism and homosexuality (most intensely where they overlap, as in a Proust or a Wittgenstein) can be seen to have been the two main generators of the entire fabric and savor of urban modernity in the West. [...] This is a vast and as yet only imperfectly understood development, of which the role of homosexuality in politics and in the world of espionage and betrayal is only a specialized, though dramatic, feature.*

—George Steiner, "The Cleric of Treason"

Our goal has been, therefore, to inform the readers of this work as precisely as possible about the true mores of individuals who are much more numerous than might be supposed, and with whom we come into contact every day, without being in the least aware of their passions.

—Henri de Weindel and F.-P. Fischer,
L'Homosexualité en Allemagne

Nations are usually unstable entities, imaginatively even when not territorially, and Jews have long been the paradigmatic "test case" troubling the edges of European national identities. In a more occluded and indirect fashion, Jews have played a similar role in the United States; furthermore, responses to male homosexuals and Communists in both Western Europe and America have been, and in the case of homosexuals continue to be, infused with the residue of memes both philo- and anti-Semitic. That is, for well over a century, representations of Jewishness, homosexuality, and Communism have been related genealogically as well as analogically. Homophobia and anti-Communism are not merely structurally "like" anti-Semitism but remain closely affiliated with it and impelled by its energies.

---

*My interpolations to quoted material in this book appear in brackets and include ellipses as well as, for translated material, terms from the French.

Eve Sedgwick has raised legitimate objections to an indiscriminate collapsing of the space between Jewishness and homosexuality in contemporary discussions of minority oppression and the function of the closet, pointing out that, among other differences, the family of origin offers a site of identity and identification for Jews that it usually does not for homosexuals.[1] And more generally, religious beliefs, ethnic background, cultural practices, sexual desires, and political ideologies are not all—or would not all seem to be—the same *kind* of attribute of individuals or communities, nor do they appear to pose the same kind of challenge to the liberal nation-state. For example, Communism, inasmuch as most of its variants envisage a total and possibly violent alteration in the form of the state, seems to represent a much more concrete threat to liberal institutions than homosexuality.

Yet even if homosexuality, a commitment to Communism, and Jewishness are not equivalent as lived, material experiences of identity, they have nonetheless occupied the same imaginary spaces sequentially when not simultaneously. Jewishness has been represented as political conspiracy or congenital abnormality; Communism has been figured as a faith, homosexuals as a race. Furthermore, sexual desire, religious belief, and political loyalty are all essentially internal and affective phenomena: they belong to that private and subjective realm that, ever since the Enlightenment, Western nations have uneasily tended to concede might not be a legitimate concern of the state. At the same time, however, the need to ensure national unity has often inspired a passionate determination to establish objective external criteria that can measure adherence to national norms. Hence the insistence that a threatening difference must be written on the body, manifested in gender deviance, disease, or physical aberration; or that there can be a standardized litmus test, like having been at any time a member of the Communist Party, that can tell us, without error, what someone's real political or religious commitments are.

In short, all of these modes of being are and historically have been discursively shaped in relation to one another as what Daniel Itzkovitz calls, in the case of homosexuality and Jewishness, "closet identities." Itzkovitz argues in response to Sedgwick that her analysis "examines neither the popularly constructed contents of the Jew's closet nor the retroactive relation these cultural fantasies have on the constitution of actual Jewish and queer identities. *Only* separating homophobia and anti-Semitism does not fully account for the ways that anti-Semitism and homophobia are inflected by one another, and the ways discourses of Jewishness and queerness speak through one another. The language of anti-Semitism utilizes and is bound up with the discourse of homophobia in particularly resonant ways."[2] Examining the histories of discourses of both Semitism and sexuality—whether anti- or philo-Semitic, homophobic or homophilic—leaves little doubt that, as numerous scholars have by now demonstrated, in the West the two have been powerfully analogous in their configuration for at least several hundred years. Most obviously, "both Jew and homosexual are other to society's Christian and heterosexual norms."[3] But "Jew" and "homosexual" are not merely comparable terms for marginality; these categories of racial and sexual difference have been mapped onto each other and then onto Communism, coconstructing each other as physiologically, socially, and politically foreign. In the next sections of this chapter I will look at some of the dominant tropes of that mutual constitution, which include the claims that homosexuals and Communists, like Jews, are alien to the nation, that Jews and Communists are particularly prone to sexual deviance and license, and that homosexual and Jewish men are equally aberrant in their gender identity—they are like women—and thus unsuited for citizenship. Jews, homosexuals, and Communists have all been associated with physical and mental disease, with threats to the family, with moral decay. And all have been understood to constitute secret societies within society, freemasonries: states within the state.

ENLIGHTENMENT AND JEWISH EMANCIPATION

The pre-Enlightenment history of Jews and anti-Semitism in Europe has been too thoroughly documented to require elaboration here, but it is worth noting several features of early modern anti-Semitism because of their continuity into the Enlightenment era. Although the legal and material status of Jews has varied considerably over time and in different regions of the world, discourses *about* Jews have remained extraordinarily consistent,[4] so that today one may encounter ideas about Jews and Jewishness easily traceable, with little alteration, to the thirteenth century; this will be my justification for making some very broad generalizations in the remarks that follow.

First and most obviously, Jews long constituted a diasporic and stateless group of people whose forced wanderings across Europe calcified their image as perpetual strangers and contributed to the assumption that their loyalties, if any, were extranational. Second, in Christian countries Jews were treated as deicides and heretics, yet while discrimination against Jews in the early modern period was usually justified on religious grounds, even converted, baptized Jews and their descendants were sometimes subject to restrictions, suggesting that well before the rise of nineteenth-century racialist thought, Jewishness was already viewed as an essential quality supplemental to religious affiliation.[5] Finally, the confinement of Jews in many places to urban ghettoes and to specific professions such as moneylending created enduring associations between Jews, cities, and capital.

Turning now to the late eighteenth century and to the three countries with which this study is particularly concerned—France, the United States, and Britain—we find that in the aftermath of the wars of religion, the Enlightenment, and the revolutions it inspired, revolutionary governments in France and America sought to decouple religious affiliation from citizenship, a project with profound consequences for the emancipation of Jews. In particular, John Locke's intellectual heirs drew a sharp distinction between citizenship as a public status and religious faith as an internal, and hence inviolably private, experience. In addition to the Déclaration des droits de l'homme et du citoyen (1789) and the Bill of Rights (1791), numerous other French and American documents of the revolutionary period expound on this critical distinction. For instance, the 1786 Virginia Statute for Religious Freedom, authored by Thomas Jefferson, states that natural rights, including the right to participate fully in the life of the nation, cannot be allocated by one person or group to other persons or groups on the grounds of shared religious conviction, since this would amount to a coercion that God Himself does not exercise over us because it is incompatible with human free will.[6] In a 1790 letter to the Hebrew Congregation of Newport, Rhode Island, George Washington spoke even more forcefully of the natural right to "liberty of conscience," decrying the apparently benign idea of religious "tolerance" on the grounds that people's natural rights are inalienable and should not depend on their being tolerated by other people: "All possess alike liberty of conscience and immunities of citizenship. It is now no more that toleration is spoken of, as if it was by the indulgence of one class of people, that another enjoyed the exercise of their inherent natural rights. For happily the Government of the United States, which gives to bigotry no sanction, to persecution no assistance requires only that they who live under its protection should demean themselves as good citizens, in giving it on all occasions their effectual support."[7]

Although the federal powers of the United States thus foreswore religious discrimination, individual states had considerable leeway to refuse Jews rights to vote and hold public office, and many of them did so well into the nineteenth century. In France, in contrast, once Jewish emancipation came it was—formally, at least—unqualified. Founding documents of the First Republic clearly established that the basis for granting Jews citizenship was the essentially private nature of religious faith. While the question of Jewish enfranchisement was being debated before the Assemblée nationale of 1789, the Comte de Clermont-Tonnerre, who favored the Jews' emancipation, contended that a sphere of privacy should protect intimate personal beliefs, and that the separation of church and state was necessary both to avoid religious warfare and for the free exercise of conscience: "The law cannot affect the religion of a man. It can take no hold over his soul; it can affect only his actions, and it must protect those actions when they do no harm to society. God wanted us to reach agreement among ourselves on issues of morality, and he has permitted us to make moral laws, but he has given to no one but himself the right to legislate dogmas and to rule over [religious] conscience."[8]

As we will see in the next chapter when we consider the Dreyfus Affair, it eventually became crucial to French republicanism to insist on the inconsequence of race and religion to any discussion of rights. Indeed, Clermont-Tonnerre argued fervently that in order to maintain the sphere of privacy, the republic must define citizens—persons considered in their public instantiation—as individuals whose religious and ethnic affiliations not only were irrelevant to their enfranchisement but should be actively suppressed in order to break up any subnational identifications that might mediate between the individual and the state: "The Jews should be denied everything as a nation, but granted everything as individuals. They must be citizens. It is claimed that they do not want to be citizens, that they say this and that they are [thus] excluded; there cannot be one nation within another nation. . . . It is intolerable that the Jews should become a separate political formation or class in the country. Every one of them must individually become a citizen; if they do not want this, they must inform us and we shall then be compelled to expel them."[9]

Clermont-Tonnerre's views won out, and the emancipation proclamation that was eventually issued in 1791 clearly defined the nation as a social

contract between neutral individuals who, other than the implicit requirements of (adult) age and (male) sex, had no other specificity and therefore
were all formally equal, in the sense of having identical relations to the
state. "The National Assembly," the proclamation declares,

> considering that the conditions requisite to be a French citizen,
> and to become an active citizen, are fixed by the constitution, and
> that every man who, being duly qualified, takes the civic oath, and
> engages to fulfill all the duties prescribed by the constitution, has
> a right to all the advantages it insures;
>
> Annuls all adjournments, restrictions, and exceptions, con-
> tained in the preceding decrees, affecting individuals of the Jewish
> persuasion, who shall take the civic oath, which shall be consid-
> ered as a renunciation of all privileges in their favor.[10]

Thus, French Jews are legally defined from the outset not as members of
a minority group within the nation but as individuals marked by a quality of Jewishness—a *Yiddishkeit* or *judaiété*—that is incidental to their
citizenship.

Jewish emancipation took place in a more piecemeal fashion in Britain
than it had under the revolutionary regime in France; in the course of the
nineteenth century various reform bills gradually lifted restrictions on the
rights of Jews to take fellowships at British universities, to hold public office,
and so on until eventually, with the elevation of Nathan Rothschild to the
House of Lords in 1884, Jews had been admitted to every level of civil society.
Thus, we do not find in Britain the same kinds of foundational documents
that we have in France defining the relationship of Jews to the state. But
although there is no British equivalent of the emancipation proclamation,
Thomas Macaulay's famous 1831 speech in Parliament calling for Jews to
be made eligible for public office can serve as a measure of the centrality of
Enlightenment thought to Whig politics, indicating that in Britain, too, Jewish enfranchisement was predicated on the assumption that religious observance and participation in the state are distinct and unrelated functions:

> We hear of essentially Protestant governments and essentially
> Christian governments, words which mean just as much as essen-
> tially Protestant cookery, or essentially Christian horsemanship.
> Government exists for the purpose of keeping the peace, for the

purpose of compelling us to settle our disputes by arbitration instead of settling them by blows, for the purpose of compelling us to supply our wants by industry instead of supplying them by rapine. [. . .] Why a man should be less fit to exercise those powers because he wears a beard, because he does not eat ham, because he goes to the synagogue on Saturdays, instead of going to church on Sundays, we cannot conceive.[11]

"By the 1870s," writes Bryan Cheyette, British "Jews were no longer 'lodgers' in a Christian nation but were able to participate in a civil society as 'Englishmen of the Mosaic Persuasion' with their religion merely a matter of personal 'conscience.'"[12] Formally, then, in France, Britain, and America, adherence to Judaism was by the late nineteenth century treated as a private affair without consequence in the public sphere, and many Jews embraced this concept. In France, for example, elite and more highly assimilated Jews tended to adopt the appellation *Israélite* rather than *Juif*, hoping that the former term would be taken to indicate a purely religious affiliation characteristic of essentially *French* citizens.[13]

Additionally, in both France and the United States we often see the projection of Jewish national aspirations onto not an indefinite messianic future in Palestine but contemporary life in France or America, reimagined as Zion. It was France, wrote one grateful Jewish patriot, "who first wiped out the disgrace of Judah and broke the shackles of all captives, she is our land of Israel; her mountains—our Zion; her rivers—our Jordan."[14] The prominent French orientalist James Darmesteter viewed Paris as the new Jerusalem, "moral capital of the world," taking over Israel's mission as a light to nations.[15] And French rabbis and religious leaders often depicted France in religious terms in sermons and speeches: "Rabbi Kahn of Nîmes, for example, referred to the Revolution as 'our flight from Egypt . . . , our modern Passover'. In the judgement of Rabbi Herrmann of Reims, France 'was designated by Him who directs the destinies of humanity to work for the emancipation of all the oppressed, to spread throughout the world the great and beautiful ideas of justice, equality, and fraternity which had formerly been the exclusive patrimony of Israel.'"[16]

American Jews, too, interpreted the national experience as the fulfillment of biblical promise. In 1825 the journalist and politician Mordecai Manuel Noah issued a public invitation to world Jewry to emigrate to upstate New York, claiming that there they would find "an asylum in a free and powerful country, where ample protection is secured to their persons, their property and religious rights; an asylum in a country remarkable for its vast resources, the richness of its soil, and the salubrity of its climate; where industry is encouraged, education promoted, and good faith rewarded; 'a land of milk and honey,' where Israel may repose in peace, under his 'vine and fig tree.' "[17] And in 1915 scholar Israel Friedländer wrote that "America was the Zion and Washington the Jerusalem of American Israel."[18]

By the nineteenth century, then, both Western Jews and the national ideologies of England, France, and America typically asserted the compatibility of Jewishness with participation in the nation-state. The point has often been made—and it is one I largely agree with, although I will try to complicate it later—that an ethos of liberalism favoring both capitalism and modernity has tended to create political, economic, and social opportunities for Jews. Consequently, this argument goes, anti-Semitism waxes and wanes as a function of public attitudes toward capitalism and liberal democracy: it is likely to diminish when these are popularly endorsed and stable and to come to the fore when they are under attack. (As we will see in the next chapter, the latter thesis was amply borne out in France during the Dreyfus Affair.) Furthermore, liberal discourses have not only affirmed the rights of Jewish citizens but also focused on those qualities that make Jews congenial to, even representative of, the liberal state as such. Colin Holmes notes that in nineteenth-century England, liberal opinion portrayed the Jewish immigrant as "a veritable symbol of self help, hard work, self denial, and deferred gratification."[19] As Holmes writes, "Liberalism was the political creed of bourgeois capitalism. As such it was particularly tolerant towards those groups whose social behaviour was regarded as bolstering capitalism and this could encourage a defence of Jews, whether as hard-working immigrants or sophisticated traders."[20]

George Fredrickson makes a similar argument about the United States, contending that anti-Semitism gained less traction there than in Europe not simply because—as has sometimes been surmised—enslaved Africans provided more numerous and visible targets for racial hatred but because the identification of Jews with the modern and black people with the primitive predisposed Americans to tolerate the former and despise the latter.[21] In fact, since the founding of the Republic, a distinct strain of philo-Semitism has viewed Jewish character as fundamentally compatible with the American spirit: mobile, urban, and committed to both modernity and capitalism.[22]

Jews themselves, like Supreme Court justice Louis Brandeis, proudly asserted that "the Jewish spirit, the product of our religion and experiences, is essentially modern and essentially American. Not since the destruction of the Temple have the Jews in spirit and in ideals been so fully in harmony with the noblest aspirations of the country in which they lived."[23]

JEWISH DIFFERENCE AND ANTI-SEMITISM

If a strong case can be made, then, that liberalism has been "good for the Jews," other scholars contend—also with cause—that anti-Semitism is actually "built into the project of modernity" because modern nation-states (in contrast to, for example, multinational empires) promote homogeneity to ensure national cohesion.[24] Whatever normative discourses proclaimed, in practice the relationship between liberal polities and anti-Semitism was always complex, and Jewishness, like other forms of sub- or supranational status, continued in the modern period to be perceived by many gentiles as a threat to national unity.

In part this was because Judaism, even considered solely in its manifestation as a religion, could not really be wholly privatized, since customs like observing the Sabbath on Saturday were incompatible with the social, cultural, and economic practices of the Christian majority. As soon as Jews exercised their Jewishness in any context other than their own minds, that Jewishness became in some way a public actuality and therefore a public problem. In addition, the argument was sometimes made that peoples could and should not be considered politically equal unless they were also socially identical;[25] by this reasoning, if a group's culture differed from that of the majority, the group could never achieve complete equality. Paul Mendes-Flohr and Jehuda Reinharz have argued that one of the bases for the development of modern anti-Semitism was the view, which persisted even in the absence of formal, legal discrimination, that "the modern state requires cultural and national integration. The Jews, possessing distinct cultural and national aspirations of their own, are hence fundamentally incompatible with the modern state that hosts them."[26]

This perspective was offered during the 1789 debates in France's National Assembly by the bishop of Nancy, Anne-Louis-Henri de la Fare. De la Fare was by no means a thoroughgoing anti-Semite, and he admitted the necessity of securing human rights for Jews. But he objected to their political enfranchisement on the grounds that whatever they might claim, they still aspired ultimately to a homeland other than France; that their religious observances, especially the dietary laws, would prevent them from entering the army or other professions; and that their religious holidays conflicted with the French national calendar.[a] A century later an American business-man would express a similar sense of Jewish inassimilability in explaining to the *New York Herald* why his Manhattan Beach Company had decided in 1879 to ban Jews from its hotels and resorts: "It is not the Jew's [*sic*] religion I object to," he specified carefully; "it is the offensiveness which they possess as a sect or *nationality*" (emphasis added).[27] These examples point to a central problem of liberal nation formation, which, as Pericles Lewis writes, "is precisely that, whereas a separation of church and state or a 'color-blind' state is at least conceivable, it is impossible to imagine a separation of state and culture."[28] Whereas Jewish individuals could hypothetically be assimilated into—for example—the French or American state, Jewish culture could not simply be assimilated into French or American culture; Jewishness per se would necessarily remain in an awkward relation to the nation.

In Britain, too, we find resentment about cultural differences and what was perceived as Jewish inassimilability; despite the country's relative political liberalism, claims historian Todd Endelman, in the eighteenth century gentiles often "viewed the Jews in their midst as a separate people, regarding even native-born, highly acculturated Jews as different in kind, marked off by a distinctive, irreducible essence or otherness that remained despite their adaptation to English conditions. In fact, the belief in Jewish distinctiveness was so embedded in popular consciousness that converted Jews, including the children of Jews baptized at birth, were commonly referred to as Jews."[29] This popular propensity to emphasize Jewish difference, which abated somewhat during the nineteenth century as Sephardic and German Jews became financially established and relatively assimilated, was then exacerbated again by the immigration to Britain of

---

a. Quoted in Mendes-Flohr and Reinharz, *Jew in the Modern World*, 115. Similar concerns continue to arise in Western democracies today; to offer just one example, there was considerable debate during the 2000 U.S. presidential race about whether Senator Joseph Lieberman could be sworn in on a Saturday if elected. Because the putatively secular calendar in the United States is largely organized around the religious calendar of the Christian majority, it cannot easily absorb minority religious observances. The incompatibility of Lieberman's religious practices with dominant cultural norms was strikingly at odds with the liberal ethos of "inclusiveness" that made it possible for him to be considered as a vice-presidential candidate in the first place.

approximately one hundred thousand Yiddish-speaking eastern European Jews in the late nineteenth century. At the fin-de-siècle, when Jews had been sitting in Parliament for forty years and the country had already had an ethnically Jewish prime minister in Benjamin Disraeli, the *East London Advertiser* could nonetheless complain that "people of any other nation, after being in England for a short time, assimilate themselves with the native race and by and by lose nearly all their foreign trace. But the Jews never do"; the paper also insisted "that Jews ignored local 'customs', 'religious observances'," and "'days of rest', and contravened established morality."[30]

So throughout the West, even as liberal societies extended more and more civic and social rights and responsibilities to Jews, a strident counter-discourse harped on the unsuitability of Jews for citizenship in a republic and argued that they could only with great difficulty be placed in the categories meaningful to the state. A citizen is supposed to be prepared to render to his nation a given quantity of loyalty that cannot be divided or multiplied. But Jewish community historically precedes nation-states; furthermore, Jewish families that extended across nations "figured importantly in the perception of Jews as having no loyalty to local communities,"[31] enforcing suspicions that Jews' allegiances were either sub- or supranational. Jews, it was frequently asserted, thought in terms of the tribe rather than the individual or the nation.[32]

A peculiar and, for my purposes, significant corollary of this view in both France and Britain was that Jews were often identified with Germany at the same time that they were seen as incapable of loyalty to any national collectivity. In France about two-thirds of the Jewish population had lived in Alsace-Lorraine, and after the Franco-Prussian war of 1870–1871, when France lost those territories to Germany, the majority of Alsatian Jews opted for French citizenship and moved to Paris and other cities. Because, like most Alsatians, they spoke German as well as French, they were "quickly assumed to be Germans," even though "their very choice of expatriation manifested their loyalty to France."[33] Because Germany (or, earlier, Prussia) had been for decades France's archenemy, the supposed affiliation of Jews with the hated foreign power helped intensify French anti-Semitism from the 1870s on. In Britain—where some of the nation's most prominent Jewish bankers and politicians were of central European extraction and had German names—the German origins of the royal family and the close political and financial connections between the two countries kept specifically anti-German anti-Semitism largely in abeyance until the Great War. But after 1914 loathing for "the Hun" authorized vehement prejudice against both gentiles and Jews with German blood.

SCIENCE AND RACE

By the second half of the nineteenth century these characterizations of Jews as culturally anomalous aliens were increasingly informed by scientific and pseudoscientific theories of race. Fredrickson argues that scientific racism flourished in post-Enlightenment France and the United States precisely because those two nations were "premised on the equal rights of all citizens," and "egalitarian norms required special reasons for exclusion." So the concept of "biological unfitness" was "applied to racial groups deemed by science to be incompetent to exercise the rights and privileges of democratic citizenship."[34] New developments in the sciences of anatomy, phrenology, embryology, neurology, and psychology encouraged the pathologization of racial (and sexual) difference, helping to "spawn [. . .] both overt and subliminal racist and sexist theories and, not least, a *nouvelle vague* in anti-Semitic imagery."[35]

Now, we should not imagine that the boundary between the domain of religious authority, which had jurisdiction over Judaism in earlier centuries, and that of science was sharply delineated, nor that the transition from one to the other was wholly accomplished by the end of the nineteenth century. But grosso modo, in the course of the nineteenth century scientific interest in the classification of biological types intensified and modernized Christian religious hostility to Judaism (and, as we will see below, to sodomy), so that Jewishness (like homosexuality) came to be viewed as a pathic conglomeration of psychological and biological traits proper to all or most of the members of the group. Summarizing Hannah Arendt's analysis of this transformation and the development of modern anti-Semitism in *The Origins of Totalitarianism*,[b] Kaplan writes, "Ultimately, Judaism was transformed into 'Jewishness': the effects of a common history and collective

---

b. Arendt's theory in this work relies on Proust and his representation of the Dreyfus Affair as almost the sole illustration of her arguments, and so, while it provides an excellent reading of *À la recherche*, *Origins of Totalitarianism* may be considered problematic as an account of such a far-reaching social phenomenon as European anti-Semitism. It is nonetheless a seminal analysis, and I use it because it is exemplary rather than because it is authoritative.

political status were attributed to individual Jews as immutable racial characteristics. [...] With the passing of a political and social system explicitly grounded in Christianity, the intimate if problematic link between Judaism and the dominant religion was severed: 'Jewishness' as a racial type was contrasted not with the Christian faith but with the 'Aryan race.' "[36]

It was not only anti-Semites, of course, who adopted the rhetoric of race or conceived of Jewishness—and, for that matter, other religious affiliations—as something inborn, a question of innate status rather than behavior or choice. The French Jew André Crémieu-Foa said of being Jewish that "if this were a fault, it would be one for which we could make no amends, since you belong to one faith or another by birth."[37] Michael Marrus observes that in general, the use of the word *race* in nineteenth century France was vague and inconsistent (as it was elsewhere in the West); writers might, even within a single text, use it to refer to anything from a linguistic group to a culture to a socioeconomic class, as well as to "biology" or what we would now call genetics.[c] Marrus claims that to most French Jewish intellectuals,

> "race" was not a precise term at all; their attempts to achieve precision collapsed in hopeless contradiction. By "race" they meant, to varying degrees, a sense of community with other Jews, a sense of some common historical fate, a "solidarity of origin with men who were the co-religionists of my fathers", as [Camille] Dreyfus put it. Almost invariably this sense of solidarity, this identification with other Jews linked the living and the dead; almost invariably it joined men who had no religious bond in common; and almost invariably it was associated with a historical tradition which transcended national boundaries and went beyond human memory. This was what Proust meant when he looked for the primary cause of some ideas in "Jewish blood."[38]

c. Marrus, *Politics of Assimilation*, 12. In 1896 the homophile writer and sexologist M.-André Raffalovich complained that many scientists were using the word *heredity* with similar imprecision, continuing to promulgate the long-discredited Lamarckian theory of the heritability of acquired characteristics: "What is truly improper is the elastic acceptance many scientific sociologists accord to the word heredity, which enables them to express willy-nilly—along with the transmission of vital characteristics by generation—the transmission of ideas, of customs, of social matters, by ancestral tradition, by domestic education, by imitation/custom" (*Uranisme et unisexualité*, 143n1).

Indeed, even the most violently anti-Semitic texts of the nineteenth century, while deeply invested in a pathologized concept of the "Jewish race," seemed similarly unsure whether Jewishness was a germ or a gene, contagious or only heritable. In Britain Jewish immigrants were viewed as a threat "to the health, physical efficiency and morals of the nation," but the threat was attributed both to the inferior physical stock they represented— and might, through intermarriage, pass on to a wider population—and more immediately to the numerous diseases they were believed to carry.[39] In France a piece published in the *Revue antisémite* in 1897 asserted that Jews were planning to accomplish their scheme of taking over the French government through, among other strategies, "foreign and Jewish infiltration that will modify our customs,"[40] as though Jewishness itself were a foreign organism capable of infecting and altering non-Jewish (cultural) entities. But at about the same time we find in the lyrics to "Nouvelles chansons antijuives" the lines "Without exception, *by nature* / Jews are usurers, traitors, grasping, / Greedy, shameless, cowardly, lying thieves" (emphasis added), indicating that the psychological traits of Jewishness are fully coextensive with Jewish bodies.[41]

By and large the difference between contagion and heredity was not particularly significant to anti-Semites, who also, for example, identified "circumcision as a 'racial' characteristic of the male Jew despite the fact that it was a result of ritual practice."[42] Pericles Lewis notes that in any case, the concepts of heredity and culture were intertwined, and both were thought of as being highly deterministic.[43] On the whole, Marrus is probably correct in saying that nineteenth-century thinkers cared less to define race precisely than they did to emphasize its centrality to social formations; whatever race was, it mattered: "Race was a convenient designation which avoided a more precise definition of the nature of the ties among peoples and which betokened, at the same time, the existence of a powerful tie— far-reaching and of great social importance."[44]

JEWS AND TREASON

The belief that Jews across the globe were bound by such a tie, coinciding with the stereotype of the wandering Jew as eternally stateless, intrinsically alien to all national communities, led easily to the inference that Jews were exceptionally inclined to conspiracy, espionage, and treason. At the height of the Dreyfus Affair the Jesuit paper *Civiltà Cattolica* thundered that "the Jew was created by God to serve as a spy wherever treason is in preparation,"[45] but that conclusion had been reached well before Dreyfus was accused. "It is indisputable that every Jew betrays the man who employs him," affirms Edouard Drumont in his famous anti-Semitic treatise *La France juive*, published in 1886. "Why would God have created the Jew, if not to serve as spies?"[46] Drumont does go on to add a curious caveat, one found not infrequently in the most radically anti-Semitic writings of the period: having indicted the Jew as a traitor, he is nonetheless forced to admit that a stateless person cannot truly betray a nation to which he does not belong. Thus, Jewish espionage really ought not to be treated as treason but rather, in Drumont's bitterly sarcastic words, as "diplomacy": "For Jews, does this constitute espionage or treason? By no means. They do not betray a country they do not have; they are engaged in diplomacy, in politics, that's all."[47]

Similarly, in a piece in *Libre parole* written a few years later, the editorialist declared that "in order for a man to betray his country it is necessary first of all that he has a country, and that country cannot be acquired by an act of naturalization."[48] So while asserting that during the Franco-Prussian war German chancellor Otto von Bismarck's spies were all Jewish Alsatians, Drumont also specifies that the treachery of these spies toward France did not, *could* not, entail any corresponding loyalty to Germany. Instead, Jews are double agents by nature, owing loyalty only to nonnational forces—international Jewry, capitalism, or their own greed.[49] In Britain the editor of the *National Review* offered the same justification for making the apparently incompatible arguments that Jews were both essentially internationalists and invariably loyal to Germany, claiming that their apparent support for Germany was purely opportunistic: "Jews could intrigue for Germany because they assumed that Germany would come to dominate Europe, in which case they would receive benefits for having worked on its behalf."[50]

In their most acute forms these fears about Jewish statelessness and treachery culminated in far-reaching conspiracy theories that attributed all manner of economic and political disturbances to the occult maneuverings of inexplicably powerful Jews, particularly in the media and in financial circles. The international popularity of the *Protocols of the Elders of Zion*, a forgery that originated in Russia in the early twentieth century, testifies to the extent to which long-standing beliefs about Jewish duplicity, secretiveness, and clannishness inclined millions of people to take seriously a document purporting to demonstrate the existence of a global Jewish conspiracy to achieve world domination.

Many anti-Semites reacted to fears of Jewish treachery by trying to render Jewish alterity less obscure, insisting not only on the distinctive psychological and moral character of Jews as a class but also on the visible manifestations of that character in a peculiar, anomalous Jewish physiology. When physical difference was not immediately visible, then discursive attention would turn to more and more subtle markers: texture of hair, nose and lip shape, posture, length of limbs, number of toes, and so on.[d] In late nineteenth-century Western Europe, in fact, we find a proliferation of texts explaining to the (gentile) public how to spot Jews. No matter how minute—or ludicrous—the alleged physical difference between Jew and gentile, it was crucial that it should be identified and that the general public should learn to recognize it. In *La France juive* Drumont wrote, "The principal signs by which a Jew may be recognized are, then: the famous hooked nose, rapidly blinking eyes, clenched teeth, prominent ears, fingernails that are square rather than almond-shape, an overly long torso, flat feet, rounded knees, extraordinarily protruding ankles, the limp and melting hand of the hypocrite and the traitor. They often have one arm longer than the other."[51]

Drumont's form of anti-Semitism was translated—quite literally—into the United States by T. T. Timayenis, an American writer whose two 1888 anti-Semitic screeds, *The American Jew* and *The Original Mr. Jacobs*, belabor the themes of Jewish treachery, espionage, sexual perversion, and sinister behind-the-scenes machinations. Timayenis's works are often cited as notable examples of American anti-Semitism, but there is nothing peculiarly American or even original about them; much of his writing reproduces *La France juive* word for word, down to the captions on the book's illustrations. In fact, most American anti-Semitic texts borrow heavily from European sources and reiterate the same motifs and stereotypes. Before the late nineteenth century, although it seems that anti-Semitism did not play a serious role in American culture and politics, "there was always a backlog of traditional anti-Semitism in America, culturally

---

d. This last item permitted gentiles to merge racial with religious prejudice in claiming that Jews had only two toes on each foot, mimicking the cloven hooves of the devil. The numerous atrocities such bizarre taxonomies of difference have endorsed should give us pause when we consider apparently benign current efforts to locate, for example, homosexual difference in claims about chromosomes, hormones or, as in one much-publicized study, the alleged difference in the length of the ring finger in lesbians and heterosexual women.

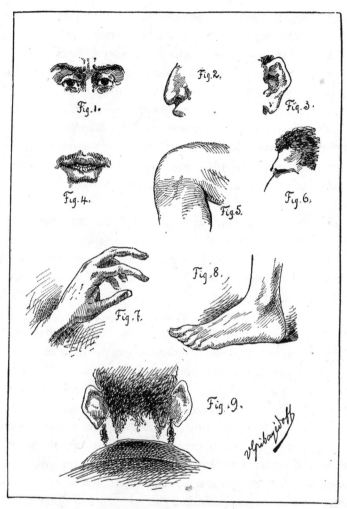

HOW WE MAY KNOW HIM.

Fig. 1. Restless suspicious eyes.	Fig. 5. Round knees.
Fig. 2. Curved nose and nostrils.	Fig. 6. Low brow.
Fig. 3. Ill-shapen ears of great size like those of a bat.	Fig. 7. Long clammy fingers.
Fig. 4. Thick lips and sharp rat's teeth.	Fig. 8. Flat feet.
	Fig. 9. Repulsive rear view.

FIGURE 1.1 *How We May Know Him.* Reproduced from T. T. Timayenis, *The American Jew: An Exposé of His Career* (New York: Minerva, 1888).

transmitted from all corners of the Western world."[52] In the United States, as in Europe, Jews were considered racially inferior to Anglo-Saxons and thus a threat to the health and morality of the "native" stock. As in Europe, they were strongly associated with urbanism, industrialization, and capitalism, and therefore, at moments in American history when populist backlashes against the evils of big cities or capitalist excesses favored a tendency toward pastoralism, anti-Semitism was also apt to flourish.[53]

With the massive influx of eastern European immigrants that began in the 1880s, anti-Semitism in the United States started to gain more political influence and also to take on the more paranoid coloration of European theories like those of Drumont and Houston Stewart Chamberlain, as Timayenis's work attests. Like Europeans, American anti-Semites adopted conspiracy theories to account for political, economic, and social phenomena ranging from the Bolshevik Revolution to anti-Semitism itself. The concept of the "monstrous Jewish pervert, familiar in European discourse," was brought to America at the same time and by the early twentieth century had had a measurable political impact.[54] In 1915 Georgia factory owner Leo Frank was lynched after being convicted of murdering a gentile girl, Mary Phagan; Frank gave an American face to the image of Jewish deviance, as he was publicly accused of unnatural practices (he allegedly forced his female employees to submit to cunnilingus). The Frank case also led to the resurrection of the Ku Klux Klan by white men protesting Mary Phagan's murder;[55] Jewish lechery thus provided the most immediate pretext for reviving an organization dedicated to anti-Semitism, anti-Catholicism, and, obviously, antiblack violence. In the 1920s Klan leadership blamed Jewish bankers for starting World War I, claimed that Jews were behind the Bolshevik Revolution, and promoted the *Protocols* and other conspiracy theories: "Some Klan leaders combined the Catholic and Jewish conspiratorial themes and suggested that Jews and Catholics were united in a plan to control the nation's press, economy, and political life. They pointed to New York as the example of an evil city controlled by Jews and Catholics."[56]

The most prominent purveyor of anti-Semitism in the United States in the 1920s was Henry Ford. Given the strong rhetorical associations between Jews and capitalism, it requires ideological ingenuity for committed capitalists to be anti-Semitic, but it is not impossible. So in the articles Ford published in the 1920s in his journal, the *Dearborn Independent*, the industrialist performs a curious rhetorical sleight of hand in order to incorporate traditional anticapitalist anti-Semitism into an American worldview. Ford explains that the owner of the means of production—that is, Ford himself—is not actually a capitalist; rather, capitalists are the Jewish financiers who control the beleaguered owning class as well as the oppressed workers and set them against each other. Jews constitute "an international supercapitalistic government."[57] The same argument was made much more successfully in Germany by Ford's admirer Adolf Hitler, but in the very different political and economic climate of the United States, Ford eventually found himself forced to disavow his claims after losing a libel suit.

Hostility toward Jewish alterity has a long history in the United States, then, even if comparative political stability and widespread acceptance of capitalism as practice and ideology have tended to mitigate the forms of anti-Semitism that Americans imported from Europe. And if figurations of the Jew as an archetypal American—deracinated, financially successful, and modern—have had an enduring presence in U.S. culture, they have also coexisted with concepts of the Jew—especially the Jewish man—as "both a disruption and a limit in the anxious construction of American notions of nationality, class, whiteness, masculinity, and culture."[58]

DEVIANCE AND THE NATION

Sexual and gender deviants[e] have for centuries been represented, like Jews, as aliens to national collectivities, and they have been similarly associated with both heresy and treason. Different European cultures characterized sodomy as a foreign aberration propagated by infidels. "In Castilian culture of the late middle ages," for example, Christians affirmed that "the Jew was the original source of sodomy: 'Sodomy came from the Jews. . . . From the Jews it went to the Muslims, to bad Christians' declares the *Libro llamado alborayque* of 1488."[59] Medievalist Allen Frantzen has found that although there is ample evidence of same-sex behavior in Anglo-Saxon England, after the Norman Conquest "sodomy acquired a specific history as a sin particular to the Norman court."[60] And if the Normans were accused of bringing unnatural vice to England, it was also suggested that they themselves had

[e]. These coincide frequently but not invariably; there have certainly been epochs and cultures in Europe in which sexual relations between men were not associated with gender deviance (see Press, "You Go, Figure," 299) or, conversely, in which effeminacy in men was taken as a sign of heterosexual immoderation rather than sodomitical tendency. In many contexts these are crucial distinctions, but for the purposes of my argument here the two so generally overlap, particularly from the nineteenth century onward, that I will usually conflate them.

learned this behavior in the Middle East during the Crusades.[61] Sodomy was also commonly attributed to heretical sects such as the Waldensians and Albigensians, or Cathars, who espoused unconventional social arrangements such as shunning marriage and procreation; Catharism was sometimes called the "Bulgarian heresy," providing the origin of the word *bugger*.

It is not surprising that sexual deviance, already viewed as both foreign and heretical, eventually came to be linked to espionage and potentially to treason: by the sixteenth century[f] we find the example of Christopher Marlowe, an accused heretic, whom rumor implicated in both sodomy and spying.[62] The sixteenth and especially the seventeenth centuries inaugurate a period where, at least in England, homosexuality "comes to figure, and to be figured in terms of, subversion of the theological order through heresy, of the legitimate political order through treason, and of the social order through disturbance of codified gender roles and stereotypes."[63] In *Homosexuality in Renaissance England* Alan Bray suggests that in a society where there is a minimal separation between church and state, or the head of one is the head of the other, a trespass against one will be considered a trespass against both; heresy and treason will not be distinct categories.[64] Thus in Anglican England—to use Bray's example—same-sex relations, because they were considered a sin, also constituted a crime against the state (and were especially likely to be associated with Roman Catholicism or non-Conformist religious sects, equally identified with both heresy and treason).

The conceptual overlap between deviance and the foreign, heretical, or subversive seems to have strengthened over the centuries. The English were especially prompt to acknowledge the existence of homosexuality in foreign cultures if they were Islamic or Catholic; if sodomy was characteristic of alien cultures, however, it could nonetheless be imported into England like any foreign custom or object. Thus Joseph Hall, bishop of Exeter and Norwich under Charles I, claimed that Spanish and Italian Catholic influence was responsible for the introduction into England of both sodomy and dueling.[65] In 1663 Samuel Pepys lamented that "buggery is now

f. If we can take the *Inferno* as an index of European Christian views on the subject, this connection would seem to have arisen some time before the sixteenth but after the thirteenth century, for Dante groups sodomites with blasphemers, the violent against God, rather than with traitors, who occupy one of the much lower circles of Hell reserved for sins of the intellect.

almost grown as common among our [English] gallants as in Italy,"[66] and in the eighteenth century John Dennis would claim that of "all the countries of the Christian world, that country has been, and is like to be, the most famous for this execrable vice [sodomy], in which idolatry has set up its headquarters"—that country being, of course, Italy, "the home of the sodomite and the pope."[67]

There was also a lengthy discursive tradition in France of projecting sexual difference onto the culturally alien, with the difference, naturally, that Catholicism was decoupled from perversion, so that Protestant England was as frequently identified with sodomy as Catholic countries like Italy. The very terms used to describe same-sex behavior—*uranisme, homosexualité*—had to be transplanted into French from other languages, lending credence to assertions that the behaviors were as foreign to France as the words describing them.[68] In Claude Courouve's dictionary of gay slang, in a list of twenty-one adjectives commonly used in French since the early modern period to modify *mœurs* ("mores" or "customs") in order to signify homosexuality, more than half of them refer to foreign nations or geographical regions, including "Arab," "Greek," "Italian," "Asiatic," "Byzantine," "Levantine," "Tunisian," and "German."[69]

In particular, the concept of *mœurs allemandes*, or "German mores," became ever more resonant in the course of the eighteenth and nineteenth centuries, as tensions grew and wars flared between France and Germany. Courouve cites an obscene ditty dating from 1784, describing a meeting place of homosexuals: "For in this place every naughty boy / Enjoyed himself just as they do in Berlin" ("Car en ce lieu chaque vilain / S'amusait tout comme à Berlin").[70] Eventually, after the Franco-Prussian War, the association of Germany with sexual deviance became deeply etched into French popular consciousness. The development of sexology as a field in Germany and the simultaneous appearance of an early German homophile emancipation movement in the last decades of the nineteenth century, as well as the eruption of several highly publicized homosexual scandals there in the early years of the twentieth, helped to reinforce the conjunction not only for the French but throughout Europe.

A few judicious fin-de-siècle French sexologists ventured to question whether homosexuality were really more common abroad than in France,[71] but more popular, less sober writers insisted vigorously on the point. In his significantly titled 1896 work *Les invertis (Le vice allemand)*, a peculiar hybrid of Gothic bodice ripper and sexological treatise, the French writer Armand

Dubarry devoted a full chapter to an inflamed attack against the sexual perversity of the modern Germans. Despite the notorious decadence of the East, he claims, "neither the inhabitants of Crete, nor those of the Levant, nor those of Naples, nor the modern Orientals have ever known this Teutonic exaltation, and one may say that in no other country does inversion have the volcanic intensity that it has acquired in Germany."[72] Dubarry is scathing on the subject of "the multitudes of barbarians who inundated our territory in 1870, burned our open cities, shot our troops [*francs-tireurs*], our women, our agèd men," and claims the barbarian horde was "swarming with sodomites."[73] We note that armed French soldiers (*francs-tireurs*) are here reduced to the same degree of helplessness as women and the elderly, making it clear that Dubarry's outrage is spurred especially by the violent effeminization of French men effected by the sodomitical German penetration of their national body. "The body politic," writes Cameron McFarlane, "like the (male) body, establishes its integrity by maintaining its impenetrability";[74] the violation of the former implies, when it does not literally entail, the violation of the latter and the loss of integrity for both.

While Dubarry's prose is purpler than most, his rhetoric draws thematically on a solidly established convention. Even those who disputed the stereotype of German deviance had to admit that it was ubiquitous.[75] So widespread was this correlation, indeed, that French homosexuals apparently came to adopt it as a coded means of self-identification; Robert de Billy recalled telling Marcel Proust that by the early 1900s the question "Do you speak German?" had become a password among Parisian homosexuals.[g] It is clear, then, that even though in France homosexuality had been formally relegated to the private sphere once consensual homosexual conduct between adults was decriminalized after the Revolution and then in the Napoleonic Code,[h] it continued to be perceived, even by

---

g. Billy, *Marcel Proust*, 176. According to Michel Rey's study of Parisian police reports in the eighteenth century, the same kind of code was used in France in an earlier period, but the foreign language mentioned was not German but Latin: "When a boy did not seem to respond to advances, 'they said to each other: Let's let him go, he doesn't understand Latin'" ("Parisian Homosexuals," 187). It seems likely that Latin was chosen because of its associations with elite minorities, arcane ritual, and recondite knowledge, just as, by the late nineteenth century, German would suggest the scientific study of, and political and cultural organizing around, deviant sexuality.

h. The code imposes a sharp legal distinction between consensual homosexual acts committed privately and without witnesses and those constituting a public affront to decency.

French homosexuals themselves, as an inassimilable anomaly within the public, national domain. Like religious or cultural difference, sexual difference threatened the liberal concept of the nation as a contract between publicly identical individuals, necessitating its sequestration as a foreign import. In an article on sexuality in the Dreyfus Affair to which I will return later, Nicholas Dobelbower observes that "in the context of French Republicanism, with its particular attachment to universalism, gay difference, like Jewish difference, metonymically portends the end of a unified notion of Frenchness, and through a process of semantic slippage tends to be assimilated to the difference represented by dangerous foreign powers. French homosexuality, in other words, is not French, but rather always symbolically foreign. From there, we are only a step away from questioning national allegiances."[76]

In Britain sexual deviance also came to be associated with Germany, partly, as in France, because of the visibility of German sexology and the German homophile emancipation movement. But as was the case with anti-German anti-Semitism, it was not until Britain was directly engaged in military conflict with Germany in World War I that anti-German homophobia assumed a prominent place in British national discourses. Michael Kettle has argued that in the face of Germany's military successes in the war, the English sought clues both to the German psychological character and to Britain's unexpected military weakness; some concluded that sexual perversion explained the German psyche and also accounted for British military defeats. If more sodomy cases were being prosecuted in Britain, then this was not because young men were "being herded together under wartime conditions" but instead because the Germans were turning Englishmen into homosexuals.[77] Late in the war right-wing journalist Arnold White warned in the *English Review* that a German victory was likely because conspiratorial homosexuals, for whom he used the German sexologists' term *urnings*, were undermining Britain from both without and within:

A great cancer, made in Germany, is eating at the heart of England and civilization. [. . .] Londoner urnings have more in common with Teuton urnings than with their own countrymen. Espionage is punished by death at the Tower of London, but there is a form of invasion which is as deadly as espionage: the systematic seduction of young British soldiers by the German urnings and their agents. [. . .] When the blonde beast is an urning he commands the

urnings in other lands. They are moles. They burrow. They plot.
They are hardest at work when they are most silent.[78]

Conservative MP Noel Pemberton-Billing added an element to White's
formula by specifying that the urnings were being directed by Jews. Pemberton-Billing used his papers, the *Vigilante* and the *Imperialist*, to promote
his view "that the British war effort was being undermined by the 'hidden
hand' of German sympathizers and German Jews operating in Britain,"
and that the weapons of choice of those he liked to call "the Shylocks of
Frankfurt" and "the Ashkenazim" were prostitution and homosexuality.[79]
In a March 1918 article published in the *Vigilante* Pemberton-Billing wrote
that "the German through his efficient and clever agent, the Ashkenazim,
has complete control of the White Slave Traffic. Germany has found that
diseased women cause more casualties than bullets. Controlled by their
Jew-agents, Germany maintains in Britain a self-supporting—even profit-
making—army of prostitutes which put more men out of action than does
their army of soldiers."[80]

Of even greater concern to Pemberton-Billing, however, was the existence of a "Black Book" in which the Germans were supposed to be keeping a list of tens of thousands of English sex perverts, in order to blackmail
prominent Britons into committing espionage and treason. In an effort to
draw attention to this alleged security crisis, Pemberton-Billing began trying to get himself sued for libel so that he could use a trial for publicity, and
eventually succeeded when he named the actress Maud Allen as a lesbian.
Yet during the subsequent trial, the prosecuting counsel made it clear that
male homosexuality and its relationship to treason were at the heart of the
case: "In this country at present," he told the jurors, "the most horrible
suggestion that you can make against any man is that he is addicted to sodomite practices. The next most horrible suggestion is that he is a traitor to
his country, and is in the pay of the Germans."[81]

Summing up the effect of the Pemberton-Billing trial on the British
public, Lucy Bland writes that it introduced to lay people the medical-
ized conception of sexual perversions, which "were not simply 'vices'
(the older moral term referring to vicious *acts*), but constitutive of genetic
make-up and personal inclination. They were also essentially non-British,
indeed *German* in essence, and their perpetrators were traitors. Xenophobia joined ranks with homophobia."[82] As we have seen, that conjunction is
neither recent nor exclusively British but derives from a long tradition of

projecting sexual difference onto the culturally alien by associating deviance with foreign languages and cultures (that which is alien *outside* the state) or with treason (the alien *within* the state).

Historians of sexuality have suggested that this phenomenon is linked to competition between European colonial powers, since the idea of sexual self-mastery played a crucial role in European colonialist narratives: those who could not discipline themselves sexually could not be considered fit to rule over the savages of Africa and the New World. But since the phenomenon predates the period of colonial expansion, there are obviously other factors at work as well. For one thing, blaming deviance on foreigners would seem to be reassuring because it holds out the possibility that perversion can be stopped at the border. When modern states started trying to forge national collectivities out of city-states, feudal domains, or multiethnic empires, it was presumably useful for them to have a way to account for the ubiquity of sexual variations while still consolidating a sense of themselves as bounded cultural entities unified by, among other things, a common, normative sexuality. At the same time, however, reiterated images of sodomitical infection or invasion reflect the persistent anxiety that national integrity is always threatened by "a dangerous and contaminating permeability."[83] If xenophobia can itself represent the fear of being sodomized—penetrated by the alien, that which is not natural to a country—then anxiety about the importation of sodomy into the homeland would reflect a kind of metaxenophobia, the fear of the nation's being unnaturally penetrated by unnatural kinds of penetration. The domestic sodomite would be an accomplice to this perverted assault on the national body and hence a traitor, requiring extirpation in order to restore national health and wholeness.

JEWS AND DEVIANCE

The Pemberton-Billing trial cast into sharp relief a discursive relationship between deviance and Jews, who were depicted in this particular instance as vectors transmitting perversion between Germany and Britain. But long before the Great War "the link between the Jew and the sexual other had been forged in the imaginative literature of Europe and England."[84] Scholars like Sander Gilman have described an entrenched European convention concatenating Jewishness with sexual or gender deviance, dating back at least to the medieval association between sodomy and usury. Later, the

myth that Jewish men menstruated arose, proving that they failed to conform to gender norms so thoroughly as to constitute an interruption not
only of the social but also of the natural order.[85]

Daniel Boyarin, Paul Breines, and others have provided a valuable
supplement to Gilman's work by proposing that Jewish male alterity was
not simply a malicious stereotype but for centuries actually represented
"an assertive historical product of Jewish culture," a deliberate resistance
to Christian norms of gendered behavior.[86] Boyarin claims that it was only
after the Enlightenment—when Jewish citizenship was facilitated by cultural assimilation—that Jewish men came to adopt dominant constructions of masculinity. Thus it was precisely "the process of 'Emancipation' [. . .] that produced both the pain and the difficulty of Jewish (male)
identity," and it was as a result of that process that "the specter of the Jewish
man as inherently queer engendered something like collective panic"—in
Jews as well as gentiles.[i] The pathologization of Jewish gender and sexuality, then, like the pathologization of Jewishness as a racial trait, can only be
fully understood within the context of both centuries-old prejudices and
new incentives to discipline difference in the service of creating cohesive
national communities of citizens.

In the course of the nineteenth century, as that project accelerated
and new national states were created throughout Europe, the sciences of
race and sex came to coincide not merely thematically but literally: "All the
race doctors were sex doctors and vice versa."[87] The scientific classification
of Jews as a race gave new authority to the figuration of the Jewish man's
body as anomalous and of Jewish sexuality as diseased: "The 'Jew's body'
was feminized and linked to a threatening sexuality. [. . .] This stereotype,
together with the association of Jews with a propensity for mental illness
and syphilis, combined to mark Jews as infectious agents of sexual corruption within the body politic. These tendencies were 'explained' in terms of
the Jewish practice of endogamy, which was conflated with incest."[88] Thus,
Drumont cites Johann Caspar Lavater's *Physiognomische Fragmente zur
Beförderung der Menschenkenntnis und Menschenliebe* (1775–1778), in which

---

i. Boyarin, *Unheroic Conduct*, 5; and Bunzl, "Book Review," 329–30. This is an important point
to bear in mind throughout the analysis I offer here, for I would not wish it to be assumed
that because I describe with sympathy the desire of Jewish and homosexual men to achieve
normative masculinity and full citizenship, I am uncritical of either masculinity or the liberal
state.

Lavater wrote that male Jews have "a sparse beard, the common sign of effeminate temperaments." Drumont follows this comment on the inadequate masculinity of Jewish men by quoting Lavater on Jewish "moral degradation": "Physical degradation [...] always follows on the heels of moral degradation; it is more noticeable in the Hebrews, the result of complete depravity."[89] Jewish moral culpability is immediately juxtaposed with, and by implication causes, the deviant gender identity of the Jewish male.

In 1903, after the birth of Zionism, the notorious Jewish anti-Semite Otto Weininger would return to the theme of Jewish men's inadequate masculinity in order to argue that Jews would never be able to commit themselves even to a *Jewish* nation, both because Jewish identity as such was necessarily diasporic and, more importantly, because Jews, like women, lacked the mature rationality necessary to form a true social contract:

> Zionism is the negation of Judaism, for the conception of Judaism involves a world-wide distribution of the Jews. Citizenship is an un-Jewish thing, and there has never been and never will be a true Jewish State. [...] The true conception of the State is foreign to the Jew because he, like the woman, is wanting in personality; his failure to grasp the idea of true society is due to his lack of a free intelligible ego. Like women, Jews tend to adhere together, but they do not associate as free independent individuals mutually respecting each other's individuality.[90]

Several modern commentators have argued that European anti-Semitism always takes Jewish men as synonymous with Jewishness itself and that the feminization of the Jewish man, paradoxically, erases Jewish women entirely. "In the implicit equation of Jews and women," writes Ann Pellegrini, "the Jewish female body goes missing. All Jews are womanly, but no women are Jews."[91] This is not entirely accurate; Weininger, for example, is obsessively concerned with the psychological and moral deficits of the Jewish woman, the sexual licentiousness of Jewish women was a common trope of anti-Semitic discourse, and many fin-de-siècle texts discuss the preponderance of Jewish female prostitutes in the respective countries of their authors.[92] But it is true that in general a good deal more rhetorical energy, more libidinal force, was expended on Jewish men and masculinity in the nineteenth and twentieth centuries, for reasons that should be clear by now: the problem posed by European Jews was above all a problem of how to define a nation, and women were not full citizens. It was men who participated, and competed, in the public institutions of national life; thus it is Jewish men, men who are perceived as feminine but are not women, who are the focus of anxiety about the nation.

HOMOSEXUALS, JEWS, TRAITORS

In the late nineteenth century the equation between effeminacy, incapacity for citizenship, and moral degradation that had been diagnosed in Jewish men at least since the Enlightenment was applied by sexologists to male inverts, increasingly identified (like Jews) as a biologically distinctive class. Work by Bray, Courouve, and others has shown that gender/sex deviants were sometimes recognized as special types before the second half of the nineteenth century, problematizing Foucault's hypothesis that the modern homosexual was an invention of that period, but they have not undermined his argument entirely. If the phenomenon is not wholly new, there is nonetheless a significant and characteristic difference in the degree to which, in the late nineteenth century, a religious understanding of sodomitical acts as discrete sins was replaced in the popular imagination by the medical concept of *homosexuality*, or *inversion*, an ontological condition almost inseparable from gender identity and described and treated as vice or pathology.[j] So too Jewishness ceased to be primarily a matter of something one practiced—Judaism—and became something one *was*, claims Arendt: "Jewish origin, without religious and political connotation, became everywhere a psychological quality, was changed into 'Jewishness,' and from then on could be considered only in the categories of virtue or vice";[93] conversely, as the individual who engaged in homosex became a "homosexual," those addicted to this vice could now also be categorized as belonging to an alien culture or race.

Kaplan neatly sums up many of the points of intersection between Jews and homosexuals in medical, popular, religious, and juridical fin-de-siècle discourses, memes that will resurface in the literary and social texts I analyze in subsequent chapters:

j. This evolution from a primarily religious conception of homosexuality to a primarily psychological one is sometimes visible within a single text, as when François Carlier writes in 1887 that "as for pederasty, it is simply a vice deriving from one of the seven deadly sins, lust" (*La prostitution antiphysique*, 90). This is the only use of the term "sin" in his work, however, and it is equally rare in other contemporary writings.

Like homosexuals, Jews were understood in terms of biologically based inherent characteristics, and yet thought to be capable of a dissembling invisibility. They shared access to a "hidden language" understood only by others of their kind; possession of a distinctive pattern of speech that involuntarily revealed their "inner nature"; propensities to mental illness and physical disease, especially those linked with sexuality; identification with urban living and with the ills of urban civilization; perception as sources of danger to normal families; incapacity to discharge the (manly) duties of citizens, especially military service; and a tendency to debilitating self-hatred.[94]

The correspondence between the two is often visible, then, in the traits they share and the comparable (and sometimes intersecting) anxieties they generate, but it is important to note that the connection was also at times imagined to be quite literal and indeed causal. The already existing imbrication of the Oriental, effeminacy, and decadence[k] permitted sexologists to speculate that Jews were, as Orientals, particularly prone to homosexuality. Dubarry lists, among the countries "infected" by homosexuality, "China, Japan, India, Persia, Babylonia, Assyria and her capital Ninevah, Palestine (Sodom and Gomorrah), Phoenicia, Asia Minor, Egypt, Greece, Rome, the Byzantine Empire," concluding his sweeping indictment of the depraved and luxurious East by observing that "the Jews, inclined to sensuality, the incorrigibly sensual Jews, were sexually unruly from early times [furent de bonne heure de désordonnés sexuels]."[95] Another early sexological text, Georges Saint-Paul's *L'homosexualité et les types homosexuels*, contains a reproduction (in discreet Latin translation) of the *Roman d'un inverti*, a sort of pornographic confession or apologia that an Italian homosexual had sent to Emile Zola, who passed it on to Saint-Paul. Commenting on the mixed parentage of the confession's author, Saint-Paul asks, "Are we not obliged to notice, in the *Roman d'un inverti*, the influence of the crossbreeding of two beings of essentially different races: the Latin father and

k. For example, Henri de Weindel and F.-P. Fischer wrote that homosexuality can be found everywhere among peoples of "exhausted blood" and high "intellectual culture," including Arabs, Persians, and the Japanese (*L'homosexualité en Allemagne*, 180). In 1909 Guy Delrouze asserted categorically that "the taste is profound, innate, universal in the races of the Orient" ("Le préjugé," 15). Even M.-André Raffalovich, usually skeptical of theories attributing homosexuality to specific races, referred casually to "the Orient of today, where pederasty can be practiced without difficulty" (*Uranisme et unisexualité*, 87).

the Jewish mother? Must we not also believe that inversion occurs more frequently in the Jewish race, which has remained, despite its infinitely variable and mobile appearances, entirely, exclusively, oriental?"[96] The same theme migrated to the United States; in *The American Jew* Timayenis concludes a chapter on "The Jew Lecher" by noting darkly that Jewish perversion cannot be satisfied by ordinary heterosexual vice but feeds on unnatural practices imported, of course, from "countries of the East":

> Not only is the Jew a liberal patron of [. . .] houses of prostitution; but such is the insatiability of his carnal appetites, and to such an extent does he give rein to his lasciviousness, that his debauches only too frequently exceed the ordinary limits of lust. Those certain hideous and abhorrent forms of vice, which have their origin in countries of the East, and which have in recent years sprung into existence in this country, have been taught to the abandoned creatures who practise them, and fostered, elaborated, and encouraged, by the lecherous Jew![97]

In 1908 another American study of homosexuality (which its author called "Uranism" or "simisexualism") succinctly observed, "The Jew, always erotic in temperament, is so frequently Uranian, or uranistic, that there is a sort of psychiatric proverb—'so many Jews, so many similisexualists.'"[98] And finally, carrying this trope of Jewish deviance to its limit, the argument was occasionally made that Jews were not only especially inclined to homosexuality but had in fact *invented* it.[99]

THE FAMILY AND THE STATE

In the whole network of relations between Jewishness and sex/gender deviance, the chain of associations that will assume the greatest significance in my argument is the one that links together the patriarchal family with national affiliation, describes Jews and homosexuals as interrelated threats to both familial and national integrity, and consequently assigns to both an overdetermined relationship to Communism. To begin tracing this series of associations let us recall that Otto Weininger argued Jewish men were unfit for citizenship because they suffered from an impairment of mature rationality that aligned them not only with women but with children. That claim relied on an older, theological representation of

Judaism as a failure of growth or maturity in relationship to Christianity; since "many Christians understood Christianity to be the fulfillment of Judaism, Jews were assumed to be immature and childlike."[100] Viewed as both effeminate and immature, Jewish men did not adequately fulfill the role of bourgeois paterfamilias; this may explain why, despite the patriarchal and family-centered culture of European Jewry, Jews were nonetheless perceived to be a threat to gentile families.[101] For example, when Alfred Naquet, who was of Jewish descent, pressed a liberalized divorce law through the French Parliament in 1884, it prompted intense Catholic hostility toward French Jews, denounced as "destroyers of the Christian family."[102] In André Gide's defense of homosexuality, *Corydon*, the protagonist Corydon shows the reactionary narrator a copy of Jewish socialist Léon Blum's controversial 1907 work *Du mariage (Marriage)*, which advocates sexual experimentation before marriage for both sexes; the narrator indignantly retorts, "The Jews are past masters in the art of demolishing our most respected, our most venerable institutions, the very ones that are the foundation and the support of our western civilization."[103]

Homosexual men, for their part, were characterized as cowardly and immature in their social and civic capacities because they shirked the duties of the bourgeois husband and father. The chief of the Parisian morals police in the 1880s, François Carlier, claimed that "the pederastic passion [. . .] debases the most vigorous natures, renders the sturdiest characters effeminate, and engenders cowardice. It extinguishes, in those whom it possesses, the noblest sentiments, those of patriotism and of the family; it makes of them creatures useless to society."[104] The same theme reappeared, as we will see in chapter 5, in a Cold War discourse that assumed the nuclear family to be integral to "democracy": both conservative and liberal cold warriors agreed in the 1950s that "homosexuals lay outside the anchoring interests of the patriarchal nuclear family, and thus outside the moral order of rational political discourse. Homosexuals were by definition not legitimate political actors in a republic. [. . .] Driven by their appetites, they lacked the ability to sublimate their passions to the requirements of civic duty and political life."[105] Thus excluded from participation in family and nation, Jews and homosexuals were, as we have already seen, assumed to be essentially cosmopolitan and without national loyalty. Dubarry waxed indignant at the lack of national sentiment that characterized nominally "French" homosexuals: "They find nothing in France to their taste, not even the fatherland, for they are internationalists. Having lost their common sense and their conception of our beautiful, limpid language, they have also lost their sense of good and evil."[106] Dubarry's formula invokes a nationalist sentiment that would express itself in the appropriate deployment of both the French language and French sexuality; misusing one, homosexuals necessarily abuse the other. Like Yiddish-speaking Jews, they do not speak the national language—or the language of nationalism—correctly.

As they transgressed national borders, Jews and homosexuals were also accused of traversing class boundaries, and consequently of favoring internationalist, left-wing political movements and of promoting the goal of social egalitarianism. Bismarck is supposed to have said that "homosexuality constitutes a grave danger for the State because it suppresses social barriers."[107] Carlier evoked an image of an international homosexual freemasonry confounding all boundaries of class: "Turkey, Italy, Germany, seem to us to be unparalleled in this regard; there, as here, the highest classes of society mingle in orgies with the working class."[108] Jews, too, were strongly associated with alien, radical, and threatening political philosophies, whether anarchism or socialism and Communism.[1] Otto Weininger argued that sympathy for Communism was another manifestation of the Jew's psychological and developmental weakness, claiming that "property is indissolubly connected with the self, with individuality. It is in harmony with the foregoing that the Jew is so readily disposed to Communism. [...] The Jew is an inborn communist."[109] Furthermore, Communism allegedly promoted free love, liberal divorce laws, and communal ownership of women and thus was consonant with and reinforced the threat homosexuals and Jews presented to the family.

There were indeed radical homosexual men, like the British socialists Edward Carpenter and John Addington Symonds, who hoped that by uniting men through an erotic bond that transcended class barriers, male homosexuality could advance the causes of democracy and socialism; in an 1893 letter to Carpenter, Symonds wrote that "the blending of Social Strata in masculine love seems to me one of its most pronounced, & socially hopeful, features. Where it appears, it abolishes class distinctions. [...] If it could be acknowledged & extended, it would do very much

---

1. Needless to say, there are numerous differences and conflicts between and within Socialist and Communist groups and movements; my only excuse for conflating them here is that those distinctions were often irrelevant to those for whom any involvement in any left-wing cause was a demonstration of Jewish or homosexual perfidy.

to further the advent of the right sort of Socialism."[110] Homosexuality, as a contemporary scholar observes, really "was one of the most important avenues by which generations of Englishmen broke through the barriers of class, privilege, and rank," as it was for American men.[111] Similarly, there is some foundation for the stereotype of the left-wing Jew: Karl Marx was of course ethnically Jewish, Jews did play a prominent role in the Bolshevik Revolution, and they were represented disproportionately in Communist parties internationally. For Jews Communism was often a response to their own oppression and disenfranchisement within brutally hierarchical societies like czarist Russia; in addition, many Jews viewed left-wing politics as a logical extension of a Jewish ethical emphasis on justice.

For anti-Semites and conservatives, however, radical politics and particularly the Russian Revolution were instruments of the international Jewish conspiracy, further evidence of the Jews' inexorable march toward world conquest. In England adventure writer H. Rider Haggard referred to Bolshevism as "a great Jewish plot,"[112] but even eminently respectable institutions like the British Foreign Office and the *Times* remarked the "pronounced Jewish involvement in Bolshevism" and asserted that three-quarters of Bolshevist leaders were Jews.[113]

American anti-Semites, who retained European suspicions of the Jews' liminal relationship to national citizenship, found their fears confirmed by the influx of Ashkenazi immigrants involved in left-wing political movements. In the American media, government agencies, and the public imagination, the Communist was often identified with the Jew as a figure of deceptiveness, political subversion, and resistance to American ideals. The 1920 report of the sixty-sixth Congress on suspending immigration notes several times the connection between Jewish immigrants and radical ideologies, claiming that the majority of Polish immigrants are Jews who "belong to the undesirable classes; that is, those who are prone to congregate in the large cities, and from whom the present type of political and labor agitators are drawn."[114]

Henry Ford's editorials in the *Dearborn Independent* emphasized that an important part of the Communist agenda in Russia was to teach "sex knowledge" to gentile children in order to corrupt them, something he warned was also being attempted in the United States.[115] Despite Ford's late-1920s recantation, the conspiracy theory he promoted remained robust for many years, disseminated in the 1930s by populist anti-Semites

FIGURE 1.2 *Whoever Assists the Jew in His Work*. Reproduced from the *American Bulletin*. Collection of the American Jewish Historical Society, New York, N.Y., and Newton, Mass.

like Father Charles Coughlin and the Reverend Gerald Winrod. And it provided ample ammunition for attacks on the New Deal as a Jewish, Bolshevist plot orchestrated by the Roosevelts—who, after all, supported sex education in the public schools and were alleged to be secret Jews themselves, descendants of a "Rosenvelt" or "Rossocampo" family.

ASSIMILATION OR EXCEPTIONALISM

In view of the ubiquity and intensity of all the pathologizing stereotypes I have enumerated, the "dissembling invisibility" of Jews and homosexuals necessarily raised complex dilemmas about (self-)revelation, assimilation, and secrecy for members of the two groups. Openly to adopt cultural practices, clothing, mannerisms, or a vocabulary that announced one's difference meant inviting hostility, discrimination, and sometimes prosecution and violence. On the other hand, to try to conform to gentile or heterosexual norms meant, precisely, to dissemble what gentile, heterosexual culture indicted as the intrinsically different nature of the Jew or homosexual and thus to confirm that Jews and homosexuals were indeed different because they dissembled: because they were secretive, untrustworthy, treacherous.

For Jews one response to this quandary was Zionism, which held out the promise of a modern, "mature" national identity equal to, but separate from, European national identities. The remedy for Jewish transnationalism was Jewish nationalism; if Communism was a symptom of immaturity, having their own nation would allow Jewish men to become adult citizens without obliging—or allowing—them to blend invisibly into a gentile culture. In 1920 Winston Churchill advocated Zionism, which would offer Jews "a national idea," as a means of siphoning off Jewish energy that might otherwise be devoted to international Communism, which he characterized as a "world-wide conspiracy for the overthrow of civilisation and for the reconstitution of society on the basis of arrested development, of envious malevolence, and impossible equality." Churchill deplored the "sinister confederacy" of "International Jews" that he described as "the mainspring of every subversive movement during the Nineteenth Century"; in contrast, Zionism would direct "the energies and the hopes of Jews in every land towards a simpler, a truer, and a far more attainable goal" than Communism.[116]

Jewish Zionists subscribed to the premise that only by becoming a distinct nation could Jews achieve acceptance. The French Zionist Jacques Bahar wrote in 1899 that the Zionists' open assertion of national difference was reassuring to French gentiles, who were mistrustful of assimilationist Jews: "The truth is that, even from the French, patriotic point of view, we [Zionists] inspire greater confidence in [gentiles] than the anti-Zionists do. The Christians sense instinctively that those Jews are denying something in themselves in order to resemble them—and that makes them uneasy. They are unconsciously right, these *goyim!*"[117] Zionism arose, of course, in response to the Dreyfus Affair; central European and German Jews like Theodore Herzl and Max Nordau were persuaded by the violent outbreak of French anti-Semitism that if even egalitarian, democratic France could not guarantee the security of its Jews, they could not be safe anywhere. The promise of liberal democracy to treat all citizens equally appeared to have failed.

Nevertheless, comparatively few French Jews embraced Zionism. If liberalism, with its ideology of universalism and privatized ethno-religious identities, left them unprepared to confront the anti-Semitism provoked by the Affair as a political problem, Jewish nationalism nonetheless presented its own troubling reinscription of a conflation between race and nation. French Jews had spent the better part of a century asserting their right to participate fully in the French national community, and few were prepared to exchange their citizenship, however contested it was by anti-Semites, for literal or metaphorical exile. Many British and American Jews were ambivalent about Zionism for the same reason, and some major Jewish organizations in both Britain and the United States were for a time strongly anti-Zionist.

This problem reasserted itself after the state of Israel was founded in 1948; if the point of a Jewish homeland was to gather Jews in from exile (and for decades Zionists had argued about whether Palestine represented *the* Jewish homeland or merely *a* Jewish homeland), what relation to Israel was obligatory, or possible, for Jews in the Diaspora who felt at home where they were? In 1950 American Jewish Committee president Jacob Blaustein pointedly told Israeli prime minister David Ben-Gurion, "I would be less than frank if I did not point out to you that American Jews vigorously repudiate any suggestion or implication that they are in exile. American Jews—young and old alike, Zionists and non-Zionists alike—are profoundly attached to America." Blaustein went on to caution the prime minister that "harm has been done to the morale and to some extent to the sense of security of the American Jewish community through unwise and unwarranted statements and appeals" to emigrate to Israel.[118]

Obviously, the position of homosexuals at the turn of the twentieth century was not precisely comparable to that of Jews; even among comparatively assimilated and politically quiescent Western Jews there were established Jewish cultures, identities, and institutions, and overt anti-Semitism was not particularly acceptable in mainstream discourse in any Western democracy. In contrast, only the nascent rudiments of homosexual identities or subcultures had arisen in most places in the West, there were few homophile organizations, and the stigmatization of deviance was

hardly questioned publicly. Nonetheless, we can perceive certain congru-
ities between the ways Jews and homosexuals framed discussions of their
relationships to the nation, for instance, and sketch the outlines of comparable assimilationist-separatist debates within the homosexual emancipation movements that had arisen in Germany, Britain, and the United States
by the late nineteenth century. Were sexual deviants, as some of them
argued, just like other citizens except for a peculiar and harmless quirk
of taste or temperament? Or did they form a distinct elite, exceptional in
either its aesthetic sensitivity or its virility inherited from the warrior cultures of ancient Greece?

Those debates took place, by and large, in the countries where sodomy laws gave sexual deviants specific goals around which to organize. In
France, in contrast—where private same-sex sexual conduct per se was
decriminalized—men who wanted and had the means to engage in consensual homosex in their homes did not run the same risk of having their
desires forcibly exposed in the public sphere. Therefore, while they had
still to confront homophobic rhetoric and repression in virtually every
realm of life, they had no specific institutional arenas in which to try to
intervene, and consequently there was no homophile movement to speak
of in France until later in the twentieth century. The privatization of central
aspects of Jewish or homosexual life—religious belief in one case, homosexual acts in the other—made it difficult to formulate collective identities
and movements.

But whether because, or in spite, of the absence in France of an ideology of minority identity, it was a Frenchman, Marcel Proust, who seems
to have been one of the first writers to imagine—if only ironically—that
homosexual desire could produce identities, relations to the nation, and
even movements in the same way that Jewishness could manifest itself in
a commitment to Zionism. In the 1890s anxieties about Jewishness, sexual
deviance, and national security had combined, reacted, and exploded in
a case that came to threaten the foundations of the French state. Writing
his magnum opus in the years just before and during World War I, when
France's national aspirations and integrity were once again crucially at
stake, Proust found in the Dreyfus Affair a rich discursive paradigm for
analyzing both Jewishness and homosexuality in relation to national identity. While many critics have discussed the novelist's lifelong interest in
the Affair, few have noticed that it was the centrality not only of Jewishness
but also of sexuality to the scandal that helped make it such a useful model

for Proust, allowing him to employ espionage as an analog for Jewish and homosexual experience and thus to offer a reading of subaltern cultural and sexual identities and practices as treason. For sexuality wove its way through the case, motivating its complicities, obscuring its conspiracies, and becoming intervolved with Jewishness in the rhetoric of treason and the process of national self-fashioning. The Affair, as we will see in the next chapter, marks a crucial moment in the becoming-modern of race, sexuality, and the state.

2

THE DREYFUS AFFAIR

> Lies and sexuality always touch so closely upon one another, be-
> cause reality belies desire, because the before and the after meet
> and contradict each other.
>
> —Marc-André Raffalovich, *Uranisme et unisexualité*

In France during the last two decades of the nineteenth century, abstract
concerns about difference and its (il)legibility in the case of Jews coincided
with material incitements to anti-Semitism in the form of several political and financial crises. Speculative bubbles popped, rousing public ire
against rich Jews who were accused of manipulating the market.[a] In particular, familiar stereotypes (newly underwritten by scientific authority) of
scheming, greedy international Jewry were easily attached to a few powerful Jewish families like the Rothschilds who were especially visible in the
financial and political worlds. When, in the midst of an economic depres-
sion, the Catholic Banque d'Union générale crashed in 1882, it was widely
believed that it had been deliberately driven into bankruptcy by the Rothschilds. During the Panama scandal members of Parliament were accused
of accepting bribes to help failed companies build the Panama Canal and
ruining many small investors in the process—and two of the Panama Canal

---

a. Interestingly, Cameron McFarlane observes that in the wake of the 1720 South Sea swin-
dle and other stock-based scams in England, charges of both conspiracy and sodomy were
leveled against stockjobbers, the representatives of what seemed in the eighteenth century a mysteriously invisible, unproductive, unnatural new "virtual" economy (*Sodomite*,
102–3). McFarlane fails to note that these charges revived the much older medieval homology between sodomites and usurers, whose investment in sterile exchange generates no
children, product, or use value and thus violates the divinely prescribed productive order of
nature. The nineteenth century recast this trope in ubiquitous representations of usurious
Jews as the embodiment of all the ills of a credit economy.

Company's wealthy directors were Jewish. More generally, the aristocracy and *grande bourgeoisie* feared they were losing economic ground to the republican middle classes, the classes to which most Jews belonged; they shared this concern with other social elements such as peasants and small-business owners, who, despite their varied economic interests, were able to develop a sense of national solidarity cemented by hostility to Jews, the Republic, and large-scale capital.[1]

Finally, even among republicans and those on the political left, the military disasters of 1870–1871 provoked acute anti-German patriotism, a sense of collective mourning for the lost territories of Alsace and Lorraine, the fear of betrayal, and a desire for revenge. While probably most French Jews shared in these sentiments, anti-Semitic ideology consistently identified Jews not only with treason but specifically, as we saw in the previous chapter, with Germany. Numerous references in the Catholic and anti-Semitic press of the time show how consistently *Jewish* was assumed to be cognate with *German*. An illustration from the virulently anti-Semitic *Calendrier des Youtres* (the "Yid Calendar"), published in 1899, depicts a large boot kicking a Jew back over the frontier from France to Germany.[2] *La libre parole* and *La Croix* refer repeatedly to "the Jewish and German syndicate" and claim that "the frightful Jews, vomited up into France by the ghettos of Germany, can barely jabber our language."[3] This (mis)identification was presumably facilitated by the fact that Jews constituted less than one-quarter of one percent of the French population, so that "most Frenchmen had never seen a Jew. In their eyes there was something monstrous about these descendants of the crucifers of the Son of God. They might be anywhere, unseen. In this they seemed like the forces of finance, pervasive and invisible."[4]

Thus, whether they were members of long-established French families or recent Russian immigrants; spoke French, German, Russian, or Yiddish; practiced Jewish rituals or were baptized—Jews were marked as German, and Germany was the archenemy. Since many French people believed that France had lost the war because of treachery, and that agents of the Kaiser were everywhere, they leaped quickly to the conclusion that the betrayers were likely to have been Jews, with their liminal racial identities and suspicious bilingualism. Later, Zola would write that Alfred Dreyfus was victimized because he seemed to represent not only treason in the present but also treason in the past, "for people burden him with the old defeat, in the stubborn belief that we could have been beaten only through betrayal."[5]

FIGURE 2.1   *Calendrier des Youtres*. (Courtesy of Houghton Library, Harvard University)

WHICH FRANCE?

The Dreyfus Affair, which began in 1894 and lasted more than a decade, crystallized these anxieties in the French national consciousness. It is crucial, however, in analyzing the Affair, to note that the stereotype of the deracinated Jew had to intersect with real improvements in Jews' legal and civic standing in France before the trope of treason could assume its full force. During the century after enfranchisement, as Jewish emancipation and assimilation became legally and culturally established realities—as French Jews gave up wearing distinctive clothing, lost their accents, were admitted to civil service positions, intermarried with gentiles, and so on—their ideological status as aliens came to collide with their legal status as citizens.

It is striking to note how careful the official representatives of both church and state were to specify, during the Affair, that they were not anti-Semitic, that they had Jewish friends and colleagues, and that they considered Jews in general to be good soldiers. Despite the vicious anti-Semitism of much of the Catholic press, the church hierarchy did not support the anti-Dreyfusard campaign, remaining scrupulously neutral; in fact the pope apparently sympathized with Dreyfus, which surely influenced the public posture of French Catholicism, if not the sentiments of individual Catholics.[6] By 1889 there were five Jewish generals in the military, which speaks not only to the success of Jews in entering the armed forces but also to the willingness of gentiles to promote them. At Dreyfus's retrial in 1899 General Auguste Mercier, the former minister of war who had helped to initiate Dreyfus's prosecution, denied vigorously that the General Staff of the Army was in any way motivated by religious prejudice and pointed to the presence of Protestants and Jews on the Staff as proof of his contention.[7] General Charles-Arthur Gonse, another of the chief architects of the campaign against Dreyfus, also testified that he was not an anti-Semite, indicating as evidence his support for a Jewish colleague whom he "would consider a very good officer."[8]

The point, of course, is not that the church and the military were hotbeds of tolerance and pluralism but that their representatives found it necessary to claim publicly that they were. While Drumont represented a large fringe, it was indeed a fringe, especially among the ruling classes; the public utterances of church and state representatives make it clear that overt expressions of anti-Semitism were not officially tolerated in fin-de-siècle France. Even Max Nordau, speaking at the Second Zionist Congress in 1898, was obliged to distinguish between the widespread and virulent cultural anti-Semitism in France and the positions adopted by its national institutions: "France is today marching at the head of the anti-Semitic movement. Not yet in her official acts and utterances, justice commands us to state thus much [...]."[9]

It seems clear, in fact, that the Affair could not have erupted in a culture of unalloyed anti-Semitism, when we recall the logic of Drumont and Weininger in claiming that Jews were so utterly alien to citizenship that they could not really betray homelands to which they would never belong. In À la recherche Proust attributes this view to the deeply anti-Semitic Baron de Charlus, who says to the narrator:

> "It is not a bad idea, if you wish to learn about life [...] to have a few
> foreigners among your friends." I replied that Bloch was French.
> "Indeed," said M. de Charlus, "I took him to be a Jew." His assertion
> of this incompatibility made me suppose that M. de Charlus was
> more anti-Dreyfusard than anyone I had met. He protested, how-
> ever, against the charge of treason levelled against Dreyfus. But his
> protest took this form: "I believe the newspapers say that Dreyfus
> has committed a crime against his country—so I understand. [...]
> In any case, the crime is non-existent. This compatriot of [Bloch]
> would have committed a crime if he had betrayed Judaea, but what
> has he to do with France? [...] Your Dreyfus might rather be con-
> victed of a breach of the laws of hospitality."[10]

In contrast, the anti-Dreyfusard diplomat M. de Norpois challenges Bloch, a Jewish character, to "perform your duty as a citizen" by condemning Dreyfus (GW, 331). The cultural anxiety about Jewish treachery could not have emerged fully from the outer limits of anti-Semitism represented by a Charlus or a Drumont. Rather, it was only when the mainstream or moderate position voiced by Norpois had shifted enough to acknowledge Jews as legitimate citizens that they could be widely viewed as potential *double*, rather than *foreign*, agents: not agents of "Judaea" working in France, but Frenchmen working for France *and* Judaea, or appearing to work for France but really working for Judaea.

The Affair, then, did not so much uncover a fundamental French xenophobia as force a critical confrontation in France between juridical, biologico-racial, and mythological definitions of the nation-state. Especially in the Affair's early years, there was a wide range of possible positions on the conflict and much disagreement even among those more or less on the same side. Nonetheless we can perceive, in general, a division between those who defined the nation as an organic union—bonded by blood, by the Catholic Church (a concordat with the papacy at the beginning of the century had officially established the church "as an organic institution of the State")[11] and, if they were royalists, by the monarchy—and those who instead understood the nation as a contractual union impartially guaranteeing specific rights to all parties to the contract. For anti-Dreyfusards (also known as antirevisionists because they opposed a "revision," or retrial, of the case), Jews were frequently viewed as an unassimilable threat to national unity. For Dreyfusards, typically, they were defined as citizens whose equal status under the law would demonstrate France's commitment to the secular values of the Revolution.

ORIGINS OF THE AFFAIR

It may be helpful at this point to backtrack momentarily and revisit some of the salient details of the Affair. After the war of 1870–1871, with its disastrous consequences for France, the War Office had established France's first formal intelligence service, innocuously named the "Statistical Section" to deter suspicion. The Section employed spies and counterspies, circulated falsified information, relied on double agents recruited from the most dubious circles of society, and had virtually no formal bureaucracy for tracking agents or documents.[12] It made up in paranoia and a passion for intrigue what it lacked in professionalism; in 1886 Colonel Jean-Conrad Sandherr was appointed head of the Section, and "advised his subordinates to have as few human ties as possible, to permanently distrust their colleagues, and to live for their mission alone. The tiny group of officers constituting the Intelligence Service thus lived apart, suspicious of all the other services, and even of the General Staff [of the Army], proudly convinced that they alone would be able to keep state secrets."[13] Interestingly, Sandherr was Alsatian, as was a very high percentage of the staff of the Statistical Section, because the critical business of spying on the Germans was obviously best conducted by German speakers; the liminality that made the French suspicious of Alsatian Jews, denoting them as double agents, really was an advantage in matters of espionage. Arguably, the necessarily multi- and equivocal identity of an effective agent is *inevitably* at odds with the desire of the nation he serves that its citizens should be clearly recognizable and monovalent in their allegiance. Certainly in the French case, Alsatians and especially Alsatian Jews in the military seem to have been a lightning rod for the anxiety produced by the nation's need to be protected by people whose borderline affiliations were themselves a potential source of danger.

Colonel Sandherr employed the maid at the German embassy, Mme Bastian—another Alsatian—as a spy; her job was to deliver the contents of the German military attaché's wastepaper basket to her superiors. These documents ranged from communiqués from spies to salacious notes from one of Maximilian von Schwartzkoppen's lovers, the Italian military attaché Alessandro Panizzardi—notes that often referred to the men's shared involvement in espionage as well as to their sexual relations. Two representative notes from Panizzardi to Schwartzkoppen read, "Dear Maximilian, am I still your Alexandrine? When will you come to bugger me?[b] I am sending you [various documents]. I will come by soon to get myself buggered anywhere at all. A thousand salutations from the girl who loves you so. Alexandrine." "My dear big bugger, Permit me to send you some Italian biscuits, which have the special property of always staying hard even if you wet them several times!! They're supposed to be good in coffee. All yours, Bugger, second class."[14]

These letters came to occupy an important place in the case against Dreyfus, but it was another document from the wastepaper basket that precipitated the Affair. In 1894 Mme Bastian turned over to the intelligence service a note—the infamous *bordereau*, or "list"—written in an unknown hand, listing classified documents to be delivered to Schwartzkoppen. Eventually, handwriting samples from a small circle of suspects led the War Office to accuse Captain Dreyfus, a Jewish officer with the General Staff of the Army, of having authored the incriminating piece. Dreyfus came from a well-to-do Alsatian family that chose French citizenship and settled in Paris after the war; he trained as an engineer and in 1892 joined the

---

b. The verb used is *bourrer* (n. *bourreur*), which literally means "to stuff" and can refer to any kind of sexual intercourse. It is perhaps slightly misleading, then, to translate it specifically as "to bugger." Nicholas Dobelbower hypothesizes that Panizzardi and Schwartzkoppen used the feminized nicknames "Alexandrine" and "Maximiliane" so that if their letters were intercepted, they would be assumed to be from women ("Petits bleus," 132), a possibility that the terms *bourrer* and *bourreur* left open. It seems to me that if this was a disguise, it was a very transparent one, and certainly it did not deceive the Statistical Section; I would assign the names instead to the same register of camp as the reference to Italian biscuits.

General Staff. Despite Dreyfus's strong academic record, a number of officers opposed his appointment to the General Staff, either because of personal anti-Semitism or because they felt anti-Semitism would interfere with his work; for example, Major du Paty de Clam, who was to play a major role in the campaign against Dreyfus, is supposed to have said, "I had very good relations with intelligent, artistic, and scholarly Jews. . . . But there are some situations in which persons who are not incontrovertibly French ought not be placed."[15]

While there is no reason to think that Dreyfus was framed for writing the *bordereau* specifically because he was Jewish, there can be little doubt that once he was mentioned as a suspect, "the fact that he was a Jew became—complementary or conclusive—grounds for presuming his guilt,"[16] particularly since the *bordereau* was addressed to a *German* diplomat. The newspaper *L'Éclair* was puzzled about what motive the wealthy Dreyfus could have for committing such a crime, but finally referred for explanation to the abnormal psychology typical of Jews: "This man would certainly make a bizarre case study for a psychologist."[17] The nationalist writer Maurice Barrès said simply, "That Dreyfus is capable of betrayal, I deduce from his race."[18] When Dreyfus's name was suggested, Colonel Sandherr is supposed to have exclaimed to a colleague that Dreyfus's "indiscreet curiosity, his continual ferreting about, his mysterious ways, and finally his sly and vain character, 'betraying all the pride and all the ignominy of his race,' had rendered him suspect for a long time." Sandherr would add, "That race has neither patriotism, nor honor, nor pride. For centuries, they have done nothing but betray."[19]

Dreyfus was tried for treason, *in camera*, in what would eventually be revealed as a thoroughly illegal court-martial. Aware that the *bordereau*—about whose authorship handwriting experts disagreed—was not enough on which to rest their case, the Statistical Section reviewed the other documents collected from Schwartzkoppen's trash to see if they could find anything more incriminating. They came up with only a few ambiguous notes, including a letter between Panizzardi and Schwartzkoppen that came to be known as the *canaille de D.*, or "scoundrel D.," letter, containing a reference to a mysterious person called "D."[c] General Mercier had his subordinates pad these questionable documents with falsified reports of the case, added his own

---

c. The identity of this individual is still uncertain, but it was certainly not Dreyfus.

highly biased commentary, and then sent the whole "secret dossier" to the court-martial without revealing its existence to either Dreyfus or his counsel.

Even without this falsified evidence, it is possible that the court-martial would have convicted Dreyfus on the sheer strength of their conscious or unconscious anti-Semitism. During the trial the prosecutor Bexon D'Ormescheville suggested through juxtaposition that Dreyfus's knowledge of foreign languages—especially his fluent German—was of a whole with his weak and un(gentle)manly character, both traits marking a suspect (and, in racialist discourse, typically Jewish) lability: "We can say that Captain Dreyfus [. . .] speaks several languages, notably German, in which he is fluent, and Italian, of which, he claims, he no longer has any but the vaguest notion; that he is, furthermore, endowed with a very pliable, even obsequious, personality, which is extremely useful in relationships of espionage with foreign agents."[20] The prosecution also characterized Dreyfus as duplicitous and sneaky, finding it remarkable, for instance, that he had told them they could search his house without finding any incriminating evidence and that, indeed, no such evidence was found.[21]

Four years after the trial, in his famous open letter to President Félix Faure, "J'accuse," Zola would sum up the almost farcical absurdity of the prosecution's effort to convict Dreyfus at all costs, if not for what he had done then for what he was. Describing the acte d'accusation quoted above, Zola writes, "I defy honest men to read the charges without their hearts swelling in indignation. [. . .] Dreyfus knows several languages, crime; no compromising papers were found in his home, crime; he sometimes returns to his birthplace [Alsace], crime; he is diligent, he is anxious to know everything, crime; he is careless, crime; he is careful, crime."[22] Not surprisingly, despite his protestations of innocence and the thinness of the evidence against him, Dreyfus was quickly convicted of treason and—since treason was no longer a capital offense in France—sentenced to deportation in perpetuity to Devil's Island, off the coast of South America. (Norman Kleeblatt notes the significance of exiling Dreyfus to an island that had been a leper colony, as if his alleged crime, so tightly intertwined with his race, were a contagious disease.)[23] Dreyfus would spend almost five years there before his supporters were able to get the case retried.

Once the guilty verdict was announced, the nationalist and anti-Semitic press lost no time in denouncing the intrinsic treacherousness of all Jews and issuing pathologizing descriptions of their distinctive physical characteristics, the equivalent of the leper's bell that would permit healthy citizens to identify and isolate the menace to national security. Given their passionate will to believe in Jewish physiological difference, anti-Semites must have been deeply distressed by Dreyfus's blond hair and blue eyes, which seemed to demonstrate, alarmingly, how invisible the race of traitors might be as they mixed among the French. As if in desperation, the nationalist press seized on his faintly aquiline—but, for Barrès, clearly "ethnic"—nose.[24] His nose was reassuring; it was not a French nose. Even more imaginatively, a cartoonist was able to create a sketch in which the phrenological indications of Dreyfus's treacherous Jewish character are superimposed on his otherwise unrevealing features. Thus, his frighteningly illegible difference could be made visible, his racialized body offered as an accurate indication of his treacherous and, above all, alien racial character. In the *Figaro* of January 6, 1895, shortly after Dreyfus's conviction, Léon Daudet (a friend of Proust's, despite their political differences) wrote with evident relief, "Above the wreckage of so many beliefs, a single faith remains real and sincere: that which safeguards our race, our language, the blood of our blood, and which keeps us all in solidarity. The closed ranks are our own. The wretch was not French. We knew it by his actions, by his demeanor, by his face."[25] Kleeblatt comments that "as treasonous criminal, Dreyfus could help exemplify that beneath every Jew—no matter how assimilated his appearance—lurked a sinister alien."[26]

THE "TWO FRANCES"

For nearly two years after Dreyfus's conviction the army's account of the incident prevailed, and after its initial barrage of anti-Semitic vituperation the nationalist press quieted down, satisfied that the matter had been resolved and that the Jewish threat was, at least temporarily, contained. In falsifying the "secret dossier" and disseminating it surreptitiously to the jurors of the court-martial without the knowledge of the defense, however, the army had already made the first of many mistakes that would eventually lead to Dreyfus's exoneration. The jurors leaked the story of the dossier to their friends, and thus within a few months of the verdict several politicians, lawyers, and journalists knew that whether or not Dreyfus was guilty, the trial had been illegal. The vice-president of the Senate, Auguste Scheurer-Kestner, and the influential newspaper editor Georges Clemenceau joined forces with Dreyfus's wife, Lucie, and his brother Mathieu and began to agitate for a "revision" of the case. Their campaign met with

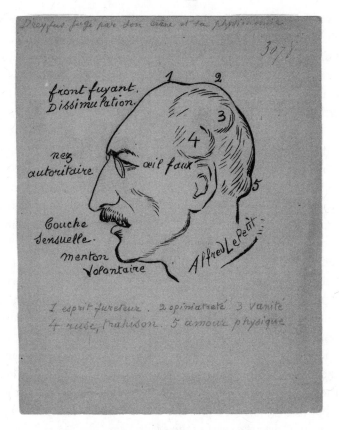

FIGURE 2.2   Alfred Le Petit, "Dreyfus judged by his skull and his physiognomy."
(Courtesy of Bowdoin College Museum of Art, Brunswick, Maine)

staunch resistance from politicians on the right, nationalist media, and, naturally, from the army, and it is with this conflict that the Dreyfus Affair as such may be properly said to have begun.

Michael Marrus, George Steiner, and others have criticized the oft-repeated view that during the Affair there were "two Frances"—the republican and the nationalist. Instead of reductively separating the parties to the Affair into the forces of reaction and those of republicanism, they claim, we should acknowledge that people, movements, and parties did not always divide along predictable lines of religious or political affiliation. "Not all Catholics, nationalists, and anti-Semites turned against Dreyfus; not all Jews, socialists, and anticlericals rallied to his side."[27] When Dreyfus was convicted, it was quite possible for republicans, socialists, even for

Jews, to believe in good faith that he was guilty; equally, it was possible for staunch conservatives to be troubled by the numerous illegalities committed by the government during his court-martial. Many anti-Dreyfusards were also ardent defenders of the Republic, and a few of the most prominent revisionists were anti-Semitic.

Furthermore, almost everyone involved evoked a commitment to the nation as the basis for his or her views. George Steiner delineates five major camps of opinion on the Affair, of which four are nationalist, including (1) "a Catholic nationalism *against* Dreyfus," (2) "a Catholic nationalism for Dreyfus," (3) "an agnostic nationalism *against* Dreyfus," and (4) "an agnostic nationalism for Dreyfus."[28] Lastly, Steiner claims, there was "a very small group, Socratic, anti-nationalist and *for* Dreyfus," a group in which he includes Julien Benda;[29] I would also put in this category both Bernard Lazare, one of the most important figures in early French Zionism, and Proust himself[d]—a point to which we will return in the next chapter. While this last group included some of the most articulate and impassioned intellectuals to participate in the Affair, their views were barely heard during the 1890s. Finally, we must note the important division, on both right and left, between those whose primary concern was maintaining the state in something like its existing form and those who hoped to overthrow the Republic and either return to theocratic monarchy or establish a socialist government. These are significant if fine distinctions and had real political effects "on the ground" over the years of the Affair.

And yet it must be admitted that the theory of the "two Frances" did not simply evolve in ex post facto analyses but was actively promulgated at the time in innumerable cartoons, broadsheets, songs, newspaper articles, and speeches on the floor of Parliament. If history has remembered the Affair largely as what Marrus calls "a titanic struggle between the 'two Frances', the one progressive, liberal and republican, and the other reactionary, highly nationalist and monarchist"[30]—that is, between groups 1 and 4 in Steiner's classification—it is because those two groups promoted that vision of their conflict tirelessly and loudly in every available forum. After a certain point, as Léon Blum would write in his memoirs, "we were no longer fighting for or against Dreyfus, for or against revision; we were

---

d. Steiner includes Proust in the fourth group, made up of secular, pro-Dreyfus nationalists, but while this may accurately describe the young Proust's personal views, I do not believe it characterizes the mature Proust's account of the Affair in *À la recherche*.

fighting for or against the Republic, for or against militarism, for or against the secularism of the State."[31]

The reactionary view, most forcefully articulated by the Catholic, nationalist right, was that France should be considered an organic entity, Gallic in race, Catholic in religion, united in one living, breathing entity and possibly with a monarch at its head; thus, Jews were obviously unassimilable to the nation, and it would be madness to admit them to crucial national institutions like the army. *Civilità Cattolica* urged Catholics to join forces against the Dreyfusards, telling them that

> the emancipation of the Jews was the corollary of the so-called principles of 1789, the yoke of which weighs on the neck of all Frenchmen. [...] Ethnic solidarity ties the Jews to each other and prevents them from becoming loyal citizens in spite of naturalization. The Dreyfus affair reveals this fact clearly. Thus anti-Semitism will become, as it should, economic, political, and national. The Jews allege an error of justice. The true error was, however, that of the *Constituante* which accorded them French nationality. That law has to be revoked. ... Not only in France, but in Germany, Austria, and Italy as well, the Jews are to be excluded from the nation.[32]

Pericles Lewis argues that this radical right nationalism derived ideologically from the same (mis)application of Rousseau's concept of the "general will" that inspired the Terror:

> The concept of the national will reverberated throughout nineteenth-century France as the claim that there could be only one interpretation of the common good, that the common good was equivalent both to justice and to the interests of all the individuals in society, and that anyone who opposed it was also opposing the nation itself. When, in the rhetoric surrounding the Dreyfus affair, this fantasy of a unified national will combined with the demand that, in order to enjoy political equality of condition as a citizen, one must be similar, or naturally equal, to all other French citizens, it helped to create modern, anti-liberal nationalism.[33]

Because in this view anything that challenged the unified will of the nation was by definition treasonous, Dreyfus—however innocent of espionage he might be—was nonetheless considered responsible for causing the Affair and the resulting national conflict. As Barrès said, speaking of the Dreyfusards, "Even if their client were innocent, they would still be criminals."[34] And indeed, even as evidence mounted that Dreyfus *was* innocent of the crime of which he had been convicted, antirevisionists intensified their campaign of violence against Dreyfusards.

On the other side, it was undoubtedly Zola who gave the most articulate public voice to the ideology of liberal republicanism; Zola, in fact, may be more responsible than almost anyone else for staking out the ideological boundaries of the Affair in starkly Manichaean terms. In particular, historians have seen the publication of Zola's article "J'accuse" in January, 1898, as the watershed of the Affair, the moment after which people could not ignore that in taking sides for or against Dreyfus, they were taking sides in a debate about the nature of France and Frenchness. As Jean-Denis Bredin writes, in Zola's letter "the reasons motivating each—on the one side, the democratic ethic, the respect for law, the idea of justice and truth; on the other, the traditional virtues whose refuge and guardian the Army took itself to be, the exaltation of national sentiment—were clearly, perhaps even crudely separated and opposed."[35] In Zola's view the antirevisionists' cause was an "aberration" forced on a deceived public by military dictatorship and clerical reaction, whereas the cause of the revisionists was that of enlightened France, rational and just.[36] In article after article published in the Dreyfusard press, Zola tried to recall France to what he saw as its identity as the birthplace of the principles of liberty, equality, and fraternity. "Are we still," he asked in 1898, "the noblest, the most brotherly, the most generous of peoples? Are we going to retain the reputation we have in Europe for fairness and humanity?"[37]

The question of France's international reputation that Zola raises here became increasingly urgent after 1898. While France itself was divided over the Affair, international opinion was firmly on the side of the Dreyfusards, as people throughout the Western world who considered themselves heirs of the Enlightenment insisted on the administration of justice. Several countries, including the United States, threatened to boycott the 1900 World's Fair in Paris if Dreyfus were not freed. France was globally castigated for failing to uphold the ideals it had brought to the world; after Zola was put on trial in 1898 for calumniating the army, the Belgian poet Emile Verhaeren wrote, "In what has by now become this historic Dreyfus Affair, all of Europe defended the spirit of France against France itself."[38]

FIGURE 2.3 René Georges Hermann-Paul, *Le bon exemple*. (Courtesy of the Fine Arts Library, Harvard University)

The media in Britain and America suggested snidely that perhaps justice was fundamentally an Anglo-Saxon concept too difficult for the French to grasp.[39] And some asked how, if France could not treat its own citizens fairly, it could be trusted with its civilizing mission to the colonized world, which helped give it such a powerful role in global politics. A French cartoon from the period, titled *The Good Example*, clearly reflects the fear of some Dreyfusards that France was embarrassing itself by failing to provide a model of enlightened republicanism to its overseas possessions: it shows three naked African children playing, one saying to another, "You be Dreyfus. We'll be the guards. We're going to play at being savages." Only by demonstrating the equality of citizens of all races *within* France could the French prove that they were morally entitled to rule over the savage races of their subject nations.

For anti-Dreyfusards, however, the vociferous foreign sympathy for Dreyfus simply played into their belief that Jews were aliens whose moral and financial support came primarily from abroad. General Gaston de Galliffet expressed the feelings of many when he said in a speech that the French majority was with the army and that only foreigners sided with

Dreyfus.[40] Anti-Dreyfusard cartoons emphasized the foreign affiliations of Dreyfus's supporters, reminding readers that Scheurer-Kestner spoke German, Clemenceau was an Anglophile, and Zola was of Italian descent; sometimes cartoons simply show the object of derision holding a sign printed in a language other than French.[41]

What eventually swayed many anti-Dreyfusards to accept compromise with the left, far more than international pressure, was the violent excesses of the most noxious elements of reaction. Conservative members of the ruling elite were in most cases unwilling to be seen to support tactics that included rioting, assassination attempts, and a failed coup d'état. The army itself appeared to some to have become a state within a state, just as the Jews were feared to be, and thus to pose a similar threat to national cohesion.[42] This view is given articulate voice in *À la recherche* by the moderate conservative Norpois, who announces his disapproval of right-wing "disturbances": "Certainly we must put a stop to the anti-militarist intrigues, but neither can we tolerate a brawl encouraged by those elements on the Right who instead of serving the patriotic ideal themselves are hoping to make it serve them. Heaven be praised, France is not a South American replica, and the need has not yet been felt here for a military pronunciamento" (*GW*, 327). It was the need for order, perhaps more than a desire for justice, that brought about Dreyfus's eventual retrial, a general amnesty, and finally his complete exoneration in 1904.[43] When all was said and done, members of the ruling class discovered that their own allegiance was primarily to the values of that class—tradition, stability, propriety, and order—rather than to a vaguely defined "nation" that included rabble with whom they did not wish to be socially associated. This conflict of loyalties between class and nation was admirably summarized by General Galliffet in a letter he wrote to his friend Princess Radziwell on the occasion of his resignation from the Union Club, after several other members were arrested for participating in the attempted coup d'état of 1899. "It isn't possible to belong to a club whose members are arrested," Galliffet huffed, in a line amply worthy of Proust. "It's not clubbable."[44]

THE AFFAIR AND FRENCH JEWRY

These frictions between class, nationalism, the desire for stability, and a commitment to justice were reflected on a smaller scale within France's Jewish population. In addition, French Jews were forced to confront questions, from within and without, about the relationship between their Frenchness and their Jewishness—and to confront these not merely at the level of ideological abstraction but as urgent political imperatives. We saw in chapter 1 that the terms of emancipation in France defined Jews not as members of a minority group within the nation but as French individuals marked by a *judaiété* that, whether it was interpreted as racial origin or religious belief, was immaterial to their citizenship. As Arendt and others have exhaustively documented, in the course of the nineteenth century most French Jews came to embrace this definition of their relation to the nation and to refocus their historic aspirations to a biblically promised homeland on France itself, defined as a "new Zion." Many of these scholars have also agreed that the failure to understand anti-Semitism as a political force, and to formulate a collective response to it, constituted near-suicidal naïveté on the part of French Jewry. In his influential *The Politics of Assimilation* Michael Marrus sums up the view that French Jews were so assimilated that they could not react coherently to the Dreyfus Affair as an expression of anti-Semitism or articulate any defense of their own community as such. Marrus's argument specifically indicts the tradition of universalism in France for failing to give Jews any positive concept of Jewish identity: "There was no pluralist tradition in France, and the Jewish community was unused to expressing its unique and distinct contribution to French life. Jews indeed became French. Their community was weakened by the corrosive effects of assimilation."[45]

In underscoring the depth of French Jewry's passionate devotion to France and Frenchness and the degree to which French Jews succeeded in entering French social, cultural, and institutional life, historians like Marrus have perhaps oversimplified the concept of assimilation and overemphasized its deleterious consequences, implying that assimilation was equivalent to apostasy, a complete and debilitating divorce from Jewish faith and culture. But in reality, Jews adopted a wide variety of definitions of their own Jewishness, framing it variously as a set of private religious beliefs, an attachment to family tradition, a sense of participation in a specific history, or "a 'solidarity of origin with men who were the co-religionists of my fathers', as [Camille] Dreyfus put it."[46] While some Jews were certainly completely secularized, and a few even converted to Catholicism, others—including Alfred Dreyfus, who is usually described as thoroughly assimilated—adopted a pattern of cultural identification and casual religious observance that would look familiar to many American Jews today:

attending synagogue on the High Holy Days, celebrating marriages and commemorating deaths in religious ceremonies, sprinkling Hebrew words or Yiddishisms over their speech, decorating their homes with Judaica. The 1987 Dreyfus exhibit at the Jewish Museum in New York included some of the family memorabilia preserved by the Dreyfus grandchildren, including "the Jewish marriage contract of Alfred and Lucie and a decorative cloth commemorating Jewish pilgrimage festivals, which hung on a wall of the Dreyfus home." Paula Hyman submits that these mementos "point to a more complex identity than is usually attributed to the ambitious young captain or to other assimilated Jews of his generation. [. . .] They suggest that bourgeois Jews, thoroughly acculturated to the mores of their class, retained a sentimental attachment to their Jewish origins and fashioned an identity from multiple elements."[47]

Of course, such an understanding of Jewish identity can invest it with considerably greater emotional importance than seems implied by the word *assimilated*, while still consigning it to a private and largely interiorized realm of domestic and affective life. It is not, then, particularly surprising that even highly devout French Jews were reluctant to negotiate the public, political territory of the Affair on the basis of their Jewishness rather than of their public identities as French citizens. There was not—or should not have been—any reason for them to believe that French citizenship, with its ironclad constitutional guarantees, would not ultimately suffice to ensure justice for Dreyfus and security for his coreligionists. "For the moment, it was held, France was being led astray. But her most fundamental principles, the principles of 1789, provided for the protection of the Jews; it could only be a matter of time before these principles reasserted themselves. From this point of view Jews would win their rights by identifying themselves on an equal basis with the other 'children' of France. All Frenchmen were equal; to claim this equality, Jews had simply to emphasize their Frenchness, their eligibility for fair treatment."[48]

In addition, French Jews considering how to respond to the Affair faced a real double bind that was not of their own making. Anti-Semitic nationalists had, from the moment Dreyfus's arrest was made public, defined a clear correspondence between race and one's view of the case; Barrès and his cohorts had immediately imposed an obligation on all those of French blood to oppose Dreyfus, while invoking the racial solidarity of the Jews as the very basis for presuming him a traitor. It was, then, very hard for Jews to voice support for Dreyfus at all—much less to offer that support *as* Jews—without appearing to lend credibility to the most racist rhetoric of his opponents. Arguing from a position of identification with Jewry would, it was feared, utterly delegitimize the argument. In sum, the faith of assimilationists in France's liberal institutions may have been, as Marrus and Arendt charge, naïve at best, self-destructive at worst. But their views reflect a dilemma intrinsic to any republicanism as undilute as France's: the very terms by which freedoms are established allow people to defend those freedoms only as neutral, fungible citizens and not from any particularity of experience.

It is in that context that we must understand what otherwise appears to be a cowardly or self-hating decision by French Jews to rely as much as possible on the advocacy of gentiles, as well as the constant efforts by both Jewish and gentile Dreyfusards to move the case away from the question of anti-Semitism and into a rhetorical sphere of nationally endorsed values like equality and justice. Scheurer-Kestner wrote to a colleague that "we must take great care to ensure that the Dreyfus question does not remain within the Jewish domain. It is too much there already. The question is one of justice."[49] And when the Ligue des Droits de l'Homme et du Citoyen, the French equivalent of the ACLU, was formed in 1898 in response to anti-Semitic riots provoked by the Affair, "the *Archives israélites* noted 'with satisfaction' that out of thirty-four members of its executive, only three were Jews. 'This proves sufficiently', the editorial declared, 'that the Dreyfus Affair . . . is in absolutely no way Jewish, but is purely humanitarian.' "[50]

Clearly, Jews who favored the revisionist cause were beset by almost paralyzing difficulties in finding a discourse, and a forum, in which they could effectively articulate their support for Dreyfus. And yet, despite that difficulty and the lack of organized Jewish protest during the Affair, a number of impassioned Dreyfusards were, in fact, of Jewish or part-Jewish descent: the grand rabbi of France, Zadoc Kahn; Victor Basch; Julien Benda; Léon Blum; Daniel Halévy; Bernard Lazare; Arthur Lévy; Gustave Kahn; the Reinach brothers, Salomon and Joseph; Marcel Proust. (In contrast, there were very few Jewish antirevisionists.) Most of these men, as Marrus points out, "made it clear that they were engaging in the struggle, not in order to defend a Jew, but to defend the basic principles of the Republic."[51] Like gentiles on all sides of the Affair, they invoked not only love for France but hatred for Germany in support of their position, arguing that it was not Dreyfusism that was undermining French national unity but a race war promoted by Germany.[52] "The same fraudulent theory that justified the conquest of Alsace," wrote Salomon Reinach, "has been the inspiration of French anti-Semitism."[53] In the eyes of at least some gentiles, this fervent French patriotism and anti-German xenophobia gave Jewish Dreyfusards a moral authority that they would not have had if they had acted in the name of their own, or Dreyfus's, Jewishness; in 1955 an historian of the Affair, Guy Chapman, received a letter from a French correspondent who wrote that "Frenchmen, notwithstanding their dislike of Jewishness *per se*, recognised in Joseph Reinach a devotion to France equal to their own. This was the secret of his personal influence. For him the Affair was not solely or even primarily a Jewish concern: it was a fight for principles he believed to be essential to save Republican, Revolutionary, Democratic France from the clutches of Reaction."[54]

Though these Jewish Dreyfusards articulated and probably genuinely understood their position as one motivated exclusively by loyalty to France, the very fact that many more Jews supported Dreyfus (if only quietly) than opposed him suggests a somewhat subtle and complicated relationship between their political position and their lived experience as Jews. It is unlikely that anyone was really galvanized into supporting Dreyfus by a reflexive, atavistic reaction of racial identification, as anti-Semites charged. But it is certainly conceivable that Jews might have been more aware of the possibility that Dreyfus was being discriminated against because of his race, more frightened by the anti-Semitism of the crusade against him and his defenders, or simply better informed about Dreyfus's character, family, and financial circumstances by virtue of belonging to the same social circles as the Dreyfuses and his wife's family, the Hadamards.[55] Proust's Duchesse de Guermantes, though hardly a Dreyfusard, nonetheless appears to appreciate the position of French Jews during the Affair, saying: "Perhaps it's just because they are Jews and know themselves that they realise that a person can be a Jew and not necessarily a traitor and anti-French, as M. Drumont seems to maintain. Certainly, if [Dreyfus had] been a Christian, the Jews wouldn't have taken any interest in him, but they did so because they knew quite well that if he hadn't been a Jew people wouldn't have been so ready to think him a traitor *a priori*."[56] Her anti-Semitic husband angrily responds that "women never understand a thing about politics," which does little to counter Oriane's (rather unwontedly) sensible point, instead leaving it as an inscription of the text's awareness that Jews might have quite practical reasons for sympathizing with Dreyfus. If Jewish identity did not unproblematically announce itself as grounds for a *prise de position* in favor of

Dreyfus, then, we may nonetheless easily imagine, as Proust does in this passage, that it informed a heightened sensitivity to the prejudice inspiring the anti-Dreyfusard campaign.

CROSSING SWORDS: THE POLITICS OF DUELING

The complexity of French Jewry's negotiations between an ethos of universalism and the specificity of Jewish identity is nicely illustrated by an exchange that took place in 1892 between Drumont and Captain André Crémieu-Foa, a Jewish army officer who challenged Drumont to a duel because of *Libre parole*'s editorial diatribes against Jews in the military. According to Daniel Boyarin, dueling was one of many aspects of gentile European culture that Jews had traditionally rejected; he writes that "violence was [...] not particularly highly regarded in traditional Jewish culture" and contrasts this attitude with the "value-system of the Protestant bourgeoisie who saw fighting (e.g., dueling) as fundamental to manly honor."[57] But by the late nineteenth century assimilating European Jewish men were anxious to demonstrate their virility by participating in duels. Jews in Germany were generally considered *nicht satisfaktionsfähig*, not worthy of or socially eligible for dueling, but French Jews enjoyed greater social acceptance,[58] and the fight between Drumont and Crémieu-Foa was only one of numerous duels fought between French Jews and anti-Semites in the 1890s.

Marrus notes that Jews were likelier to respond to anti-Semitism by issuing a challenge than by organizing a protest, implicitly defining anti-Semitism as a personal (and elite) concern rather than treating it as a systemic, mass, political issue. Dueling, in Marrus's view, actually distracted attention from the political problem of anti-Semitism: duels "drew energy away from the attempt to construct an organized Jewish opposition to anti-Semitism. Attention was focused, if at all, upon the personal insult; the interested public concerned itself with the confrontation of individuals, with duelling protocol, and with other extraneous personal issues."[59] Marrus, though, neglects to consider the ways that Jewish challenges to anti-Semites also represented a way for French Jewish men to use the class and gender ideology of dueling to form their own identities as gender-normative European men without relinquishing their sense of ethnic particularity and pride.

The duel originally arose in the early Middle Ages as a type of trial by ordeal; it was presumed that God would intervene on the side of right, so death in combat was proof of the divine condemnation of the dead man.

This conception of the duel was already disappearing by the fifteenth century, but the religious belief that the defeated party was by definition guilty of a sin was easily accommodated to an ethic that pronounced victory an honor and surrender shameful. That is, if a man refused a challenge or fought but lost, then he was still guilty of cowardice or inadequate masculinity, if not of whatever had first provoked the challenge.[60] Thus, the duel was transformed into a primarily secular test of honor—of *virtù*—rather than of moral virtue, and as such was an essential feature of late feudal culture.

Despite its origins in the rigid hierarchies of the feudal era, dueling also eventually evolved into a way of accommodating the increasing social mobility of the modern era. With the rise of the bourgeoisie, engaging in duels became a potent symbol of the bourgeois man's assimilation into the culture of aristocracy. Furthermore, whereas in the feudal period a man was supposed to duel in the name of his liege or his family, as nations and national identities began to coalesce in Europe the concept of dueling in the name of one's country took hold. In conjunction with duels motivated by nationalist impulses, we also see the advent of duels that signal a claim by nonnationals to assimilation into a nation or race; for instance, men of African descent who issued challenges in response to racist insults were able to demonstrate their comfort with and parity within European cultural traditions.[61] Similarly, French Jews who participated in duels in the nineteenth century were marking the thoroughness of their own assimilation into both the upper class and French culture. (In addition, dueling had the advantage of aligning Jewish duelists with a medieval and distinctly European past, thus antidoting at one blow hostile images of the Jew as either too ancient and oriental or too implicated in modernity.)

Notions of personal and collective honor overlap in such cases; anti-black or anti-Semitic insults challenge the honor of the group as a whole and hence of anyone identified with the group. The individual issuing the challenge defends his own honor as a member of the insulted collectivity but also claims to demonstrate the honorability of the group in acting as its exemplar. The logic involved is necessarily synecdochal; it relies on the assumption that all individuals associated with a particular racial or national identity have some essence in common such that any one of them can, in acting or speaking, claim to act or speak for the collectivity. What we observe in the exchange between Crémieu-Foa and Drumont is, among other things, a dispute over the validity of such a notion of identity, as well as over the nature of the French nation.

After the second article appeared in the series of vitriolic editorials that *Libre parole* directed against Jews in the military in 1892, Crémieu-Foa issued a challenge to Drumont that begins, "In insulting the three hundred French Army officers on active duty who belong to the Israelite faith, you insult me personally." Drumont responded that

> you do not have the right to proclaim yourself the champion of the Jewish officers in the army; you are not the most senior among them, nor have you been delegated [to such a position]. [...]
>
> If the Jewish officers of the French Army are wounded by our articles, let them choose by lot the number of delegates they wish and we will oppose them with an equal number of French swords.
>
> As for you, if, as a Jew, you challenge me, you will find me at your disposal.[62]

There are two particularly interesting points to make about these letters. First, they appear to limn a sharp distinction between Enlightenment liberalism and organicist, racist nationalism. Crémieu-Foa considers himself a "*French* officer belonging to the Israelite faith," a participant in the French national community whose minority religious affiliation is private and irrelevant to his public status as a citizen and a soldier. His brother Ernest wrote of hearing the captain say that "nothing irritated him like the *Libre Parole*'s systematic insistence on confusing, and on making others confuse, the idea of religion with the idea of nationality"(Crémieu-Foa, *La campagne antisémitique*, 25). As a citizen—more importantly, as a soldier—Crémieu-Foa wants to consider himself absolutely neutral, unmarked by race or religion, fungible with all other soldiers: "The uniform covers a soldier, and *nothing but a soldier*" (ibid., 27; his emphasis).

Furthermore, and somewhat counterintuitively, Crémieu-Foa seems to feel that his religious affiliation is contingent to his identity precisely because it has not been chosen; it is "natural" rather than contractual and thus should have no bearing on his Being (in the sense of *Sein*) as a rational individual, in liberal terms. In his account Jewishness is an accident of birth rather than a set of beliefs or practices, a question of status rather than conduct, and so anti-Semitism unfairly attacks something over which one has no control. "It's strange!" his brother Ernest remembers him saying; "Whether we're *practicing* or not, I am and we are Israelites. If this were a fault, it would be one for which we could make no amends, since you belong to one faith or another by birth" (ibid., 24; his emphasis). In Crémieu-Foa's challenge to Drumont we notice that Jews *belong* to the faith rather than *being* of the faith; the ontological category here, in fact, is "officer." In Crémieu-Foa's construction, being a French officer—a voluntary participant in a national institution—trumps Jewishness as his essential identity. Indeed, the procès-verbal of the duel specifies that Captain Crémieu-Foa was "offended, *as an officer*, by the articles" in the *Libre parole* (ibid., 29; emphasis added).

In contrast, Drumont names Crémieu-Foa and his collectivity "Jewish officers," to be opposed by "French swords," thus making racial/religious identity coextensive with public, national identity. Furthermore, Drumont's construction clearly opposes Judaism and France as hostile national entities. Jews are thus both essentially defined by their Jewishness and, by virtue of that Jewishness, excluded from the French national body. All Jewish officers have something in common that makes them essentially unlike all Frenchmen.

The two Frances—one liberal and republican, the other reactionary and *völkisch*—seem, up to this point, to be perfectly represented by Crémieu-Foa and Drumont. Both men change tactics, however, in the course of their correspondence, revealing the discrepancies embedded in their respective positions. The second interesting point to observe about their exchange of letters is the way the two approach the relation of the individual to the collectivity. Strictly speaking, if Jewishness were truly not, or were only trivially, constitutive of identity, then there would be no compelling reason for the captain to feel implicated in attacks on Jews in general or even in attacks on Jewish soldiers more specifically. Yet he does, and if "belonging to the Israelite faith" only modifies the substantive "officer," it nonetheless is the modifier, freighted with a sense of communal, extranational identity, that must be seen to constitute the motivation for this particular challenge. In his account of his brother's quarrel with Drumont, Ernest Crémieu-Foa admits as much when he characterizes the anti-Semitic media campaign, though directed against a collectivity, as an act of aggression to which individual Jews may legitimately respond by dueling in self-defense (ibid., 10). So while André Crémieu-Foa disavows Jewishness as grounds for identity/identification, he simultaneously declares himself insulted as an individual by insults offered to a group (French Army officers belonging to the Jewish faith) with which he identifies.

Certainly, Crémieu-Foa's construction of identification works only from the whole to the part. It does not explicitly work in the other direction; though it is possible to infer that in demanding reparation for himself he is demanding it for the collectivity, he does not actually say so. This is, however, the way that Drumont construes the challenge and then rejects it because he does not acknowledge an essential synecdochal relation between part and whole in the case of this particular collectivity (i.e., Jewish officers in the French Army). When Drumont wants to argue as a racist nationalist, then, he argues that Jews as a whole constitute, essentially, a national body distinct from the French national body. But in order to counter Crémieu-Foa's implicit claim to a distinctive racial/religious identity *within* the French national collectivity, Drumont switches gears and maintains that Jewish officers in the French Army are not, in fact, essentially related to each other, but only contractually, and that the terms of the contract are identical to those of the army as a whole: the right to represent the group depends on seniority or appointment, not mere religious identity. Thus, Drumont will acknowledge the legitimacy of a national conflict between "Jewish" and "French" swords or an individual conflict between Crémieu-Foa as a Jew and him as a Frenchman. But he will not allow Crémieu-Foa to speak and act, as a Jewish Frenchman, on behalf of other Jewish Frenchmen and to offer a challenge to Drumont as a Frenchman of a different racial/religious identity—for to do so would be to admit, first, that race and nation are not equivalent, and second, that individuals within a national body may speak from extranational identity positions, on behalf of extranational collectivities. What we see mapped out in this exchange, then, is not only the incommensurability of Enlightenment and pre- or anti-Enlightenment constructions of the nation but also the tensions and irregularities in the discourses of liberalism, nationalism, and racial identification that are at play in both Crémieu-Foa's and Drumont's rhetoric. The ideology of dueling is not, at least in this case, as completely privatized as Marrus indicates; instead, it steers a complicated, uneven course through notions of personal, racial/religious, and national identities.

There is one other point that bears mentioning about the ramifications of dueling in this context. After Crémieu-Foa and Drumont fought (both survived), Drumont praised his opponent's courage in the *Libre parole* (ibid., 30). Throughout the history of dueling agreeing to participate in a duel has always signaled a recognition of class commonality between the participants, even if they were of somewhat uneven social status: to accept a challenge was to acknowledge that both parties obeyed the same social

codes. It was an honor that the whistle-blower in the Dreyfus case, Lieuten-
ant Colonel Georges Picquart, refused to grant to the man he knew to be
the real author of the *bordereau*,[e] his fellow officer Major Ferdinand Walsin
Esterhazy, when Esterhazy challenged him in 1898.[f] And yet it was an honor
Drumont conceded to one of the Jews he loathed. Whatever his hostility
to Jews in general and to Crémieu-Foa, as a Jew, in particular, in agreeing
to fight at all Drumont was admitting his identification with someone who
shared the values of his class and culture—someone who, if not quite a
Frenchman, was at least a European, and a gentleman.

Such an acknowledgment of social parity is reminiscent of the duel's
origins as a trial by ordeal. If the secular equivalent of divine sanction was
social approval, then a Jew who dueled was proving that though Jewish, he
could not be what anti-Semites designated as "a Jew"—degenerate, feminized, without honor, and alien to Europe. And a gentile who fought him
was tacitly admitting the same thing. By agreeing to meet Crémieu-Foa on
the field of arms, by fighting him, and by publicly praising him after they
had fought, Drumont, in a sense, disproved his own argument.

A similar logic may have been operating in the case of duels fought
in this period over allegations of homosexuality. During the notorious
Eulenburg Affair, which Proust followed with great interest, a number of
challenges were issued by men accused of homosexuality. Proust himself
fought several duels in his life, generally provoked by insinuations about
his homosexuality. In *À la recherche* he has the Baron de Charlus—avatar of
the premodern—threaten to fight a duel for the same reason. These duels
were, prima facie, very different from those fought over anti-Semitism,
since the offended parties did not offer their challenges in order to
defend the honor of homosexuals but, on the contrary, to show that they
were not homosexual. If, however, we interpret these engagements in the

e. It has never been proved beyond all doubt that Esterhazy prepared the *bordereau*, and
periodically arguments have been advanced proposing other sources for the document, but
the technicalities involved in that debate need not concern us here. The fact is that the hand
in which it is written is indistinguishable from his, and most people at the time who knew
that Dreyfus had not written the piece believed that Esterhazy had, including the anti-Dreyfusard officers who went to great and illegal lengths to protect Esterhazy.

f. Burns, *France*, 106. It is one of the most striking ironies of the whole history of the Affair
that Esterhazy served as one of Crémieu-Foa's seconds in the latter's duel with Drumont.

context of the trial by ordeal, they read somewhat differently, as efforts to "prove" the challengers' innocence, not of homosexual acts, but of the effeminacy associated with them. When in 1920 a reviewer characterized Proust as "feminine," Proust angrily responded, "It is just one step from feminine to effeminate. Those who have served as my seconds will tell you if I have the softness of effeminate men."[63] If a Jewish man who duels is not what is meant by "a Jew," similarly, a man who desires men but is willing to participate in the virile activity of dueling is not "an invert." Thus, European men with subaltern social positions (by virtue of race, religion, or sexual practices) were not simply "defending their honor," in some vague way, by challenging those who insulted them. Instead, the mere fact of issuing a challenge allowed them to lay claim to a normative European masculinity that anti-Semitic and homophobic discourses vigorously denied them.

THE SECRET DOSSIER

The question of homosexuality brings us back to the Dreyfus Affair and the role played in it by a discourse about sex/gender deviance that is more encrypted, more subterranean than the discourses of Semitism that informed it, but closely interwoven with them. Two scholarly pieces have offered the theory that homosexuality more or less preceded Jewishness in the paranoiac imaginary of the French General Staff. Norman Kleeblatt suggests that the exiled Dreyfus, made safely legible in his difference and segregated from the body politic, might have been serving as a "surrogate" onto which the army could displace an even more profound and less nameable hostility toward the sexual difference manifested in Schwartzkoppen and Panizzardi. "As archetypical Jew, a secure stereotype and carefully researched specimen for the medical science of the time, Dreyfus could displace the homosexual. [. . .] So the reinscribed body of Alfred Dreyfus, the 'passing' Jewish soldier, offered a surrogate for the 'passing' homosexual and military bodies of Schwartzkoppen and Panizzardi. As homosexuals and foreigners, these two men may have been ultimately even more threatening, and certainly less controllable, than French Jews."[64] Kleeblatt accounts for this sense of "threat" by reasoning that while the French officers who had access to the Schwartzkoppen-Panizzardi correspondence *might* have been pleased to discover that one of their German archenemies was "less than [a man]," it is equally plausible that they would have been disturbed by the implication that the French Army could have been vanquished in 1871 by, so to speak, a nation of pansies.[65] By disciplining and exiling one effeminate, alien body, then, they could symbolically master the much larger problem of France's military inferiority to Germany.[g]

Nicholas Dobelbower makes a somewhat similar argument, writing that "the anti-Semitic attitudes that eventually colored the Affair were actually superimposed upon an existing set of preconceptions pertaining to the alterity (otherness) of homosexuals."[66] Dobelbower's thesis rests in part on the fact that in the years that followed Dreyfus's conviction, the secret dossier was augmented with hundreds of additional documents (many of them forged), intended to convince new members of the General Staff and the government of Dreyfus's guilt, and that, curiously, these documents included nearly fifty erotic letters between Schwartzkoppen and Panizzardi having no bearing on Dreyfus or even, in most cases, on espionage. The envelope containing the letters bears the legend, "Nature of the relations existing between the two attachés"; there is no other commentary. Dobelbower notes that the letters' "presence in the dossier as a sort of erotic excess certainly requires some consideration of their intended use" and points out that "the possibility that Dreyfus was in association with Panizzardi and Schwartzkoppen was undoubtedly rendered more believable by the similarity of the ways in which Jews and homosexuals figured into French ideology at the turn of the century."[67] He proposes, therefore, that the letters were added to the file purely to evoke a visceral and irrational homophobic response in readers that would condition their reactions to Dreyfus.[68] Thus, after the original dossier had served its purpose by establishing for the jurors of the court-martial that there was a connection (however spurious) between the *foreign* military attachés and someone designated as "D.,"

g. It weakens Kleeblatt's thesis that there is little evidence that Schwartzkoppen *was* perceived as effeminate. References to his sexual conduct in contemporary sources use the same terms in describing his "scandalous" and "dishonorable" correspondence with both his mistress, Hermance de Weede, and Panizzardi, which might indicate that his sexual behavior was considered inappropriate not because it was unmanly but because it was promiscuous, indiscreet, or indiscriminate in its objects.

the augmented dossier could, and did, continue to circulate among military and government personnel, providing officials who still needed persuading with a textual connection between the *homosexual* military attachés and the exiled Dreyfus.

In view of the centrality of this secret dossier to the Affair—a dossier with the erotic correspondence between two men at its core—it is not completely implausible that the Affair was somehow really about homosexuality rather than Jewishness: that homosexuality is the repressed that persistently resurfaces to trigger a paranoia that must then be redirected against Dreyfus. But what we actually find in the Dreyfus Affair is that homosexual practices and effeminacy circulate *alongside* heterosexual promiscuity, a taste for sadomasochism, racial or religious difference, and so on as nearly equivalent signifiers of unreliability. The play of transference between Jewishness and sex/gender deviance in the Affair extended far beyond, and was far more complicated than, a single symbolic substitution of *Jew* for *homosexual*. Surrogacy—a person, thing, or sign standing in for another person, thing, or sign—is, after all, integral to espionage, as are other forms of "code switching": disguise, encryption, secrecy, pretense. In the intertwining discourses generated by the Affair, sexuality and Jewishness always "stand (in) for," point to, both each other and treason.

In addition, illicit sexuality, like espionage, obviously tends to involve people in deception; in a case like the Dreyfus Affair, entailing both sex and spying, there was neither any way to guarantee that witnesses with various pressing reasons to lie were telling the truth nor any means of determining, if they *were* lying, whether their motivation was espionage or sex. Thus, sexuality seems often to have operated as a kind of *Zweifelprinzip*, an element of doubt ramifying through the already intricate tangle of evidence, testimonies, and competing epistemes the Affair comprised.

Let us consider some of the other ways that sexuality functioned during the Affair, taking the history of the "scoundrel D." letter as a salient example. Although the actual contents of the secret dossier were known only to military officials and their intimates, the information that secret evidence had illegally been shown to the jurors of the first court-martial without the defendant's knowledge had been leaked to several people by late 1895. In September 1896 *L'Éclair* referred publicly to the secret dossier for the first time and printed an incorrect version of the "scoundrel

D." letter containing the line, "Decidedly, this scoundrel Dreyfus has been demanding," a sentence that appears nowhere in the original document, which actually reads as follows:

> My dear friend
>
> I truly regret not having seen you before my departure. For the rest, I will be back in eight days. Attached [are] 12 master plans of Nice which that scoundrel D. gave me for you. I told him that you did not intend to resume relations. He claims there was a misunderstanding and that he will do all he can to satisfy you. He says he was stubborn and you don't hold it against him. I responded that he was mad and that I did not believe that you wanted to resume relations with him.
> Do whatever you wish!
> Good bye, I am in a great hurry.
>
> Alexandrine
> Don't bugger too much!!![69]

While glossing the letter's opaque reference to "D." to translate it into transparent evidence of Dreyfus's guilt, however, the paper also theorized that the letter was written in secret code and thus could not be made public without jeopardizing the work of French intelligence:

> In September [1894], the military attachés of the German embassy addressed a letter in code to their colleagues in the Italian embassy. [...] It was a letter encrypted in the code used by the German embassy. That code was in our possession, and it may be imagined that it was of too great a usefulness for such a secret to be publicly divulged. [...] Such was the reason for which the letter in question was not included in the official dossier and was communicated to the judges of the Court Martial only in secret and in the deliberation room, outside the presence even of the accused man.[70]

In fact, though, as we can see, the only "code" in this particular document was the use of Panizzardi's pet name, "Alexandrine," and, in the postscript, the word *bourrer*.[h] Thus, the semiotics of homosex was read as code; the words function as the sign of secret knowledge, simultaneously involving sexuality and espionage. Buggery could not merely name itself; it must instead, or also, be made to name an act of treachery.

Over the next few years the "scoundrel D." letter—or rather, what was imagined to be the "scoundrel D." letter—was subjected to several more constructions in which the document's sexual import morphed fantastically depending on the political views of its interpreters, almost none of whom had seen the original text, judging from their misconstruals of its contents. It was clearly considered vital to the Dreyfusard cause to deny that the document pertained to espionage (although in fact it did), so as to foreclose the possibility that it pertained to Dreyfus. A year and a half after the *Éclair* article, Zola referred to the letter in "J'accuse," rejecting the notion that it had anything to do with spying and reading its mention of "D." as a reference to heterosexual prostitution: the letter, he writes, is "a ridiculous piece of paper, yes, perhaps the piece where there's talk about women of easy virtue, about a certain D. who's becoming too demanding: no doubt some husband who thinks he's not being paid enough for his wife's favors."[71] So in the letter's first metamorphosis its sexual tenor remains but is transposed onto the wrong sentence and into the wrong category of illicit sexuality.

During Zola's 1898 trial for calumniating the army in "J'accuse," the attorney general made remarks to the effect that everyone knew that *L'Éclair*'s account of the letter was inexact, but that the only inaccuracy in the article was that it indicated a full name, "Dreyfus," where the original had an initial.[72] He also affirmed Zola's hypothesis that the letter was about loose women, adding that "we are all going to be in agreement about the

---

h. A contemporary copy of another of Panizzardi's letters transcribed the salutation, "Mon cher bourreur," as "Mon cher bonneur [sic]" (the "sic" included), indicating that the word was unfamiliar to the copyist, who was therefore unable to decipher Panizzardi's difficult handwriting accurately (Archives nationales, BB19 84). Presumably the word *bougre* would, in contrast, have been known to the copyist or any other sophisticated adult, suggesting that *bourreur* was a fairly heavily encoded term. It is conceivable, then, that some of the military officials who had direct access to these letters did not fully grasp their sexual significance. But Maurice Baumont claimed that "the intimacy of their relations was a secret to no one" (*Aux sources de l'affaire*, 15), and in view of the contents of the secret dossier it is clear that the overall import and tenor of the correspondence were understood even if some of the specific words were not.

import of this 'scoundrel D.' document."[73] The attorney general was not, it seems, particularly concerned with the content of the letter, but rather with arguing that the *Éclair* article had been planted by Dreyfusards trying to force a revision (on the grounds that the first court-martial had been illegal); it was, then, in his interests as well as those of the Dreyfusards to dismiss the letter as unimportant.

Meanwhile, Zola's defense lawyer, Fernand Labori, strenuously denied that the letter was in code, trying to dispel the smokescreen that the anti-Dreyfusards had created by their insistence that the letter was highly classified material so that they could justify its illegal use during Dreyfus's court-martial. Strangely, Labori implied that he had seen the original, yet he too misquoted it, claiming, significantly, that the line "Decidedly, this scoundrel D. has been demanding"[i] was contained in a postscript.[74] Where Zola displaced the letter's erotic valence from homo- onto heterosexuality, Labori now replaces the breezy reference to sodomy in the original with an invented line that erases the real postscript's sexual significance entirely, while bearing the symbolic trace of the confusion it continued to generate. A few months later Dreyfusard Yves Guyot, editor of *Le siècle*, repeated Labori's new version of the postscript but seemed to fear that it ran the risk of introducing something other than sex—perhaps espionage—into the story. Therefore, Guyot reprised Zola's earlier suggestion and ingeniously proposed that the problematic postscript *too* had to do with the heterosexual prostitutes he imagined to inhabit the body of the letter, thus unwittingly restoring to the postscript the function its author had originally assigned to it, of talking about sex: "It would not require, it seems, a great deal of perspicacity to imagine that the postscript might pertain to the text of the letter, that is to say, to the pleasure parties, the women of easy virtue, and the blackmail with which their imprudent friends might, at times, be menaced."[75]

Postscripts work paraleptically, both presenting themselves as something superfluous to the import of a letter proper and drawing heightened

---

i. Members of the Dreyfusard camp were claiming that the pejorative term used in the letter was "animal" rather than "*canaille*" at least as early as January 1898, before Zola's trial (see J. Reinach, *L'affaire Dreyfus*, 44); this further distortion of the language of the original is interesting in view of Dobelbower's argument that *canaille* had, in addition to its common meaning of "scoundrel," a connotation in homosexual slang of effeminacy ("Petits bleus," 136–37). Were Dreyfusards, consciously or not, heterosexualizing "D."?

attention to themselves by virtue of their location. The real "scoundrel D." postscript—"Don't bugger too much!"—introduces sex as the thing extraneous to the letter's actual content, which was about espionage. The postscript's falsified surrogate focused everyone's attention on the question of how the line should read—"D." or "Dreyfus"—and thus of whether Dreyfus was guilty of espionage, while obscuring the fact that the line was standing in for a reference to homosex.

Eventually, at an 1898 appeals court hearing that helped overturn the 1894 verdict, Georges Picquart—one of the few witnesses who one can be sure had seen the original letter and had too much integrity to lie about its contents—paraphrased the document, quite accurately, from memory, including the signature "Alexandrine," but omitting the sodomitical postscript. Asked about the signature, Picquart said only that "'ALEXANDRINE' was a signature known to the [Statistical Section] office. It would be impossible for me to tell you, at this time, whether it was that of A . . . [Schwartzkoppen] or of B . . . [Panizzardi]."[j] The letter thus makes, in Picquart's testimony, its first public appearance in anything like its real form, but with its sexual content reduced to a sort of vestigial appendage, the mere acknowledgment that "Alexandrine" was the nom de plume of a man.

Later during the appeals court hearing, and then again at Dreyfus's 1899 retrial at Rennes, the original letter was finally read aloud, but the postscript was omitted again and Schwartzkoppen and Panizzardi were identified only as "foreign agents."[76] After five years the letter was allowed to speak the truth about espionage, but only in exchange for stifling what it had to say about sex. It is as if, in order for Dreyfus to be made to disappear from Schwartzkoppen and Panizzardi's correspondence, sexuality had to disappear from it, too. The unvarnished truth of the "scoundrel D." letter—that it really was about both espionage and homosexuality, but it was not about Dreyfus—seems to have been inadmissible in the context of the Affair, so invariably did homosexuality, treason, and Jewishness evoke one another.

The exegetical history of the "scoundrel D." letter is evidence of the General Staff's difficulty in spinning evidence so that it would yield the result that they wanted, and no other—for evidence about espionage, like

---

j. Dreyfus, *La révision du procès Dreyfus: Enquête*, 137. In the written transcripts of the trials the attachés' names are always given as "A" and "B," but the media and the public knew who they were, and Picquart may have identified them by name in his oral testimony.

evidence about sex, is slippery, undependable, and the sources the army was relying on had to do with both. In attempting to make treason unambiguously legible the military was, in fact, putting itself in an untenable position. First, to acknowledge the secret dossier at all meant admitting that Dreyfus's court-martial had been illegal, which could, and eventually did, lead to a retrial. Furthermore, they could not prove Dreyfus's guilt beyond all doubt without presenting documents that stated in unequivocal language that he was guilty. But no one knew better than people who worked in intelligence that documents pertaining to espionage are highly unlikely to be couched in unequivocal terms; the minister of war, General Jean-Baptiste Billot, effectively if unintentionally undermined the army's own case when he testified at Rennes: "I will say very plainly to the court-martial that when it comes to espionage, two out of three spies are always double agents; consequently, in general, any document pertaining to espionage is suspect to some degree."[77]

In short, even if Dreyfus had been guilty, documents clearly demonstrating his guilt would not have existed because any actual correspondence about a spy would have been in code. After the *Éclair* piece appeared what puzzled those who knew anything about espionage was that "intelligence officers never mentioned the most minor agent by name in any communication";[78] Picquart explained to the court of appeals that these were his grounds for believing that "D." could not possibly be Dreyfus.[79] After all, secret agents are, by definition, supposed to have opaque identities. Thus, whether Dreyfus was innocent or guilty, there ought not, logically, to have been any unambiguous—uncoded—evidence against him. The General Staff could only prove its case by disproving it, "translating," for example, the homoeroticism of the "scoundrel D." letter into treason to make something clear that actually should have been occulted if they had been right—or wrong.

The problem of the mistranslation of erotic language surfaces again in another document in the secret dossier, an 1894 telegram sent from Panizzardi to his superiors in Rome just after Dreyfus was arrested. Panizzardi wired that "if Captain Dreyfus has never been in contact with you, it would be advisable to instruct the ambassador to publish an official denial."[80] This telegram actually *was* encrypted, written in a cipher that French intelligence had managed to crack by decoding another, unrelated, correspondence between two heterosexual Italian lovers. A French official, Maurice Paléologue, said of that correspondence that it was "entirely clear and frank, for it expressed only the simplest, most natural feelings."[81] Hetero-sex, it would seem, is "clear and frank" even when it is in code, but homosex is read as code even when it is entirely clear! Despite the alleged transparency of the eroticism affiliated with this cipher, however, the General Staff still garbled its translation of Panizzardi's telegram so that rather than exculpating Dreyfus, it explicitly named him as a spy: the first line now read "Dreyfus arrested, precautions taken, our emissary warned."[82] Not surprisingly, it was the mistranslation that made its way into the secret dossier, although Paléologue at least, and probably others in French intelligence, had copies of the correct translation and sent them to the Staff.

A few other scraps in the secret dossier seem to have been included solely to reinforce the connection between proscribed sexuality and the enemies of France. Classified reports on the activities of diplomats and spies dwell on their sexual affairs; women with more than one lover, prostitutes, and demimondaines were subjected to close scrutiny, and foreign, especially German-speaking, mistresses of Frenchmen were also considered suspicious. A copy of a note dated September 24, 1894 (the month before Dreyfus was arrested), mentions a "Schoenfeld," adjunct of the Archduke Albert, who "has passions like those of the Marquis de Sade" and then adds that he is well-known among the *filles publiques* of Vienna. A clipping headed "Allemagne, le 27 Septembre 1898," and captioned "Les scandales aux ateliers militaires de Spandau" cites reports that military workmen "are idle and debauched; they earn a great deal of money for doing nothing. Their time is spent gorging themselves with beer and engaging in debauches that recall those of Sodom and Gomorrah."[83] None of these materials has to do with Dreyfus, or any of the other principals in the Affair; none of them is even embedded in commentary *purporting* to make logical connections between these texts or between them and Dreyfus. Instead, all of these documents serve, like the Schwartzkoppen-Panizzardi letters, as "erotic excess," creating an almost subliminal paralogical chain of associations between spies, perversion, Germanness, licentiousness, treason, and sexually undisciplined women that threads its way through, or under, the explicit narrative of the case against a Jew, Alfred Dreyfus.

Oddly, the sexual contents of the secret dossier were taken as an indication of the authenticity and veracity of *all* the materials in the file, many of which were actually forgeries. At different times various members of the General Staff testified that they had believed the charges against Dreyfus precisely because of the erotic nature of some of the materials in the file[84]—

even though the documents that pertained to sex had nothing to do with Dreyfus. In 1897, for example, General Gonse wrote in a note that all of the material allegedly taken from Schwartzkoppen's wastepaper basket must be assumed to be authentic: "There are even some [documents] that are of such an intimate character that doubt is impossible, and the persons whom they concern have such an obvious interest in keeping them secret that the mere fact that they have been delivered to the Service is superabundant proof of their authenticity and, consequently, that of all the documents from the same source."[85] The frank eroticism of the Schwartzkoppen-Panizzardi letters is thus presumed to demonstrate their transparency: only people who believed themselves to be acting in secrecy would write such things, so everything they wrote can be taken as equally candid. Gonse proceeds by the same metonymic logic that informed the use of these letters to inculpate Dreyfus; as their queerness implicitly implicated him, interpolated him into a series of discourses about foreign deviance, so their truth-effects radiate outward to the other contents of the wastepaper basket. Yet the reasoning is as faulty in one case as in the other; sex, which appeared to Gonse and others as a guarantee of certainty, in fact acts here only to distract attention from the glaringly obvious forgeries in the dossier, making the case against Dreyfus not clearer but infinitely more opaque.

SEX, LIES, AND ESPIONAGE

The secret dossier, with its excessive, decrypted, reencrypted, mistranslated erotic texts and their surrogates, is a singularly clamant instance of sexuality's centrality to the Affair, but by no means the only one. If, in the case of the "scoundrel D." letter, a homoerotic text was made to convey "sensitive" information, homosexual men were also important conduits for that information, with a number of consequences for the Affair. Political and sexual secrets were transmitted through a covert network of male friends and lovers in which personal relationships were shaped by the exigencies of the closet and the pressures of homophobia; the vicissitudes of those relationships changed political history. The most curious example of this is that after Oscar Wilde's release from prison, he became involved in the Affair through his good friend Carlos Blacker, who was also close to Panizzardi. Now, Panizzardi was, like Schwartz-koppen, distressed by what they both knew to be Dreyfus's wrongful imprisonment, but neither could reveal the truth without betraying the real traitor, Esterhazy. Probably a more important consideration (since Schwartzkoppen had no fondness for Esterhazy, though he was willing to use him as an agent) was that the attachés could not set the record straight without revealing the fact that they were involved in espionage, in defiance of international law, and also potentially exposing their own sexual relationship.

But when Esterhazy, after being publicly accused of writing the *bordereau*, was court-martialed and acquitted of treason, Panizzardi and his friend Blacker conceived of a plan to leak their inside information about Esterhazy to the international media, hoping to persuade the general public of his guilt and, consequently, of Dreyfus's innocence. Blacker discussed this plan with Wilde, apparently hoping to spur him to a sense of sympathetic outrage that would inspire him to write something in Dreyfus's defense; here, Blacker would seem to have come close to acknowledging a correspondence between Wilde's unjust imprisonment for committing sexual acts that would not have been criminal in France[k] and Dreyfus's unjust imprisonment for a political act that he had not committed at all.

Wilde, however, broke with Blacker soon afterward because the latter disapproved of his continued involvement with Lord Alfred Douglas, and Wilde passed on his former friend's confidences to two other homosexual men: the journalist Rowland Strong, who was a friend of Esterhazy's, and Strong's lover, Chris Healy. Healy in turn gave the information to Zola, through whom it eventually passed to Dreyfusard journalists who published it, but Strong tipped off Esterhazy, who was thus able to preempt the Dreyfusards by announcing that what was about to be published about him was false. Strong and Healy broke up over the incident,[86] and these multiple betrayals of confidence deflected what might have been a major coup by the Dreyfusards.

Relations among the circle of acquaintances were apparently close enough that Esterhazy, although decidedly heterosexual, occasionally

k. Proust's friend Robert de Billy pointed to the fact that homosexuality was "natural" in some countries and "punished" in others as one of the things that inspired, and legitimated, Proust's interest in it. Billy is thinking in particular of the Eulenburg Affair, but he could equally well have mentioned the Wilde scandal, which had prompted acute indignation in France at the same time that the Dreyfus Affair was arousing such ire in England. See Billy, *Marcel Proust*, 174; and Langlade, *La mésentente cordiale*.

vacationed with Strong, Wilde, and Lord Alfred.[87] It was to Strong that Esterhazy confessed, in an interview published in the *London Observer*, that he had indeed authored the *bordereau*. When Esterhazy was called to serve as a witness during the appeals court hearings in 1899, however, he denied making this confession and suggested, with typical audacity, that Strong was not only a homosexual but also an alcoholic:

> I must mention that M. Strong has, as his intimate friends, two very intelligent men with whom he lives nearly constantly, Lord Alfred Douglas and Sir Oscar Wilde. Since, *even though I have been accused of all the crimes and vices in the world, I have not yet acquired the one that could make such relations particularly agreeable to me*, I took an interest in M. Strong only because he was well-informed, because he put the English newspaper with which he was associated at my disposition and at that of my superiors; [. . .] when I got out of prison, he was one of the first to come to congratulate me, and, what's more, he was thoroughly drunk at the time; as he was wont to do, he had consumed an enormous quantity of whiskey. (emphasis added)[88]

Clearly, Wilde's name serves here as a perfectly recognizable synonym for homosexuality, and in turn homosexuality is recognized as, in and of itself, evidence of unreliability and mendacity. Esterhazy can thus argue, for all intents and purposes, that he is not a traitor because he is not a homosexual.

This logic helps explain the liberality with which both sides in the Affair, but especially the antirevisionists, accused those on the other side of homosexuality and effeminacy. Cartoons of the period often represent the caricaturists' chosen villains in the case as lisping cross-dressers. The Statistical Section kept a file on Maurice Weil—a prominent Jewish officer who was a friend of Esterhazy's—that included speculation that he was the lover of General Félix Saussier, the military governor of Paris; the contents of the file were leaked and became widely known. These accusations reached as far as the German monarch: the anti-Dreyfusard Cécile Dardenne-Cavaignac, daughter of the 1898 minister of war, wrote in her unpublished memoir of the Affair that there was a Jewish conspiracy to force Kaiser Wilhelm II to exculpate Dreyfus by threatening to publish the Schwartzkoppen-Panizzardi correspondence. This attempt at blackmail would succeed, she indicated, "because the shame that would result from the publication affects [*atteint*] the sovereign as much as the military attaché himself."[89]

In particular, Georges Picquart, as the army insider turned voluntary pariah, was repeatedly singled out for vituperative commentary about his gender identity and sexual practices. General Gonse wrote a hostile report about Picquart claiming that "*Picquart* is known in certain circles under the name of *Georgette*" and mentioning an alleged morals charge against him, which "would explain the attitude of Picquart in the Dreyfus Case."[90] An anti-Dreyfusard poster of the period titled "Les remparts d'Israël" levels the same accusation against Picquart and, implicitly, the pro-Dreyfus lawyer Alphonse Bard; it shows Picquart dressed in flamboyant drag, with a little ditty below him that reads, "Accompanied by his friend Bard, / The former Lieutenant-Colonel Picquart / In front of the court, at his first chance, / Starts to do a belly-dance" ("En compagnie de son ami Bard / L'ex lieutenant-colonel Picquart / Devant la cour sitot qu'il entre / S'met a danser la danse du ventre").[91] And when she was covering the Zola trial the anti-Dreyfusard journalist Gyp tied Picquart's alleged sexual deviance to both Protestantism and Jewishness, which registers in her remarks not as a race or faith but as an ontological condition of effeminacy and treachery: "Colonel Picquart is the pretty Jew, or rather the pretty Jewish blond. About his religion I have no hint, though I'd wager Protestant. He sways back and forth at the witness rail, moving his hips, which he shows off a bit too much."[92] As in Esterhazy's testimony, the connection between homosexuality and untrustworthiness is apparently considered too obvious to require any further explanation.

Meanwhile, numerous sources have claimed that one of the most mysterious figures in the Affair, a "veiled lady" who supposedly met several times with Esterhazy, was actually Du Paty in full drag, and they have further suggested that his transvestism was habitual.[93] The pissoirs of Paris, notorious sites of homosexual activity, also played a role in the Affair: Du Paty met with one of his informants, Esterhazy's cousin Christian, "in dark corners of the city, on bridges or in public lavatories, where messages were read and answers written by match-light," and Bredin says that "in public urinals, du Paty would read Esterhazy's notes."[94] As Proust would later emphasize, secret documents weren't the only form of classified information men exchanged in the pissoirs; in that light, what are we to make of the fact that during Dreyfus's retrial there were accusations of influence peddling after a judge and Picquart were found "meeting" by the urinals?[95]

Heterosexual adultery played an important role in the Affair, too, as mistresses of the male principals were often involved in their skullduggery or presumed to be their motive for lying about a particular incident. During his trials prosecutors hounded Dreyfus about his alleged extramarital liaisons, especially with German-speaking women, as the supposition that he was cheating on his wife was adduced as further evidence that he was leading a double life. As in the case of Dubarry's inverts—who, having lost their moral sense along with their sense of the national language, have become "internationalists"—we find illicit sexuality and foreign tongues intercalated again in the legal charges against Dreyfus, which insinuate that a man who would betray his wife is eminently capable of betraying both French and France itself: "The private conduct of Captain Dreyfus is far from being exemplary [. . .] he admitted to us that he stopped the woman 'Y' in the street in 1893, and became acquainted with the woman 'Z' at the race track, in 1894; the first of these women is Austrian, speaks several languages, especially German."[96]

Although Dreyfus was—rather surprisingly—never accused of homosexual tendencies himself, in many other cases allegations of heterosexual adultery appear in conjunction with intimations of homosexuality, the two often appearing to reinforce each other. Any indulgence in aberrant sexuality was likely to be taken as an indication, at least by someone's enemies, that he was inclined to other forms of sexual license, as well as to treachery. In the same report in which Gonse suggested that Picquart was homosexual, he proposed incriminating Picquart by informing his mistress's husband of their adulterous affair, which was in fact done, bringing about the dissolution of the marriage.[97] General Saussier's intimacy with Maurice Weil was attributed not only to their supposed sexual involvement but also to Saussier's alleged sexual relationship with Mme Weil. Similarly, Paléologue ascribed Major Henry's fondness for his colleague, Captain J. M. Lauth, to Lauth's affair with Mme Henry,[98] which surely only a Frenchman could consider a sufficient explanation for a masculine friendship.

The peculiarity of this claim might tempt us to look for the "truth" of a homoerotic relationship veiled by Paléologue's naïveté or disingenuousness, but to do so would be, again, to give priority to homosexuality as that which must always be concealed, to assume that heterosexual adultery must always be a smokescreen for sodomy rather than to read the two as comparable surrogates for untrustworthiness in the vocabulary of obloquy. It is true that in these contemporary accounts of the role of sexuality in the Affair, the reader often has a sense that something is being concealed; but (homo)sexuality is as likely to be the thing doing the hiding as the thing being hidden.

For example, in the years after the 1894 trial, as efforts to prove or disprove Dreyfus's guilt took on truly byzantine complexity, numerous people on both sides of the Affair threatened to blackmail Panizzardi and Schwartzkoppen, but it is not always evident that their homosexual relationship was the (sole) basis for the threat. The word *blackmail* did have at one time a specifically homosexual meaning, according to Courouve; he quotes one dictionary that defines *chanteur*, "blackmailer," as "a man who, by pretending to share the tastes of the sodomites, ends up obliging them to pay him off according to their means by threatening to denounce them."[99] Courouve claims that this connotation died out after the 1860s, but it is possible that we observe its lingering traces in the ambiguously worded accounts of the "blackmail" with which the attachés were so frequently menaced. At the same time, however, heterosexual promiscuity is as likely to motivate these threats as sodomy. For instance, in the rare sources where Schwartzkoppen's bisexual relationships are openly acknowledged, hetero- and homosexuality are equally and explicitly described as potential grounds for blackmail: Dardenne-Cavaignac wrote that to accomplish its ends, international Jewry was prepared to use "blackmail, the threat of publishing the scandalous correspondence exchanged by Schwartzkoppen and Panizzardi; or Schwartzkoppen's amorous correspondence with Mme X, wife of a foreign diplomat."[100]

Heterosexuality's role in these narratives about attempted blackmail is often nearly as ambiguous as that of homosexuality. At one point during the Affair the General Staff tried to exert pressure on the Italians by showing the Italian ambassador letters Schwartzkoppen and Panizzardi had allegedly, in Panizzardi's words, "addressed to women in society."[101] Panizzardi wrote Schwartzkoppen an indignant note about these accusations, assuring his lover that he had written no such letters and sounding slightly put out that Schwartzkoppen might have more mistresses than Panizzardi had realized: "I've been told that the Syndicate[1] possesses letters from you addressed to a lady who is not the one with whom I am acquainted, so you see that they know more about it than I do."[102] Since Panizzardi apparently did not have sexual relations with women, what

---

1. A name commonly given to what were imagined to be the conspiratorial forces of international Jewry.

were the letters shown to the Italian ambassador? Letters to men, as David Levering Lewis hypothesizes?[103] Was Panizzardi describing these as "letters to women" only to avoid compromising himself further if this missive to Schwartzkoppen should be intercepted (as it obviously was)? Was Panizzardi, intending his letter to be private, anxious only to affirm his sexual loyalty to his lover and perhaps to reproach Schwartzkoppen for his lack of it? Or did he, on the contrary, assume the note would be read by French authorities and believe that it would persuade them of his innocence of any sexual indiscretion?

Questions like these puzzled contemporaries but became even more impenetrable in the decades after the Affair, when the secret dossier disappeared into the obscurity of the army's archives, and historians had to rely solely on (often cryptic) written documents rather than their personal knowledge of events. They were, in addition, constrained by reticences sometimes more acute than those of the late nineteenth century. Cécile Dardenne-Cavaignac's memoir, for example, while occasionally elliptical in its approach, makes it clear that at the turn of the century even a well-bred Frenchwoman might be thoroughly informed about the sexual peccadilloes, real or imagined, of her father's enemies. In contrast, well into the twentieth century most historians would describe Schwartzkoppen's mistress, Hermance de Weede, only as "a lady" rather than giving her name. And until Bredin published *The Affair* in 1983, historians made almost no reference to Schwartzkoppen's relationship with Panizzardi, either being unaware of it or choosing to suppress it in deference to the prejudices of their own age. In 1961 Marcel Thomas, who wrote the most exhaustive chronicle of the case to appear since Joseph Reinach's monumental *L'affaire Dreyfus* had been published at the turn of the century, ventured only to suggest tentatively that the attachés might have been bound by "an intimacy closer, and of an even more unmentionable nature," than their partnership in espionage.[104] But even though Thomas had unearthed the letters between the two from the military archives, he seems to have remained unconvinced that they were lovers, in part because of Schwartzkoppen's relationships with women—as if what an earlier period could not see at all, the 1960s could see only through the filter of a highly polarized conception of sexual orientation.

What is most striking about the treatment of sexuality in the Affair by twentieth-century writers, though, is not how suppressed it was but the degree to which sexuality continued to function, as it had during the Affair itself, as an element of doubt persistently sowing confusion through narratives striving for coherence. Some historians, attempting to explain the fact that a note from Schwartzkoppen to Esterhazy is not in Schwartzkoppen's handwriting, assert that he dictated it to one of his mistresses, others to a boyfriend; strangely, few surmise that it might have been transcribed by someone with whom Schwartzkoppen was *not* sexually involved, such as a secretary. David Levering Lewis says flatly that Schwartzkoppen "was homosexual" and speculates therefore that he denied knowledge of the *bordereau* simply because he wanted "to cast doubt upon the validity of all information obtained through the wastebasket leak,"[105] including his ribald correspondence with Panizzardi. And Thomas explains a particular piece of testimony by Weil by saying it really had to do with his wife's affair with Saussier and adds, "It is assuredly here, rather than in the improbable complicities of espionage, that we should look for the explanation of Weil's reticence,"[106] still assuming that illicit sex, albeit heterosex, is what is being covered up by something else—that what appears to be espionage is really sex instead.

It has not been my intention here to claim that I, unlike these other chroniclers of the Affair, have somehow gotten at the truth of the sexual discourses tangled in it. Instead, I have tried to suggest that sexuality in general, and homosexuality in particular, is a *Zweifelprinzip*, one of the things that keeps us, as it kept Dreyfus's contemporaries, from ever being quite sure what the truth of the Affair really was. Perhaps Schwartzkoppen never fingered Esterhazy because he couldn't admit that he himself was involved in espionage; or because he feared exposing his homosexual relationship with Panizzardi, or his heterosexual relationship with Mme de Weede; or because he did not want his superiors to know that he was careless enough to throw away compromising documents instead of burning them. Maybe General Saussier was, as some have claimed, a "known homosexual," the lover of Maurice Weil, or perhaps a confirmed adulterer, lover of Weil's wife and other married women,[107] or both, and either or both of those things might have influenced his testimony, or Weil's, in court. Possibly Dreyfus was a womanizer, Picquart bisexual, Du Paty a transvestite. Any or all of these things could be grounds for dissimulation, as is being guilty of spying, treason, forgery, or perjury. Thus any of the explanations offered for the intrigues and deceptions involved in the Affair could be accurate, but (what we presume to be) the need to conceal the evidence of both espionage and prohibited sexuality keeps us from ever being able to say with certainty, "This is what really happened." Sexuality is not the reality of the Affair waiting to be known; it is what has always made the reality of the Affair, in some measure, unknowable.

3

SECRET DOSSIERS

Men must be capable of imagining and executing and insisting on social change, if they are to reform or even maintain civilization, and capable too of furnishing the rebellion which is sometimes necessary if society is not to perish of immobility. Therefore all men should have a drop of treason in their veins, if the nations are not to go soft like so many sleepy pears.

—Rebecca West, *The New Meaning of Treason*

It was Emile Zola who explicitly put sexual deviance, Jewishness, and treachery back together again after the Dreyfus Affair had settled down, who conjoined them and made them completely legible; Zola, passionate advocate of religious tolerance and the man so well known for his sympathetic interest in sexual nonconformity that the anonymous Italian homosexual who authored *Roman d'un inverti* chose him to receive his confession; Zola, heroic defender of the liberal Republic or treasonous pornographer, depending on one's perspective. Zola fictionalized the Affair in 1903 in a roman à clef entitled *Vérité*, *"Truth,"* and changed the crime with which the innocent Jewish protagonist is wrongly charged from treason to pederastic rape and murder—as if one could simply stand in for the other. Crucially, the protagonist's alleged crime is not only illegal but also unnatural, for only thus could it be an adequate surrogate for betraying one's nation. A few years later Proust, like Zola, would choose in his own fiction to access the elaborate discourses of race and sexuality that the Affair had mobilized. But where Zola's aim was to attack the anti-Semitic prejudice that associated Jews with crime, disloyalty, and deviance, Proust was more interested in exploring, exploiting, and sometimes, as we shall see, even affirming that connection.

The Eulenburg case[a] and the trials of Oscar Wilde both contributed to Proust's work on "La race maudite," the long disquisition on homosexuality

---

a. An early twentieth-century scandal in which Prince Philipp zu Eulenburg-Hertefeld and other intimates of the German emperor were accused of treason and homosexuality.

that eventually became the opening section of *Sodom and Gomorrah*, but more central to *À la recherche* than either is the Dreyfus Affair. In addition to exposing the role played by sexuality in the Affair itself, Proust uses the Affair as one of the most frequently recurring terms of comparison for illicit sexuality in the novel, a metaphor whose full relevance is evident only in light of the correlation between Jews and homosexuals in the cultural, and Proust's, imagination. Eve Sedgwick has written that in *À la recherche* Dreyfusism and illicit sexuality are "the organizing principles for one another as they are for the volumes through which they ramify,"[1] interlaced in explicit allusions (the pissoirs, the veiled lady, the secret dossier), implicit juxtaposition, and especially the recurrent themes and images of espionage, spies, secrets, false identities, and changing loyalties. Furthermore, these two tropes involve myriad other plots of treason, assimilation, desire, and (be)longing and ultimately contribute to the novel's destabilization of any fixed conception of personal, cultural, or national identity.

HOMOSEXUALITY AND HERMENEUTICS

One way that Proust evokes the centrality of sexuality to the Dreyfus Affair is simply by representing the way that, as we saw in the last chapter, sex circulated—especially via rumor and gossip—as an explanatory device, which usually obfuscated what it claimed to reveal:

> "You know," [the Duc de Guermantes] went on, "why they can't produce the proof of Dreyfus's guilt. Apparently it's because he's the lover of the War Minister's wife, that's what people are saying on the sly."
> "Ah! I thought it was the Prime Minister's wife," said M. d'Argencourt. [...]
> "No, it was the War Minister's wife; at least, that's the talk of the coffee-houses."[2]

Elsewhere, and more frequently, sexuality—and especially homosexuality—is interpolated into conversations about Dreyfusism, acting not hermeneutically as it does in the quote here but through contiguity. Referring to an incident during Zola's trial in 1898, when Prince Henri d'Orléans embraced Esterhazy after the latter had given evidence, M. Norpois says that, in contrast, "'you would never have found the Prince of Bulgaria clasping Major Esterhazy to his bosom.' 'He would have preferred a private soldier,' murmured Mme de Guermantes" (GW, 328). At the reception held by the Prince and Princesse de Guermantes, conversations about the Affair are interwoven with allusions to homosexuality or staged against the backdrop of a homosexual scene; as Swann discusses the prince's conversion to Dreyfusism with Marcel,[b] for example, Charlus is cruising Mme de Surgis's sons in the background, and Swann himself segues smoothly between denying Charlus's homosexuality and telling Marcel about the conversation in which the prince confessed his change of heart (a point the full significance of which will emerge only once we learn later that the prince, too, is an invert):

> "[Charlus] is more sentimental than other men, that's all; on the other hand, as he never goes very far with women, that has given a sort of plausibility to the idiotic rumours to which you refer. Charlus is perhaps greatly attached to his men friends, but you may be quite certain that the attachment is only in his head and in his heart. [...] Well, the Prince de Guermantes went on to say: 'I don't mind telling you that this idea of a possible illegality in the conduct of the trial was extremely painful to me, because I have always, as you know, worshipped the Army.'"[3]

In addition to thus placing the Affair and sexuality next to each other, or in the same frame, Proust also develops an extended comparison between (homo)sexuality and espionage that draws part of its effect from the rhetorical nexus between the two established by the Affair. In our first glimpse of the Baron de Charlus, for instance, Marcel metaphorically describes him as a spy because of the way Charlus is looking at him, with a singular expression that he can not yet interpret as homoerotic desire: "[Charlus's] eyes were shot through by a look of restless activity such as the sight of a person they do not know excites only in men in whom, for whatever reason, it inspires thoughts that would not occur to anyone else—madmen, for instance, or spies."[4] Most significantly, Proust invokes the secret dossier as a sign and representation of the homosexual experience at the

---

b. For the sake of convenience I will adopt the conventional, though disputed and inadequate, practice of referring to the novel's protagonist and sometime first-person narrator as "Marcel."

heart of the Affair. He first alludes to the secret dossier in *The Guermantes Way* in describing Albert Bloch's political naïveté, his desire to believe that the truth of the Affair can be recovered *tel quel* from the infamous dossier: "Naturally, Bloch thought that the truth in politics could be approximately reconstructed by the most lucid minds, but he imagined, like the man in the street, that it resided permanently, beyond the reach of argument and in a material form, in the secret files [*le dossier secret*] of the President of the Republic and the Prime Minister, who imparted it to the Cabinet" (GW, 325)

In fact, however, establishing political truth requires that we subject data to a process of trained exegesis; and the training required, we are about to discover, is a crash course in homosexuality. Seventy-odd pages later—in an allusion that would have been instantly recognizable to readers who had lived through the Affair even if Proust had not earlier reminded them of its significance—Charlus analogizes his own sexual experience to a "secret dossier" that he would like to communicate to a deserving young man in need of instruction. He says to the as-yet-oblivious Marcel, who will not realize that the baron is an invert until the following volume:

> "I have often thought, Monsieur, that there was in me [. . .] a wealth of experience, a sort of secret dossier of inestimable value, of which I have not felt myself at liberty to make use for my own personal ends, which would be a priceless acquisition to a young man to whom I would hand over in a few months what it has taken me more than thirty years to acquire. [. . .] And I do not speak only of events that have already occurred, but of the chain of circumstances. [. . .] I could give you an explanation that no one has dreamed of, not only of the past but of the future." (GW, 389)

In Charlus's account, then, the secret dossier of homosexual experience is the key to decoding everything, a kind of master hermeneutics that can explain not just the Dreyfus Affair but all of history.

Arguably, homosexuality serves this very function in the novel, especially for Marcel but also to some extent for the (heterosexual) first-time reader. If we examine the relation of "La race maudite" to the overall structure of the novel and especially to the sections that treat the Dreyfus Affair, we are struck by its placement. There are only three scattered references to the Affair in the first two volumes of *À la recherche*, but fifty in *The Guermantes Way*, which covers the years when the case was at its height. Simultaneously, as Roger Shattuck has observed, the last sections of *The Guermantes Way* represent the point where the theme of homosexuality is bubbling irrepressibly to the surface and "Marcel's naïveté [about Charlus] has been stretched to the limit";[5] he, and we, simply can't go on any further without "getting it," or at least, without coming to understand that there is something to get.

The first forty pages of *Sodom and Gomorrah* provide the necessary, transformative revelation of Charlus's sexual relationship with Jupien; Marcel learns that Charlus is an invert and the reader is provided with Proust's most extended explanation of masculine homosexuality. This section is immediately followed by the scene of the Guermantes' reception and about thirty-five further references to the Affair, most of them grouped closely together within a hundred pages. After that, the Affair gradually disappears again from the text; there are but ten allusions to it in *The Captive* and *The Fugitive* together, and only six in the final volume of *À la recherche*. We see, then, that the sexual encounter between the two men is placed not only in the exact center of the novel but, like the secret dossier itself, in the center of the Affair as well. Nestled in the middle of the dense clusters of references to the Affair in volumes 3 and 4, "La race maudite" stands in the same spatial relation to them as the Schwartzkoppen-Panizzardi correspondence does to the historical case: and it does similar kinds of metonymic and explanatory work.

Shattuck points out that at the Guermantes' soirée, just a few hours after Marcel has observed Charlus and Jupien in the morning, his ability to apprehend both homosexuality and "political depravity" has suddenly become acute: "Beneath the resounding titles, the magnificent surroundings, and the polite conversation, Marcel soon detects not only snobbery and political depravity (the Dreyfus case is at its height) but also ubiquitous homosexuality that destroys some of the most honorable names."[6] Listening to a conversation between M. de Vaugoubert and Charlus about the staff at a certain embassy, Marcel realizes that Vaugoubert is himself homosexual, and that the embassy staff are as well, something that even Vaugoubert, despite his own predilections, does not understand as clearly as Marcel. In this next passage the phrases "in time to come" and "my trained ear" belong to the older narrator, but the protagonist is already well on his way to becoming an accomplished exegete:

It was [. . .] the voice of M. de Vaugoubert talking to M. de Charlus.
A skilled physician need not even make his patient unbutton his

shirt, nor listen to his breathing—the sound of his voice is enough. How often, in time to come, was my ear to be caught in a drawing-room by the intonation or laughter of some man whose artificial voice, for all that he was reproducing exactly the language of his profession or the manners of his class, affecting a stern aloofness or a coarse familiarity, was enough to indicate "He is a Charlus" to my trained ear, like the note of a tuning-fork! (*SG*, 86)

One reason it is important for Marcel to acquire this expertise is that it enables him to transcend Bloch's naïve faith in the authority of others, by becoming something of an expert himself. Jessica Berman notes that "one of the key threats to identity in *A la recherche* [is] passive, social acquiescence."[7] Inasmuch as it is necessary, in order for Marcel to become an individual, an adult, and an artist, for him to escape the stultifying uniformity of the social world he originally longed to join, it is also necessary for him to learn to evaluate and analyze data independently of others. In *Time Regained* Proust mocks the credulity of those who, like Bloch, "empower social authorities to judge for them,"[8] renouncing their own responsibility to interpret the world: "I had seen everybody believe, during the Dreyfus Affair or during the war, and in medicine too, that truth is a particular piece of knowledge which cabinet ministers and doctors possess, a Yes or No which requires no interpretation, thanks to the possession of which the men in power *knew* whether Dreyfus was guilty or not [. . .] in the same way that an X-ray photograph is supposed to indicate without any need for interpretation the exact nature of a patient's disease."[9]

Learning to read the secret dossier of homosexuality is, therefore, a crucial element—perhaps *the* crucial element—in Marcel's political, sentimental, and aesthetic education. Jeanne Bem has written that the episode between Charlus and Jupien is widely acknowledged to be an "inaugural" moment in the text, and, noting both that their union is referred to as a fertilization and that Proust describes a writer as being pregnant with his own work, she speculates that what Charlus and Jupien inaugurate, the product of their union, is nothing less than (the meaning of) the novel—either *À la recherche* itself or the novel Marcel is planning to write at the end of the *Recherche*.[c] It may be, then, that Marcel cannot even read his own text

c. Bem, "Le juif et l'homosexuel," 102. These are frequently assumed to be the same work, but a cogent argument can be made that they are not; see, for example, Landy, "Proust."

(either the one he appears in or the one he will write) until he has learned to decipher the secret dossier.

Even after the pivotal scene in *Sodom and Gomorrah*, of course, it will take Marcel—and the reader with him—a while to master this cipher. Marcel has to spend a good deal of time in the central volumes of *À la recherche* learning the "foreign tongue" of inversion, which poses a challenge to his linguistic abilities in the sheer bewildering variety of its vocabulary. After all, in just one single, breathtaking, three-page sentence in "La race maudite," Proust refers to it as a crime, a disease, a race, an innate disposition, a freemasonry, an identity, an anachronistic fiction, and a vice (*SG*, 21–24). And in addition, like Jewishness, inversion is described elsewhere in the novel as a psychological state, a colony, a culture, a fact of nature, a genetic tendency—but also as a germ, something that can and does spread.

The multiple valences of homosexuality and Jewishness contribute to, where they do not directly create, the opacity of both identity categories and the consequent difficulty of interpreting them. The novel itself, however, serves as a decoding device, helping to illuminate the myriad manifestations of homosexuality and other occulted identities. In particular, part of the novel's project is to involve the putatively heterosexual, gentile reader in the unveiling of the mysteries of inversion and Jewishness, so that she can piece together the proleptic fragments of information in the earlier volumes and reinsert them into a coherent narrative later on. This requires that the reader, like Marcel, take on the identity of a spy herself, peering in at these presumably alien beings and learning to decipher their codes. "Marcel is not only a bourgeois interloper in the beau monde, he is also an outsider and spy within the homosexual demi-monde. [. . .] Likewise the bourgeois or proletarian reader, on being 'drawn into' the Hôtel de Guermantes; likewise the heterosexual reader, on 'entering' Jupien's whore house."[10] Furthermore, if we accept Hannah Arendt's argument that Proust's own identity as a (partially) closeted homosexual and (largely) assimilated Jew positioned him particularly well as an observer of—a spy on—salon society,[11] we might figure Proust's relationship to the world he describes in terms of espionage as well.

Espionage is, in fact, a productive metaphor, not only for the relationship of both the writer and the reader *to* the text, but for all the human relationships *within* the text. Because every social group has its own codes of conduct—because, moreover, the experience of individuals is almost completely unfathomable to others—all of Proust's characters find themselves in the position of spying on others in an effort to apprehend the secrets of both their social and their personal being. The narrator refers to his own surveillance of his lover, Albertine, as "espionage";[12] as Leo Bersani writes, "The need to become familiar with Albertine's desires is so intense that the activity of loving turns out to be something like a compulsive intellectual investigation."[13] Merely entering society means doing intelligence work, given the "cryptographical aspect of polite conversation."[14]

We recall that the incessantly reiterated phrase used to evoke the specificity of communal and personal identities, and the complicated play of the characters' affiliations with them, is *en être*, "to be one of us" or "one of them." But literally it means "to be of it" or "to be in it," to be inside; so that someone *qui n'en est pas*, "who is not one of them," is then necessarily outside, looking in: spying. *En être* was time-worn slang, dating back to the late sixteenth century, used to describe being homosexual;[15] Proust expands on this meaning and uses the phrase to designate other kinds of hermetic difference as well. Thus *il en est* means, at various points in the novel and frequently simultaneously, he's one of us; he's one of them; he's an invert; he's a Jew; he's a member of a particular social class; he's a Dreyfusard. And each of these identities has its own slang, mannerisms, and rules of engagement, all requiring careful decoding and interpretation on the part of those who are not "inside," *ceux qui n'en sont pas*—especially if they aspire to be.

The task of decryption is made infinitely more difficult by the fact that in Proust's vision, dissimulation is as fundamental to social life in general as it is to espionage in particular. Nearly everyone in *À la recherche* is a double agent, assuming multiple identities and invested in multiple loyalties, which is at least partly an effect of the fact that everybody is viewed by others in multiple contexts, so that, for example, Swann is both "the intimate of the Prince of Wales and the butt of Madame Verdurin's jokes."[16] Disruptions in the social order—what Proust calls the turn of the kaleidoscope—can suddenly expose a double agent's hidden identity, but without putting a stop to the ongoing game of transvestism that Proust shows to be fundamental to our constitution as social beings. "All simulate and dissimulate, lie or lie to themselves, all have a secret life, a vice, a passion, a virtue, a hidden genius, all are Dr. Jekyll and Mr. Hyde, lending themselves from one day to the next to the most spectacular revelations. Certain historical events (the Dreyfus affair, the War), certain social facts (Sodom and Gomorrha [*sic*]) seem to take place only to provide further surprises: this ladies' man cared only for waiters, this violent anti-Semite was a Dreyfusard, this hero was a coward, this man was a woman, etc."[17]

Lying—or what in some contexts we would call "passing"—is essential to assimilation into any group. One step in the narrator's process of assimilation into society is learning a language of disingenuousness: "I was beginning to learn the exact value of the language, spoken or mute, of aristocratic affability. [. . .] That one should discern the fictitious character of this affability was what [the Guermantes] called being well-bred" (SG, 84). Sometimes it is necessary for subalterns, especially homosexual men, to communicate in code in order to dissimulate potentially incriminating speech acts, as, for example, when Charlus tries to seduce Marcel with his opaque reference to his secret dossier. Sometimes the use of encoded language is itself a (failed) attempt to pass by demonstrating that the speaker has equal facility in multiple linguistic registers and therefore cannot be identified with any one in particular, as is the case in *Guermantes Way* when Charlus uses gay slang in conversation with Marcel to try to convey his indifference to homosexuality. (Note, incidentally, the temporal split here between the narrator recounting the incident, who obviously now understands the term Charlus used, and Marcel, who didn't.) "'At least he's a man,'" says Charlus,

> "not one of those effeminate creatures one sees so many of nowadays, who look like little rent boys [*truqueurs*] and at any moment may bring their innocent victims to the gallows." (I did not know the meaning of this slang expression, "rent boy"; anyone who had known it would have been as greatly surprised by his use of it as myself. Society people always like talking slang, and people who may be suspected of certain things like to show that they are not afraid to mention them. A proof of innocence in their eyes. But they have lost their sense of proportion, they are no longer capable of realising the point beyond which a certain pleasantry will become too technical, too flagrant, will be a proof rather of corruption than of ingenuousness.) (*GW*, 400–401)

Charlus's blunder illuminates the paradox that the knowledge of these codes, used to conceal—Hebrew, Yiddish, the semiotics of cruising—can also reveal too much. Indeed, Marcel always fears that Charlus, in insisting on his specialized knowledge of homosexuality, will betray himself— and he does, repeatedly. Similarly, the ability of Jews to dissimulate their meaning can become the thing that exposes—that keeps them from dissimulating—their identities, as when they inadvertently use a Hebrew word in front of gentiles.

> "Meschores," in the Bible, means "the servant of God." In the family circle the Blochs used the word to refer to the servants, and were always delighted by it, because their certainty of not being understood either by Christians or by the servants themselves enhanced in M. Nissim Bernard and M. Bloch their twofold distinction of being "masters" and at the same time "Jews." But this latter source of satisfaction became a source of displeasure when there was "company." At such times M. Bloch, hearing his uncle say "meschores," felt that he was over-exposing his oriental side. (WBG, 484)

Thus, these coded verbal communications, normally reserved for members of the freemasonry—*pour ceux qui en sont*—can sometimes be recognized as code or even deciphered by others, a fact that is not without its risks for the subaltern whose ability to pass is thereby threatened.

Inevitably, the play of concealed meanings, and the efforts of people from different social groups to decode the meanings of others, yield innumerable misunderstandings that are some of the richest sources of humor in the novel. A number of the funniest scenes in *À la recherche* rely for their comedic effect on the malentendus generated by M. and Mme Cottard's persistent confusion about both sexual deviance and Jewishness, categories that Mme Cottard, in particular, is unable to distinguish. When she overhears her husband gossiping about Charlus, she "picked up only the words 'a member of the confraternity' and '*tapette*' [both "chatterbox" and "fairy"], and as in the Doctor's vocabulary the former expression denoted the Jewish race and the latter a wagging tongue, Mme Cottard concluded that M. de Charlus must be a garrulous Jew" (SG, 594). Mme Cottard then endeavors to convey her enlightened philo-Semitism to the devoutly Catholic and anti-Semitic Charlus, relentlessly working the conversation around to topics that she assumes will interest him as a Jew. Mme Cottard's gaffe provides one of many occasions for a shared joke between the narrator and the reader—assumed to be not only heterosexual and gentile but also less knowledgeable than Marcel—whom he is in the process of initiating into the mysteries of these foreign languages.

LEARNING THE LANGUAGE

Let us now examine some of the ramifications of treating homosexuality, in particular, as a language. There are several different manifestations of what Proust calls the "strange tongue" (*SG*, 36). First, there is the visual language of the body, which Marcel sees; then there are the sounds produced by the (homo)sexual body, which he hears; finally, there is a discourse, or more accurately there are multiple discourses, *about* homosexuality. All of these pose their own interpretive problems. In particular, the visual and the audible manifestations of homosexual identity and practice, while quite distinct, seem to be oddly interdependent and mutually illuminating in Marcel's understanding. I have argued that in general, anxieties about "passing" have to do with the visual illegibility of Jewish and homosexual difference, and indeed, Proust acknowledges this at many points in the novel. And yet, while the visual opacity of difference does on occasion confound comprehension (especially, as we shall see, in the case of Jews), what actually seems to be most epistemologically problematic when it comes to sex, at least for Marcel, is the aural.

There is in *À la recherche* a frequently iterated concern about the aural perceptibility, or imperceptibility, of homosex. The first question is whether it will be overheard: when Charlus and Morel stay with Mme Verdurin, who is aware of their sexual relationship, she "would then give them adjoining rooms, and, to put them at their ease, would say: 'If you want to have a little music, don't worry about us. The walls are as thick as a fortress, you have nobody else on your floor, and my husband sleeps like a log'" (*SG*, 602). But a more pressing question is always whether those who hear it will recognize it, which Marcel often does not, and here it is usually the visual that comes to his rescue. On two occasions Marcel overhears sexual acts between men, first when he listens to Charlus and Jupien having sex, the second time when he hears Charlus being beaten during an S/M scene. And both times he believes at first that what he is hearing is a criminal act, probably a murder—perhaps someone having his throat slit (*SG*, 12; *TR*, 177).

It is highly significant in this context that *entendre* can mean both "to hear" and "to understand." Marcel's mishearing registers his complicity with a misunderstanding, the prejudice that associates inverts, like Jews, with certain crimes to which they are assumed to be predisposed: "Murder in inverts and treason in Jews" (*SG*, 20). This misconception requires a visual corrective; on both occasions the supposed "crime" eventually becomes visible, literally and figuratively, and can be recognized as sex. The narrator peers through a little window at the S/M scene; we are not told what he is able to see of Charlus and Jupien, but he tells us that while they are having sex, "I had stealthily hoisted myself up my ladder so as to peep through the fanlight which I did not open" (*SG*, 12). In both cases, once the "dissembling invisibility" of male homosex becomes visible, Marcel is able properly to interpret what he has heard as sex rather than violent crime. In describing the incident with Charlus and Jupien, in fact, he says that "from the beginning of this scene my eyes had been opened" (*SG*, 17), although at the beginning of the scene his perception was actually auditory; later he will refer to the scene as "what I *saw*," as though the primarily aural event registers retroactively as a visual memory once its meaning has been clarified by visual perception. He cannot see homosex until after he has heard it, but he cannot understand what he has heard until after he has seen it.

The epistemological unreliability of the aural in these scenes suggests a richly productive play on words in French: a *malentendu* is a misunderstanding, but literally could also mean, among other things, "badly heard," "ill-intended," or "evil overheard."[d] To (mis)hear homosex as evil or pain is to misunderstand its intent, its meaning as pleasure. "I concluded later on," the narrator says after spying on Charlus and Jupien, "that there is another thing as noisy as pain, namely pleasure" (*SG*, 12)—later on, after he has learned the language. As Yiddish is to the Jew, then, audible sex is to the homosexual: it is the language that those who have not been initiated, *ceux qui n'en sont pas*, cannot understand.

It is interesting that much later in the novel when the narrator arranges and watches a sexual encounter between two women for his own edification, he is completely unable to understand the sounds of their pleasure, even though he is looking right at them. The violence, even apparent criminality, of male homosex is less alien to him than the spectacle of female homosex. Lesbianism resembles male homosexuality in its resistance to hearing/understanding, and both male homosexuals and lesbians are described as foreign races with their own distinct national languages, cultures, and sign systems. The nation of Gomorrah, though, is *so* essentially, ontologically foreign that Marcel never does learn to speak the language;

---

d. *Mal*: adv., badly or ill; adj., wrong, bad; n., evil, pain. *Entendre*: v., to hear, to understand, to intend, to mean.

lesbians are not so much another nation as a different species altogether. After Albertine's death he thinks to himself that she always concealed her lesbianism from him "as a woman might conceal from me that she was a native of an enemy country and a spy, and *far more treacherously even than a spy*, for the latter deceives us only as to her nationality, whereas Albertine had deceived me as to her profoundest humanity, the fact that she did not belong to ordinary humankind, but to an alien race which moves among it, hides itself among it and never merges with it" (emphasis added).[18]

Female homosexuality, indeed, remains visually, aurally, and epistemologically impenetrable to the narrator throughout the novel.[19] Lesbianism can be looked at, but never seen, its meaning "concealed from my eyes," Marcel tells us, "by the curtain that is for ever lowered for other people over what happens in the mysterious intimacy of every human creature" (F, 741–42). While at one level the incident with the two women demonstrates to Marcel the unknowability of *all* other human creatures as individuals, it also illuminates the sharp distinction between his utter bafflement at the spectacle of female homosexuality and the relative ease with which he eventually learns to decode the signs of male homosexuality. The metaphor of espionage breaks down when confronted with the limit case of lesbianism, because successful intelligence work requires that we share an epistemic universe with those we spy on: we can spy on foreigners but not on Martians or fruit flies. But Marcel can, it seems, meaningfully subject *male* homosexuality to investigation, as he can Jewish culture or the mores of salon society; these sign systems are alien to him, yet not entirely beyond decryption.

The comparative skill that Marcel eventually acquires as a cryptographer may be in part attributable to the "uncodedness" of his own speech; he has to learn many different discourses in the course of the novel but not to unlearn any (whereas Bloch, for example, has to abandon his family's Yiddishisms in order to assimilate). Confronted with the number of characters in À *la recherche* who resort to slang, jargon, malapropisms, Yiddish, or Anglicisms, we might well ask what has happened to the "beautiful, limpid" French language that Armand Dubarry accused homosexuals of abandoning in *Le vice allemand*, for here it is not only inverts who commit all manner of linguistic assaults on the beauty and limpidity of French. Indeed, Gérard Genette has pointed out that what he calls "linguistic deafness" is something of an epidemic in the novel, especially afflicting, in his view, people who refuse to conform or assimilate, a tendency he speculates might have to do with not belonging to the middle class. Noting that this "deafness" is shared by Basin, Duc de Guermantes, and the narrator's butler, for example, Genette writes that "one may suppose that ignorance of the language is maintained on Basin's part by the proud feeling that a Guermantes 'does not have to' bend himself to so common a norm as usage. Thus, with perhaps the same measure of bad conscience and bad faith, working-class self-assertion and aristocratic arrogance meet."[20]

I would argue that linguistic deafness is a particular feature, not just of those who are not middle-class, but of all those who, as anti-Semites in the novel say of the Jews, *ne se nationalisent pas*, by which I mean those who cannot easily be assimilated into the modern, liberal nation-state: Jews and homosexuals as well as aristocrats, servants, and rural peasants. In fact, one of the few characters who, by his own account (his speech, of course, is very rarely reproduced directly in the text), speaks a correct, standardized French, free of slang or other verbal "tics," is Marcel. His uninflected French is symptomatic of his middle-class status, his heterosexuality, his Christian faith, and the relationship to citizenship that these allow him. He is one of the few neutral, liberal bourgeois subjects in the novel, not distinguished by aristocracy, sexual deviance, Jewishness, or any other identity markers that would mediate between him and the Republic. There is a sense, then, in which Marcel is *without* (remarkable) identity; he is simply a citizen.

MAKING SELVES: HEREDITY, SOCIETY, AGENCY

Personal and group identities as Proust conceptualizes them have three distinct, and not particularly harmonious, aspects. First, there are components of identity bestowed by race, history, nature, and other apparently suprahuman forces; second, there is the question of how we, as individuals or members of collectivities, are viewed by others; and finally, there is in every identity some degree of self-fashioning, of agential intervention in the way our Being signifies in the world. The most intelligible reading of what the text has to say about identity can be achieved only if we try to imagine that all three of these components of selfhood are always at least potentially in play.

Proust clearly lends considerable weight to factors he often describes as hereditary, those characteristics we inherit bon gré mal gré from our personal or collective histories. He describes the ubiquitous homosexuality in certain families as hereditary and inevitable, one member after another of the aristocracy succumbing despite the efforts of their uncles and fathers to save them from the destiny to which the latter have themselves long since capitulated. Male homosexuality itself is described in terms of inversion, the belief that the homosexual is a woman wrongly but irresistibly assigned by nature to a man's body, *anima muliebris in corpore virili inclusa*. Proust conjoins this trope with the theme of heredity by explaining that in particular, it is usually "the spirit of a relative of the female sex" that possesses the invert (*SG*, 414). After witnessing Charlus and Jupien together in the courtyard, the narrator says that "I now understood, moreover, why earlier, when I had seen him coming away from Mme de Villeparisis's, I had managed to arrive at the conclusion that M. de Charlus looked like a woman: he was one!" (*SG*, 19), and tells us that Charlus is quite unable to defy the mandate of his nature:

> As for M. de Charlus [...] it was with a fluttering, mincing gait and the same sweep with which a skirt would have enlarged and impeded his waddling motion that he advanced upon Mme Verdurin with so flattered and honoured an air that one would have said that to be presented to her was for him a supreme favour. [...] One might have thought that it was [his sister] Mme de Marsantes who was entering the room, so salient at that moment was the woman whom a mistake on the part of Nature had enshrined in the body of M. de Charlus. Of course the Baron had made every effort to conceal this mistake and to assume a masculine appearance. (*SG*, 415–16)

Proust proposes that such influences shape us in ways that limit our objectivity, our understanding of others, and our ability to recognize and prevail over our prejudices. In this he coincides with both nineteenth-century naturalists and twentieth-century modernists who tended to emphasize the restricted capacity of the individual to overcome her circumstances: Pericles Lewis, who treats this issue at length in *Modernism, Nationalism, and the Novel*, writes that "the sense, in modernist novels, that consciousness is always overdetermined by what T.S. Eliot called 'vast impersonal forces' reflects the growth of a conception of individuals as the playthings of such collective identities as national wills."[21] In particular, Proust frequently resorts to the concept of race as such a force, employing the word in a very broad sense:

> The narrator uses the term to describe a category of social roles that are apparently intractable. Jews, homosexuals, aristocrats,

peasants, and inhabitants of provincial towns are all described as belonging to "races." [. . .] The word "race" seems to apply to whatever group fails to be assimilated into the nation and maintains a distinctness the narrator associates with echoes of a distant past. [. . .] More than any of the other roles played in the novel [. . .] those roles associated with the term "race" draw attention to the "situatedness" of the self. They are roles that one has not chosen and is not free to renounce, as even the assimilated Jews discover.[22]

These "racial" affiliations are one of the things that make it most difficult for us to obey Kant's imperative that we universalize our own experience. In particular, Proust intimates on several occasions that people's political and ethical decisions about the Dreyfus Affair are motivated by racial or emotional drives that are implicitly irrational, whether in Jews, nationalists, or aristocrats; he puts into play in the text assumptions about the atavistic roots of our beliefs, while at the same time, as we will see in the following quote, explicitly denouncing such assumptions as "follies." In a passage on the famous Dreyfusard Joseph Reinach (whom, in reality, Proust greatly admired) the narrator wonders if

perhaps this rationalist crowd-manipulator was himself manipulated by his ancestry. When we find that the systems of philosophy which contain the most truths were dictated to their authors, in the last analysis, by reasons of sentiment, how are we to suppose that in a simple affair of politics like the Dreyfus case reasons of that sort may not, unbeknown to the reasoner, have ruled his reason? Bloch believed himself to have been led by a logical chain of reasoning to choose Dreyfusism, yet he knew that his nose, his skin and his hair had been imposed on him by his race. Doubtless the reason enjoys more freedom; yet it obeys certain laws which it has not prescribed for itself. (*GW*, 402–3)

Swann, too, feels an "ardent conviction as a Jew" (*SG*, 152) of Dreyfus's innocence; the fact that he, Bloch, and for that matter all the other Jewish characters are Dreyfusards appears to validate the view that Jewish support for Dreyfus was conditioned by a primitive racial solidarity. For his part the most prominent gentile Dreyfusard in the novel, Robert de Saint-Loup-en-Bray, seems equally driven by irrational and unacknowledged emotional factors—in his case, the fact that he is, when the Affair erupts, at odds with his family about his Jewish mistress.[23] Familial conflict is thus sufficient to override the influence of Saint-Loup's aristocratic upbringing and to make him an impassioned Dreyfusard, as long as his affair with Rachel lasts. Once the love affair ends, so does his commitment to Dreyfusism, now revealed not as a rational political choice but as a petulant attempt to annoy his mother.

On the other hand, we learn that Mme de Guermantes "was anti-Dreyfusard (while believing Dreyfus to be innocent)" (GW, 653); the emotional positions people adopt in the Affair fail to reflect even their own conscious *beliefs* about the case. Swann ascribes similarly irrational sentiments to all anti-Dreyfusards. When the narrator asks Swann why all the Guermantes are antirevisionists, Swann responds that it is because they're all anti-Semites, even though he

> knew very well from experience that certain of them were not, but, like everyone who holds a strong opinion, preferred to explain the fact that other people did not share it by imputing to them preconceptions and prejudices against which there was nothing to be done, rather than reasons which might permit of discussion. [. . .] [Swann continued,] "But after all, young or old, men or women, when all's said and done these people belong to a different race, one can't have a thousand years of feudalism in one's blood with impunity. Naturally they imagine that it counts for nothing in their opinions." (GW, 796–98)

Swann then denounces the idiocies of anti-Semitism, while illogically deducing that the Duc de Guermantes must be anti-Semitic because he's anti-Dreyfusard (GW, 797). When Marcel responds to his remark about the feudalism of the Guermantes by pointing out that after all, Saint-Loup is a Dreyfusard, Swann attributes this to the young man's intelligence; later that day, when Robert has changed sides but his uncle the Prince de Guermantes has been revealed to be a Dreyfusard, Swann argues that only moral integrity can account for the prince's change of heart. "Swann was forgetting that during the afternoon he had on the contrary told me that people's opinions as to the Dreyfus case were dictated by atavism. At the most he had made an exception on behalf of intelligence, because in Saint-Loup it had managed to overcome atavism and had made a Dreyfusard of him. Now he had just seen that this victory had been of short duration and that Saint-Loup had passed into the opposite camp. And so it was to moral uprightness that he now assigned the role which had previously devolved upon intelligence" (*SG*, 151).

Swann's assumptions about the irrationality of his opponents' opinions are themselves described as irrational follies. Yet, as the narrator says, "the anti-Dreyfusards were in no position to criticise these follies. They explained that one was only a Dreyfusard because one was of Jewish origin" (*GW*, 799)—as if he himself were not suggesting the same thing about Reinach, Bloch, and Swann. If all sides in the Affair arrogate objectivity to themselves and specious prejudice to their opponents, while in fact all sides are simply driven by atavistic emotion, the prospects for rational discussion of this or any political point, for the consensus building essential to the cohesion of a liberal republic, would seem extremely dim.

But there are nuances, even contradictions, in these passages that suggest that something more complicated is at work here than a purely deterministic view of the subjection of reason and selfhood to "vast impersonal forces." For one thing, "the reason enjoys more freedom" from the laws of heredity than the body, the narrator tells us; not a great deal more, but some. That this is so is suggested by the fact that Marcel is himself revealed to be a Dreyfusard, although we learn this only indirectly; he says merely that his father was an antirevisionist, and that "he refused to speak to me for a week after learning that I had taken a different line" (*GW*, 200).[e] Unless we are to infer that Marcel, like Saint-Loup, is motivated by familial conflict, the text does not seem to ascribe Marcel's support for Dreyfus to any of the irrational or primitive compulsions that impel others—nor would it be likely to, given his status as a bourgeois, heterosexual gentile and therefore his neutrality and immunity to atavism.

It is admittedly curious that in the sole instance when Marcel articulates his political position the statement is deflected, as it were, off his father. But the line just quoted clearly attributes the tension with his father to his Dreyfusism, not vice versa, and while their quarrel lasts only a week, Marcel's Dreyfusism never wavers; later he tells us that he fought several duels over the Affair (*SG*, 11). The point seems to be, not that he is driven by hostility to his family like Saint-Loup, but, on the contrary, that he is able to overcome

---

e. The Moncrieff and Kilmartin translation actually reads, "I had *chosen* to take a different line," which buttresses my point but is not quite faithful to the original, in which he says simply that "j'avais suivi une ligne de conduite différente" (Proust, *À la recherche*, vol. 2, *Le côté de Guermantes I*, 450).

the influence of his heritage and upbringing in order to *choose* to become a committed Dreyfusard. Marcel can thus stand for the possibility of a rational, objective, and freely chosen Dreyfusism—precisely the position that, historically, Jewish Dreyfusards sought gentile supporters to occupy. This is undoubtedly one of the reasons Proust opted to make his protagonist heterosexual and gentile; far from being a reflection of the author's internalized anti-Semitism or homophobia, as some have argued, his choice would seem to represent a strategic recognition that French republicanism demanded neutrality of its citizens, and consequently a shrewd decision to let the text endorse Dreyfusism through the one character who is completely unmarked in relation to the novel's categories of identity.

The second major factor bearing on identity in the novel is the way that we are perceived and our identities constructed by others. A specificity of identity is enforced, and "assimilation is undone," in the moment when one's difference is "sighted" by others,[24] as if identity were something "done to" one by, in this case, society rather than by nature. The power of the characters' perceptions about each other's identities is such that they exert pressure even on those intractable forces like race that we might, wrongly, assume to be static and monovalent. If a Jew becomes acculturated, even his nose will become French; "his manners [will] become so Gallicised that on his face a refractory nose, growing like a nasturtium in unexpected directions, will be more reminiscent of Molière's Mascarille than of Solomon" (GW, 253). In addition, people project fantasies and desires onto others that, even if unfounded, nonetheless affect how their identities are construed; Charlus suggests that Swann is homosexual by evoking his prettiness in their schoolboy days, while the Prince de Guermantes phantasmically constructs Swann as a gentile aristocrat by inventing for him an illegitimate descent from the Duc de Berry.

The idea that identity is socially constructed is, then, quite literal in Proust: we are what we are in part because of how we are seen in society. And since different people see us differently, our identities are always at least double if not multiple. Swann's Dreyfusism reads differently depending on the standpoint of others; he refuses to sign a petition that Bloch is passing around in support of Georges Picquart, "with the result that, if he passed in the eyes of many people as a fanatical Dreyfusard, my friend found him lukewarm, infected with nationalism, and jingoistic" (SG, 153).

One consequence of this social constructionism is that people whose identities are strongly, and negatively, socially overdetermined exhibit

particularly distinctive identity characteristics. Proust depicts both Jewishness and the fatal predisposition to inversion simultaneously as innate,
or "natural," and as constructed by the dominant culture: "The paradox is
inescapable: this 'innate disposition' results in 'Jewishness' or 'homosexuality' only under social conditions of Christian orthodoxy or compulsory heterosexuality."[25] And one is no more tractable than the other; contra the fac-
ile assumption often made that "culture" is more malleable than "nature,"
Proust shows that "the 'homosexual' or the 'Jew' is a powerful social category precisely because of the imbrication of what appear to the narrator
to be 'natural' categories (race, descent, and heredity) with more evidently
cultural categories, such as religious belief."[26] Clearly, Charlus cannot evade
his inversion, nor Swann his Jewishness. But the bodily manifestations of
their difference become increasingly visible as they age, not only provoking
but also *provoked by* the increasing awareness others have of their difference.

Finally, however, the novel indicates that there is a way that people can
shape or recuperate the identities imposed on them by heredity, God, or society. Nearly every passage already quoted that seems to describe identity as
something dictated to us also goes on to intimate that there is another process involved as well, some way in which we form our identities in an ongoing
dialectical engagement with ineluctable fate or social pressure. I edited those
passages in order to isolate and clarify their emphasis on the external constraints on selfhood, but consider how differently, how strangely and con-
tradictorily but also how much more richly, they signify if we read on further.
The passage about the baron's gender identity, for example, continues thus:

> One might have thought that it was Mme de Marsantes who was
> entering the room, so salient at that moment was the woman
> whom a mistake on the part of Nature had enshrined in the body
> of M. de Charlus. Of course the Baron had made every effort to
> conceal this mistake and to assume a masculine appearance. But
> no sooner had he succeeded than, having meanwhile retained the
> same tastes, he acquired from this habit of feeling like a woman
> a new feminine appearance, *due not to heredity but to his own way
> of living.* [. . .] Although other reasons may have dictated this
> transformation of M. de Charlus, and purely physical ferments
> may have set his chemistry "working" and made his body gradu-
> ally change into the category of women's bodies, nevertheless
> the change that we record here was of spiritual origin. By dint of

imagining oneself to be ill one becomes ill. [. . .] By dint of thinking tenderly of men one becomes a woman, and an imaginary skirt
hampers one's movements. The obsession, as in the other instance
it can affect one's health, may in this instance alter one's sex.
(*SG*, 416–17; emphasis added)

Indeed, if we examine Proust's use of this concept of inversion
closely, even the apparently stable and determinate gender identities
that the theory enforces begin to disintegrate, so that gender itself starts
to seem less like something bestowed (correctly or in error) by nature
and more like something we fashion both individually and collectively.
If Proust asserts that an invert is a woman trapped in a man's body, he
also undermines any certainty about what a woman is. Inhabiting a male
invert's body, she can manifest herself as "feminine temperament"—
whatever that is—or in socially feminine traits, like the impulse to clutch
"an invisible muff" or swish one's skirts about (*SG*, 414–15). She can also
appear as the trace of a primeval anatomical hermaphroditism: "The race
of inverts, who readily link themselves with the ancient East or the golden
age of Greece, might be traced back further still, to those experimental
epochs in which there existed neither dioecious plants nor monosexual
animals, to that initial hermaphroditism of which certain rudiments of
male organs in the anatomy of women and of female organs in that of men
seem still to preserve the trace" (*SG*, 40). Thus, it is unclear whether gender identity is primarily biological, social, spiritual, or sartorial in nature.
Individuals, in fact, have a kind of imaginative power over their own gender; gender in Proust's account is not only simultaneously biological *and*
socially constructed, it is also, perhaps even primarily, a product of individual creativity: an art(ifice).

This may help explain how it is that in Saint-Loup the hereditary condition of inversion, while as inescapable in his case as in Charlus's, manifests
itself very differently than it does in his uncle, perhaps a result both of their
different "ways of living" and of how they are seen by others. Saint-Loup
becomes *more* masculine, with "the grace and ease of a cavalry officer," after
becoming homosexual (*TR*, 12); only his object choice is inverted, not his
gender identity. So whatever Saint-Loup inherits from his uncle, it is not
the "same" homosexuality that the baron—supposedly so representative
of his type that "a Charlus" becomes code for "a homosexual" in the
novel—experiences himself.

Additionally, Aimé, the maître d' who oversees much of the homosexual activity in the novel, describes Robert's inversion, unlike Charlus's, as a temporally locatable event: a moment of turning, not a condition of being turned. Marcel thinks that Aimé places the moment too early: "I was convinced that Saint-Loup's physiological evolution had not begun at [the time Aimé indicates] and that he had then been still exclusively a lover of women" (*F*, 928). There is a strange overlapping and overloading of categories here in the suggestion that there must be a physiological, ontogenetic "evolution"—a word usually applied to a phylogenetic process—in an individual in order for him to experience homosexual desire, now described as a "taste" and therefore placed, in *À la recherche*, in the realm of the aesthetic and the gustatory as well as the erotic. Thus, homosexuality is not so much a simple hereditary compulsion as one possible outcome of a predisposition that, in a particular environment and given specific choices on the part of the homosexual himself, will alter the body in such a way as to produce certain sensual preferences and behaviors.

Jewishness, too, turns out to be a more yielding category than some of the passages quoted earlier at first seem to imply. Even a marked subject may enjoy some freedom, not perhaps from the identity category to which he is assigned but in the way he chooses to assume his ineluctable destiny, and Jews can intervene in how their Jewishness manifests in at least two distinct ways, as we see in the contrasting cases of Bloch and Swann. Bloch begins the novel heavily marked by Jewishness but by the end has nearly vanished as a Jew, so thoroughly has he assimilated—and this assimilation is indicated not only by his eventual adoption of a gentile pseudonym and changes in his class status, speech, and comportment but also by the disappearance even of the physical signs of his racial difference, thanks to the deployment of the same kind of artifice by which normative gender may be constructed. "Indeed an English chic had completely transformed his appearance and smoothed away, as with a plane, everything in it that was susceptible of such treatment. The once curly hair, now brushed flat, with a parting in the middle, glistened with brilliantine. [...] And thanks to the way in which he brushed his hair, to the suppression of his moustache, to the elegance of his whole figure—thanks, that is to say, to his determination— his Jewish nose was now scarcely more visible than is the deformity of a hunchbacked woman who skilfully arranges her appearance" (*TR*, 384).

Swann's trajectory heads in the opposite direction from Bloch's: the former becomes more and more visibly Jewish as the latter assimilates.

Given the multiple approaches to identity that the novel sets up, we cannot know whether Swann is "really" becoming more Jewish-looking as his Jewish nature emerges, either against or because of his will, or whether others simply *perceive* him as more Jewish. But we do know that he has options about how he takes on his accentuated Jewishness. By the time of his death Swann seems to have accepted, as an ethical choice, his solidarity with other Jews, his moral calling as a prophet—and his nose.

> Swann's punchinello nose, absorbed for long years into an agreeable face, seemed now enormous, tumid, crimson, the nose of an old Hebrew rather than of a dilettante Valois. Perhaps, too, in these last days, the physical type that characterises his race was becoming more pronounced in him, at the same time as a sense of moral solidarity with the rest of the Jews, a solidarity which Swann seemed to have forgotten throughout his life, and which, one after another, his mortal illness, the Dreyfus case and the anti-semitic propaganda had reawakened. There are certain Jews, men of great refinement and social delicacy, in whom nevertheless there remain in reserve and in the wings, ready to enter their lives at a given moment, as in a play, a cad and a prophet. Swann had arrived at the age of the prophet. (SG, 121–22)

As Jonathan Freedman writes, "Like Bloch, [Swann] too undergoes a metamorphosis, but one with an utterly different outcome. As a result of this choice, he grows physiologically into a racial identity he has chosen to avow."[27] While racial identity is here clearly generated by history or nature and structured by the social context of anti-Semitism, it also appears as a source of cultural and spiritual value. Drawing on Arendt's analysis of the pariah, Jessica Berman argues that in this passage Swann's trajectory converges with that of those inverts in the novel who, similarly, choose to affirm their marginal identities and to recognize themselves in community with other pariahs: "It is only in avowing their status as either *invertis* or pariahs, rather than simply being revealed as such, that the marginalized characters in *A la recherche* come to resemble turn-of-the-century Zionists, moving beyond assimilation to the strength of membership in the community of conscious pariahs. If Swann becomes a Dreyfusard it is *not only* through atavistic return to the blood of his ancestors, as the Guermantes presume, but rather through his control of his bodily expression, his consciousness of his status."[28] In sum, then, although Proust's designation of homosexuality and Jewishness as "races" may seem to lodge them firmly in the realm of the biological, his representation of both types embraces possible identifications with the concepts of heredity, culture, political solidarity, and elective affinity.

INVERTS, JEWS, AND DREYFUSARDS

Using this framework for understanding the complexity of identity formation in À la recherche, let me turn to a closer examination of the way homosexuality and Jewishness are imbricated in Proust's text and the analogical relation Proust establishes between them. The analogy is unidirectional; that is, homosexuals are frequently compared to Jews, but not the other way around: "One should note that in comparisons using 'like' or 'in the same way as,' the homosexual is always the thing compared, the Jew the standard of comparison."[29] Judaism, or more generally Jewishness, as a term already somewhat familiar in early twentieth-century France, is the means by which homosexuality can be mentally assimilated—in the first instance by Marcel, whose imagination creates the metaphor, and in the second instance by Proust's readers.

Judaism may, then, give Proust a vocabulary to talk about homosexuality and provides him also with a history that he appropriates and revises in order to create a history of homosexuality, which he grounds in his thoroughly unauthorized, tongue-in-cheek rewriting of the biblical story of Sodom. In his myth the Sodomites, condemned to destruction, are allowed out of Sodom by a naïve heterosexual angel who believes their cover stories about wives and children and lets them go out into the world to "engender a numerous progeny," as numerous as the descendants of Abraham (SG, 43). "Homosexuality," writes Bem, " has no discourse of its own. Homosexual discourse can constitute itself only as a *parasite of another discourse*. In search of a discourse to parasitize, homosexual discourse encounters Jewish discourse."[30]

One might suppose that "Jewish discourse" would resist being parasitized in this way, for the comparison between Jewishness and homosexuality would appear, for several reasons, to be a highly problematic one. For example, the narrator's own textual inspiration for his creation myth, the account in Genesis 18–19 of the destruction of Sodom, seems to discourage us from conflating Jews and homosexuals, given that Sodom represents a non-Hebraic culture destroyed for transgressing against the Hebrew God; as one critic notes, "the inhabitants of Sodom are 'other' to the Jews."[31] Also, while the connection between Jews and homosexuals is ubiquitous in À la recherche at the rhetorical level, it is comparatively underrepresented at the "literal" or biographical level of the characters, among whom there is only one Jewish homosexual man, Nissim Bernard. Indeed, Swann and Bloch, the most prominent Jewish characters, are two of the only exclusively heterosexual men in the novel. Finally, as I note in chapter 1, even though both groups unquestionably have a fraught relation to secrecy and dissimulation in life as in literature, Sedgwick challenges the usefulness of the metaphor of the closet in discussions of Jewish identity. Unlike homosexuality, she points out, an individual's Jewishness, however occulted in gentile society, still derives from and is presumably known to his or her family: "Vibrantly resonant as the image of the closet is for many modern oppressions, it is indicative for homophobia in a way it cannot be for other oppressions. [...] A (for instance) Jewish or Gypsy identity, and hence a Jewish or Gypsy secrecy or closet, would nonetheless differ again from the distinctive gay versions of these things in its clear ancestral linearity and answerability, in the roots (however tortuous and ambivalent) of cultural identification through each individual's originary culture of (at a minimum) the family."[32]

And yet. While Sedgwick's point that most homosexuals do not grow up in homosexual families as Jews grow up in Jewish families seems commonsensical, in À la recherche, as we have already seen, they actually do just that, as one member after another of France's titled families assumes his hereditary homosexuality. Here Proust was merely following the nineteenth-century sexologists in their emphasis on heredity,[f] and so in the novel even the best efforts of homosexual fathers to guard their sons from the familial proclivities are bound to fail in light of the overwhelming pressures of genetic destiny: "For the Prince de Foix had succeeded in preserving his son from the external influence of bad company but not from heredity" (*TR*, 200).

Despite what appear to be the obvious limits of the comparison, homosexuality and Jewishness are in fact bound to each other at so many different junctures in Proust's novel that the force of the reiterated comparisons

---

f. In 1898 Léon-Henri Thoinot, for example, had written, "there are *families of uranists*, just as there are families of degenerates; the former result from the latter" (*Attentats aux moeurs*, 329).

transforms homosexuality into a phenomenon that can hardly be understood outside its relationship to Jewish identity. In addition, while it is true
that there is little overlap between Jewishness and male homosexuality in
the biographies of the characters, if we consider those characters not as
discrete persons but as textual effects, we see that the semiotic boundary
between Jews and gentiles (not to mention that between homosexuals and
heterosexuals) is sufficiently blurred that even Swann's evident heterosexuality or Charlus's pious Catholicism may be destabilized by their textual proximity to one another. Julia Kristeva points out that Charlus and
Swann, and Charlus and Jewishness more generally, converge at several
points, beginning with the phonetic resemblance of the name "Charlus" to
that of one of the real-life models for Swann, Charles Haas. Mme Cottard's
belief that Charlus is "a garrulous Jew" and her misapprehension that he
and Swann "are on familiar terms" may reveal something more interesting than her stupidity: "This 'reverberation,' a sort of shady contagion, is
a union between characters," between Charlus and Swann.[33] Charlus is not
"really" Jewish any more than Swann is "really" homosexual, but the difficulty that other characters, and the text itself, experience in remembering
this speaks to the way homosexuality and Jewishness saturate each other,
bleeding into each other throughout the novel.

The parallels between the two are elaborated through a series of rhetorical effects that, through a process of accretion and transposition, coat
Proust's tropes of sexuality and Jewishness with such heavily sedimented
layers of value that both inversion and Jewishness are finally invested
with vast aesthetic, metaphysical, and political significance. They are connected, of course, through the ubiquitous metaphors and similes that ultimately serve as "a network of transversals" linking every term in the novel
to every other, like the "communicating paths" that ultimately link all the
individuals and events in Marcel's life (TR, 502, 504). In addition, the two
terms may be associated by metonymy, by apposition, by being placed in
equivalent relationships to a third term, or by a kind of syzygy, where terms
are repeatedly lined up in a certain order until, in the course of the novel,
we learn to expect one once we have seen the other(s).

Proust explicitly announces the comparison of Jews with homosexuals, suggested briefly in earlier passages, in *Sodom and Gomorrah*'s biblical title and carries it on in the long passage in "La race maudite" where
he creates the myth of his Sodomites. Additionally, Proust often likens
revelations of homosexuality to revelations in Racine's plays that certain
characters are Jewish. In particular, the biblical story of Esther serves as a

model for the epistemology of the closet: after Marcel begins to be aware of the homosexuality all around him, he thinks that "these rapid revelations [of homosexuality were] similar to those which in Racine's tragedies inform Athalie and Abner that Joas is of the House of David, that Esther, 'enthroned in the purple,' has 'Yid' parents" (*SG*, 87). Proust also describes both Judaism and homosexuality as freemasonries, secret societies with elaborate rituals and private codes.

On occasion the comparison is furthered by a homology between two terms, in which *A* and *B* are not explicitly analogous but rather have the same *function*. Thus, Jewishness and the vice of homosexuality are both used as examples of another phenomenon, the persistence of traits across time and generations: "I had seen the vices and the courage of the Guermantes recur in Saint-Loup [. . .] as in Swann his Semitism" (*TR*, 352–53). In another scene we learn that conversation with a homosexual can give the *same* pleasure that is generated by travel in the "Orient," including Palestine: "Brichot, who had often expounded the second *Eclogue* of Virgil without really knowing whether its fiction had any basis in reality, belatedly found, in conversing with Charlus, some of the pleasure which he knew that his [literary] masters [. . .] had felt when travelling in Spain, Palestine and Egypt" (*C*, 441).

This passage illustrates the role played in the text by the larger trope of the Oriental, of which Judaism and Jewishness are one aspect, and represents only one of many instances in which oriental or, more properly speaking, orientalized, languages, sites, objets d'art, literatures, and peoples furnish the scenery (the stage props, as it were) for a discussion or enactment of the homoerotic in the novel—recalling the frequency with which the Orient appeared as a topos of homosexuality in other literary and sexological texts of the period. In *À la recherche* the "strange tongue" of homosexuality is most frequently compared to Eastern languages understood by only a few Westerners: Sanskrit, Japanese, Russian, Hebrew. Saint-Loup, at a point when we already know that he is homosexual, nonetheless insists to Marcel, when pressed, that "as for the sort of thing you allude to, it means about as much to me as Sanskrit" (*TR*, 21). When Marcel first realizes that Charlus is an invert, he describes that point "when, upon the smooth surface of an individual indistinguishable from everyone else, there suddenly appears, traced in an ink hitherto invisible, the characters that compose the word dear to the ancient Greeks," that is, *pœderastia*. A few lines later, he compares *this* sort of revelation to those that can save people from social gaffes, as when someone conveys, to a speaker about to insult a lady, the whispered information that she is the lover of someone present. That information appears, Proust writes, like the mysterious words *Mene, Tekel, Upharsin*—words written by the hand of God, which only a Jew, Daniel, can translate for the Babylonian king (*SG*, 18–19). Knowledge about other people's secret sexual identities, relations, or behaviors, like knowledge about Jewish culture, is transmitted in code, invisible or untranslatable except to initiates. The language of sexuality is the property of a minority, and power accrues to those who learn, like the narrator, to decipher it.

By the novel's final volume the Orient and the homoerotic have both erupted as explicit and dramatic sites of signification, staged in elaborate theatrical fantasies that underline their contiguity. As Marcel strolls through Paris one night during the Great War, for instance, he has "the impression of an oriental vision"; allied troops including Africans and Indians are walking by, and he writes that they are "enough to transform for me this Paris through which I was walking into a whole imaginary exotic city, an oriental scene," which he compares to Jerusalem or Constantinople. In a typical gesture of unglossed apposition, Marcel then tells us in the next sentence that as he walks he sees a man "to whose purplish face I hesitated whether I should give the name of an actor or a painter, both equally notorious for innumerable sodomist scandals" (*TR*, 106). The contiguity between the Oriental and the homosexual is reinforced a few pages later when Marcel thinks of the *Arabian Nights* before setting off for Jupien's brothel and comments that all the taxis he sees are "driven by Levantines or negroes" (*TR*, 173). Later on, after he has seen Charlus engaged in sadomasochistic homosex, he will return to the *Arabian Nights*, comparing the scenes of sadism he has witnessed during the evening to tales from the story.

Proust adds one more twist to what would otherwise be a somewhat conventional, albeit brilliantly elaborated, association between the exoticism of the colonized Orient and the exoticism of deviance. He brings perversity back home, as it were, by describing homosexuals themselves as an "oriental colony" within any nation they inhabit: "Certainly they form in every land an oriental colony, cultured, musical, malicious, which has charming qualities and intolerable defects" (*SG*, 43). And in the end their loyalty to that "race," that other, mythical country—Sodom—is much stronger than their acculturation within heterosexual society, stronger even than the loyalty of Jews to *their* colony in the face of pressure to assimilate to gentile culture. "Possibly even the example of the Jews, of a different type of colony, is not strong enough to account for the frail hold that their upbringing has upon them, and for the skill and cunning with which they find their way back [. . .] to a life whose compulsive pleasures the men of the other race not only cannot understand, cannot imagine, abominate, but whose frequent danger and constant shame would horrify them" (*SG*, 33). Here Proust undercuts two of the central premises of fin-de-siècle French universalism: that citizens, internal subjects, are not differentiated within the nation, and that the goal of colonialism is to mold external subjects in the image of the colonizing nation. Colonized subjects exist, he suggests, both inside and outside the nation, and their difference is not, is never, recuperable. They can perhaps be *nationalized*—the text ultimately seems to disagree with the view that it is impossible for the "Jewish race to be assimilated into a nation" (*TR*, 325)— but they cannot be fully homogenized.

Because members of both Jewish and homosexual "colonies" have at least some ability to *pass* as undifferentiated citizens, however, their lives are governed by the question of secrecy—how much secrecy is possible, or desirable, and under what circumstances—and by the codes they develop to maintain community even under the crushing pressure of the injunction to effect an assimilation that is both mandatory and impossible. This is especially true, as Proust shows us, in the context of the Dreyfus Affair, when a political choice is likely to be viewed as an indicator of ontological status; recall General Gonse's assertion that Picquart's alleged homosexuality "would account for his attitude in the Dreyfus Case."[g]

g. Proust registered the same view in a manuscript passage excised from the original print edition, which caricatures those who attribute the Dreyfusism of the Prince de Guermantes to his wife's German heritage and her infatuation with her husband's homosexual cousin, Charlus:

> When some wavering spirit pointed out in favour of Dreyfus's innocence the fact that a nationalist and anti-Semitic Christian like the Prince de Guermantes had been converted to a belief in it, people would reply: "But didn't he marry a German?" "Yes, but . . ." "And isn't that German woman rather highly strung? Isn't she infatuated with a man who has bizarre tastes?" And in spite of the fact that the Prince's Dreyfusism had not been prompted by his wife and had no connexion with the Baron's sexual proclivities, the philosophical anti-Dreyfusard would conclude: "There, you see! The Prince de Guermantes may be Dreyfusist in the best of good faith; but foreign influence may have been brought to bear on him by occult means. That's the most dangerous way. But let me give you a piece of advice. Whenever you come across a Dreyfusard, just scratch a bit. Not far underneath you'll find the ghetto, foreign blood, inversion or Wagneromania." And cravenly the subject would be dropped, for it had to be admitted that the Princess was a passionate Wagnerian. (*SG*, Addenda, 731)

Although Proust did not restore the excised passage before his death, it nonetheless provides a useful index of his sensitivity to the way anti-Semitism, homophobia, and xenophobia conspired in anti-Dreyfusism.

Indeed, the most political ramifications of Proust's analogy between inversion and Jewishness are made explicit when homosexuals are compared not just to Jews but to Dreyfusards, that is, people both Jewish and gentile who have a particular, deliberate, ethical, and political relation to Jewishness in a given historical moment. The Affair gives Proust a way to articulate the experience of having one's political choices attributed to one's pathological being, of being excluded from the national body by virtue of what one *is*. He counters with a representation of Dreyfusards as a subaltern group constituted only weakly by race, more strongly by political affinity and by their characterization in the anti-Dreyfusard imagination as a secret society of traitors. In Proust's usage the Dreyfus Affair both confirms a correlation between blood and political affiliation—all Jews in the novel are Dreyfusards—and ruptures it—not all Dreyfusards in the novel are Jews, and furthermore, even the different Jewish characters support Dreyfus with varying degrees of enthusiasm inflected, among other things, by their differing attitudes toward the nation and the military.

For example, Swann does side with Dreyfus as if instinctively, "as a Jew." Yet he also negotiates his political relationship to Jewish identity much more carefully than Bloch does, fearing that his opponents will perceive Jewish support for Picquart as illegitimately biased or, worse, as evidence that the entire Affair is indeed a conspiracy by international Jewry.

> Swann interested Bloch greatly by telling him that the Prince de Guermantes was a Dreyfusard. "We must ask him to sign our appeal on behalf of Picquart; a name like his would have a tremendous effect." But Swann, blending with his ardent conviction as a Jew the diplomatic moderation of a man of the world, whose habits he had too thoroughly acquired to be able to shed them at this late hour, refused to allow Bloch to send the Prince a petition to sign, even on his own initiative. [...] Furthermore, Swann withheld his own name. He considered it too Hebraic not to create a bad effect. (*SG*, 152)

We can also assume, though we are not told, that Swann is afraid of the consequences for his own position in society if his Dreyfusism becomes public. While he is known to be Jewish, his Jewishness has not hitherto been (re)marked; it has not *signified* as a statement about his relation to his class or to the nation. On this occasion, then, Swann is still trying to control and contain the signs of his Jewishness.

Eventually, however, Swann finds his Dreyfusism and his Jewishness making each other mutually visible, and his political opinions retroactively attributed to his race. In the view of his anti-Dreyfusard friends, for a Jew to support Dreyfus is to demonstrate that he belongs to a nation, a race, indeed a biological type alien to France; to prove, as the Duc de Guermantes says, that the Jews are "all secretly united and are somehow forced to give their support to anyone of their own race, even if they don't know him personally." Swann is "almost the only Jew that anyone knew" (*SG*, 108), the token Jew welcomed in the salons, a man whose essential Frenchness has until now been demonstrated by his ability to master the codes of the Faubourg: "I should never have believed it of him," the duke says of Swann's Dreyfusism; "an epicure, a man of practical judgment, a collector, a connoisseur of old books, a member of the Jockey [Club], a man who enjoys the respect of all, who knows all the good addresses and used to send us the best port you could wish to drink" (*SG*, 104). In other words, the duke has believed that to be truly French is to pass satisfactorily as *un homme du monde*. That world is united entirely by personal and familial ties that cross national boundaries (the Guermantes family, for instance, is partly German), just as those among Jews supposedly do. We have already noted that aristocrats, like Jews, are defined in the text as a "race," and there would seem to be no obvious imperative for an international aristocracy to express nationalist sentiment: *ils ne se nationalisent pas*. Yet according to the duke's logic, in the social formations temporarily imposed by the Affair, the Faubourg becomes equivalent to the French nation. Thus when Swann defends Dreyfus, "who, guilty or not, never moved in his world," he betrays a lack of *personal* loyalty to his society friends, which is, in this equation, taken as the sign of his lack of *political* loyalty to France.

> "Yes, after the friendship my wife has always shown him," went on the Duke, who evidently considered that to denounce Dreyfus as guilty of high treason, whatever opinion one might hold in one's heart of hearts as to his guilt, constituted a sort of thank-you for the manner in which one had been received in the Faubourg Saint-Germain, "he ought to have dissociated himself. [. . .] It's true that Swann is a Jew. But, until today [. . .] I have always been foolish enough to believe that a Jew can be a Frenchman, I mean an honourable Jew, a man of the world. Now, Swann was that in every sense of the word. Well, now he forces me to admit that I was

mistaken, since he has taken the side of this Dreyfus (who, guilty or not, never moved in his world, whom he wouldn't ever have met) against a society that had adopted him, had treated him as one of its own. There's no question about it, we were all of us prepared to vouch for Swann, I would have answered for his patriotism as for my own. And this is how he repays us!" (*SG*, 104–5)

The key phrase in the Duke's speech is, of course, "a society that had *adopted* him": Swann belongs to the salons, *il en est*, not by blood but through an adoption that guards the trace of his irreducible difference even as those around him marvel at the success of his assimilation. He is, precisely, passing; he is enacting a highly successful performance of *un homme du monde*. But the fine port and the membership in the Jockey Club are revealed as mere disguise, the mask Swann has worn to conceal his more essential racial identity. In the moment that Swann's Jewishness is taken to translate itself into political terms, he falls from grace, having proved that he always "really" belonged not to the salons, or the nation, but to a group known for its intrinsic untrustworthiness. Swann believes that his support for Dreyfus is an act of political affinity and moral choice; to his friends it constitutes the revelation of his true, and treasonous, racial being.

We might compare Swann's attempts to control the significations of his own difference to the way, in Proust's account, some inverts deliberately allow the signs of their effeminacy to circulate publicly, but in a highly circumscribed manner. Like Swann and Bloch, homosexuals need to make decisions about how they permit their difference to signify. While the narrator describes the men in the passage below as "extremists" and tempts us to contrast their flamboyance with Swann's reserve, we note that their feminine accoutrements appear only in the interstices of their masculine dress, semaphoring their meaning rather than spelling it out:

On certain evenings, at another table, there are extremists who allow a bracelet to slip down from beneath a cuff, or sometimes a necklace to gleam in the gap of a collar, who by their persistent stares, their cooings, their laughter, their mutual caresses, oblige a band of students to depart in hot haste, and are served with a civility beneath which indignation smoulders by a waiter who, as on the evenings when he has to serve Dreyfusards, would have the greatest pleasure in summoning the police did he not find profit in pocketing their gratuities. (*SG*, 26)

It is important to observe that these "extremists" are only one of three tables of homosexuals in the café; there is also a group there described as "correct," "cold," "reserved," and "modest" and a table of young aristocrats "the most attractive" of whom will end up, we are told, being homosexual (SG, 25–26). Clearly, inversion, like Jewishness, can be performed in a number of different ways.

That variability problematizes Marcel's suggestion that Dreyfusism is necessarily easier to conceal than inversion, where "there is a more direct relation between the revealing sign and the secret" (SG, 498). Marcel asserts that the signs of Charlus's effeminacy emerge directly and, as it were, irresistibly from the secret of his homosexuality, whereas the secret of someone's political opinions may, he claims, be kept concealed.

> It is curious that a certain category of secret impulses has as an external consequence a way of speaking or gesticulating which reveals them. If a man believes or disbelieves [...] in the innocence of Dreyfus [...] and wishes to keep his opinion to himself, you will find nothing in his voice or in his gait that will betray his thoughts. But on hearing M. de Charlus say, in that shrill voice and with that smile and those gestures, "No, I preferred its neighbour, the strawberry-juice," one could say: "Ah, he likes the stronger sex," with the same certainty as enables a judge to sentence a criminal who has not confessed. (SG, 497–98)

In view of the varied manifestations of inversion on display in the café scene, however, and given that it takes Marcel four volumes to realize that Charlus is homosexual—as well as the fact that others remain unaware of his homosexuality—we may ask whether inversion does not actually resemble Dreyfusism in its opacity a good deal more closely than Marcel here allows. Both inverted and Dreyfusard subjects have some—if only limited—autonomy in deciding how to signal the political or sexual choices to which their natures have led them; in neither case do they have much control over how those choices will be taken up, framed by others.

GERMAN TENDENCIES

As À la recherche progresses through the early 1910s—by which time Dreyfus had finally been exonerated—Proust indicates a turn of the kaleidoscope of political life by showing how the spot marked "traitor," previously filled by Dreyfusards, is now open for full-time occupation by homosexuals. Increasingly, as the narrative moves toward the Great War, the code word signifying both homosexuality and treason comes to be *German* more than, or at least as much as, it is *Jewish*. To be sure, there are passages where the transition from one to the other modulates, like a chord being transposed into another key, because Dreyfusism was always marked, in Proust's novel just as it was in history, as both Jewish *and* German. Then during World War I the connection between Jewishness, Germanness, and treason resurfaces when Gilberte de Saint-Loup—Swann's daughter and Robert's wife—writes to Marcel and praises the courteous behavior of the German regiment that has requisitioned the Guermantes' ancestral manor. Marcel is uncertain whether her sympathy for the Germans should be attributed to her own partly Jewish ancestry or to her marriage into the partly German Guermantes family:

> Whether the German staff had really behaved well, or whether it was right to detect in Gilberte's letter the influence, by contagion, of the spirit of those Guermantes who were of Bavarian stock and related to the highest aristocracy of Germany, she was lavish in her praise of the perfect breeding of the staff-officers [. . .] a good breeding which she contrasted with the disorderly violence of the fleeing French troops, who had pillaged everything as they crossed the property before the arrival of the German generals. [. . .] Gilberte's letter was in some ways impregnated with the spirit of the Guermantes—others would say the spirit of Jewish international-ism [. . .]. (*TR*, 89)

Finally, and most frequently in the last volume of the novel, the Jewish or Dreyfusard part of this chain of equivalences drops out, and we are left with Germanness and homosexuality. As a half-Bavarian invert, Charlus—who was rabidly anti-Dreyfusard—falls under suspicion of being a double agent himself. As Mme Verdurin, Morel, and others campaign to destroy Charlus, the narrator tells us that Mme Verdurin "affected to believe that [Charlus] was not French. 'What is his nationality exactly, isn't he an Austrian?' M. Verdurin would ask innocently. [. . .] 'No, he is Prussian,' the Mistress would say" (*TR*, 109). His German blood, we are told, makes him a liar, "guilefully provocative and arrogantly bellicose" (*C*, 487), and his homosexuality merges with his Germanophilia to designate a traitor.

Mme Verdurin sows mischief between Charlus and his lover Charlie Morel by telling the latter, untruthfully, that Charlus has lied to him and has been spreading rumors about his family. Mme Verdurin is thus the real traitor here, but Morel believes her and exclaims to her, "I was betrayed by a wretch and you, you're good [. . .] [this] proves that he's a traitor" (C, 424). Charlus and his friends are accused of being spies for Germany, and hostile newspaper articles with titles like "Une Allemande" characterize him as "Frau Bosch," feminizing the homosexual and/as the national enemy: "Not only was the Baron's inversion denounced, but also his alleged Germanic nationality: 'Frau Bosch,' 'Frau von den Bosch' were the names habitually used to designate M. de Charlus" (TR, 112).

Once his mind starts going Charlus himself begins publicly to announce his pro-Germanism and his homosexuality, characterized by Marcel as aspects of a single phenomenon: "He was no more capable of checking the flow of his pro-German feelings than of his other inclinations" (TR, 162). At another point Marcel explains, "Needless to say, when, at the moments when he was 'not quite all there,' M. de Charlus made these avowals of his *pro-German or other tendencies*, anybody from his immediate circle who might be with him would interrupt the imprudent remarks and interpret them for the benefit of others" (TR, 252–53; emphasis added). Here, we notice, the "interpretation" that takes place is not a decoding but a recoding of Charlus's overly transparent, treasonous, deviant utterances. Only those *qui en sont*—in this case, Charlus's friends—are allowed to understand what he really means, and their concern is to *mis*interpret it for those *qui n'en sont pas*.

Charlus conflates his personal desires and his national affinities; the Duc de Guermantes asserts that Swann betrays his nation in betraying the Faubourg, and vice versa; Mme Verdurin mistakes the microcosm of the salons for the macrocosm of international politics. René Girard points out that if "Charlus and Mme Verdurin confuse social life with the First World War" (as the duke confused it with the Dreyfus Affair), "the novelist [. . .] methodically assimilates them to one another."[34] Thus, the constant tracking back and forth between the social, personal, and private realms, on the one hand, and the geopolitical, on the other, that has led some to accuse Proust of trivializing the political can be more usefully interpreted as a strategy that enables him to examine the ways social prejudices ramify through the political sphere. J. E. Rivers, for example, reads the passages concerning Mme Verdurin's feud with Charlus as Proust's moral allegory of the Eulenburg scandal, which had demonstrated so clearly how homophobia could be used politically. Like the journalist who had unleashed the accusations of treason and perversion against the Kaiser's friend Eulenberg, Rivers writes, "Mme Verdurin cleverly bases her assertions about Charlus on precisely the sorts of stereotypes that will make them credible and frightening to a homophobic mind [. . .] drawing upon the superstition which connects homosexuality with subversive foreign ideologies."[35]

Numerous passages in the later volumes, especially *Time Regained*, invoke that "superstition," underlining the view that homosexual being and homosexual acts are potential sites of treason. We are told that committing homosexual acts is either just like committing treason or different from it only in degree, not in kind. "Thus it was," the narrator writes, "that the former lift-boy at Balbec would now not have accepted for silver or gold propositions which he had come to regard as no less criminal than treasonable proposals from the enemy" (*TR*, 132). And Jupien tells Marcel that Charlus needs to be careful about how he words his propositions:

> "Only the other day there was a page-boy from a hotel who was absolutely terrified because of all the money the Baron offered him if he would go to his house! [. . .] The boy, who in fact only cares about women, was reassured when he understood what was wanted of him. Hearing all these promises of money, he had taken the Baron for a spy. And he was greatly relieved when he realised that he was being asked to sell not his country but his body, which is possibly not a more moral thing to do, but less dangerous and in any case easier." (*TR*, 204)

Charlus is also not the only character whose double affiliation, as a German(ophile) and a homosexual, draws accusations of subversion. During the war Robert de Saint-Loup incriminates himself through a correspondence with a German officer, the tenor of which we can infer to have been erotic, but which was assumed instead—or, rather, precisely because—of this to have been treasonous. When Marcel stumbles on a male brothel that he takes at first for a den of spies, he sees a military man who might be Saint-Loup leaving the establishment and thinks to himself, "I recalled involuntarily that [Robert] had—unjustly—been involved in a case of espionage because his name had been found in some letters captured on a German officer. He had, of course, been completely exonerated by the military authorities. But in spite of myself I associated this recollection with what I now saw. Was this hotel being used as a meeting-place of spies?" (*TR*, 175). And indeed, the clients of the brothel all go to great lengths to conceal their identities—though not for the reasons Marcel imagines. But it is Marcel himself who becomes the spy now, passing as a homosexual in order to enter the hotel and spy on homosexuals he thinks are spies so that he can relay this information back to "his" side, the heterosexual side he supposedly shares with the reader. His hope of uncovering a plot, like his recurring belief that he is overhearing crimes, turns out to be a malentendu; the gigolos who work in the establishment, whom Marcel assumes to be part of the spy ring, are revealed to be fervent patriots anxious to go to war against Germany. If *Sodom and Gomorrah* invoked the belief that inverts are predisposed to murder as Jews are to treason, it was so that this view could be systematically debunked by the end of the novel: Marcel finds out (repeatedly) that inverts are not literally either criminals or traitors, any more than Jews are. (During the Great War Bloch's father dies "from grief, it was said, at seeing France invaded" [*TR*, 347]; a Jew can be a more passionate patriot than any cosmopolitan aristocrat).

NATIONAL BODIES

The question of treason is particularly urgent in *Time Regained*, of course, because the backdrop of the war gives Proust the opportunity to engage the idea of the nation, and debates about nationalism, more intensively than anywhere else in the novel. In several lengthy pieces the narrator reflects on the meaning and function of the nation, often resorting to metaphors of the nation-as-body that appear to rely on a Barrèsian, organicist nationalism. "Just as there are animal bodies and human bodies," the narrator says, "so there exist huge organised accumulations of individuals which are called nations [. . .] and anybody who is incapable of comprehending the mystery, the reactions, the laws of these smaller lives, will only make futile pronouncements when he talks about struggles between nations" (*TR*, 118). Furthermore, these "great collections of individuals called nations themselves behave to some extent like individuals. The logic that governs them is an inner logic, wrought and perpetually re-wrought by passions, like that of men and women at grips with one another in an amorous or domestic quarrel, the quarrel of a son with his father, or of a cook with her mistress, or a wife with her husband" (*TR*, 121). This formulation permits him, among other things, to reaffirm the value of his own parallels between private and public spheres.

Patriotism, then, appears in this construction to be an almost physiological matter of inclusion within the national body; individuals are to the nation as cells are to the individual, and so a patriot cannot think or act independently of the "national interest" any more than a cell could normally opt out of its obligation to, say, the kidney in which it is located: "We [. . .] form but one flesh [. . .] since patriotism accomplishes the miracle that we are 'for' our country as in a quarrel between lovers we are 'for' ourself" (*TR*, 124).

> To remain blind to the unjustness of the cause of the individual "Germany," to recognise at every moment the justness of the cause of the individual "France," the surest way was not for a German to be without judgment, or for a Frenchman to possess it, it was, both for the one and for the other, to be possessed of patriotism. M. de Charlus, who had rare moral qualities, who was susceptible to pity, generous, capable of affection and devotion, on the other hand for various reasons—among which the fact that his mother had been a Duchess of Bavaria may have played a part—did not have patriotism. He belonged, in consequence, no more to the body France than to the body Germany. (*TR*, 122)

Kristeva suggests that Charlus's lack of patriotism is consequent upon his gender inversion: "Charlus is not only a sexual hermaphrodite but a national hermaphrodite. Since he cannot be of a single sex, he cannot be of a single nation."[36] The correlating factor would appear to be homosexual desire rather than inversion, however, because the virile Saint-Loup is as disinterested and "unpatriotic" as his uncle: while he dies courageously fighting for France, his heroism is motivated by a passionate erotic attachment to his men, not by any hostility toward Germany. It is even implied that pacifism and homosexuality are cognate, at least in Saint-Loup's mind; he believes that the Kaiser is homosexual and therefore assumes that he opposed the war: "Never had any man felt less hatred for a nation than [Robert] (and as for the Emperor, for particular reasons, very possibly incorrect, he thought that William II had tried rather to prevent the war than to bring it about). Nor had he hated Germanism; the last words which I had heard on his lips, six days before he died, were the opening words of a Schumann song which he had started to hum in German on my staircase, until I had made him desist because of the neighbours" (*TR*, 226–27). In contrast, Marcel compares Charlus's detachment with his own (implicitly irrational) participation in the French national body. Like his unproblematic relationship to the French language, the narrator's untroubled patriotism is apparently enabled by his neutral, unmarked status as a Catholic heterosexual of pure French descent.

Up to this point Marcel's view of the nation, and to a certain extent that of the text, seems perfectly in accord with Barrès. *À la recherche* as a whole, however, suggests two significant objections to Marcel's (and Barrès's) view of the nation as an organic whole. The first is that national attachments are revealed to be as arbitrary and transitory as erotic ones, and the second is that the unity of the individual (notably, Marcel), on which his organicist metaphors rely, is similarly revealed to be a fiction of singular instability.

As we have seen, when confronted with Charlus's lack of patriotism, Marcel first ascribes it to a quality peculiar to the baron himself: his German blood, perhaps, or, less explicitly, his homosexuality. But Marcel eventually has to concede that all national(ist) passions, like romantic passions, are necessarily both subjective and fungible. Carefully differentiating this position from moral relativism, which he rejects, Proust nonetheless insists on the subjectivity ineluctably informing our moral, political, and erotic choices:

The Germanophilia of M. de Charlus [. . .] had helped me to free myself for a moment, if not from my Germanophobia, at least from my belief in the pure objectivity of this feeling, had helped to make me think that perhaps what applied to love applied also to hate and that, in the terrible judgment which at this time France passed on Germany—that she was a nation outside the pale of humanity—the most important element was an objectification of feelings as subjective as those which had caused Rachel and Albertine to appear so precious, the one to Saint-Loup and the other to me. What, in fact, made it possible that this perversity was not entirely intrinsic to Germany was that, just as I as an individual had had successive loves and at the end of each one its object had appeared to me valueless, so I had already seen in my country successive hates which had, for example, at one time condemned as traitors—a thousand times worse than the Germans into whose hands they were delivering France—those very Dreyfusards such as Reinach with whom today patriotic Frenchmen were collaborating against a race whose every member was of necessity a liar, a savage beast, a madman. [...] This subjective element in the situation struck one forcibly if one had any conversation with neutrals, since the pro-Germans among them had, for instance, the faculty of ceasing for a moment to understand and even to listen when one spoke to them about the German atrocities in Belgium. (And yet they were real, these atrocities: the subjective element that I had observed to exist in hatred as in vision itself did not imply that an object could not possess real qualities or defects and in no way tended to make reality vanish into pure relativism.) (*TR*, 324–26)

Charlus is thus the instrument for teaching Marcel two crucial and related lessons about what Girard terms "the infinitely active void of metaphysical desire."[37] This is one of the most important stakes in Proust's interweaving of homosexuality, the Dreyfus Affair, and World War I: *amor patria* is persistently compared to sexual love, and sexual love in Proust is capricious. The object of both loves is equally arbitrary, and in addition, the qualities ascribed to the object do not really inhere in it: the mistress is not necessarily more beautiful than other women, the nation not more enlightened than other nations. Proust uses the comparison between sexual and national desire to denaturalize both normative sexuality and patriotism, emphasizing the purely performative aspect of our attachments to countries as well as lovers.

Several critics have made the claim that Proust distinguishes between "good" nationalism, which Girard calls patriotism, and "bad" nationalism, or chauvinism and "racist jingoism."[38] In the view of these critics, only the latter provokes Proust's "disgust": "Patriotism already contains elements of self-love and therefore self-contempt but it is still a sincere cult of heroes and saints. Its fervor is not dependent upon rivalry with other countries. Chauvinism, on the contrary, is the fruit of such rivalry. It is a negative sentiment based on hatred. [...] Proust's remarks on the First World War, despite their extreme caution, betray a profound disgust."[39] If patriotism is "sincere," however, it would appear to be so only in the same sense in which it is described as "genuine" in the passage in which the baron has himself flagellated by gigolos. When Marcel observes—or, more accurately, overhears—Charlus being beaten in the brothel, he reflects that this sado-masochistic game playing is a kind of madness, but it also reveals a profound truth about the irrational and erotic charge underlying feelings of patriotism. "This madman knew, in spite of everything, that he was the victim of a form of madness and during his mad moments he nevertheless was playing a part, since he knew quite well that the young man who was beating him was not more wicked than the little boy who in a game of war is chosen by lot to be 'the Prussian,' upon whom all the others hurl themselves in a fury of genuine patriotism and pretended hate" (TR, 215).

The psychological equivalent to the little boys' "pretended hate" is Charlus's feigned fear of his dominator, whom he knows in reality to be a decent lad who is simply trying to earn a living. The equivalent to "genuine patriotism" is presumably the real desire for pleasure that drives Charlus. Both S/M and nationalism are games, inspired by sincere and authentic feelings that have, in the text's view, grievously misplaced objects. At most, then, we can say that the sentiment of patriotism is indeed legitimate, but the nation should not be its object, at least not ultimately. Instead, Proust sketches a picture of a historical progression to increasingly large circles of human association, so that the nation, instead of appearing particularly natural, shows up only as one stage en route to a global state and universal brotherhood.

> The Queen [of Naples] was a woman of great kindness, but she conceived of kindness first and foremost in the form of an unshakeable attachment to the people she loved, to her own family, to all the princes of her race. [. . .] No doubt this is a narrow conception of kindness, somewhat Tory and increasingly obsolete. But this does not mean that her kindness was any less genuine or ardent. The ancients were no less strongly attached to the human group to which they devoted themselves because it did not go beyond the limits of their city, nor are the men of today to their country, than those who in the future will love the United States of the World.
> (C, 431–32)

If the object of (nationalist) desire is misplaced or at least provisional, and the feeling of desire itself arbitrary, the desiring subject offers no more secure repository for a Barrèsian investment in nationalism as a coherent source of values. The subject in Proust is at least divided, often multiple, in its physical as well as its psychic aspects. "I had always considered each one of us to be a sort of multiple organism or polyp," the narrator writes, "not only at a given moment of time—so that when a speck of dust passes it, the eye, an associated but independent organ, blinks without having received an order from the mind, and the intestine, like an embedded parasite, can fall victim to an infection without the mind knowing anything about it—but also, similarly, where the personality is concerned and its duration through life, I had thought of this as a sequence of juxtaposed but distinct 'I's' which would die one after the other or even come to life alternately" (*TR*, 352). This emphasis on the plurality of the individual body seriously undermines the notion of the nation as an organic whole: if the individual is not one, either psychically or corporeally, then presumably the national body analogized to it cannot be either.

Proust's stance can be read as a direct response to the organicist racism of a Barrès, a Charles Maurras, or a Léon Daudet. He agrees with the nationalist view that we are traversed and molded by social forces beyond individual control, but whereas Barrès, for instance, thinks that the nation is the only one of those forces that really matters, Proust believes we negotiate among numerous different, and sometimes opposed, forces, and that furthermore the nation is itself a multivalent and provisional construction. The nationalists' mistake is to insist that what is necessarily only their partial and subjective perspective is, instead, a monovalent truth; like the Citizen of the "Cyclops" episode in James Joyce's *Ulysses*, nationalists fail to realize that their vision is monocular. "It is the claim to a panoramic and objective view of the truth that undermines the nationalist cause," writes Berman.[40] Proust's response is not necessarily to try to offer a *more* effective master narrative, but rather to propose that stereoscopic vision can only be achieved by acknowledging our own multiple, and partial, positions. "The narrative never attempts to present a new, all-inclusive version of identity or to connect the many strands of affiliation that trail behind each character. *A la recherche* never seeks to posit another world where relationships remain untainted by a lurking otherness. The novel [. . .] not only creates worlds of belonging out of the *inverti* and the pariah, but presumes that these worlds contain only partial and subjective truths."[41] As Berman here suggests, the case of the invert is paradigmatic in this regard; even when the homosexual is offered as an example of a universal truth, that truth often turns out to be a revelation of, precisely, the impossibility of apprehending a universal truth uninflected by perspective.

EST-CE QUE VOUS EN ÊTES?

For several decades after its publication, critics discussed the treatment of homosexuality in *À la recherche* as either a cautionary tale about the wages of sin or a reflection of Proust's own pathological psychology; in either case, there was no question that inversion was the curse of a minority. By the 1980s critical works like J. E. Rivers' *Proust and the Art of Love* were instead offering interpretations of the novel's view of sexuality that emphasized its "universalizing" tendencies. Homosexuality, in this account, is merely an exacerbated version of the drama of all romantic desire and its frustration, an allegory of the impossibility of communication between self and non-self. But such readings fail to notice that even when Proust is being "universalizing," his universalizing works in a particular direction: to imply not that homosexuals (or Jews) are just like everybody else, but rather that everybody else is just like them.

The result is that everyone in *À la recherche* eventually finds him- or herself implicated in the radical indeterminacy bearing on homosexuality, and all identity categories, by the novel's end. For identity is not only multiple but also tenuously bounded; the dichotomies mapped out by nationalism, racism, and identity politics are constantly being blurred. Just as Swann and Charlus often shade into each other, so too do the narrator and Bloch in the last volume: "Sometimes it even happens that after a time we confuse one person with another. 'Bloch? Oh yes, he was someone who used to come to Combray,' and when he says Bloch, the speaker is in fact referring to me. Conversely, Mme Sazerat was firmly persuaded that it was I who was the author of a certain historical study of Philip II which was in fact by Bloch" (*TR*, 419). Women and men are frequently transposed in the text, as when Gilberte is transformed into a young man in Marcel's dream (*WBG*, 282), and homosexual men are analogized to pregnant women. Heterosexuals become homosexual, homosexual men become lesbians, Bloch becomes (very nearly) a gentile. Dreyfusards and nationalists merge or switch sides; Mme Verdurin becomes a Guermantes. Furthermore, these alterations in political, racial, and sexual identity are often effected with the same ease with which any taste or fashion may alter with time. And so by the end of *À la recherche*, nearly all categories of sexual, racial, class, and political affiliation have either disintegrated or gone topsy-turvy. Positions that once seemed radical, whether in political views or sexual style, may be adopted by more and more people, even a majority—which raises the question of how marginal "minority" identities or behaviors can really be. As Berman writes, "the potential for pariahdom lurks within all members of society."[42]

In Sedgwick's analysis in *Between Men* "homosexual panic" is propelled by the impossibility of ever knowing whether (some)one *en est* or *n'en est pas*: "No man must be able to ascertain that he is not (that his bonds are not) homosexual."[43] In *À la recherche* this principle is generalized, as people, and signs, continually cross boundaries, so that there is finally no way out of the question that lies at the heart of homosexual (or Jewish? or gender?) panic: "After the revelation-revolution of *Sodom and Gomorrah I*, and through to the end of *Time Regained*, one can no longer find one's way in the metonymic delirium of signs, no one escaping henceforth from the paranoiac question: 'Are you one of them?' "[44]

If no one—potentially not even the reader—can be sure whether s/he's one of us or one of them, what happens to community, national or otherwise? After all, "*A la recherche* remains resolutely anti-nationalist."[45] In the emphasis on instability, flux, and fragmentation that Proust offers instead of nationalism, we can, if we are so inclined, find something profoundly emancipatory, as Proust embraces—if only momentarily and with his tongue held firmly in his cheek—a vision of a world without prejudice and hence without war: "If the social position of individuals is liable to change (like the fortunes and the alliances and the hatreds of nations), so too are the most deeply rooted ideas and customs and among them even the idea that you cannot receive anybody who is not chic. Not only does snobbishness change in form, it might one day altogether disappear—like war itself—and radicals and Jews might become members of the Jockey" (*TR*, 393–94). And, we could add, the perverse might turn out to be normal—if only in a strictly statistical sense.

I add that caveat to make it clear I am not claiming that Proust wants to move subaltern identities into the category of the "natural," now vacated by both heterosexuality and patriotism. Proust's antinationalism would have no more truck with the Queer Nation or Zionism than with French xenophobia. For some Jews, including Theodor Herzl, the Dreyfus Affair definitively undermined the project of assimilation, leading them to conclude "that a Jew would never be able to live in complete happiness and tranquillity anywhere other than in a Jewish State."[46] For others, like Joseph Reinach, Zionism represented an atavistic ethnic solidarity incompatible with the modern nation-state to which he owed allegiance, the French Republic.

But for Proust *any* notion of a nation or homeland seems to be suspect. In an often-quoted "disclaimer" at the end of "La race maudite," he
writes: "I have thought it as well to utter here a provisional warning against
the lamentable error of proposing (just as people have encouraged a Zionist movement) to create a Sodomist movement and to rebuild Sodom.
For, no sooner had they arrived there than the Sodomites would leave the
town so as not to have the appearance of belonging to it" (*SG*, 43–44). Make
sexual perversion into Sodomism, or Jewishness into Zionism, and one
would only have reinstituted an illusory, and potentially coercive, model of
organic wholeness. The diasporic rootlessness of Jews and homosexuals,
Proust seems to say, is necessary to the constitution of their Being *as* Jews
or homosexuals.

We must bear in mind that desire in Proust, whether for an individual
or for a collectivity, is never reciprocal. Whether the object of desire is a
woman, a man, salon society, or the French nation, no one in *À la recherche* ever really wants to belong to any club that would have someone like
him as a member. Identities, in this novel, are thus necessarily differen-
tial and diasporic, and homosexual or Jewish "community" represents, at
most, a sort of anticommunity. But this is not to say that inverts or Jews
represent only an absence, a void. There is something vital that emerges
from these anticommunities. For one thing, if the novel makes it clear that
individual Jews or homosexuals are not literally likely to commit treason,
it nonetheless suggests that one of the virtues of Jews and homosexuals
in a more abstract sense is that, under conditions of compulsory heterosexuality, Catholicism, and French patriotism, they really are traitors to the
nation: they do, in fact, form bonds that traverse and sometimes take pre-
cedence over national boundaries. Just as Armand Dubarry and François
Carlier feared, homosexuals are indeed internationalists. Jupien's brothel,
for example, attracts a cosmopolitan clientele indulging in cross-class and
cross-national orgies, and the text does not rule out the possibility that the
world is a better place for it.[47]

So it is possible to claim that Proust articulates a radically mobile and
contingent model of desire and identity that dispenses with the calcified
ontologies he attacks, and that this gesture has great emancipatory potential. But is this too optimistic a reading, overlooking both the text's darkness (and cattiness) and its resistance to recuperation by a progressive
political agenda? And is it not frustrating, even defeatist, to imagine that
"next year in Jerusalem" must always be indefinitely deferred, realized

only as abstract and unfulfillable promise, because its concretization will necessarily recapitulate the oppressive conditions of exclusion to which Zionism was meant to put an end? After all, expressing all desires and antipathies as fungible, and all identities as a succession of arbitrary and temporary object choices, can seriously undermine political organizing and progress, and it is perhaps this point that critics have responded to in arguing, as many have, that Proust was "apolitical"—not that the novel does not treat political questions, for it is clearly obsessed by them, but that it does not propose political solutions. Furthermore, reacting against Bersani's claim that "we might almost see [in *Sodom and Gomorrah*] a Queer Nation poised for revolution," Lewis contends that "this position does not seem to have all the positive connotations Bersani associates with it. Queerness, racial identity, is a curse in Proust."[48] And to some extent one is obliged to agree.

Lewis continues, however: "But [it is] a curse that is at any rate truer than the fictional identity, equality, and moral unity of the nation-state."[49] It is finally the privileged relation of Jewishness and inversion to truth that succeeds in at least partially counterbalancing the desolate portrait the novel paints of individual Jewish or homosexual lives. Rivers points to the way "the 'chosen race' and the 'race accursed' become metaphors for each other in Proust's work" and claims that "one of the results is to lend homosexuality some of the same power of survival, some of the same sense of a paradoxical interweaving of cursedness and election which have characterized Jewish history."[50] If there can be little doubt, especially in view of Charlus's grotesque and tragic final decline, that homosexuals are in *À la recherche* a *race maudite*, the analogy to Jews nonetheless permits us to imagine that they are also the elect. Admittedly, Proust parodies that sense of election when it manifests itself in the deluded belief of some misogynist and evangelical homosexuals that homosexuality is both a privilege and a mission, requiring them to try to convert the heathen; he ridicules these homosexuals "who, the exceptional character of their inclinations making them regard themselves as superior to the other sex, look down on women, regard homosexuality as the appurtenance of genius and the great periods of history, and, when they wish to share their taste with others, seek out not so much those who seem to them to be predisposed towards it [. . .] as those who seem to them to be worthy of it, from apostolic zeal, just as others preach

Zionism, conscientious objection, Saint-Simonianism, vegetarianism or anarchy" (*SG*, 27–28).

But despite Proust's mockery, there is another sense in which Sodom, in all its depravity and squalor, may truly be viewed as a city on a hill. Homosexuals, like Jews, have a defamiliarized perspective that others need desperately; in particular, it is crucial for artists (Elstir, for example) to tap into ways of seeing that are not those of the world at large, so as to resist "the stultifying, bourgeois principles of group uniformity and upward mobility that predominate in *Belle Epoque* France."[51] This is not necessarily to imply that there is *a* "Jewish" or "homosexual" way of seeing, of course; if there were, it would only reinforce conformity within a group. Rather, the difference of subalterns registers as a formal discrepancy, a sense of outsiderness.

For Marcel, especially, the lessons he learns from that "unique experience," that outsider's perspective, will be invaluable in enabling him eventually to disengage himself from the salons, a process essential to his education and development as an artist. The understanding that history, beauty, desire, the nation all look profoundly different from the margins helps Marcel to shake off the *idées réçues* that still stunt and enervate his imagination until the final epiphanies of *Time Regained* set him free to write. Thus, by teaching Marcel how to see, homosexuals, like Jews, teach him truth—not, again, *a* truth or *the* truth, but how to find his way to his own stereoscopic vision of "the truth which is before him," which is the sole obligation of the artist. The narrator's rebuke of Barrès for forgetting precisely this point is famous: "At the beginning of the war M. Barrès had said that the artist [...] must first and foremost serve the glory of his country. But this he can do only by being an artist, which means only on condition that, while in his own sphere he is studying laws, conducting experiments, making discoveries which are as delicate as those of science, he shall think of nothing—not even his country—but the truth which is before him" (*TR*, 280).

Not coincidentally, Proust's notion of artistic integrity here corresponds precisely to the ideal of justice that he and other Dreyfusards embraced during the Affair. In response to the antirevisionists' argument that Dreyfus's case must not be reopened for the sake of the unity, security, and honor of the nation, the Dreyfusards said, as the artist does here, that the principle of truth at any cost must outweigh raisons d'état. The nationalists' fears were neither trivial nor unrealistic: the Affair *did* very nearly bring about the collapse of France. But the Dreyfusards staked, and won, their battle, as the narrator does in *Time Regained*, on the belief that only truth, whether political or aesthetic, could ultimately be good for the nation, and that a nation that could not tolerate the truth, while it might be stable and secure, would finally represent a kind of social contract not worth preserving.

4

TRUTH BREATHING DOWN THE NECK OF FICTION

I occasionally practise [...] my speech for the defence (magnificent but unsuccessful) on your arrest for high treason and subsequent execution at the Tower.

> —Christopher Isherwood to Stephen Spender,
> November 15, 1936

I know exactly why Guy Burgess went to Moscow. It wasn't enough to be a queer and a drunk. He had to revolt still more to break away from it all. That's just what I've done by becoming an American citizen.

> —W. H. Auden to Robin Maugham

In the second half of this book I turn from the work of Marcel Proust to that of W. H. Auden and from fin-de-siècle France to Great Britain and America between the wars, with two consequent shifts in perspective. One is that in the next two chapters the topic of Jews and Jewishness will be held in abeyance until it resumes its crucial place in my argument in chapter 6, and in its place I will be dealing with Communism. This is primarily because Jewishness was not central to Auden's prewar poetry, my subject here, and also because I need to map out the itineraries of midcentury discourses about Communism and homosexuality before I can adequately assess their relationship to Jewishness. The second readjustment I will ask of my reader is to remember that there is a wide gap, culturally though not chronologically, between Proust's France and Auden's England with regard to male same-sex relations, and not only because these were illegal in England. Although Auden's earliest publications are virtually contemporaneous with the appearance of the final volumes of *À la recherche*, he and Proust inhabited quite different sexual cultures—partly because whereas a young Proust would have had only the classics and medical literature to read on the subject of sexuality, the young Auden also had Proust. Thus, while Proust struggled with, revised, and resisted the category of the invert, Auden and his contemporaries had little doubt that the word *homosexual*, like the words *bugger* and *queer*, designated what they felt themselves to be; even as adolescents they were able to negotiate their sexual desires and self-conceptions in relation to a socially well-articulated category that persists, grosso modo, to the current day. Auden's "homosexuality" is, to a great extent, the same homosexuality as ours, whereas Proust's "inversion" is only a distant, if recognizable, ancestor to both.

THE SPIES' CAREER

Auden once told Robin Maugham, in words quoted at the beginning of this chapter, that he felt his own adoption of U.S. citizenship was comparable to the 1951 defection of the notorious Soviet spy—and Auden's friend—Guy Burgess.[1] We might think that in saying this the poet was merely engaging in a spot of typical Audenesque exaggeration; a writer who happens to emigrate (even during wartime, as Auden had) is surely less disloyal to his native country than a man who spent more than fifteen years spying for the Soviet Union. Yet if we take Auden's remark seriously as an analysis of his position—that of a homosexual man who, like Burgess and the other Cambridge spies, had been drawn to Communism in the early 1930s and later left England—we perceive that it is informed by homologies between male homosexuality, espionage, and treason that were already circulating widely in the work of Auden and his literary contemporaries in the late 1920s and the 1930s. Long before Burgess, Donald Maclean, and Kim Philby defected, even longer before Anthony Blunt was unmasked as the fourth man in the spy ring in 1979, British writers had helped fashion an image of the left-wing intellectual—particularly the homosexual intellectual—as a subject exceptionally inclined to disloyalty and alienated from the dominant national culture; these writers both responded to and helped invent the context within which they, and the Cambridge spies, would be understood as traitors.

Auden's early poetry relies on obsessively reiterated images of conspiracy, secrecy, frontiers, passports, treachery, disguises, sentries, wars, and espionage. Critic Monroe Spears identifies "The Spy" as a governing trope of *all* the work in the 1933 edition of Auden's *Poems*, which collected many of the important poems from 1927 on. Spears writes that in that collection, "the chief figure [. . .] is the Spy, the Secret Agent."[2] Auden himself acknowledges his earlier fixation on espionage in the 1935 poem "August for the people," in which he reminisces about his adolescent friendship with Christopher Isherwood, saying, "Our hopes were set still on the spies' career."[3] Clive James has written that this line of the poem "gains luminosity once we have accustomed ourselves to the close identification in Auden's mind of homosexuality with clandestine activity and all its apparatus of codes and invisible inks"; he continues: "Auden's artistic indulgence in the 30's vocabulary of espionage—a vocabulary which was a matter of life and death to those from whom he borrowed it—seemed then, and can still seem now, trivial beyond forgiveness. It's worth remembering, though, that Auden was in a war too, and needed to hide himself just as deep."[4] With that in mind, I would argue that for Auden comparing himself to Burgess was neither melodramatic nor trivializing; rather, the trope of espionage really was for him a particularly resonant way of describing what it meant, in interwar England, to flout the paradigms of compulsory heterosexuality, and his sense that to do so constituted an act of treason against England. Yet by the time Auden "betrayed" England definitively by leaving her, that trope had nearly vanished from his work, rendered supererogatory by Auden's new vision of the more productive possibilities that queered forms of national identification could offer the homosexual.

THE 1930S: TEXTS AND CONTEXTS

Critic Valentine Cunningham has described the tendency of 1930s texts and contexts to fuse so that "the dominant images of the 1930s do have a way of turning out to be intimately one with the events of that time, and vice versa."[5] He offers several examples, including the prevalence of themes of public school life in 1930s writing by authors just returned to schools as masters; metaphors of frontiers, at a time when frontiers recently redrawn by the Great War were once again threatened with violent rearrangement; images of gigantism in the work of writers who were either physically small or preoccupied with their own moral smallness in comparison to men of an earlier generation; and so on. Espionage and the whole apparatus of war had a similar status "not only as signifiers of an external reality," in Bernard Bergonzi's words, "but also as metaphors and recurring formal constituents."[6]

In Cunningham's view these recursive factual/figurative loops constitute a single massive field of meaning within which 1930s literature must be understood—or, as Cunningham puts it in a vocabulary that is itself borrowed from espionage, "decoded": he concludes, "It certainly is not hard for the intellectual historian to perceive that the facts and fictions offered for his decoding comprise, in large measure, something like a connected field, a whole text, a set of diverse signs adding up [...] to a single semiotic."[7]

Cunningham's argument provides a useful departure point for any analysis of the literature of this period, but the sheer five-hundred-page sprawl of his *British Writers of the 1930s* suggests that other critics might try to select smaller subsets of signs within which to situate more sharply delineated readings. My own critical focus in this chapter is on Auden and his use of the figure of the spy, though it is difficult to read him in isolation from the other writers to whom he was closest, so strongly conscious were they of themselves as forming a like-minded and often collaborative group. Thus, I will also acknowledge the work of Auden's contemporaries, and particularly Isherwood and Stephen Spender, as an essential part of the context within which I read Auden. And I will place them, and in the next chapter the Cambridge spies, against the whole text, the connected field of "facts and fictions" that was the world of the public school– and Oxbridge-educated British upper-middle-class: the class whose sons became teachers, clergymen, barristers, imperial administrators, and civil servants.

The "Auden group"—like the Cambridge spies—might more properly be described as a large network,[a] a few of whose members have become especially well known. These are the five who remain today the canonical Auden group: Auden himself, Spender, Cecil Day Lewis, Louis MacNeice, and the only novelist in the group, Isherwood, who chronicled the lives of the others in numerous romans à clef and did as much as anyone to create the mythology of the Auden Generation. All of them contributed, though, to the powerful literary mystique that arose around the figures of the spy and the traitor—roles that the Cambridge spies then donned, as if their treachery had been made imaginatively necessary or at least possible by the cultural representations of espionage and treason that preceded it. If the writers' work was a "signifier of external reality" inasmuch as it responded

---

a. A network including, among others, the Lehmann siblings (John and Rosamund), Cyril Connolly, Isherwood's cousin Graham Greene, Edward Upward, Rex Warner, Geoffrey Grigson, Naomi Mitchison, John Cornford, and Christopher Caudwell.

to specific political and social pressures of the times, it also helped to create the ideational universe both the writers and the spies inhabited.

John Lehmann thought that his generation's obsession with the theme of espionage reflected their confrontation in the 1930s with unbridled, amoral political power: "I was [. . .] convinced that the great theme of our time was this problem of power running amok, power without moral sanction or restraint; and that there was something in the claim that the real image of the world we lived in was to be found in a certain class of detective and spy stories."[8] So he and his peers responded to political conflict and instability with stories about spying that had a privileged relation to reality, generating *the*—not *a*—real image of the world. And then the writers were taken aback by the uncanny degree to which the lives of Burgess and Maclean followed the narrative track laid down by those stories. John Pudney, a close friend of both Auden and Maclean from public school, has told the story of meeting Maclean for drinks the week before the latter fled to Moscow, when Pudney was writing his spy novel *The Net*. Asked by Maclean what he was working on, Pudney answered:

> "A novel," I said. "It came to me after a job I was doing among the research people at the Royal Aeronautical Establishment at Farnborough. It's about treachery . . . or perhaps that's not the word . . . defection. A Farnborough type of scientist taking off and offering himself and his bag of tricks to Russia."
>
> How often have I gone back over that in vain searching my memory for some trace of tension, some catch of breath, any indication at all that this was Donald's last Sunday in Kent. [. . .] Then we read about [his defection] in the papers. It made the closing chapters of *The Net* singularly difficult to write, with this bizarre truth breathing down the neck of fiction.[9]

"I UNDERSTAND YOU ARE AN AUSTRIAN": THE INTELLECTUAL AS ALIEN

In addition to writing about spies and traitors, the members of the Auden group were themselves publicly identified with these terms. Auden's biographer Richard Davenport-Hines reports that during World War II American neighbors of Auden's told the FBI that he was a spy; Davenport-Hines hypothesizes that Auden's towheadedness gave him "a Nordic look" and mentions that "the agent who came to interview him asked, You're a Scandinavian, aren't you?"[10] In 1942 four German saboteurs had been arrested after being dropped off on Long Island by a submarine, so it seems likelier that the neighbors were worried that Auden looked *German*—his own explanation was that "they obviously thought I'd come off a submarine"— but in either case, what is interesting is that the very English Auden "read," to Americans, like the agent of a foreign country.

While Auden was being interrogated as a spy in the United States, the same thing was happening to Cyril Connolly in England. Military police accused Connolly of spying on a group of officers in a hotel lounge in 1940, and when their suspicions were further aroused by the conjunction of his Irish name, his British passport, and the fact that the passport had been issued in Vienna, they searched his hotel room. After learning that he was a writer, and finding nude sketches in the journal he edited, the police decided that he "should be put in the Coop for the night." Connolly apparently represented a confusing intellectual cosmopolitanism that the state was anxious to assimilate to simpler categories of national identity: the inspector who searched his room opened his interrogation in much the same way as the FBI agent who questioned Auden, saying, "Good evening, sir, I understand you are an Austrian."[11]

Auden had also been denounced by his compatriots as a traitor, along with Isherwood, after the two men left for America in January 1939. At the time they were not sure whether they were leaving for good, and of course they did not know that Britain would be at war within a year. But in the event they did stay in the States, and once war had broken out even some of their friends joined the chorus of criticism attacking them for everything from cowardice to sedition. Referring to Isherwood, Auden, and their fellow emigrés Gerald Heard and Aldous Huxley, Harold Nicolson—previously on warm terms with them—complained in the *Spectator* that "four of our most liberated intellectuals refuse to identify themselves either with those who fight or with those who oppose the battle" and suggested that they might even exercise a pernicious influence on international politics, since "their presence in the United States may lead American opinion, which is all too prone to doubt the righteousness of our cause, to find comfort in their company."[12] Hostile letters from the public poured into the newspapers; finally, Conservative MPs launched a Parliamentary debate about whether Auden and Isherwood should be forcibly recalled to Britain to perform military service. Sir Jocelyn Lucas asked in Parliament "whether British citizens of military age, such as Mr W.H. Auden and Mr Christopher Isherwood, who have gone to the United States and expressed their determination not to return to this country until war is over, will be summoned back for registration and calling up, in view of the fact that they are seeking refuge abroad?"[13]

In fact, Isherwood and Auden had never "expressed their determination not to return" to Britain, and as we will see later, they made repeated efforts to contribute to the war effort for both the British and the Americans. Nevertheless, the charges of espionage and treason were hardly shots in the dark. Lehmann viewed the accusations directed against his friends as part of a wider Anglo-American backlash against artists and intellectuals whose work, especially during wartime, was difficult to enlist in support of the values of capitalist productivity or the national welfare.

> The intellectuals of the 'thirties were by no means popular at that time with members of Parliament, influential Civil Servants and Generals in authority. [. . .] One sensed an only just undivulged wish to put us in front of a firing squad, or at least to clap us into prison for the duration. [. . .] The suppressed emotions of hostility broke violently into the open over the "Auden-Isherwood affair". Christopher and Wystan were suddenly branded as traitors and cowards in a campaign that was waged with the utmost fury against them.[14]

In Davenport-Hines's judgement "the force behind the campaign was a loathing of mental or sexual heterodoxy,"[15] which is probably fair but elides the degree to which Auden and his friends deliberately cultivated and performed heterodoxy as an aesthetic and political principle. If, during the war, Auden, Isherwood, Connolly, and other artists looked so much like spies and traitors, this is surely at least in part because as early as the late 1920s, they themselves had begun to synthesize their own sexual and political oppositionality in carefully constructed fictional and poetic figures of alienation, treason, and espionage. It was not just the public that thought of them as spies and traitors; they thought of themselves that way, too.

THE TEST

When the younger generations of the British governing classes collectively shifted to the political left in the late 1920s and early 1930s, they—especially the men[b]—acquired a peculiarly liminal social status as both consummate insiders and defiant outsiders: immensely powerful by global standards yet, at least in their own minds, rebellious against power, and enjoying all the perquisites of expensive educations and comfortable lifestyles while passionately (and apparently sincerely) committed to overthrowing the economic system that funded these luxuries. These juxtapositions sometimes produced almost irresistibly humorous incongruities, as in the case of Francis Edward Hovell-Thurlow-Cumming-Bruce, later the eighth Baron Thurlow and governor of the Bahamas, who joined the Communist Party at Cambridge in the 1930s. At Cambridge he was in a "cell" with Donald Maclean and Maclean's brilliant friend from Gresham's School, James Klugmann, known today for his work as the official historian of the British Communist Party and the fact that he, too, may have been acting as a double agent while working for British intelligence during the war. These were men who were, evidently, serious about Communism. But interviewed decades later, Lord Thurlow remembered his own stint in the party as if it had been just another club membership, and the caption to his photo in Barrie Penrose and Simon Freeman's *Conspiracy of Silence* admirably sums up all the potential absurdity in the image of the upper-crust left-wing militant: "In term time he sold the *Daily Worker*, while in the holidays he went fox-hunting and shooting."[16]

If the paradoxes of ruling-class radicalism occasionally terminate in caricature, however, they also fecundated much of the work of the Auden group, whose members expressed both an acute consciousness of their privilege as bourgeois Englishmen and a strong sense of estrangement from their nation and their class. They attributed their feelings of alienation and outsiderhood to a range of factors, including artistic sensibility and, in some cases, their ethnicity (MacNeice and Day Lewis were Anglo-Irish, Spender partly German and Jewish). From Connolly's perspective simply being intellectuals was enough to set them at odds with their class and to require that they adopt a strategy of subterfuge: "To be 'highbrow'

---

b. Obviously, numerous women of all classes also dedicated themselves to left-wing causes; women's involvement in the various Left parties and movements of the 1930s has been well documented. But since even very privileged women had never been raised with the same relationship to power as ruling-class men, their investment in radical political ideals of social and economic equality was necessarily very different from—and frankly less paradoxical than—that of their brothers, as Virginia Woolf demonstrates in *A Room of One's Own* and *Three Guineas*.

was to be different, to be set apart and so excluded from the ruling class of which one was either a potential enemy or a potential servant. Intelligence was a deformity which must be concealed; a public school taught one to conceal it as a good tailor hides a paunch or a hump."[17]

But above all, it was the crisis of masculinity experienced by many men of Auden's generation that made them feel like exiles from the nation. Homosexuality was a particularly fraught aspect of that crisis, and Spender, Auden, and Isherwood all found that their homosexual desires and practices sometimes put them at odds with both familial and social norms and the institutions of the nation-state, particularly the police and immigration authorities. Conflicts over the meaning of masculinity were, however, shared by many in Auden's circle, whether they engaged in homosex or not. MacNeice, for instance, though a passionate lover of women, was far from orthodox in his gender expression—as the campy banter he exchanged in letters with gay friends like Auden and Anthony Blunt suggests—and was once forcibly debagged at Oxford by a gang of hearties who assumed he must be homosexual.[18]

A crucial factor in the group's uneasy negotiations with masculinity was, on their own account, the fact that they had been too young to fight in the Great War that had allowed their older male relatives to attain a now unreachable ideal of heroic virility. Connolly wrote that during the war, whenever boys at his preparatory school misbehaved, "the example of brothers or cousins now in the trenches was [. . .] produced to shame us."[19] Isherwood, whose father was killed in combat, described the relationship of his generation to the war in terms of "The Test," the sense that their own manliness was unproved and indeed unprovable once the war was over: "Like most of my generation, I was obsessed by a complex of terrors and longings connected with the idea 'War.' 'War,' in this purely neurotic sense, meant The Test. The test of your courage, of your maturity, of your sexual prowess: 'Are you really a Man?'"[20] In his 1929 poem "On Sunday walks" Auden writes that "Father by son / Lives on and on," but over the "motto on the gate" of the ancestral home, "The lichen grows / From year to year," suggesting the gradual effacement and decay of hereditary values and warlike virility (*EA*, 33–34). Richard Bozorth proposes that in poems like this Auden satirizes "anxieties about living up to the father" and concludes that the sons of heroic fathers are driven to "make-believe masculinity. What the fathers were, the sons can only emulate in distended, artificial form."[21]

The perception that these writers had failed to achieve normative adult masculinity is evident in the ubiquitous and enduring characterization of their work, and sometimes of their lives, as "immature." Homosexuality was understood to be central to the Auden group from the outset (hence the sobriquet "the Homintern," bestowed on them by Connolly), but the subject was usually addressed only by reference to their "immaturity." So widespread was the theory that homosexual desires were typical of an early stage of human psychosexual development, however, that the term *immaturity* in criticism of the Auden group can be understood as nearly synonymous with *homosexuality*, more than as a euphemism for it. Indeed, at times the writers used this terminology themselves: influenced by Freudian psychology, Auden would say to the end of his life "that he believed homosexuality was a symptom of arrested development, a continuous prolonging of adolescence, a refusal of full maturity."[22]

The writers' vocabulary and imagery, their preoccupation with espionage, and their attraction to Communism were all attributed to this arrested psychosexual development. Some have argued that what Isherwood calls the "all-consuming morbid interest in the idea of 'war'" in the Auden generation's work is not only a kind of make-believe but also an essentially juvenile attempt to compensate, via fantasy, for their feelings of insufficiency.[23] Robin Skelton, himself a poet of the 1930s, found "something curiously adolescent in the use of phrases like 'The Enemy', 'The Struggle', and 'The Country', and in the deployment of such words as 'Leader', 'Conspiracy', 'Frontier', 'Maps', 'Guns' and 'Armies' in much of the writing of the period."[24] Given that war-making is the adult male activity par excellence, the vocabulary cannot be "adolescent" in and of itself; rather, it becomes so when adopted by writers who did not have the wartime experience to lay legitimate claim to that rhetoric.

The Leavisites pressed especially hard on this theme; reviews of the Auden group's work in *Scrutiny* often exhaust their supply of synonyms for *immature* within the first couple of paragraphs. To "irresponsible," "adolescent," and "schoolboy" are occasionally added "neurotic," "unsound," "sentimental," or "unbalanced," conjuring the image of hysterical effeminacy in conjunction with arrested development and thus reinforcing the suggestion of sexual deviance. Even more sympathetic critics reiterated these ideas: in the 1937 special issue of *New Verse* dedicated to Auden, many of those who contributed commentaries carefully balanced their praise with criticism of his immaturity. Dylan Thomas, for instance, wrote, "I sometimes think of his poetry as a great war, admire intensely the mature, religious, and logical fighter, and deprecate the boy bushranger."[25]

This reading surfaced as recently as the late 1980s in the work of Valentine Cunningham, who frequently refers to "the lingering juvenility of which the homosexuality was arguably a part."[26] Cunningham does not hesitate to mix criticism of the Auden group's writing with hostile commentary on their personal immaturity and irresponsibility, fulminating that "a whole generation of writers refused to countenance the normal family in their work, as they refused in their lives to acquire wives and become fathers."[27] He goes so far as to characterize the *mariages blancs* that several British homosexual writers contracted in the 1930s with German and Austrian women as "practical jokes,"[28] even though these marriages were performed so that the women could acquire British passports and escape the Nazis. (One rather doubts that under the circumstances, Erika Mann viewed her marriage to Auden as a practical joke.) And for Cunningham the Auden group's poetry, and their Left politics, are equally compromised by their immature homoeroticism: "Much of the period's writing about the proletariat is vitiated by the bourgeois bugger's specialist regard. Spender's attitude to the Spanish Civil War soldiery [. . .] is deeply mixed up in homosexual affections (the fighting and the Commissars put his ex-boyfriend specially in danger, and 'the boy lying dead under the olive tree' in the poem 'Ultima Ratio Regum' is no simple object of general humanitarian sympathy: 'He was a better target for a kiss')."[29] Presumably if Spender had written about a dead girl instead, his poem might have aspired to both universality and maturity, and thus to genuine literary distinction.

But there are also less hostile and more interesting readings of the writers' putative immaturity. Day Lewis claimed that Auden's "irresponsibility" was a function of his socialist realism, as he was simply reflecting in his work the life of his own decaying social class: "His satire has been criticised at times as irresponsible: this is to misunderstand its motive and aim: in so far as it proceeds from the life of one social class, a class which has lost its responsibility and civilising impetus, the terms of this satire are bound to be superficially irresponsible."[30] Writing twenty years later, Joseph Warren Beach reversed the causal relation between immaturity and Marxism, holding that schoolboy games produced the taste for conspiracy that in turn made Auden and his friends so receptive to Marxism: "As a boy Auden and his intimates played for years the game of spies and conspirators, and the delight in conspiracy gives its tone to his poetry for many years. It was perhaps this fancy for the conspiratorial that made so attractive to these young men the Marxian ideology."[31]

In making a connection between immaturity and Left politics, Beach and Day Lewis point us toward an entirely different understanding of these terms: the view that a revolt against adulthood—or, to be precise, against a very specific form of adult bourgeois masculinity—can have a radical political valence. In their memoirs Louis MacNeice and Anthony Blunt both recall how, at their public school, an embattled minority of "precious" aesthetes and intellectuals deliberately set out to provoke the school toughs and hearties, disliked not only in themselves but also as representatives of an adult world whose values the aesthetes abhorred.[32] So MacNeice, Blunt, and their friends embraced the "child-cult," carrying stuffed animals in public and playing with hoops and babies' rubber balls, the children's toys their weapons of choice in a parodic yet fundamentally serious campaign against normative heterosexuality, anti-intellectualism, the cult of sports, and the militaristic logic of sacrifice.[33]

The "immaturity" manifested in a refusal of particular forms of adult masculinity became, for these men, a way of separating themselves from the expectations of their class, nation, and families, individuating themselves and thus achieving emotional and artistic maturity on their own terms. In the synthesis of Freud and Marx common to their generation, they often formulated their political theories in terms of familial relations, investigating how psychological patterns established within families are related to larger social and political institutions and, not infrequently, indicting the patriarchal family as the origin of repressive social structures associated, at best, with cultural Philistinism and at worst with fascism. A necessary separation of oneself from the family and familial roles is therefore equated with alienation from one's class or nation.

Thus, writers like Isherwood took their failure to measure up to the standard of masculinity established by their fathers as the starting point for an impassioned revolt against patriarchal nationalism: "By denying your duty toward the Hero-Father, you deny the authority of the Flag, the Old School Tie, the Unknown Soldier, The Land That Bore You and the God of Battles."[34] Auden frequently attributed his own decision to emigrate to his desire to escape England's "family life," using the family as a metaphor for everything that is both seductive, and dangerous, about the English bourgeoisie and the political and social cultures they oversee. In a 1963 BBC interview he explained that he had left because "I felt the situation for me in England was becoming impossible. I couldn't grow up. English life is for me a family life, and I love my family but I don't want to live with them."[35] Equating loyalty to the family—and thus to England—with immaturity, he implies that disloyalty to both is a necessary step into adulthood. Thus, in Auden's formulation it is the heteronormative, nationalist man who is "immature" rather than the homosexual, expatriate aesthete.

Emigrating was a particularly dramatic way of expressing one's disloyalty to the homeland. (Committing treason as the Cambridge spies did was another.) But skepticism about national loyalties was common to Auden's generation of leftists. George Orwell famously called Communism "the patriotism of the deracinated,"[36] an ideology that attempted to substitute identification with a class for identification with a nation. The antinationalist stance Isherwood expresses in the line just quoted from his autobiography, *Kathleen and Frank*, does not seem to be simply a matter of an older man retroactively attributing his later political positions to his ten-year-old self, given that as an adolescent at public school he "proposed a motion before the debating society that 'in the opinion of this House, patriotism is an obstacle to civilization.'"[37] Others in Auden's group expressed a similar antipathy toward, or even sheer incomprehension of, nationalist sentiment in the conventional sense of a strongly cathected relation to "The Land That Bore You." Day Lewis wrote that as a young man, "I had no feeling of patriotism—I mean, no real sense of attachment to a country or even to a place. Patriotism in the sense of 'my country, right or wrong' remains a meaningless thing to me, and 'the Nation', 'the Empire', 'the British way of life' are generalisations to which I cannot respond [. . .] a collective noun like 'the Nation' must be translated into known, flesh-and-blood human beings before I can feel concern."[38]

In work written soon after he emigrated Auden indicted patriotic sentiment as superstition and idolatry, suggesting that by then his antinationalism could be referred to his newfound Christian convictions as easily as to his earlier materialism. In an early draft of "New Year Letter" (1940) Auden accuses the rhetorical concept of the nation, which he associates with outdated folk superstitions, of motivating a fatally misplaced libidinal attachment: "'England', 'La France', 'Das Reich', their words / Are like the names of extinct birds / Or peasant-women's quaint old charms / For bringing lovers to their arms, / Which would be only pretty, save / That they bring thousands to their grave."[39] And even in a 1944 article in which he concedes that in view of the mass slaughter of European Jews, the establishment of a Jewish state might be necessary, Auden writes that "to regard national statehood as anything more than a technical convenience of social organisation [. . .] is idolatry."[40]

ALL THE CONSPIRATORS

Auden and his circle incarnated their skepticism about territorial rootedness, filial piety, and the political and economic culture of the interwar period in figures like the exile, the bohemian, the stranger, the wandering Jew. But of all these tropes none figured more prominently in their writing than that of the spy, which had the virtue, among others, of imbuing the unhappy experiences of isolation and alienation with glamour and romance. It was also a flexible symbol, available for service to such a broad range of political and narrative positions that it could almost be defined as the master trope of the liminal, the oppositional, the secretive. In a literary work the spy could be an individual acting on his own behalf or on behalf of any group with which his creator wished to identify him, against any other group, or against the state; he could represent a loner, an insurgent, or a double agent, depending on the themes or narrative line that the text required him to carry. If John Lehmann was right in thinking that spy stories reflected his generation's vision of a world in which they found themselves confronting "power running amok," there was no shortage of the forms such power could take and therefore almost no limit to the uses "spy stories" could serve. There is one notable exception, however: almost never, in the literature of the interwar period, does the spy appear as a straightforward, and as it were "legitimate," agent of a state power. The one perspective that, it appears, the Auden generation were not interested in exploring via the metaphor of the spy was that of formal identification with state interests and institutions. MI6 agents James Bond and George Smiley are decidedly post–World War II creations.

In Isherwood's work the motif of the spy appeared very early; his first novel, published in 1928, is titled *All the Conspirators*. But years before, he and Edward Upward had already sketched the whole landscape of espionage, with its dangerous frontiers, mysterious enemies, and secret codes, in the Mortmere fantasies they created together at their public school. In that looking-glass world, which provided so much of the raw matter of the Auden group's early work, Isherwood and Upward alone constitute the unit that in later texts would become a "gang," a "team," or a "class," and "treason" is defined as a violation of an entirely personal loyalty to one other human being. When the two boys traveled up to Cambridge University to interview for admission, Isherwood writes,

> we had got to stick together, we told each other. We were venturing, like spies, into an enemy stronghold. "They," our adversaries, would employ other tactics down there; they would be sly, polite, reassuring; they would invite us to tea. We should have to be on our guard. [. . .] the whole establishment seemed to offer an enormous tacit bribe. We fortified ourselves against it as best we could, in the privacy of our rooms; swearing never to betray each other, never to forget the existence of "the two sides" and their eternal, necessary state of war.[41]

It is striking that at this stage, Isherwood's "side" consisted solely of himself and Upward, for no particular reason except that they were best friends, and also that their bond was not attributable to what Wyndham Lewis snidely called the "*esprit de corps* of the pathic,"[42] since Upward was not homosexual. At the same time, the "enemy" was not simply adults, Cambridge, or anything else so specific; it was "the whole establishment." If these retrospective accounts of their adolescence can be believed, this generation's orientation toward espionage—the us-versus-them militancy and the rhetoric of treason—long preceded their articulation of specific oppositional identities and political stances, arising from a primal and undifferentiated sense of alienation. By the time they began to publish they already took it as given that the artist/spy/hero and his side must always be involved in a perilous undercover campaign against the other side, however those sides were defined and whether the stakes in the battle being waged were aesthetic, political, or sexual.

Sometimes, then, their writing pitted the alienated artist against the Philistines, the British bourgeoisie in the twentieth century. For instance, Richard Hoggart attributes the group's preoccupation with espionage to their positions as writers in an age when there was no appropriate and useful social place for a poet: "Why [. . .] were they all so interested in the apparatus of the spy story? [. . .] In some degree the fondness for the climate of war arose from the sense of menace which all had in the 'thirties, from the sense of being in enemy country. Briefly, these poets felt that they did not properly belong, that in this century less than ever the poet is able to assume an audience or his own place in society."[43]

Contrasting his generation's position with the more comfortable role of the Augustan poet, Auden writes in "Letter to Lord Byron" that in the modern age the artist must conceal his vocation; no longer permitted to be one among peers, he is alienated from the crowds among whom he must pass as a spy: "On this point he must differ from the crowd, / And, like a secret agent, must keep hidden / His passion for his shop" (*EA*, 186). Isherwood felt that the job of a novelist is to observe, minutely, his society. Yet as a young man he could not move among English people of his own class without betraying his hostility toward them, so he determined to learn how to disguise himself (which he did for a time by feigning a slight Cockney accent): "The most I shall ever achieve, I thought, will be to learn how to spy upon [the English], unnoticed. Henceforward, my problem is how to perfect a disguise."[44] Spender, too, imagined the "Historians of the future"—artists?—who reject national allegiances and are killed because they foresee the possibility of a future that the ruling class resists: "The allies of no city, / O man and woman minute beneath their larger day; / Those burrowing beneath frontier, shot as spies because / Sensitive to new contours."[45]

While the spy could represent poet-artists as outsiders to bourgeois norms, he could also symbolize their uneasy relationship to insider status. Spears has hypothesized that the idea of the spy held particular power for Auden as a schoolmaster, because in that role he was an agent of the state, responsible for transmitting the culture and values of England's ruling class to his pupils—but since he was also a political radical hypothetically dedicated to overthrowing the state, he was acting as a double agent.[46] This reading accords with Auden's own comments about the dilemma of a master in a public school who is embedded in a system that makes it impossible for him to do his job, which is to teach his students about the world. Public schools, Auden writes in his 1934 essay "The Liberal Fascist," cannot give boys "any real sense of the problems of the world, or of how to attack them. [. . .] Indeed it is impossible to see how any school [. . .] where boys and staff are both drawn from the monied classes, can hope to see the world picture of that class objectively. The mass production of gentlemen is their *raison-d'être*, and one can hardly suggest that they should adopt principles which would destroy them" (*EA*, 322–23).

If the privileged writer abandoned his own class as a bad job and tried instead to pass among the proletariat, he might, like a spy, feign an accent (Isherwood's Cockney) or go under an alias, like Christopher St. John

Sprigg, who became Christopher Caudwell so his name would sound less tony. (Cecil Day-Lewis abbreviated his first name and dropped the hyphen from the second for the same reason.) Cunningham considers these forms of self-disguise a manifestation of the way bourgeois writers—and most especially bourgeois homosexual writers—experienced the ambiguity of their own social position, the tensions of passing, and the proximity of their own forms of duplicity to the criminality of the Cambridge spies. "The sense of disguising [...] as an immoral faking, obviously reached out via the anxious writer's general feeling of class guilt over his class's privileges, to touch those guilty disguisings that were actually criminal: the converging world of the spy, the masked agent or double-agent that so many '30s Leftists fantasized themselves as, and that some (like Guy Burgess and Anthony Blunt) actually were, and the world of the homosexual that so many '30s Leftists and writers (including Burgess and Blunt) also were."[47] Invoking the intersections between class, sexuality, guilt, and duplicity, Cunningham thus points to what is, for my reading of Auden, the most pertinent function of the metaphor of the spy: to represent the anxious position of the ruling-class male homosexual.

PERSECUTION AND PRIVILEGE

The feelings Auden expressed, in both private writings and published texts, about the relation between state and social institutions and homosexuality are ambivalent and sometimes contradictory. In this he differed from Isherwood, who was unequivocally enraged by institutionalized heteronormativity, writing in *Christopher and His Kind*, "Damn Nearly Everybody. Girls are what the state and the church and the law and the press and the medical profession endorse, and command me to desire. [...] In their will is my death."[48] In contrast, Auden sometimes seemed indifferent to legal and religious injunctions against homosexuality, sometimes amused by them; occasionally guilty, remorseful, or self-flagellating. But his early writing conveys an understanding of homosexuality that is both psychologically nuanced and politically acute in its recognition of the double burden of self-loathing and public contempt bearing down on the homosexual. He wrote in his journal that "all buggers hate each other's bodies as they hate their own, since they all suffer under the reproach, real or imaginary of 'Call yourself a man,' "[49] and he often identified his own sexuality with criminality, referring to himself as a "crook." Then again, he also wrote poems like the unpublished "Chanson," which equates homosexuals' confrontations with the law with the struggles of fascism's victims[c].

In 1940 James Southworth wrote that Auden's work was notable for its sensitivity to both the proletariat and homosexuals (whom Southworth quaintly calls "Urnings"), and implicitly for the way it draws together the interests of those two subaltern groups in its social critique: "There is little question in my mind," said Southworth, "but that Mr Auden is the foremost of the younger group of poets. He has done much to quicken our senses toward two groups—the workers and the Urnings, and to point out where many of the evils of contemporary civilization lie."[50] In 1973 Clive James argued even more explicitly that radical politics and sexuality are indissociable in the interwar poetry: "Auden's radicalism, such as it was, was at one with his sexuality, with the subsequent result that he spent the 30's experiencing Communism as sensual and sex as political."[51]

But if we can legitimately read sexual radicalism, a protest against the oppression and marginalization of the homosexual, into Auden's prewar work, we should also remember the suggestion made by a good many of his contemporaries that, in their time, to be homosexual was more an advantage than otherwise among certain influential British elites. Cyril Connolly complained that at Eton "the potentially homosexual boy was the one who benefited, whose love of beauty was stimulated, whose appreciation was widened and whose critical powers were developed; the normal boy, free from adolescent fevers, missed both the perils and the prizes; he was apt to find himself left out."[52] John Pudney wrote of realizing that his friends Auden and Benjamin Britten both "belonged to that homosexual world which closed certain doors to strangers" and that he himself, despite his occasional same-sex affairs, "would always be a stranger."[53] And then there was MacNeice's quip that "I discovered that in Oxford homosexuality and 'intelligence,' heterosexuality and brawn were almost inexorably paired. This left me out in the cold and I took to drink."[54]

More broadly, it can be argued that male homosexuality was built into structures of domination in England and that the erotic power relations practiced at public schools and university were simply a preparation for the

c. The last two stanzas of this poem, which Auden penned in French and sent to Isherwood, read, "Salut aux Rouges / Qui combattent en Espagne / Et à la Chine / Cette belle campagne; Salut à tous / Qui ont triché la Police / Nous sommes pour l'Amour / Et la Justice" ("Chanson," 1938–1939? Christopher Isherwood Papers, 2790).

exercise of power in the administration of empire. Far from being a marginalizing factor, on this account homosexual experiences would be essential to the formation of the ruling class. Auden himself suggests as much in describing the way the public schools operated to produce a governing class that was both emotionally retarded—so (implicitly) homosexual—and instinctively elitist, having learned to identify the national interest exclusively with the interests of privileged men. In "The Liberal Fascist" Auden described his time at Gresham's School as the equivalent of life in a fascist state. This was not because it was exceptionally brutal; on the contrary, Auden was quite happy there. But Gresham's enforced an honor code that demanded boys should not only abstain from swearing, smoking, and indecency but also confess if they broke the rules and turn in anyone else they suspected of doing so. Auden argues that such a system is bound to produce neurotics whose emotions are forced "backward"—that is, homosexuals (*EA*, 325). And in the later essay "How Not to Be a Genius"—a review of Connolly's account of his own experience at Eton in *Enemies of Promise*—Auden noted that "from the six percent [of the British population] who undergo this education, come most of England's rulers and writers. [. . .] The public-school boy comes away with a first-class political training, but one which he can only use in the interests of six percent of the nation, for that is all the nation he knows."[55] We might conclude, then, that England was governed between the wars by a small clique that was inordinately powerful, narrowly self-interested, and as Connolly said, "in the last analysis homosexual."[56]

Bozorth navigates between these conflicting readings of the status of male homosexuality in Auden's work by placing "The Liberal Fascist" alongside *The Orators* in order to argue that Auden's early poetry inscribes an awareness of both homosexuality's privilege *and* its marginality. Bozorth acknowledges that "the political implications of homosexuality in *The Orators* are themselves contradictory. Same-sex desire at once preserves the political order and makes the homosexual a criminal according to that order."[57] I suggest that the figure of the spy offers a way for Auden to represent, though not to resolve, both the ambiguous social position of the homosexual and the social, political, and psychological pressures operating on him. It is telling that the figure of the spy, his representation, his attributes, are very different from those of the petty criminal, the gangster, the armed rebel, or other icons of delinquent masculinity. The spy can look like, indeed can *be*, a gentleman. Thus, the inside/outside status of the spy is analogous to that of the ruling-class homosexual, who is thoroughly embedded in the very social regime that makes him a criminal.

1928–1935: THE RISE AND FALL OF THE SPY

I want to turn now to a closer examination of the uses of espionage in Auden's work of the late 1920s and the 1930s. Auden's preoccupation with espionage inscribes an epistemology of the closet that simultaneously camouflages its subject and reveals the mechanism of that camouflaging. This inquiry cannot be limited to an explication of the way illicit sexuality is signaled to readers "in the know" by the use of coded language, however tempting it is to imagine that homosexuality might prove to be a kind of critical magic decoder ring that could render all the obscurities of Auden's writing en clair. True, there are a few terms current not only among Auden and his coterie but also in period slang that refer to homosexuality and that, once recognized, make certain passages more coherent: "crooked," "backward," "left-handed." And it is helpful to learn, from the keys that Auden wrote in friends' copies of his poems, that some of his verses refer to specific men with whom he or his friends were involved. But to assume that there is a transparently clear, "gay" text underneath the encoded and obscure language of Auden's early poetry is to misunderstand the relationship between sex and text. Rather than being arcane indices of an occulted sexuality that constitutes the real meaning of the texts, the metaphors of spies and frontiers, treason, alienation, and secret codes—even perhaps the difficult and semaphoric syntax of the poems—are instead articulations of the way sexuality itself signifies within a context of which secrecy is one, but not the only, determinant.

This is dramatically evident in the 1928 sonnet "Control of the passes," later titled "The Secret Agent," in which the figure of the spy makes his very first appearance in Auden's work. The poem opens on an authoritative note (the first word is, after all, "control") that emphasizes the perceptiveness of the "trained spy": "Control of the passes was, he saw, the key / To this new district" (*EA*, 25). But his acuity is immediately revealed to be futile, the assertiveness of the first line undermined by its conclusion in a question in the second line: "But who would get it?" For the spy, despite his training, has "walked into the trap"; now, solitary ("he often had / Reproached the night for a companion"), he anticipates punishment for a sexual consummation desired but never achieved: "They would shoot of course / Parting easily who were never joined." Even if the spy/lover has exceptional skill and acumen, there is no one to understand his insights, no one who will "get it," and the mere dream of sexual fulfilment is apparently enough to merit death by firing squad. The spy thus makes his entrance into Auden's œuvre under the sign of danger, frustration, loneliness, and violent death.

Spears has written of this poem that "the spy in enemy country symbolizes [...] the adolescent in the adult world, the intellectual among Philistines, perhaps the political radical in a bourgeois society—the alienated of all sorts."[58] Spears neglects the most obvious interpretation of the symbol, the spy as alienated lover—a reading fully authorized by the poem's own conclusion, with its image of the longed-for companion and the quotation, in the final line, from the Anglo-Saxon poem "Wulf and Eadwacer," which is about the unconsummated and illicit love of a heterosexual couple.[59] Furthermore, Bozorth has glossed the (homo)sexual connotations of the poem's diction—"passes," "seduced," "tricks"—to reach the persuasive conclusion that the poem "allegorizes cruising as espionage."[60] In other words, it illustrates the risks endemic to homosexual seduction in the 1920s, when mistaken identities and missed signals might lead to something much worse than loneliness and rejection—to imprisonment, for instance, or even to death.

This much was clear in the earliest drafts of the poem, which contained only ten lines and did not include the second quatrain.[61] These drafts strip the "story" of the poem to its essentials: the trapped spy, the nighttime loneliness, the anticipation of violence. In adding the second quatrain Auden introduced several significant new elements. First, by making the poem a sonnet he invites the reader to anticipate a thematic or tonal shift after the octave; now a full eight lines are devoted to building the sense of tension, frustration, and menace ("The bridges were unbuilt and trouble coming") that gives way to the melancholy reminiscences and resigned despair of the sestet, greatly heightening its emotional impact. Michael O'Neill and Gareth Reeves also suggest that the sonnet form creates a kind of false or covert identity for the poem itself since, "along with the assonance and consonance, it gives the mistaken impression that the poem rhymes," which contributes to the work's uncanny, off-kilter effect.[62]

In addition, in the new quatrain Auden introduces a "they," the spy's own side, who seem to have betrayed him or at least let him down: "They ignored his wires." This complicates the poem's narrative by making it unclear who is responsible for the spy's downfall—the "bogus guide"?

(And who sent the guide?) The recipients of the spy's wires, who ignored his crucial communiqués? An enemy? The spy himself? No longer a simple, if tragic, story of entrapment by the "other side," "Control of the passes" now opens onto the more complex and paranoid vision of the poems that followed it, in which anyone might turn out to be an enemy, including one's friends, or oneself. No matter how we decide to allocate guilt in this poem, it seems undeniable that "frustration has both 'internal' and 'external' sources [. . .]. This conjunction of psychic and social borders defines the closet, where social prohibition reinforces psychic inhibition, and vice versa."[63] From the outset, then, the spy functions in Auden's poetry to point to both external conflicts (whether these are conceived in terms of homophobic oppression or class warfare) and to the internal conflicts they engender and are engendered by. He certainly works as a figure for paranoia, bearing in mind that in Freud's analysis of Paul Schreber's memoirs, Freud attributed paranoia to the subject's attempt to negate homosexual desire.[64] But as the old joke goes, just because you're paranoid doesn't mean they're not out to get you, and so the spy can successfully be used to figure both the angst of the neurotic and the anxiety of the persecuted.

For seven or eight years after publishing "Control of the passes," Auden continued to litter his work with references to espionage, sometimes working out an extended allegory around the spy, sometimes—especially toward the end of this period—evoking the spy only in passing. Some have argued that over the years there was a transformation of the figure from an embodiment of psychological distress to one of political struggle, reflecting Auden's embrace of Communism in the early 1930s.[65] But this overstates the sharpness of Auden's shift from Freudianism to Marxism, which was less a real change in his ideology than a question of how he accented analyses that drew on both perspectives. My own readings suggest that the Freudian-Marxist synthesis—or, to put it more generally, the integration of materialist, political considerations with psychological concerns—was always central to Auden's views of homosexuality and the private-public tensions shaping it, and thus to his treatment of espionage.

When the spy makes a second appearance in Auden's work, in the "charade" *Paid on Both Sides*, the emphasis of the metaphor does shift somewhat toward psychomachia,[66] the internal psychic struggle, though it is a psychomachia synchronized with the family feud the play describes. That the spy and the psychological conflict he represents play an important if obscure role in *Paid* is indicated by the fact that he does not appear in Auden's first draft of the work, composed during the summer of 1928, which deals exclusively with the feud between the Nowers and the Shaws. This first version is also, interestingly, clearer in its syntax than the final draft that Auden sent to Faber in December of 1928; by then he had added the spy and the dream sequence in the center of the play and also rewritten or added numerous passages in the dense, elliptical language, inspired by Anglo-Saxon and Old Norse poetry, that MacNeice dubbed "telegraphese."

Both the introduction of the spy and the tortuous syntax point to something troubled and difficult of expression in the final, more "psychological," version of the piece. Certainly, it is significant that between composing the first draft and submitting the second for publication, Auden had moved to Berlin and met John Layard, an anthropologist and psychologist who introduced him to Homer Lane's theory that disease is invariably psychosomatic in origin. As the play begins John Nower has just been killed by the Shaws while on his way to visit "Layard." The play's premise, then, is that a quest for a cure of some kind has been violently suppressed, and its drama is no longer simply motivated by a social conflict, as in the first draft, but now poses larger questions about the possibilities for social and psychological healing, and the relationship between them.

The spy first appears in *Paid* as a "real" character, the older brother of Seth Shaw, who is apprehended by the Nowers and immediately shot (*EA*, 7). This scene is followed by a fantasy or dream sequence in which "The Spy" (played by the same actor) is put on trial by John Nower, shot again, and eventually revived by a doctor; the Spy and John Nower then plant a tree together (*EA*, 8–11). Critics agree that the spy from the Shaw family or the Spy of the dream, or both, represent a repressed aspect of John Nower's psyche, "a manifestation of unconscious forces—the 'Other' within himself—in conflict with his conscious ego."[67] The executions would then be a kind of psychic suicide and the dream resurrection of the Spy a metaphorical rebirth and self-healing: "Nower, that is, shoots himself, and is then reconciled to himself in a psychological resurrection ('The Spy gets up') heralding his awakening to his buried self."[68]

In his analysis of *Paid* Edward Callan reads backward from a line in *The Orators* (1931) that describes "perverted lovers" as those "who when the saving thought came shot it for a spy," a juxtaposition suggesting at least two possible conclusions (*EA*, 63).[69] First, the spy in *Paid* could represent a repressed homosexual impulse that might save Nower from the fatal cycle of violence if acknowledged. Alternatively, Nower himself might be a homosexual who could be saved from his perversion, *and* from the feud, by the thought of marrying Anne Shaw. Trying to decide between these possibilities is made more difficult by the ambiguity of another mysterious figure who appears during the dream sequence, the Man-Woman, described "as a prisoner of war" (*EA*, 9). The Man-Woman can certainly be taken as an emblem of the reconciliation of male and female, and thus as a foreshadowing of the marriage of John and Anne and the short-lived reconciliation it brings about between their families before John is assassinated by Seth Shaw. But knowing that while in Berlin Auden was reading the newly translated *Sodom and Gomorrah*, one is tempted to equate the Man-Woman with Proust's *homme-femme*, and even more specifically with Charlus. Auden jested that he fancied himself a modern-day Charlus, and in a letter to Spender he said that he himself was the Man-Woman.[70] In this case, it would not be the heterosexual love affair that has been kept a prisoner of war but the hermaphroditic homosexual man, and the play's impulse toward reconciliation would be enacted not through the attempted heterosexual marriage of John and Anne but through the symbolic homosexual union of John with the Spy as they plant a tree together.

The second interpretation is given more weight by the fact that Seth Shaw kills John Nower, terminating the heterosexual marriage celebration, in revenge for the murder of his brother, the spy. If the spy does represent a homosexual desire that John has killed (while subconsciously wishing he could revive it, as indicated by his dream), then it makes sense that this attempt to suppress homosexuality directly provokes the violent disruption of a heterosexual marriage. Put simply, Auden's point might be that the conflict, both social and psychological, at the heart of the play cannot be resolved through heterosexual love because John Nower is really homosexual, will never happily marry a woman, and ought to come out of the closet instead. On the other hand, it also seems possible that the different conclusions to be drawn from the figures of the Spy and the Man-Woman do not merely seem contradictory but are genuinely so, and that the play is really "about" psychosexual ambivalence—a confusion reflected in its sometimes impenetrable syntactical obscurity.

In Auden's other long work from this early period, the brilliant and bizarre *The Orators*, there is no single spy, but there are a number of provocative references to spies and spying. In the section called "The Initiates" Auden, following Dante, divides the diseased into excessive lovers, defective lovers, and perverted lovers; we saw above that those in the last category "are they who, when the saving thought came shot it for a spy" (*EA*, 63). Though his taxonomy is based on the *Commedia*, Auden's analysis of the perverted lovers owes more to nineteenth-century sexology, Freud, and Layard than it does to Dante, and so it is unclear—as it was in *Paid*—whether his perverted lovers are equivalent to Dante's sodomites, rejecting the saving thought that could restore them to sexual normalcy or if, on the contrary, they are unhealthily repressed homosexuals who reject the idea that they should embrace "life" and their own sexual desires.

Later in *The Orators*, in "Journal of an Airman," "spying" is equated with "introspection" and appears to be a quality of "The Enemy," who may or may not be a Fascist. Introspection abuts narcissism, and thus homosexuality, in Auden's thought, suggesting that the Enemy is homosexual. In addition, as Bozorth points out, in the visual "test" preceding the lines about introspection, which presents us with a choice of geometric shapes, we are cautioned that those who select the symmetrical drawing are our friends, whereas anyone who prefers the oblique, crooked (queer?) diagram should be shot "at once."[71] That would seem to put homosexuality in the camp of the enemies and the diseased, except for the obvious problem that our "protagonist," the Airman, is homosexual, too. So while it is clear overall that espionage in this text is a psychological phenomenon, that the frontiers the spy is crossing are boundaries between different psychic realms, and that the danger to the spy comes from the irreconcilability of some aspects of the personality with others, the route out of this impasse—whether psychological or, ultimately, political—is not clearly marked. As in *Paid*, the spy ends up reading as a symbol of the agon associated with homosexuality, without indicating how that struggle can or ought to be resolved.

A slightly later poem, "The earth turns over, our side feels the cold" (1933) reiterates the association of espionage with both social pressures and psychic discord. This poem describes a Christmas visit home where the speaker finds himself torn between family and his absent, implicitly male, lover, "The one an aunt refers to as a friend." The family home is a false mirror world—Auden later titled the poem "Through the Looking-Glass"—in which the parents appear as "enormous comics" enacting surreal Lewis Carroll–esque scenes. But the world his lover inhabits, "Love's daytime kingdom which I say you rule," is also false, a totalitarian realm in which the lover is dictator or perhaps headmaster: "The total state where all must wear your badges" (*EA*, 145).

The comparison that Auden drew in "The Liberal Fascist" between a totalitarian state and a boy's school is critical to understanding the poem's reference to espionage. In that essay Auden argues that Gresham's honor code, with its requirement that students report on others who violate the code (for instance, by masturbating), created not only neurotics but, "much the more serious" consequence, young men with the mentality of informers, instruments of a (perfectly internalized) panopticon (*EA*, 325). So in "The earth turns over," when Auden describes "Love's daytime kingdom" by saying that there, "All lust [is] at once informed on and suppressed," he is invoking a disciplinary regime that works on homosexuals from the inside out. The speaker can experience desire but knows he is spied on, perhaps even by himself, and that his lust will instantly be "suppressed" by a power both political and psychological, external and internal.

Since in his parents' fantastically distorted mirror world his lover is not even "present as a character," it is clear that there is no legitimate space for homosexual desire on either side of the looking-glass. There is also no way the two sides can communicate honestly, for in love's world, "*family* affection" is "the one in cypher," implying that in the heterosexual world of the family it is homosexual affection that is in code (*EA*, 145; emphasis added). When Auden revised this poem, he added a line in which he describes himself caught "between these dreams, / Unable to choose either for a home,"[72] underlining the fundamental rootlessness and alienation of the homosexual. Only the poem's final stanza, with its lovely but entirely hypothetical vision of a "natural" and "untransfigured" world where he could bring his lover home to meet his parents, offers any hint of harmonious and integrated homosexual love—a homosexuality freed from the conspiracies, surveillance, and encodings of espionage.

In several other early 1930s lyrics spies make brief appearances. "Having abdicated with comparative ease" (1930) addresses a figure who has "Escaped in a submarine / With a false beard," assuring him that despite his disguise, "no one will take you for a spy" (*EA*, 45). In "A Happy New Year (To Gerald Heard)" (1932) we read an account of a bizarre dream that incorporates all the characteristic elements of the early work: a brooding sense of paranoid anxiety; an emphasis on secrecy; a flight from nameless enemies; secret police; battles between factions of schoolchildren, performing artists, and saxophone players; and finally, a strange companion who says, mysteriously, "I gave them lessons in deciphering codes, / I warned them of spies in acrostic odes" (*EA*, 450). Auden's 1935 play *The Dog Beneath the*

Skin, written in collaboration with Isherwood, also alludes once or twice to secret agents. But in these instances the spy seems to serve no particular function except to evoke a complex of images and ideas already activated by earlier work like "Control of the passes" and *Paid on Both Sides*, creating a recognizably Audenesque atmosphere: in short, it is an easy way of saying "Hey, look! This is an Auden poem." The rhetoric of covert operations is thus repurposed as a brand identity or marketing device.[73]

THE SPY'S DEMOTION

In these texts the figure of the spy seems to be, as it were, running out of steam; arguably, in fact, the trope was never again used with quite such eerie, unsettling force as it had been in "Control of the passes," and its later manifestations were all attempts, some successful and some not, to work out the connections that the earlier poem created between espionage, sexuality, and the conflicting private and public pressures operating on the homosexual subject. In my view, if the symbol became gradually etiolated and was then discarded, it was not necessarily because Auden had made it carry all the weight it could for his purposes but because his purposes had changed: by the mid-1930s he was already less worried about what it meant to be homosexual than about what it meant to be politically active, an artist, and, ultimately, a citizen, and the spy was a less potent metaphor for these concerns.

At the beginning of this chapter I referred to Auden's 1935 birthday poem for Isherwood, "August for the people," which marks a crucial transition in Auden's thinking about the spy. The spy's isolation begins to seem, here, a willfully chosen self-alienation more than the enforced isolation of the persecuted, and so in this poem "Auden tries to come clean about his and Isherwood's earlier arrogance in thinking they could stand apart from their society and adopt 'the spies' career.'"[74] "August for the people" was composed during a summer holiday trip with Isherwood, and in it Auden recalls a vacation they had taken together nine years previously, when they were, as he writes, "Half-boys"; Isherwood would have been about twenty-two at the time, Auden nineteen. They were naïve and overprivileged ("behind us only / The stuccoed suburb and expensive school"), and he characterizes their obsession with spying, disguises, and the intrigues of love as "false," a kind of excitingly illicit but artificial stimulant like cocaine:

> Our hopes were set still on the spies' career,
> Prizing the glasses and the old felt hat,
> And all the secrets we discovered were
> Extraordinary and false; for this one coughed
> And it was gasworks coke, and that one laughed
> And it was snow in bedrooms [...] (*EA*, 156)

As they face the growing crisis in European politics, however, Auden asserts the shortcomings of the refuges they once found in private humor, the erotic, and the aesthetic; the external world is now encroaching relentlessly on their boyish idyll ("Louder to-day the wireless roars"), demanding the more mature response of which, he says, only Isherwood's "strict and adult pen" is capable (*EA*, 157). Whether this is an accurate characterization of Isherwood's writing is debatable; it is true that in 1935 he was perfecting the limpid, flat, ostensibly objective prose style that he used to such great effect in *Mr Norris Changes Trains*, but of course that small masterpiece is a story of espionage, intrigue, and treason. Nevertheless, what is important for our purposes is that at this stage of his own development, Auden was beginning to manifest discontent with what had been one of his own most significant and recognizable tropes, feeling it an inadequate metaphor for the role of the contemporary artist.

Two years later, in the poem "Schoolchildren" (1937), Auden also seems to reassess his own earlier comparisons between public-school life and state politics, questioning the efficacy of schoolboys' posturing. He writes, about the schoolchildren of the poem's title, that "their conspiracies [are] / Weak like the vows of drunkards" (*EA*, 216) and asks in the end, "The improper word / Scribbled upon the fountain, is that all the rebellion? / The storm of tears shed in the corner, are these / The seeds of the new life?" (*EA*, 217). Humphrey Carpenter points out that Auden wrote this poem after returning from the civil war in Spain;[75] Auden never said very much about what he saw or did in Spain, but most critics have inferred that his experience there contributed to his growing doubts about how, and even whether, the artist could engage in politics.

In two of his last appearances in Auden's writing the spy is explicitly associated with the artist, and in both cases the tone in which the spy is invoked is comic, almost devoid of the haunted resonances it calls up in the earlier work. In "Poetry, Poets and Taste," a 1936 essay that was originally published for a mass audience by the Workers' Educational Association,

Auden describes the artist as "a mixture of spy and gossip, a cross between the slavey, with her eye glued to the keyhole of the hotel bedroom, and the wife of a minor canon; he is the little boy who comes into the drawing-room and says, 'I saw St. Peter in the hall' or 'I saw Aunt Emma in the bath without her wig'" (*EA*, 359). The spy has been demoted here from an icon of tormented masculinity caught in dramatic public conflict to a figure compared to a female servant, a petty bourgeoise, and a little boy, concerned only with local trivia and childish fancies. If there is a misogynist reflex in the association of the feminine with the insignificant, it is nonetheless interesting that Auden is analogizing *himself*, as an artist, to these female figures, suggesting a much less anxious relationship to his own masculinity than he had felt in the late 1920s. Additionally, there is nothing political about this figuration of the spy, and nothing particularly psychological either; if the spy in this case is a symbol of the artist, it is not the alienated, psychically conflicted, and politically radical homosexual artist speaking for a revolutionary generation but instead an artist modestly focused on the minutiae of ordinary domestic life.

Auden wrote the "Letter to Lord Byron" at about the same time as "Poetry, Poets and Taste," and in lines that I quoted earlier he again compares the artist to a secret agent. Describing the function of the poet in the contemporary age, he writes,

> To be a highbrow is the natural state:
> To have a special interest of one's own. [...]
> But to the artist this is quite forbidden:
> On this point he must differ from the crowd,
> And, like a secret agent, must keep hidden
> His passion for his shop. However proud,
> And rightly, of his trade, he's not allowed
> To etch his face with his professional creases,
> Or die from occupational diseases. (*EA*, 186)

I said before that these lines reflect a conception of the artist-as-spy as an alienated and romantic figure estranged from his natural audience under the material conditions of capitalism. And so they do, but humorously, and with a twist: the artist *is* different from his fellows, but the way in which he differs is that he is not allowed to behave as though he is different, to make a pose of being "A Poet." Auden came to disdain the notion of the suffering and exceptional artist, writing dismissively, in a 1959 review of Vincent Van Gogh's letters, about the nineteenth century's "myth of the Artist as Hero, the man who sacrifices his health and happiness to his art and in compensation claims exemption from all social responsibilities and norms of behavior."[76] In contrast, Auden urges modesty and discretion on the artist, and if the explicit import of his simile in "Letter" is still that contemporary artists need to work undercover, the thought seems to be motivated not by a sense of the perils they confront but by a growing distaste for the role into which he himself had been thrust in the 1930s—that of the poet as political guru, mouthpiece for a movement.

PERMANENT BUT LIVABLE EXILE:
FROM SPIES TO CITIZENS

Within three years of writing "Poetry, Poets and Taste" and the "Letter to Lord Byron," Auden left for America with Isherwood, or, as some people thought of it—including, perhaps, the writers themselves—they defected. The two were characterized by both the political Right and their own leftist friends as traitors, and they did not disagree; when Auden compared himself to Burgess, we remember, the comparison hinged on the equivalence between Burgess's defection and his own adoption of U.S. citizenship. But this was a peculiar form of treason, because for both Auden and Isherwood the ultimate goal of defecting was to be able to abandon the subterfuge of the spy and to become citizens in the fullest and most meaningful sense—not by the accident of birth but by deliberate, careful, conscious, and moral choice.

The two were not certain, at first, that they would stay in the States; a few months after they emigrated Isherwood wrote to E. M. Forster that they were both trying to find jobs, but that "that doesn't commit us to becoming American citizens. In fact, you have to have been on the quota two years before you can even make your first application. And, in the meantime, you can return to England if you wish. So nothing irrevocable has happened."[77] But both of them were—despite what their detractors in England claimed—concerned about how to contribute to the war effort as what they had always wanted to prove they could be: responsible adult male citizens. If only for bureaucratic reasons, this required making decisions about national affiliation. So just a few months later Isherwood wrote to Forster again that he was thinking of joining a U.S. ambulance corps, as "I

am half an American citizen, anyway."[78] And in December of that same year
I. A. Richards heard Auden give a lecture at Harvard that he opened "by saying how proud he was to speak to the 1st University in the country of which
he hoped to become, in a few years, a citizen."[79]

In 1939, of course, the United States had not yet joined World War II,
and the writers' interest in assisting the war effort is in one sense a measure
of the degree to which they were still English, concerned with a war being
fought by their "native" country. It took several more years for the two
to work their way through both British and American bureaucracies, trying to find something they could do. If anything illustrates the investment
they had in meeting the requirements of adult male citizenship, in fact, it
is the perseverance they showed in offering their services to uninterested
bureaucrats. Isherwood, who had become a committed pacifist, dutifully
registered as a conscientious objector and was eventually allowed to join a
Quaker group assisting German-speaking refugees. Early in the war Auden
went to the British embassy in New York to ask if he could be useful and was
told that he was not technically qualified for any of the positions needing
to be filled. Then he was called before an American draft board in 1942 but
was rejected for service after a psychiatric interview, because he was homosexual.[80] It was, writes one of his biographers, "humiliating to be excluded
because of his homosexuality. [...] He resented his categorisation as a deviant on a par with public exhibitionists."[81] When, in 1944, it appeared that
age limits might be lifted to increase available conscripts, Auden reflected
bitterly to Isherwood that even under the new conditions he would not be
considered for service: "I [...] suspect that in this extraordinary country,
they will set the halt, the maimed and the blind to work, before they touch
the morally unfit 4F's with a pair of tongs."[82]

Once Auden received U.S. citizenship in 1946 he exercised the pre-
rogatives of citizenship such as voting and serving on juries with great dili-
gence.[83] He was emphatic about his identification as an American citizen
and the political import of that position; Margaret Gardiner remembered
that during the Vietnam War, when she was trying to collect signatures on
a petition "urging an immediate end to Kissinger's long-drawn-out pro-
crastination over the signing of the Paris peace agreement, Wystan signed,
with a gloss in his covering letter to me, 'I can sign this because I am an
American.'"[84] Isherwood, too, quickly came to identify himself as, specifically, a Californian; in 1940, writing to John Lehmann about the changes he
was going through both spiritually and as an artist, he said he felt sure that

"there will be something to show for this exile. Or perhaps I shouldn't call it exile—for I love California. If a dozen people I know were here, I couldn't imagine a better home."[85]

The United States was no more hospitable toward queers (or leftists) than Britain, of course—quite the contrary—but then as Auden indicated to Robin Maugham, for him, and he imagined for Burgess, the point of leaving was not to find a more welcoming society but rather to "break away" from all the norms, expectations, and pressures of a society they were supposed to adhere to by birthright; not to trade in one nationalism for another but to revolt against the nation altogether. Auden and Isherwood, like Day Lewis, were more responsive to "flesh-and-blood human beings" than to collective nouns such as *nation* and *class* (which was one of the factors that eventually divided them from Marxist orthodoxy). They sought, therefore, after an ideal of loyalty and identification that was nonorganic, consciously chosen, and detached from history and tradition. Both men tried to reconceptualize "family" and "country," divorcing each from their institutional embodiments in the biological family, on the one hand, and the nation-state, on the other, and imagining each instead in terms of chosen communities of friends. (After all, in fleeing both his family of origin and the metaphorical English family, Auden nevertheless brought the most significant member of his own literary family, Isherwood, with him.)

"I am simply *delighted* that you're coming to America," Isherwood wrote to Spender in 1946, anticipating their reunion after a seven-year separation. "Oh, it'll be so nice, and I shall see my stepfatherland all over again through your eyes."[86] "Stepfatherland": the coinage signals Isherwood's belief that both families and nations can be dislocated from their origins and rearranged in new configurations, where filiation is not necessarily equivalent to blood relation. In fact, any organic or "natural" relationship to the nation precludes, in Isherwood's construction, a genuine apprehension of the nation's meaning, which is accessible only to natural*ized*—that is, artificially constructed—citizens. In another letter to Lehmann he wrote that "I love California more than ever, and I wouldn't wish any other permanent home. [...] I shouldn't like to have been born here. That would be different. You must arrive, with Europe inside you, to understand it properly."[87]

For Auden, too, citizenship—like Christianity—had to be something chosen in a deliberate leap of faith. He might be English, but he *became* American consciously and in the most literal sense artificially—creating his citizenship as an act of artifact making, like crafting a poem. Building on Auden's own claim in 1940 that life in the United States allowed him "to live deliberately without roots,"[88] Robert Caserio suggests that for him American citizenship entailed "not a state of inclusion, but a state of allegiance-on-the-move, a refugeeism. [...] The dignity of citizenship inheres in a concretely enacted state of being *between* or *among* nations, and not *in* or *of* one."[89] Auden combined, then, a punctilious observance of his responsibilities to the civic polity with a refusal to fetishize the state.

Bozorth reads two of Auden's major poems from the 1940s, the decade in which he became a U.S. citizen, in terms of "queer citizenship," arguing that in "For the Time Being" (1942) "Auden suggests that the homosexual should not be at home in the world," and that "In Praise of Limestone" (1948) represents "homosexuality less as arrested development—the inability to leave one's psychic home—than as permanent but livable exile."[90] Permanent, but livable, exile also seems like a way to construe Auden's relationship to the nation—never fully at home anywhere in the sense of being unreflectively patriotic, as Day Lewis defined patriotism: "my country, right or wrong." Rather, by virtue of accepting a permanent condition of alterity, Auden was able to make many homes (New York, Ischia, Oxford, Austria) and stand in loving yet critical relation to all of them. He began with that condition of alienation that had made him feel like a spy and ultimately transmuted it into a claim that the obligation of the alienated, the queer citizens, is to model civic duty for others, writing to his lover Chester Kallman in 1969 that

> We, Chester,
> and the choir we sort with have been assigned to
>   garrison stations.
>
> Whoever rules, our duty to the City
>   is loyal opposition. [...]
>
> Let us leave rebellions to the choleric
> who enjoy them: to serve as a paradigm
> now of what a plausible Future might be
>   is what we're here for.[91]

The vocabulary of war remains in place, but how different is the context from the earlier work so frequently derided as "immature." Now the homosexual has gained maturity in part by abandoning the closet, announcing his community with other homosexuals ("the choir we sort with"), and asserting their loyalty—albeit a critical loyalty—to the polis they defend from their position on the margins, their outlying garrison stations, instead of either rebelling against it or spying on it from within its walls.

I want to conclude this chapter with one other image of Auden's eventual, "adult," relationship to the nation-state. In 1945, with the fighting in the European theater coming to an end, he sent an excited letter to Isherwood, writing "Top Secret" in the left-hand margin. "Dearest Christopher," Auden began, "There is just a possibility that I may be going to Germany within the month as a bombing survey analyst with the rank of captain. [...] Actually I think it unlikely because though I have had all my anti-typhus-tetanus etc shots and got my passport renewed, I have now to be investigated by the F.B.I. and I shall be very surprised indeed if my Homintern-Comintern Axis affiliations don't sink me. But keep your fingers crossed for me."[92] The addendum "Top Secret" indicates that the letter itself forms part of the discourse of espionage between the two would-be secret agents, still acutely conscious that their "Homintern-Comintern" affiliations are likely to exclude them from the kind of participation in state power that men of their class and education might otherwise expect. And since the state espionage bureaucracy, infinitely more powerful than a lone spy, is bound to find out about their homosexuality and their radical politics, they cannot even be effectively undercover; instead Auden intimates that he will be associated with the Axis, the known state enemy, not the surreptitious conspirator.

But as it happened, Auden was wrong; his Homintern-Comintern-Axis affiliations did not sink him, and he went to Germany proudly wearing the uniform of a U.S. Army officer, even though technically he remained a British subject until the following year. His friend Lincoln Kirstein, in Germany on another mission, met with him there and later offered this portrait of the man who, as a teenager, had had his hopes set on the spies' career: "In the army, he behaved exactly as an off-beat intelligence officer is supposed to behave. I first fancied he cast himself as such in a token or symbolic rôle, to be played to the hilt. Soon, however, I realized that this was merely what I, myself, was doing—'acting-like' a soldier, or attempting to disguise myself, while always feeling like an amateur civilian. Wystan, on the other hand, exactly incorporated Intelligence—in a personification rather than an impersonation."[93]

The job offered, in fact, a perfect reconciliation of Auden's profound sense of alterity and oppositionality with his commitment to citizenship. He could use his proficient German and knowledge of Germany—the marker of the cosmopolitan and in the 1940s still, perhaps, faintly redolent of the homosexual—in the service of a legitimate national mission. He could fulfill the military duties from which he had formerly been excluded as a homosexual, thus finally passing "The Test" and demonstrating his right to participate as a mature man in the life of the nation, but he did so wearing the uniform of a country of which he was not actually a legal citizen. And he got to be an intelligence agent, embodying in his own person the figure he had so often deployed as a metaphor for alienation—yet he was acting, not as lone maverick or leader of an insurgency, but as an officer of the state. Queer citizenship, indeed.

5

THE GANELON TYPE

Homosexuals make natural secret agents and natural traitors.
—Countess Rosa Goldschmidt von Waldeck,
"Homosexual International"

You can't hardly separate homosexuals from subversives.
—Senator Kenneth Wherry

Four Englishmen are known with certainty to have been involved in the
Soviet spy ring recruited at Cambridge University in the early 1930s: Guy
Burgess and Donald Maclean, who defected to Moscow together in 1951;
H. A. R. "Kim" Philby, "the Third Man," who defected in 1963; and Anthony
Blunt, who was publicly denounced by Prime Minister Margaret Thatcher
in 1979 but, because of an immunity agreement secretly arranged in the
1960s, was never prosecuted. All four were double agents, working for British intelligence for varying periods of time while also spying for the Soviets.[a]
Numerous people have been named as "the Fifth Man" of this group, so that
the ring is often called "the Cambridge Five"; John Cairncross, Victor Rothschild, and Leo Long are those most frequently mentioned as potential
coconspirators. But over the years various deathbed confessions, posthumous accusations, and the fall of the Soviet Union and consequent opening
of new intelligence archives to scrutiny have made it clear that there may
have been scores of "Fifth Men"—and women—since many Cambridge
undergraduates were approached by Soviet recruiters and a fair number

a. Technically, they were spying for the Comintern, the international Communist organization; in the early days of the recruitment drive in England recruiters were often central
European rather than Russian, and they emphasized to prospective recruits that they would
be working for the international Communist cause, not for the Soviet Union. This was, of
course, merely a pretense, and by the late 1930s most operatives who were not hopelessly
naïve must have known that the information they supplied went directly to the NKVD or
another of the Russian intelligence groups.

of them passed at least some sensitive information to their contacts in the Soviet Union before going on to respectable careers and quiet lives. I will confine my discussion, then, to the four proven spies, and in particular to Guy Burgess and Anthony Blunt, the two who were most closely connected to members of the Auden group.

In addition to having publicly espoused Communist views as undergraduates, Blunt was known by most acquaintances to be homosexual and Burgess was overtly and outrageously so, in addition to being a heavy drinker. Donald Maclean seems to have been conflictedly bisexual, or perhaps simply a repressed, and alcoholic, homosexual. Yet despite the fact that by some accounts British intelligence was not particularly hospitable to sexual deviants, all three men managed to obtain sensitive diplomatic and intelligence jobs in government offices including MI5, MI6,[b] and the Foreign Office. Sir Vernon Kell, director of MI5 from 1909 until 1940, is supposed to have run the intelligence agency as what he considered a gentlemen's club, excluding homosexuals: "He was a decent, honest man, though he had strong, obstinate prejudices. His officers had to be of good character—which ruled out men who had not been to public school, homosexuals and Catholics. Homosexuals, Kell thought, were disgusting and unreliable and Catholics were habitual intriguers with loyalties that extended beyond Britain."[1]

But while public school credentials and formal religious affiliation could be checked, sexual tastes were harder to verify, and so before the war, despite Kell's prejudices, quite a number of homosexuals were undoubtedly employed in intelligence work. Investigative journalist Andrew Boyle, like many others who have written about the Burgess-Maclean scandal, indignantly blames a class-based old-boy network for the fact that in 1938, the Eton- and Cambridge-educated Guy Burgess was given a job doing propaganda for the War Office without either his homosexuality (he had already been brought up once on morals charges) or his previous Communist Party affiliation ever coming up: "Trust, the right academic and social

b. Very roughly speaking, MI5 (the "Security Service") corresponds to the FBI in the United States, and MI6 (the "Secret Intelligence Service") to the CIA, charged respectively with internal and external security matters. Both organizations have numerous branches, whose names and responsibilities have changed over the years. Scotland Yard's Special Branch handles important security and counterterrorism functions as well. Since the distinctions and conflicts between these groups are not usually relevant to this discussion, I will refer to all of these operations collectively as "British intelligence."

background, and evidence of clubbability and good fellowship were criteria enough; so Burgess was enrolled without questioning."[2]

The Soviets may have actively sought sexually deviant recruits—not, as many have assumed, because they could be easily blackmailed, but on the contrary, because the Soviets believed their homosexuality would open so many doors to them among British elites. Soviet administrator Alexander Orlov supposedly wanted Burgess recruited specifically for this reason, since—believing that "the majority of [England's] most polished sons are pederasts"—Orlov thought Burgess would be useful as "'a cultural pederast' who could exploit 'the mysterious laws of sex in this country.'"[3] However dubious this theory, it appears that in one way the Soviets were right to think that homosexuality might be an asset in a spy, because, as it had in the Dreyfus Affair, sexuality could work to sow confusion about the causes of deception and illicit behavior. In the case of the Cambridge spies, certainly, homosexuality seems at times to have constituted a convenient smokescreen for espionage.

For example, Boyle suggests that when Donald Maclean went out for unexplained assignations at night, his wife, Melinda, worried that the men he met were his lovers,[4] but it seems at least equally likely that they were NKVD agents. And Guy Burgess relied on his legendary flamboyance to divert any suspicion that he could be involved in something so serious as treason; as one writer has noted, "his flaunted indiscretions were, indeed, part of his cover."[5] In a kind of "purloined letter" approach to espionage, Burgess announced from time to time that he was working for the Comintern, blithely spilled confidential information, and on one occasion interrupted a luncheon to put secret documents in an NKVD drop box in full view of his companions, who—reminding us of the fungibility of sexuality and spying in the secret dossier on Dreyfus—assumed he was leaving a note for a boyfriend.[6] Burgess being Burgess, no one ever paid attention. It is difficult to imagine a better alibi, and indeed, in 1955 Foreign Secretary Harold Macmillan admitted as much when he told the House of Commons that "until the day of [Burgess's] disappearance, there were no grounds for suspecting that he was working against the security of the State. He had been indiscreet, but then indiscretion is not generally the characteristic of a secret agent."[7]

THE KEY TO THE SCANDAL

As the spies were discovered over the years, their sexuality became a focal point for explanations of their treachery, no longer a smokescreen for espionage but rather, now, assumed to be its proximate cause. In June 1951, almost as soon as the story broke that Burgess and Maclean had disappeared, some newspapers raised the spectre of rampant sexual perversion in the Foreign Office and hinted that the two men had run away to have an affair. The charges were taken seriously enough that the newly appointed foreign secretary, Herbert Morrison, was obliged to address them in the House of Commons. Intelligence agencies on both sides of the Atlantic made careful note of the press reports and also pursued the matter in their researches; indeed, the majority of the documents in the files of both British intelligence and the FBI describe the two men as homosexual, at times reiterating the point four or five times in as many pages.

Sometimes the FBI, echoing the British and U.S. media, offered the homosexuality of the "missing diplomats" as an explanation for their disappearance: one FBI teletype sent in June 1951, just after they vanished, refers to press reports "that both Maclean and Burgess were 'pansies' and were probably out together on an affair."[8] More sensationally, a memo sent later in June by FBI associate director Clyde Tolson reported an informant's claim that Maclean had belonged to a ring of cross-dressing, homosexual "dope addicts" and that he had now fled with Burgess to Buenos Aires, dressed in women's clothes.[9] Usually, however, information about the men's sexual habits is offered without commentary; a memo FBI director J. Edgar Hoover sent to the director of the CIA about the case states simply, "We intend to give you in more detail at a later date the developments in the investigation regarding these two individuals. [. . .] It is believed that you will be interested in the fact that both individuals are reported to have been homosexuals."[10] By 1951 the thesis that homosexuals constituted a security risk was already well established in the United States, and American intelligence personnel investigating the diplomats' disappearance hardly needed to belabor the point in their interdepartmental communications.

The British government was more reticent about the issue, at least publicly, which frustrated both the British media and the Americans. In September 1955, when a Soviet defector finally confirmed that Burgess and Maclean had fled to Moscow four years earlier, Whitehall belatedly issued a white paper about the pair to try to account for the breaches in intelligence their defection had revealed but did not comment on their sexual proclivities. British newspapers loudly criticized the report's omissions, the *Sunday Pictorial* particularly complaining that "this sordid secret of homosexuality—*which is one of the keys to the whole scandal* of the

Missing Diplomats—is ignored by the Government White Paper" (empha-sis added).[11] The belief that homosexuality was an essential and perhaps even sufficient cause, not only of the Burgess-Maclean scandal, but of trea-son more generally, was then given renewed impetus in 1962 by the convic-tion for espionage of John Vassall, a homosexual naval attaché working at the British embassy in Moscow who had been blackmailed into spying for the Soviets.

In 1979 the speculation that homosexuality had in some way caused the Cambridge spies' Communism, and consequently their treachery, intensi-fied again when Andrew Boyle precipitated Anthony Blunt's exposure by publishing *The Climate of Treason*, his book about the other three spies. (Boyle did not name the "Fourth Man" in the group but provided so many clues that others immediately identified him as Blunt, a well-respected art historian with close ties to the royal family.) Describing Burgess's ardent relationship with a boy called David Hedley while both were at Eton, Boyle writes, "Hedley, under his bosom friend's influence, became a homosexual and remained a passionate Communist until his early death."[12] We note the verbal slippage here from homosexuality to Communism ("*became* homo-sexual and *remained* Communist") and additionally, the fact that Boyle assumes that both are, equally, something to which one can be inclined by another person's influence—into which one can, in other words, be recruited. When Thatcher denounced Blunt in Parliament less than two weeks after Boyle's book was published, the press reports of the scandal relentlessly reiterated both the theme of political and sexual recruitment and the idea that Communism and sexual deviance are mutually constitu-tive aberrations that dispose men to treachery. The press quoted former acquaintances and colleagues who underlined Blunt's homosexuality and questionable virility and their propinquity to his Communism and acts of treason, describing him as a "pansy aesthete," "a hopeless officer [in World War II]" and a "treacherous Communist poof."[13]

In addition, investigators publicly speculated about whether Blunt had seduced Burgess into homosexuality and treason, or vice versa. (In fact, there is no good evidence that the two friends were ever sexually involved, nor is it known who recruited whom.) Blunt gave a press conference a few days after Thatcher's speech to try to account for his actions, and the inter-viewer brought the issue up again, asking whether he had been lovers with Burgess in the early 1930s. When Blunt answered, "No, absolutely not," the interviewer asked with obvious scepticism, "So what *was* the leverage, then, that made you join as a Russian spy? Was it not homosexuality?" The word "leverage" might seem to suggest that the interviewer was hinting at blackmail, but nothing else in the exchange indicates this; rather, "homosexuality" is simply left vaguely implicated as something that somehow makes people become Russian spies.[14]

In 1985 Barrie Penrose and Simon Freeman interviewed Dick White, who had headed MI5 in the 1950s and then later directed MI6. White continued to argue that the key to understanding the Cambridge spies was "the homosexual subculture,"[15] and in particular its sexual promiscuity, incarnate in Guy Burgess, with whom he persisted in believing Blunt had been in love. "It had always been evident to me that Blunt was under the influence of Burgess," White told the two journalists. "I could not understand why he was besotted by Burgess. But I had no idea at the time about the gay scene and its incredible promiscuity."[16]

Donald Maclean's former colleague and friend, David Cecil, devotes several passages of his 1988 biography of Maclean to expressions of regret that neither he nor anyone else realized earlier that Maclean's sexual proclivities were indicators of his unreliability, but he offers the excuse that it was only Maclean and Burgess's defection that had made the correlation between homosexuality and treason clear. A psychiatrist treating Maclean for a nervous breakdown in 1950 reported to his superiors that his symptoms were caused by "overwork, marital troubles and repressed homosexuality"; Cecil comments that "with hindsight one might perhaps suppose that a guarded mention of homosexual tendencies would have alerted the Personnel Department to the risk of employing such an officer on highly secret and responsible work. It would be unhistorical to think in this way: it was indeed the defection of Maclean and Burgess, followed by the prosecution in 1962 of John Vassall, the homosexual Admiralty clerk, that finally drove home the lesson that a deviation in one direction may indicate deviation in another."[17]

As when General Charles-Arthur Gonse claimed that Georges Picquart's alleged homosexuality "would explain the attitude of Picquart in the Dreyfus Case," most British commentators on the scandal, from the 1950s to the 1980s, seem to have felt that *treacherous*, *Communist*, and *poof* are self-evidently cognate. This belief was so widespread that in 1980 one author of a well-known book about the case felt the need to point out dryly that "contrary to the current public view, homosexuality is not an essential qualification for being a spy." He then reminds his readers that "Philby was always a womanizer,"[18] which raises the significant point that (in marked difference to the Dreyfus Affair) *heterosexual* irregularities did not appear to register in the case of the Cambridge spies. When Philby defected in 1963 the media could have commented on his philandering, but didn't. In the late nineteenth century in France, as we saw in chapter 2, the specific distinction between the abnormal and the merely naughty was of less interest than the way in which sexual indiscretions in general could usefully be attached to national or racial differences. Fifty-odd years later, in a culture that criminalized homosex and that in addition was saturated in both Freudian and Protestant conceptions of normative sexual behavior, only homosexual conduct was assumed to be relevant to the psychological and moral profile of the traitor.[c]

The focus on the deviant sexuality of three of the Cambridge spies, especially in the absence of any coherent explanation of the relationship between homosexuality and spying, clearly manifests a desire to find some marker of difference or exceptionality that could, if only ex post facto, help to identify a spy. Other Soviet agents had been uncovered in Great Britain since the war, notably the scientists Alan Nunn May, Klaus Fuchs, and Bruno Pontecorvo. But as an editorial in the *Observer* noted in 1955, the British response to these earlier cases was tepid in comparison to the reaction to the Burgess-Maclean defections, making it clear that what was manifested in the latter case was less a concern about actual security breaches than a fundamental anxiety about national cohesion: "Dr. Klaus Fuchs, the socially colourless *emigré*, was probably a far more valuable Soviet agent than Maclean or Burgess. How he escaped detection for so long provoked far less demand for inquiries. It seems to be the social, rather than the security, significance of such cases that excites."[19] Alan Nunn May, too, was socially undistinguished and a known Communist, and Pontecorvo, like Fuchs, was a foreigner, and Jewish to boot. It was ideologically unremarkable that they should be spies; their treachery could be accounted for by their marginality.

Burgess and Maclean, in contrast, were not only formal representatives but also figuratively representative of the nation-state they were

---

c. This is not to say, of course, that heterosexual scandal was uninteresting to the British public, which was enthralled by the Profumo Affair the same year that Philby defected. Even illicit heterosexual behaviors like adultery and prostitution were not, however, taken as a marker of someone's essentially treacherous nature, nor were adulterers and call girls assumed to be prone to treason as a group.

suspected of betraying. In 1952, before it was known with certainty what had happened to them, their old acquaintance Cyril Connolly wrote that "they are members of the governing class, of the high bureaucracy, the 'they' who rule the 'we' to whom refugees like Fuchs and Pontecorvo and humble figures like Nunn May belong. If traitors they be, then they are traitors to themselves."[20] More accurately, he might have said "traitors to our class," and to the political and economic interests with which that class is identified; reactions to the scandal reflect the fear that of all possible security threats to the state, the deadliest is the betrayal by its ruling class of its own interests. Confronted with the possibility that two members of the British establishment—native born, white, Protestant, upper middle class, and Cambridge educated—had committed treason, public reaction adapted the racial discourses circulating in Europe to a more psychologized characterization of sexual difference. The suggestion that homosexuals as a psychological or moral type are compulsively inclined to treachery works similarly to the argument that Jews are a race of traitors. Both theses seem to offer the reassurance that treachery is a behavior specific to identifiable groups of people and thus that those people can, with sufficient vigilance, be cordoned off—a proposition that was fundamental to the rhetoric and ideology of the Cold War, to which we will return later in this chapter.

CONTEMPORARY FICTION AND THE CAMBRIDGE SPIES

More sympathetic readings of the relationship between homosexuality and treason in the case of the Cambridge spies are also possible, readings that draw on tropes and themes disseminated by the Auden group to suggest that homosexuals might in fact be more disposed to treachery than others, not because of their innate unreliability or moral weakness, but as a response to a social and political climate that engaged them in an obligatory relationship to both duplicity and criminality. As we saw in the last chapter, the work of the Auden group during this period suggests that this relationship informed the way they, and probably the spies, understood themselves; unquestionably, it informs the way all of them have been understood by others, including British writers who have continued to be fascinated by the Cambridge spy ring. Indeed, the two most eloquent investigations of the impetus homosexuality might have given to the treason of the Cambridge spies are both works of fiction and so tell us nothing at all about the men's actual motives. They do, though, tell us a great deal about the way in which homosexuality has come, inescapably, to be overdetermined in all readings of the scandal, fictional and nonfictional.

Julian Mitchell's 1982 play *Another Country* and John Banville's 1997 novel *The Untouchable*, which fictionalize the lives of Guy Burgess and Anthony Blunt, respectively, illustrate distinctly post-Stonewall conceptions of the closet-as-oppression (in Mitchell's case) and the closet-as-pathology (in Banville's). In Mitchell's play a youthful "Guy Bennett" is caned, humiliated, and denied admission to Eton's elite "Pop" society, not because he practices buggery—most of his schoolmates do as well—but because he is too openly in love with another boy, James Harcourt, based on David Hedley. The shock of being excluded from privilege for the first time in his life, because he avows what the rest of his class practices furtively, drives Bennett to embrace the Communist views of his friend Tommy Judd, a character modeled on John Cornford, the young poet who was killed in the Spanish Civil War. The play does not follow Bennett/Burgess from Eton to Cambridge, so we are not shown his decision to become a spy, only its emotional genesis.

As a rationale for treason some critics found this theory inadequate; when the play was made into a movie in 1984, film critic David Denby reviewed it skeptically, saying that "surely a good many public-school homosexuals must have been double-crossed by friends and even unfairly caned without becoming Soviet agents."[21] Obviously, this is true, but Denby misses Mitchell's point: what he illustrates persuasively is that political rebellion *can* have its origin in the moment when someone whose identity has been defined by access to power first finds that power curtailed. Chantal Mouffe has described the kind of social antagonism that can arise when "subjects constructed on the basis of certain rights [. . .] find themselves in a position in which those rights are denied by some practices or discourses. At that point there is a negation of subjectivity or identification, which can be the basis for an antagonism."[22] Mitchell's play suggests, as does much of the early work of the Auden generation, that some ruling-class homosexual men like Burgess found themselves in this kind of antagonistic position in adolescence and became politicized when they found that the full range of entitlements to which they had been bred could be denied to them unless they kept their sexual desires and behaviors within oppressively restrictive bounds.

John Banville takes another approach in *The Untouchable*, intimating that rather than being swayed to Communism by homophobic oppression, his protagonist, Victor Maskell, uses his experience of being a double agent as the libidinal testing ground for his eventual explorations of homosex:

> When I began to go in search of men it was all already familiar to me: the covert, speculative glance, the underhand sign, the blank exchange of passwords, the hurried, hot unburdening—all, all familiar. Even the territory was the same, the public lavatories, the grim, suburban pubs, the garbage-strewn back-alleyways, and, in summer, the city's dreamy, tenderly green, innocent parks, whose clement air I sullied with my secret whisperings. Often, at pub closing time, I would find myself sidling up to some likely looking red-knuckled soldier or twitching, Crombie-coated traveling salesman in this or that George, or Coach, or Fox and Hounds, at the very same corner of the bar where earlier in the day I had stood with Oleg and passed to him a roll of film or a sheaf of what the Department supposed were top-secret documents.[23]

In Banville's reading, the causal relation between homosexuality and espionage on which commentators had insisted for decades is cleverly inverted; homosexuality does not necessarily lead to spying, he suggests, but spying can be a rehearsal for homosexuality. Thus Banville, like Mitchell, acknowledges the discursive relation between the two, without assuming that there is necessarily an ontological *correlation* between them.

LITERATURE AND POLITICS: THE OLYMPIC RINGS

If contemporary British writers continue to find fertile material in the stories of the Cambridge spies, this may be a measure of the degree to which the spies partook of—and in Blunt's case, contributed to—a literary and intellectual culture in which their lives intersected with those of now canonical writers. Far more than either Alfred Dreyfus or the Rosenbergs, the Cambridge spies were involved in the very intellectual circles that shaped the context within which their crimes would be understood; they form a part, if only a tangential part, of the literary tradition British writers today inherit.

In chapter 4 we saw that the Auden group writers took on the perspectives of the spy and the traitor as they inscribed their own vexed relationship to their nation and class in their work, during roughly the same years when the Cambridge spies were first recruited. The two groups were already biographically connected by that point and remained so both literally and imaginatively for decades. There has been a certain amount of contention about how well the writers and the spies actually knew one another; given the prestige of one group and the infamy of the other, it is unsurprising that whereas the biographers of the spies and the spies themselves have tended to emphasize the social and psychological background they shared with the writers, partisans of the writers are more apt to downplay the connection. Perhaps we can best visualize the traffic between the two groups in terms of the metaphor of the interlocking Olympic rings, an image provided by a figure who himself constitutes an interesting biographical link between the writers and the spies. A former chorus boy, Jacky Hewit had affairs with both Guy Burgess and Christopher Isherwood in the 1930s and remained friends with them long afterward. When Hewit was interviewed by Penrose and Freeman in the 1980s for their research on the Cambridge spies, he confirmed that what Dick White called the "gay scene" was a "freemasonry" epistemologically inaccessible to heterosexuals, but he revised the stereotype of "incredible promiscuity" by emphasizing that sexual relations were secondary to the intellectual stimulation and emotional support the freemasonry offered its members. Hewit warmly described the friends he had met through Burgess: "E.M. Forster, for instance, was very kind to me. You have to understand that the gay world then had style which it doesn't now. There was a sort of gay intellectual freemasonry which you know nothing about. It was like the five concentric [*sic*] circles in the Olympic emblem. One person in one circle knew one in another and that's how people met."[24] Incidentally, that a working-class man like Jacky Hewit should not only be lovers with men named Guy Francis de Moncy Burgess and Christopher William Bradshaw-Isherwood but also mingle socially with an E. M. Forster underscores the phenomenon of cross-class mixing within the freemasonry that Bismarck had deplored and Proust, arguably, celebrated. This *social* promiscuity, which was invariably read as sexual promiscuity whether sexual relations were involved or not, reinforced the perception that homosexuality and Communism were homologous assaults on the class structure, or, even more literally, that homosex was the means by which Communism accomplished its ideological agenda of social leveling.

The sexual connection of Burgess, Hewit, and Isherwood is only one of many points of intersection between the Cambridge spies and the Auden group. Certainly, it would be an exaggeration to suggest that the writers and all four of the spies formed part of a single intimate social set, and yet the world they inhabited—what one commentator on the Burgess-Maclean case called "that section of the London world where literature and politics converge"[25]—was in fact much smaller even than the comparatively closed loops that have long operated in the United States between the Ivy Leagues and Washington. (In the context of the present work it is an especially pleasing coincidence, suggesting just how closely connected the Anglo-European elites of the early twentieth century were, that Anthony Blunt's elder brother Wilfrid was secretary to the Comtesse de Greffuhle, on whom Proust modeled Mme de Guermantes.)

The spies and the writers attended the same preparatory and public schools, though not always at the same time, and Louis MacNeice and Anthony Blunt became close friends at Marlborough. Through their boyhood friendships the spies, who were all at Cambridge, and the poets, who were at Oxford, came to know one another during their university years and even once played hockey against each other, their teams captained by Blunt and Spender.[26] As adults they attended political events together and went to each other's weddings. Burgess read Auden devotedly, and Auden read Blunt's Marxist art criticism, finding that his own aesthetic views coincided with Blunt's.[27] Blunt was in the group that came to see Auden and Isherwood off when they emigrated to America in 1939, and he visited Auden and MacNeice on Ischia in the late 1940s, when Auden had taken a summer home on the Italian island. Burgess dined with Isherwood when the latter came to Britain in 1947, and visited Auden in New York in 1948. Most significantly, from the point of view of later events, Spender was one of the few people Burgess telephoned, twice, immediately before he defected in May 1951; according to the story Burgess would tell in later years he was desperately trying to reach Auden, then visiting from the States, in order to find out if he could hole up at Auden's house on Ischia after fleeing England rather than going on to the Soviet Union with Maclean.

If there were no bosom friendships uniting the two groups, then (with the exception of MacNeice and Blunt's), there were clearly warm and sustained relations among several of their members. Yet judging not only from their public statements but also from their private correspondence and diaries, none of the Auden group ever had the faintest idea that their friends were working as Soviet agents during this time. After Burgess and Maclean disappeared, however, the writers quickly found themselves implicated in the affair. The story of the two "missing diplomats" broke in the press within a fortnight, and the papers also picked up on the men's associations with Auden's circle. At the same time, the intelligence services on both sides of the Atlantic began trading information about Burgess's and Maclean's literary acquaintances, in some cases going so far as to wiretap their telephones.

Numerous internal memoranda, letters, and teletypes in the files of British intelligence and the FBI refer to Connolly, Auden, Isherwood, and Spender either by name or obliquely, often mentioning the last-minute phone calls Burgess made to Spender, identified as "the poet and former Communist."[28] MI5 and MI6 were most interested in the writers' Communist leanings but also duly noted that Isherwood, Auden, and Auden's wife, Erika Mann, were reported to be members of "a group of persons engaged in sexual perversion."[29] And the FBI files allude to the writers' homosexuality, as well as their Communist sympathies, nearly every time their names are mentioned. For instance, an internal FBI teletype dated June 10, 1951, summarizes an interview with a witness who reported that Burgess "boasted of friendship" with an "English poet" and an "English novelist, both probably homosexuals," presumably a reference to Auden and Isherwood.[d] It seems especially likely that Isherwood was the novelist named in that document, because another teletype shows that five days later the FBI interrogated him at his home in Santa Monica about his relationship to Burgess and grilled him about Burgess's homosexuality, though they apparently did not ask him directly about his own.[30] Auden, already in Italy by June, was questioned by Italian police, who swarmed over Ischia and briefly arrested a friend of his who they thought was Burgess.

In the course of that summer of 1951 Spender and Auden were also besieged by journalists who interviewed them repeatedly and printed their astonished reactions to the affair. For example, in a *Manchester Guardian* interview on June 11, Auden—described as "a fellow-member with the two missing men of the Institute of Contemporary Art in London"—acknowledged that Burgess had been a Communist but insisted it was "absolutely fantastic" to think that he had defected.[31] As the reference to the institute suggests, press accounts went out of their way to emphasize and sometimes exaggerate the closeness of the writers' connections to the presumed spies, wrongly claiming that Auden had been both at Gresham's

---

d. FBI, *Philby/MacLean/Burgess*, 1a:126. Most names in the FBI files have been redacted, but it is often possible to read traces of the lettering or to deduce the names from addresses and other identifying information.

when Maclean was there and at Cambridge with Burgess, for instance. Humphrey Carpenter writes that "the general impression created by the press during these weeks was that Auden, though professedly now out of sympathy with the Communist cause, had nevertheless been intimate with Burgess—who, it was later revealed, was homosexual—and had been privy to whatever plans Burgess had made."[32]

Contemporary accounts of the Cambridge spies have continued to flag their relationship to Auden. In a 1980 *New Yorker* article titled "The Cleric of Treason," George Steiner took exception to the apologies for Anthony Blunt then appearing in England, which tended to take the form of claiming that after all, pretty much everybody had been a Communist in the 1930s. Summarizing this viewpoint in the rhetorical question "Why should an Auden depart in the odor of sanctity and a Blunt be hounded?" Steiner implies that perhaps Auden deserved hounding, too.[33] Biographies of the spies make much of their connections to Auden, and in addition, the biographers themselves often rely discursively on Auden to recreate the atmosphere of 1930s bohemia. David Cecil, for instance, opens his book on Maclean with an epigraph from Auden and Isherwood's play *The Ascent of F6* and litters the text itself with more Auden quotes, as if to stress the intellectual sympathy between his subject and the poet. In the 2003 BBC movie "The Cambridge Spies" the scriptwriters indicate the spies' horrified reaction to the bombing of Guernica in a scene where Burgess, Blunt, and Philby listen to Jacky Hewit reciting Auden's "Epitaph on a Tyrant." Clearly, the poem was used because it functions both to establish the characters' sensitivity and intellectual bona fides—even an audience that does not know the piece will grasp that these are the kind of men who turn to poetry at times of moral crisis—and, for those viewers who would recognize Auden and his affiliation with left-wing politics in the 1930s, to mark the spies not as aberrant exceptions but as typical products of what has been called the Age of Auden. More recently, when British intelligence released previously classified files on Auden in the spring of 2007, newspapers around the world seized on the Auden-Burgess connection, running dramatic headlines like "Poet WH Auden Suspect in Soviet Spy Ring."[34] In reality, the files are not especially incriminating and contain little information that was not already public, but the excitement with which the press greeted the story indicates the degree to which Auden remains reflexively tied to the Cambridge spies by a series of associations, sometimes quite romanticized, between aesthetes and intellectuals, homosexuality, a commitment to left-wing causes, and illicit conspiracy.

THE AMERICAN CONTEXT

That in the 1950s British and American political and intelligence organizations perceived the same connections (although they certainly did not romanticize them) is not particularly surprising. When David Cecil wrote that Britain's diplomatic service first learned from Burgess and Maclean to take notice of homosexual tendencies as indices of treachery, he overlooked the fact that associations between homosexuality and political unreliability were centuries old and in Britain had been revived and revised by the Auden group as recently as the 1930s. In the United States, furthermore, a clamorous political and cultural campaign identifying sexual deviance with Communism had roared into life in 1950—a campaign that in its more erudite expressions explicitly referred to both Auden and Proust for its conception of homosexuality. When Burgess and Maclean disappeared a year later they did not create the nexus of homosexuality, Communism, and treachery in the minds of the British and American publics but merely confirmed its existence.[e]

At this point I want to backtrack a few years to discuss the political climate in the United States in the period just before Burgess and Maclean defected. It is not my intention to rehearse the entire history of the countersubversive witch hunts targeting homosexuals and political radicals in the 1950s, episodes that have been exhaustively documented by others. But as I turn here and in the following chapter from Europe to the United States, it is important to look a little more closely at this crucial midcentury juncture that serves, in a sense, as a switch point both in history and in my own project: a moment when the Western political and cultural landscape was transformed as power was definitively transferred from Great Britain to the United States, and American political and cultural views began to hold global sway. The rest of this book will focus on the reiteration, adoption, and transformation of Anglo-European discourses about homosexuals and

e. The case does seem to have reinvigorated a crusade that was already underway; just a month after Burgess and Maclean fled, U.S. newspapers reported that purges at the State Department had been renewed: "In the background of the State Department's re-examination of 500 members of its staff from top to bottom, including the suspension of several career diplomats pending security hearings, was the mysterious disappearance of the two British diplomats. [...] The State Department [...] is taking precautions, lest the same thing happen to the American diplomatic service" (Pearson, "Here Wilson" B13).

Jews in an American context; the 1950s represent a watershed moment in the process of that discursive translation.

What has become known as the Lavender Scare, when thousands of Americans accused of sexual and gender deviance were fired or forced to resign from their government jobs, had begun stirring soon after the end of the war, around 1947—the year President Truman also set up the Employee Loyalty Review Board, and when the new U.S. policy toward Soviet Communism was first defined as "containment," signalling the increasing importance to national affairs of strategies for dealing with internal and external Communism. In June 1947 the Senate Appropriations Committee presented a memorandum to Secretary of State George Marshall warning that his undersecretary, Dean Acheson, was protecting Communists, Soviet spies, and homosexuals working in the State Department, the American equivalent of the Foreign Office that employed Burgess and Maclean.[35] Homosexuals are described in this memo as "security risks," a designation that distinguished them, theoretically, from "loyalty risks." A Communist supposedly constituted a loyalty risk on the basis of conduct; that is, it was alleged that Communists deliberately engaged in treacherous behavior. In contrast, security risks like homosexuals or alcoholics were believed dangerous because their abnormality made them prone, however inadvertently or unwillingly, to "divulge secret information, because they were either careless or coerced."[36]

In both practice and rhetoric the distinction between loyalty risks and security risks, Communists and homosexuals, was frequently blurred. In February 1950 Senator Joe McCarthy made the infamous speech in Wheeling, West Virginia, in which he claimed that two hundred and five State Department employees were Communists—and that two of them were homosexual, a point he made to illustrate his belief that "practically every active Communist is twisted mentally or physically in some way." From that point on, as David K. Johnson writes, the "Red Scare [. . .] had a tinge of lavender."[37] The chiefs of the D.C. Metropolitan Police's Vice Squad and Subversive Squad helped to reinforce this assumption when they testified in the spring of 1950 before a Senate subcommittee headed by ultraconservative Nebraska Republican Kenneth Wherry. Responding to a line of questioning about subversion, Chief James Hunter executed a neat pivot from "loyalty" to "security" risks, raising the question of homosexuals' loyalty as if by accident:

SENATOR WHERRY: You mentioned 1,000 [people] that you say are
dangerous. What was the word you used? Loyalty risk?
MR. HUNTER: They are bad security risks. That is right, sir.[38]

In a larger ideological sense Hunter's confusion of the two terms was
not accidental at all but instead revelatory of the strategic and rhetorical
logic underlying the 1950s witch hunts. First of all, practically speaking, the
state apparatuses already in place for investigating Communist activity
could easily be engaged to monitor and discipline sexual conduct. Journalist Max Lerner spoke to this point in a series of articles on the Lavender
Scare he published in the summer of 1950, writing that when the unprecedented problem arose of "hunting down [. . .] job-holders on a mass scale
for their private sexual life," the investigators modeled their tactics on
the treatment of political subversives: "As always with a new problem, the
impulse is to treat it with the same techniques with which familiar problems have been treated. Since the problem of the Reds in government was
tackled by Congressional inquiries, lists, dossiers, sleuthing, and rumors
the problem of homosexuals in government is being tackled by Congressional inquiries, lists, dossiers, sleuthing and rumors."[39] Historians have
shown that, among other groups that found these strategies useful, Republicans were able to deploy them especially effectively to undermine New
Deal institutions, policies, and politicians and, more generally, to begin to
position themselves as the party of the "common man," while depicting
Democrats as effete and treacherous elitists.[40]

The second reason for the persistent correlation of Communism and
homosexuality is that they provided such robust, coherent conceptual
models for understanding one another. John D'Emilio notes that "the
incorporation of gay women and men into the demonology of the McCarthy era required little effort. [. . .] The congruence of the stereotypical
communist and homosexual made scapegoating gay men and women a
simple matter."[41] Also, while Jewishness was rarely invoked explicitly in
these discussions, many of the ideologemes circulating in the discourses
of the Red and Lavender Scares are familiar features of anti-Semitic rhetoric, a point to which we will return in the next chapter. Homosexuals and
Communists, like Jews, were supposed to be concentrated in Los Angeles
and New York, where they controlled the culture industry; they were distinguished by the peculiarity, excessiveness, or exoticism of their speech;
they were psychologically stunted and physically pathological; they were

devious and surreptitiously manipulative; their gender was anomalous. In addition, as Robert D. Dean writes, "both [Communists and homosexuals] were closeted, secretive, conspiratorial, and the activities of each were proscribed by law. Both insidiously infiltrated government and society because those outside the group could not easily recognize either a communist or a homosexual by any set of 'outward characteristics or physical traits.' [. . .] Despite their ability to 'pass' in 'normal' society, each group had subtle and secret means of identifying their own members."[42] Consequently, just as charts and pamphlets on how to recognize a Jew had begun to circulate with the rise of political anti-Semitism at the end of the nineteenth century, the postwar period saw a surge of magazine articles with titles like "Ten Ways to Spot a Homosexual" (Levine) and "How to Spot a Communist" (Cherne).

Like Proust's comparisons of homosexuals and Jews, rhetorical links between homosexuals and Communists were produced through analogy, metaphor, the attribution of similar traits or functions to both, and ascriptions of causality. All of these devices are exploited in a little piece titled "Homosexual International," published early in 1952 by R. G. Waldeck and read in its entirety into the *Congressional Record* a few months later. Waldeck was German by birth and a member of the Austro-Hungarian aristocracy by marriage, and her article purveys European constructions of sexuality, citing long passages of Proust's "La race maudite" almost verbatim. Waldeck's central thesis is that homosexuals, "welded together by the identity of their forbidden desires, of their strange, sad needs, habits, dangers, not to mention their outrageously fatuous vocabulary [. . .] constitute a world-wide conspiracy against society."[43]

This Homosexual International shares the aims of the Communist International, as Waldeck explains, in its "rebellion" against bourgeois capitalism, in its "passion for intrigue for intrigue's sake," and finally, because of "the social promiscuity within the homosexual minority and the fusion it effects between upperclass and proletarian corruption" (Waldeck, "Homosexual International," 137). Victims of "arrested emotional development," homosexuals come to hate society and so collude with a Communist movement that seems to offer them both liberation and the possibility of revenge (ibid., 138–39). In turn, the international homosexual conspiracy benefits the Comintern in several ways: it "puts at her disposal a network which, superior to her own in scope and flexibility, is almost impenetrably obscure"; homosexuals "diffuse their particular brand of

moral and physical corruption through the media of entertainment," lay-
ing the groundwork for Communist conquest; and above all, male homosexuals constitute "natural secret agents" by virtue of their effeminacy,
their double lives as both men and women (ibid., 140). Homosexuals are
literally duplicitous, double-gendered; double agency is for them a status
as much as an activity. For a homosexual man, "spy" is less a job description
than an ontology.

Waldeck affirms that homosexual men are conspirators by nature
and that treason ensues from their "astonishing understanding" of and
for one another, which transcends all other social or national affiliations.
"The mysterious laws which rule this condemned portion of humanity
are more binding on its members than any national, spiritual, social loyalties," she claims, and then adds, in another passage lifted from Proust,
"What is the unifying force of race, of faith, of ideology as compared to
the unifying force of a vice which intimately links the press tycoon to the
beggar, the jailbird to the Ambassador, the General to the Pullman por-
ter?" (ibid., 137–39). Ever since the 1930s this "sinister, mysterious and
efficient International" has been "gnawing away at the very sinews of the
state" and now, given the stresses of the Cold War, constitutes an intolerable "peril" to the security not just of America but of the entire Western
world (ibid., 137–38).

In addition to the obvious influence of Proust, we observe that
Waldeck's historical examples are nearly all European: she refers to the
Eulenburg scandal, the case of Alfred Redl—a homosexual Austrian officer
who committed suicide in 1913 after he was caught selling military information to the Russians—and the disappearance of Burgess and Maclean,
whom she correctly assumes to be Soviet agents, although in 1952 that
was still unproven. Furthermore, the congresswoman who had Waldeck's
article read into the *Congressional Record*, Katharine St. George, was born in
England and educated in Europe, and she married an American descendant
of an Anglo-Irish aristocratic family. Both women were, then, European
by birth and attuned to a conservative European ethos, and they relied on
European history to help make their case that 1950s America now faced
the same threats that had, in their view, brought down the empires of the
Old World. "The Countess Waldeck knows the background in Germany
of this kind of vice in government," said Representative St. George when
introducing the piece during House debates. "Many people believe that the

infamous Eulenburg scandal dealt a death blow to the empire of the Hohenzollerns. Be that as it may, the dangers to our own country and our whole political structure from this kind of an international ring is [sic] dangerous in the extreme and not to be dismissed lightly."[44]

Homegrown American analyses typically depart from Waldeck's in two significant regards, indicative of the difference between the European context with which we have hitherto been dealing in this book and an American conceptual framework. First, they are generally much less concerned with homosexuality's social promiscuity, its assault on class distinctions. (Oddly, this was equally true of anti-Communism in America, which, as a putatively classless society itself, was less offended by the idea of eradicating class barriers per se than by the prospect of doing so through state-enforced economic restructuring.) And second, perhaps as a substitute for that explanation of the specific appeal of Communism to the homosexual, they are much more focussed than Waldeck on blackmail as the means by which homosexuals are pressured into espionage.

In the United States the contention that homosexuals were vulnerable to Communist blackmail was ubiquitous in government and media reports. Homosexuals were said to be liable to blackmail because they were less emotionally resistant than the sexually normal, because their speech was inherently excessive and indiscreet, or just because their lives would be wrecked if their homosexuality should be revealed. Even reactionary muckrakers Jack Lait and Lee Mortimer conceded that homosexuals might not be traitors by nature ("Fairies are no more disloyal than the normal," they wrote) but still asserted that they were less able to control their sexuality and its social ramifications than others: "Homosexuals are vulnerable, they can be blackmailed or influenced by sex more deeply than conventional citizens; they are far more intense about their love-life."[45] Nearly every government report on the subject of homosexuality, every expert interviewed, and every newspaper article alludes to the possibility of blackmail—and early on during the Lavender Scare the old legend of the Black Book was revived. No one knew of, or at any rate mentioned, the rumor's origin in Noel Pemberton-Billing's campaign against German-Jewish infiltration of Great Britain during World War I. Instead, in the new version of the story, the Nazis had compiled lists of homosexuals; these lists had supposedly been seized by the Soviets when Berlin surrendered in 1945, and Communists were now using the lists, again dubbed the "Black Book," to identify blackmail targets worldwide.[f]

If most U.S. commentators were less interested in class warfare than Waldeck and more preoccupied with blackmail, however, they agreed with her analysis in several other important regards, demonstrating strong consistencies between European and American discourses on sexuality. First, they shared her view of the conspiratorial social relations of homosexuals and Communists; three years before her piece was published Arthur Schlesinger Jr. had also drawn on Proust's description of the semiotic subterfuges homosexuals use to communicate in order to depict the social relations and peculiar idiom of covert Communists and fellow travellers: "A curious freemasonry exists among underground workers and sympathizers. They can identify each other (and be identified by their enemies) on casual meeting by the use of certain phrases, the names of certain friends, by certain enthusiasms and certain silences. It is reminiscent of nothing so much as the famous scene in Proust where the Baron de Charlus and the tailor Jupien suddenly recognize their common corruption."[46]

Like Waldeck, Americans also relied on the enduring trope of immaturity, or arrested development (now, in a Freudian age, blamed on childhood trauma or faulty parenting), to explain departures from political or sexual normativity. The Hoey Committee, a Senate subcommittee appointed in the summer of 1950 to investigate the employment of homosexuals in government, reported in its findings, "Psychiatric physicians generally agree that indulgence in sexually perverted practices indicates a personality which has failed to reach sexual maturity."[47] A year later the Congress's Joint Committee on Atomic Energy, in the report *Soviet Atomic Espionage*, delved into the "warped mentalities" of spies like Fuchs and Pontecorvo and commented on their "immature minds" before concluding that "it is evident that a lack of moral standards, combined with an overweening and childlike arrogance—all induced by exposure to Communist

---

f. While the Black Book was presumably an overheated fantasy, in view of the overwhelming prejudice against homosexuals it does not seem improbable that they really might have been vulnerable to blackmail intended to pressure them into revealing state secrets. Yet in the 1950s, with the Vassall case still a decade in the future, there was no proof that this had ever actually happened in either the United States or Great Britain. The unhappy Captain Redl was the sole example invoked to prove the point; that the incident had taken place in another country forty years earlier and that the Russian regime in question had been czarist rather than Communist was usually glossed over.

recruiting techniques during early manhood—characterizes the atomic spy."[48] Notice here the impulse to attribute Communism, like other personality defects, to formative influences during development, even though doing so requires extending the period of childhood impressionability all the way into "early manhood."

U.S. pundits shared Waldeck's concern that cadres of Communists and homosexuals—sometimes referred to as "colonies," after Proust—exercised covert and pernicious influence over the entertainment industry. In the late 1940s and early 1950s House Un-American Activities Committee (HUAC) investigations into Hollywood radicals were motivated by the fear that, in the words of Committee member John Rankin, "we have [Communists] in Hollywood spreading their poisonous propaganda through the moving pictures. We have them on the radio sending their poisonous propaganda into every home."[49] While HUAC fretted that Los Angeles–based Communists dominated film and radio, others, like "Alfred Towne" (a pseudonym for joint authors John Clellon Holmes and Jay Landesman), deplored the stranglehold a powerful homosexual coterie supposedly had on both Hollywood screenwriting and the New York publishing world.[50]

Towne warned that effete characters in film and other surreptitious manifestations of the covert homosexual presence in the media "resemble a kind of fifth column who sell dissension by refusing to name the cause for which they do so. [. . .] A gradual effeminization of artistic and sexual values [is] the foreseeable result."[51] According to Towne, the monopoly exercised by this "fifth column" implicitly accounts for the interpretive difficulties posed by modern literature, as all straightforward, virile writing is rejected by editors who prefer the allusive, ornamented, and effeminate because their own sex lives have trained them in the exegesis of encoded sign systems. The end result is that the "machinery of [artistic] success in the hands of people who by their nature cannot experience the single biggest emotion in life, not only assembles reputations like so many automobiles, it also alters values, until at the present moment the 'new taste' dominates the cultural scene."[52] Homosexuals thus become the medium for transforming the genuine and organic into the automated and artificial, reprising a common theme of the Kulturkampf that in a slightly earlier era had contrasted authentic, rooted national values with Jewish materialism and sterility. According to Towne, this "new taste" in literature is exemplified by Auden, "now living in New York" and "so fashionable that he has developed his own coterie within the coterie. [. . .] Widespread acceptance" of the values implicit in Auden's style, Towne concludes, "can only lead to a gradual corruption of all aspects of American culture."[53]

Finally, American commentators overlapped with Waldeck's more Eurocentric analysis in their view that homosexuality challenged gender distinctions and consequently posed an unconscionable threat to Americans' collective virility. A few countersubversives even continued to insist on the *physiological* femininity of the male homosexual, recalling not only nineteenth-century medical theories but the even older myth of Jewish male menstruation: Representative Arthur L. Miller, himself a physician, opined that "it is found that the cycle of these individuals' homosexual desires follow [*sic*] the cycle closely patterned to the menstrual period of women. There may be 3 or 4 days in each month that this homosexual's instincts break down and drive the individual into abnormal fields of sexual practice. It has been found that if the individual can be given large doses of sedatives and other treatments during this sensitive cycle, that he may escape performing acts of homosexuality."[54] In the same speech Miller informed his colleagues in the House that homosexuality "is practiced extensively among the Orientals," confirming that his deeply essentialist model owed more to nineteenth-century sexology than to more recent psychological theories. Among Miller's contemporaries it was more common to concentrate on gender-anomalous *behavior* as both cause and consequence of perversion. Lait and Mortimer, for instance, blame feminism, as well as the culture industry and Marxism, for promoting sex/gender deviance: "Under a matriarchy men grow soft and women masculine. The self-sufficient girl who doesn't want to become an incubator or 'kitchen slavie' for a man is a push-over for a predatory Lesbian. The shortage of men is an aggravating factor. Marxian teachings, the examples of women in high political and social places, and the propagandized knowledge that many of the movie set prefer it that way are contributory."[55]

NO ENTRY: THE PARADOX OF CONTAINMENT

This constellation of ideologemes, bolstered by rigid gender norms, helped to underwrite the conceptualization of the Cold War as a politico-sexual conflict between gendered bodies in which homosexual and Communist aggression against the American body politic were not merely analogous but a single phenomenon. Softening up a nation's men made the whole country vulnerable to sabotage. Discussing a United Press story about a "Communist blueprint for the destruction of Washington" that allegedly contained "detailed instructions for the bombing of key Government offices, destroying public utilities and poisoning the city's water supply," the *Washington Daily News* quoted Senator Wherry's explanation that Communists had used "homosexuals to pry out Government secrets" in forging their plans.[56] The ever-excitable Wherry also told Congress that the government needed to protect "the security of seaports and major cities against sabotage through conspiracy of subversives and moral perverts in Government establishments."[57]

The concern with seaports, as well as the countersubversives' focus on the Voice of America, overseas embassies, the Commerce Department, and above all the State Department as the loci of Communist/homosexual infiltration, suggests particular anxiety about points of contact and interchange between the American self and the foreign other that could jeopardize the integrity of the nation, closely identified with the bodies of its adult male citizens in Cold War rhetoric. And that rhetoric relied on a normative conception of the male body as absolutely impenetrable. The eightieth Congress passed a sweeping sodomy law for D.C., in recognition of "the dangerous spread of moral perversion in the Nation's Capital," that criminalized every possible form of sexual contact except penis-in-vagina intercourse and emphasized that "*any penetration, however slight, is sufficient to complete the crime* specified in this section" (emphasis added).[58] A similarly absolutist vision of the impermeable boundary between U.S. capitalism and Soviet Communism governed foreign policy and motivated an obsessive preoccupation with the places, people, and institutions charged with foreign trade and diplomacy.

It seems especially evident that the State Department—characterized as "the epicenter of conspiratorial subversion and perversion"[59]—must have been targeted for reasons other than an actual preponderance of homosexuals and Communists on its staff when we consider the fact that many more members of *other* branches of government were arrested on morals charges without initially precipitating witch hunts in those departments. In April 1950 J. Edgar Hoover sent one of Truman's assistants a list, culled from Vice Squad records, of people with important government positions who had been arrested for sexual offences. Dean notes that twenty-two people on the list of sixty-six were in the military, "far outnumbering any other federal agencies"—yet, as he points out, "right-wing attacks on homosexuals never mentioned the Defense Department as a haven for homosexuality, while the State and Commerce Departments (three names on Hoover's list) came under particular scrutiny."[60] Dean offers a compelling explanation of the regional and class antagonisms that fueled attacks on the eastern establishment at the State Department by western congressional isolationists. But in addition to these material factors, we ought also to consider the crucial metaphorical function that the State Department, like Commerce and the seaports, served within Cold War rhetoric.

Other critics have noted the dual valence of *containment*, explicitly meaning a policy of keeping Communism sequestered away from the United States, its allies, and its satellites, but also implying that the threat is always already inside, contained within national boundaries/bodies.[61] The psychological tension inherent in Cold War policy might be expressed by the conundrum "We are afraid of not containing the Russians; we are afraid of containing the Russians." And how would the Russians get inside us, if not through the orifices represented by the nation's points of contact with the foreign outside? In *Containment Culture* (1995) Alan Nadel observes that diplomat George Kennan's original formulation of the doctrine of containment figures Soviet power as "a source of essential fluids and Soviet aggression [as] a form of incontinence," and that "Kennan's rhetoric suggests that the fluid's fearful nature is its seminal quality."[62] Furthermore, Dean argues that "in its external imperial incarnation" Communism was "depicted as an implacable, expansionist, militarily threatening enemy," while in contrast, *domestic* Communism was represented as an infection, "a conspiratorial, protean invasion."[63] Placing these readings in relation to one another, we can ask whether the language of "expansion" and "implacability" does not denote the external menace as phallic and thus the source of a seminal fluid that, introduced into the (male/national) body, can only be understood by the homophobic imagination as disease, infection.

Certainly, Arthur Schlesinger's famously eroticized description of Communist infiltration as "these half-concealed exercises in penetration and manipulation" vividly evokes an image of a male Soviet aggressor with perverted, as well as subversive, intentions—especially given that it falls in a passage immediately preceding his citation of Proust.[64] But unlike the rampaging German sodomites whom Armand Dubarry denounced in *Les invertis*, Schlesinger's Communist apparently prefers to spend some time on foreplay.[g] Thus, reiterated concerns during the Cold War about homosexual "susceptibility" to persuasion, about the "moral weakness" of homosexuals and subversives and the "softness" of liberals, speak not just generally to a nationalist valorization of manly vigor but to the very specific horror provoked by the idea of male orifices open to and even welcoming the advance(s) of Communism. When a "Harvard professor" interviewed by Max Lerner explains that "it takes a virile man [. . .] to be able to meet Russian diplomacy today. It requires the kind of toughness that an effeminate man simply would not have,"[65] he tacitly assumes that men who would allow other men to enter their own bodies would not be able or even willing to maintain the corporeal impenetrability of the homeland. And right-wing columnist John O'Donnell of the *New York Daily News* used telling words when he claimed in 1950 that "the foreign policy of the U.S., even before World War II, was dominated by an all-powerful, supersecret, inner circle of highly-educated, socially high-placed sexual misfits, in the State Dept., all easy to blackmail, all susceptible to blandishments by homosexuals in foreign nations."[66] A powerful, hidden, sexualized inner circle yielding to homoerotic seductions: this image of the State-Department-as-sphincter portends the violation of the national body in quasi-pornographic terms. Isolationism, then, reveals itself not just as a theory about America's appropriate place in the world order but as a desperate desire to keep the nation intact, safe from penetration by foreign objects.[h]

CAN YOU SPOT A HOMOSEXUAL?

Informing all of these readings of the correspondences between homosexuals and Communists and the threats they posed to the Western world, implicitly or explicitly troubling every strategic plan for controlling the danger, is the same apprehension that dogged anti-Semites—that the Other

g. See K. A. Cuordileone's analysis of "eroticized imagery" in *Vital Center* (Cuordileone, *Manhood*, 18, 27–28).

h. The conjoined fears of Soviet phallic dominance and America's anal vulnerability obviously persisted after the 1950s. Consider Schlesinger's warning that "by the early '60s the Soviet Union . . . will have a superiority in the thrust of its missiles and in the penetration of outer space" or President Johnson's response to the suggestion that he ease up on bombing the Vietcong: "Oh yes, a bombing halt, I'll tell you what happens when there is a bombing halt. I halt and then Ho Chi Minh shoves his trucks right up my ass" (quoted in Dean, *Imperial Brotherhood*, 172, 239).

might not be distinguishable from the Same. This fear was exacerbated by the publication of the two Kinsey reports, which undermined normalizing schemata of sexual behaviors and identities; in particular, *Sexual Behavior in the Human Male* (1948) revealed that homosexual experiences and desires were apparently widespread among American men. Kinsey and other scientists further claimed that, in the words of the director of the National Institute of Mental Health when he testified before the Hoey Committee, "all available evidence indicates that homosexuality can be found in all parts of the country, both urban and rural, and in all walks of life,"[67] rebutting assumptions that homosexuals could be isolated in urban locales and stereotypical professions. Countersubversive conservatives, progressives, and homosexuals themselves all understood the challenge such scientific claims could pose to the rigid binarisms of Cold War discourses. Conservatives denounced Kinsey, saying that the studies "pave the way for people to believe in communism and to act like Communists."[68] Meanwhile, Guy Burgess fell on the report with glee, and Max Lerner wondered in his column how exactly—if "there is no simple division of men into homosexuals and heterosexuals, into 'perverts' (or 'inverts') and 'normal' men"—countersubversives were going to succeed in ferreting out "anywhere from four to thirty-seven per cent of the adult male population."[69]

Yet the implications of the Kinsey Report and other scientific findings were complex and did not always lend themselves clearly to one partisan political end. If Lerner could use Kinsey's data to argue that homosexuals were not a distinct class and that the witch hunts were therefore quixotic if not patently absurd, countersubversives could proclaim that the ubiquity and indistinguishability of homosexuals made them even more dangerous and draconian security measures even more necessary, as Robert J. Corber observes:

> One of the ways in which the discourses of national security tried to contain the impact of [Kinsey's] findings was by using them to justify the construction of homosexuality as a security risk. If gay men did not differ significantly from straight men and were to be found in every level of American society, then they could infiltrate the nation's cultural and political institutions and subvert them from within. [...] The possibility that gay men could escape detection by passing as straight linked them in the Cold War political imaginary to the Communists who were allegedly conspiring to overthrow the government.[70]

Corber claims that the security state actually emphasized homosexual invisibility, writing that "the Cold War era was marked by a project to make the gay male body *il*legible. [...] The discourses of national security exploited fears that there was no way to tell homosexuals apart from heterosexuals."[71] To attempt to render homosexuality illegible so as to exploit the (already existing) fear of its illegibility is a chicken-and-egg proposition to begin with. But in addition, we find materials produced during this period by both government and non-state entities that attempt to render homosexuality *legible*, asserting that it is possible to learn to identify the signs of deviant difference. How do we reconcile these apparently contradictory strategies?

In truth, the belief that homosexuals could not be identified and the insistence that they could, the fear of their ubiquity and the certainty that they could be quarantined, appear to be Janus-faced aspects of an escalating paranoia; the effort to contain difference is spurred by, precisely, the dread of containing difference. As anti-Semites had wavered between theories of gene and germ, imagining Jewishness to be both essential to specific bodies and contagious, countersubversives oscillated between characterizing homosexuality as an abnormal, freakish condition and condemning it as an all-too-common vice, expressing abhorrence of its foreignness while warning of its intolerable proximity. So it is not only during the same period but sometimes in the same sources that we find, for example, an emphasis on homosexuals' anomalous gender alongside an acknowledgment that homosexuals do not always violate gender boundaries. Even while claiming that "many [male homosexuals] aren't men," Lait and Mortimer caution their readers on the very next page of *U.S.A. Confidential* that stereotypes about homosexual effeminacy are misleading: "Any cop will tell you that among the fairies he arrests are tough young kids, college football players, truck-drivers and weather-bitten servicemen. [...] Many queers are married, fathers of families."[72] Government investigators asked references for job applicants, "Have you any reason to doubt his masculinity?"[73] and people turned their coworkers in for security screening because their mouths, hips, or gait did not seem to conform to gender norms.[74] Yet the Hoey Committee's report also admitted that "most authorities believe that sex deviation results from psychological rather than physical causes, and in many cases there are no outward characteristics or physical traits that are positive as identifying marks of sex perversion. Contrary to a common belief, all homosexual males do not have feminine mannerisms, nor do all female homosexuals display masculine characteristics in their dress or actions. The fact is that many male homosexuals are very masculine in their physical appearance and general demeanor, and many female homosexuals have every appearance of femininity in their outward behavior."[75]

Countersubversives also turned to sociology and linguistics for help in identifying homosexuals: a manual for security officers in the State Department published in 1952 devotes nine pages to the problem, instructing personnel that however difficult it might be to establish procedural rules "due to the lack of a well-established pattern of appearance, behavior, education, position, etc.," agents should still interview male job applicants in order to obtain information about their "hobbies, associates, means of diversion, places of amusement, etc.," and should take note of "any unusual traits of speech, appearance, or personality."[76] Even while security officers were being trained to discern the markers of profound social and behavioral difference, however, congressmen, journalists, and psychiatrists fretted that heterosexuals could be so easily converted to perversion that just "one homosexual can pollute a Government office," as the Hoey Committee warned[77]—and how could one keep track of a deviant population whose numbers were constantly expanding to include the until-very-recently normal?

The paradoxical quest to ascertain something while simultaneously emphasizing its resistance to verification produced fantasies of technological or scientific interventions that might carry irresistible probative weight. What had once been the province of phrenologists was now delegated to machines that could, it was imagined, chase difference from the surface of the body into its interior and even to its intangible manifestation in the sound waves of speech. During the Hoey Committee hearings Senator Margaret Chase Smith wondered if there were not a "quick test like an X-ray that discloses these things," conjuring an image of the homosexual body rendered literally as well as figuratively transparent.[78] Senator Karl Mundt was impressed by a medical professional's suggestion that homosexuals had a specific "vocabulary, which only they use," but became concerned when the witness insisted that "an individual can have all of those characteristics which you connect with homosexuality and not be homosexual at all." Mundt hoped, therefore, that a polygraph test would be more accurate than a human interviewer in distinguishing surface mannerisms from essential perversity; unfortunately for him, his skeptical medical witness rejected this suggestion.[79]

Failing technological miracles, congressional investigators relied heavily on the presumed expertise of medical and judicial professionals, hoping that the two fields would complement each other's efforts. The Hoey Committee advised that psychiatrists were most successful in identifying homosexuality "in those cases where information concerning the patient's life and activities has been made available to them as a result of collateral investigations."[80] Reading on, however, we discover that these "collateral investigations" relied largely on police arrest records, which identified, at most, only cross-dressers and men who engaged in public cruising (or who happened to be in the wrong place at the wrong time); they provided little information about women, or men who had sex in private. It is not clear, therefore, what value psychiatrists added to an already problematic investigative process. Furthermore, psychiatrists and other medical professionals had a regrettable tendency to dwell on the complexity and nuances of human sexuality, which was unhelpful to elected officials who wanted to be able to reassure their constituents that they were firmly in control of the security crisis. During the hearings Mundt complained that while "unanimous testimony from the security officers of the Government" described homosexuals as "the worst conceivable security risk," medical professionals said "there is no means of detecting them," and they constituted a large percentage of the population. In Mundt's view the obvious but unacceptable conclusion was that "we just are not going to have any security in this country."[81]

In the end, then, every instrument available for calibrating deviance was too precise or too crude—either leaving too many of the perverse unidentified or, at the other extreme, inculpating so many that the purges threatened to yield to indefinitely expanding mission creep.[i] The risks of that expansion may have been suggested to some when one of the medical witnesses for the Hoey Committee testified that a signal characteristic of latent homosexuals was their "extreme antagonism toward the homosexual or toward deviates of any kind," a description in which Mundt, at least, might well have recognized himself.[82]

---

i. This is in fact what happened when, in 1953, the new secretary of state John Foster Dulles began to extend the department's investigation of sexual subversives to heterosexual adulterers, leading liberal columnist Anthony Lewis to protest that unlike homosexuals, adulterers were not "likely to divulge government secrets" (quoted in Dean, *Imperial Brotherhood*, 118). Dulles's antiadultery campaign was not long lasting.

THE UNDETECTABLE VIRUS

In the contours of its progression and its built-in tendency toward escala-
tion, the consternation over homosexual invisibility obviously mirrored
anxiety about Communist invisibility, which in turn was exacerbated by the
fact that the United States' most fearsome enemy was defined by ideological rather than visible, racial difference from the majority of Americans in
the 1950s. Russians are white Europeans, after all, and Beria himself could
probably have walked down the street unnoticed in any American city. Yet
Cold War rhetoric in the United States relied on the premise that Communism was the moral, political, indeed existential antithesis of "the American way of life"—and how could something utterly different look exactly
the same? When *Look* magazine ran its story "How to Spot a Communist," it
rendered this disquieting paradox at the heart of the Red Scare graphically
by depicting cartoon Communists who are identical to non-Communists,
except that they are helpfully wearing black suits to demonstrate their difference from their white-suited opponents.[83] Real Communists, however,
were not color-coded.

Not only were Communists themselves visually unidentifiable, but
party affiliation did not overlap neatly with national loyalty or with actual
or potential treasonous behavior. There was, on the one hand, the question
of whether all Communists were potential traitors, as countersubversives
insisted; the existence of thousands of former Communist Party members
and sympathizers who never engaged in espionage or attempted to overthrow the U.S. government would suggest otherwise, but that is not the
sole issue at stake. For there were also, on the other hand, the genuine spies
whose connection to Communism had been erased or was only tenuous
to start with. Prospective Soviet agents were advised not to join the Communist Party, or to distance themselves from it if they had already joined
before being recruited as spies—to stop reading the *Daily Worker*, cease
going to meetings or rallies, and drop Communist friends. Some, like the
courier Harry Gold, seem never to have been close to the party or much
interested in Communist ideology. So not only did Communists look just
like non-Communists, but actual Soviet spies might not even be Communists at all.

The same situation obtained in Great Britain, with the added com-
plication that since the Communist Party was never banned there, as it
was in the United States, more law-abiding citizens retained their party

membership. Many Britons who were party members—probably the majority of them—were loyal subjects; indeed, it is not uncommon in this period in England to come across the phenomenon, so foreign to most of the rest of the world, of the committed Marxist who is also sentimentally devoted to the monarchy. Conversely, Burgess, Maclean, and Philby all went to considerable lengths to disavow their youthful Communism, even associating themselves with extreme right-wing movements as part of their cover. As Rebecca West remarked, "It is not formal membership or conviction which makes the spy and the traitor."[84]

This problem prompted both American and British commentators to argue that the advent of Communism, as a belief system rather than a formal political affiliation, entailed newly covert forms of treason distinct from the open radicalism of the 1920s and 1930s; that is, Communist traitors were now by definition double agents rather than rebels. It is unclear whether the claim that this was a new development is historically accurate, since an image of the duplicitous, conspiratorial Red had coexisted with the stereotype of the violent Bolshevik revolutionary since well before the Cold War. But it is important that it was widely *thought* to be true, or in other words, that by the 1950s the former characterization had largely superceded the latter in reference to the domestic Communist. In reaction to the Alger Hiss case Leslie Fiedler wrote that after the mid-1930s, "for the first time, a corps of Communists existed for whom 'treason,' in the sense of real deceit, was possible. These were not revolutionaries but Machiavellians, men with a double allegiance, making the best of two worlds."[85] And in England the *Daily Telegraph*, responding to the September 1955 white paper on Burgess and Maclean, bemoaned the fact that Communism made possible a new kind of treason, a corruption of affect so wholly internal—as "faith" or conscience is necessarily private—that it left no identifying external signs: "The problem is entirely different since the cold war started. Before, treason was a matter of corruption, or grievance, or mental instability. To-day the Marxist faith has proved capable of subverting men otherwise of upright character and balanced mind. How are they to be detected in time to save the country from them, and them from themselves?"[86] In the same month an article in the *Spectator*—specifically dismissing the fantasy that subversive difference might be technologically controlled—concluded grimly, "Communism is a virus that cannot be detected by any security microscope: screening will only tend to exclude those who have avowed themselves Communists—not, now the most dangerous strain."[87]

Communist traitors could not, then, be reliably identified even as Communists, much less as traitors. The hope that they might instead be identifiable as sex deviants was, in a sense, a fallback position. But as we have seen, homosexuality proved to be as difficult to find and verify as Communism, forcing the search for the indices of treachery to sweep in ever-broadening circles. Viewed in this light, the interest that intelligence agencies demonstrated in the sex lives and political interests of the Auden group in the wake of their diplomatic friends' disappearance seems neither wholly prurient nor simply paranoid. Clearly, the intelligence community was trying to establish a set of personality traits, behaviors, and cultural affiliations that could explain Burgess and Maclean's otherwise inexplicable actions and help to identify other weaknesses in the security systems of the Western nations. That is, they were trying to work out a usable system of what we now call profiling.

But it would be hard to argue that the attempt to develop an accurate profile of the traitor or potential traitor—whether based on his or her political affiliation, sexual desires, literary tastes, or physiological peculiarities—was successful, despite all the inquisitions and purges of the Red and Lavender Scares. That the effort would be futile was, like so much of Cold War politics, already foreseen in the literature of the 1930s, text predicting context once again. Alluding to Ganelon, the traitor in the *Chanson de Roland*, Graham Greene writes of the protagonist of his 1939 novel *The Confidential Agent*, "He had seen many people shot on both sides of the line for treachery: he knew you couldn't recognise them by their manners or faces: there was no Ganelon type."[88]

Yet for a nation to accept that world-weary pronouncement is nearly impossible, for it means that the danger of betrayal can never be averted, that there is no way of recognizing a traitor until after he has committed treason. And while some perceived threats to security are illusory—homosexuals no more conspired to poison America's water supply in 1950 than Jews really poisoned wells in the Middle Ages—not all of them are. For much of the twentieth century Soviet agents really were working to promote the military superiority of the Soviet Union and encourage the collapse of Western governments (as, of course, Western agents were doing inside the Soviet bloc). From the point of view of the British and American governments, and no doubt of most of their citizens as well, to suggest that there was no way to avoid occasionally placing such agents in positions of power, no means of detecting their treachery until after security had already been breached, was intolerable. There simply had to be a Ganelon type.

THE BURGESS-MACLEAN SCANDAL AND ANGLO-AMERICAN RELATIONS

Before turning in the next chapter to the Rosenbergs and then to Tony Kushner's response to McCarthyism in *Angels in America*, I want to take a last look back at the political consequences of Burgess and Maclean's defection in Britain and the United States. The scandal affected Anglo-American relations and the rise of new political formations in both countries that culminated in the simultaneous ascent to power of Margaret Thatcher and Ronald Reagan. By the early 1950s Americans had become incensed by what they considered lapses in British intelligence and security enforcement, especially after the disappearance of Burgess and Maclean, and U.S. officials encouraged the adoption of their own security protocols in Britain. In 1953 Scotland Yard sent one of its top officers to the United States for three months to consult with the FBI "about the strategy and methods of a homosexual purge,"[89] with the result that for the first time candidates for intelligence and government posts in Britain were subjected to vetting intended to screen out Communists and homosexuals. Additionally, in 1954 the Admiralty issued orders mandating that officers search sailors for physical evidence of homosexual activity, and the "War Office also introduced new regulations against homosexuality."[90]

Despite this intensified (if ineffective) security screening in Britain, U.S. politicians and the American press increasingly promulgated the view of Great Britain as a nation of effete, left-leaning, and unreliable pederasts, in marked contrast to the deference they had generally shown the British before World War II. Eisenhower's secretary of state John Foster Dulles saw Foreign Secretary Anthony Eden "as 'a weak sister' more to be scorned than trusted,"[91] an attitude that hardened when Eden, as prime minister, headed the government's bungled response to the Cambridge spy scandal with the white paper of 1955. During that episode J. Edgar Hoover was so irate about Britain's refusal to name Kim Philby as the Third Man that he took matters into his own hands and planted the story in U.S. newspapers, deeply embarrassing Foreign Secretary Harold Macmillan.[92] When Philby then actually defected in 1963, *Newsweek* wrote that "Americans are worried [. . .] about the treacle-footed way that the British Government—

whether Tory or Labor—moves on information supplied by its own or friendly agents, the sloppy handling of secrets by the British civil service, the chummy reluctance of one Harrovian or Etonian to doubt the integrity of any other Old Boy."[93] This article, which touches on the Profumo Affair and the case of John Vassall as well as Philby's defection, is illustrated with a cartoon in which a businessman, with a pencil moustache denoting his upper-crust Englishness, is saying to what appears to be a well-dressed woman in his office, "Look here old chap . . . have the Russians got some sort of secret hold over you?" Thus, even though of the three cases dealt with in the article only one involved homosexuality and none cross-dressing, British political scandal in general is implicitly associated with British effeminacy.

This view of the British both reflected and validated the transferal of global hegemony from Britain to the United States. The empire that had ruled the world now was seen by Americans as, at best, a rather hapless junior partner and at worst a dangerous liability. Conservative media in the United States argued strenuously against sharing sensitive information, especially information about nuclear weapons, with the British. British politicians and newspapers—with the exception of a few right-wing papers that bitterly agreed with the American assessment of Britain's failings and called for a domestic version of McCarthyism—responded with pointed criticism of America's own security lapses. Some commentators specu-lated that the Soviets had decided to acknowledge the Burgess-Maclean defections in 1955 purely in order to create this kind of tension in the Anglo-American alliance; even if this was not their goal, it was presumably, from the Soviet point of view, one happy consequence of the entire Cambridge espionage experiment.

ANTI-INTELLECTUALISM AND THE NEW RIGHT

The Burgess-Maclean affair also played a role in the evolution of a conser-vative populism in Great Britain and the United States and in the post-war ascendancy of previously excluded classes to political power. In Britain the 1950s and subsequent decades saw a gradual loosening of the iron grip that the Oxbridge-educated haute bourgeoisie had had on governance since the nineteenth century, a shift that came about in part because the spy scandal demonstrated to many on both Right and Left the unfitness of that class for leadership. In the attacks on the Cambridge spies and the government that

"*Look here old chap . . . have the Russians got some sort of secret hold over you?*"

FIGURE 5.1   Bill Tidy, *Look Here Old Chap*. Reproduced with permission of Punch Ltd. (www.punch.co.uk).

had apparently failed to pursue them—or, worse yet, actively protected them—working-class antipathy toward ruling elites merged with Tory antagonism to left-wing radicals. Newspapers everywhere on the political spectrum from the eminent *Sunday Times* to the socialist-backed *Daily Herald* joined the populist chorus, denouncing (in terms nearly identical to those used in America to disparage State Department diplomats) the intellectual, Eton-educated, aesthete cabal that allegedly controlled British foreign policy. As the *Daily Mirror* wrote in 1955, "The British Foreign Office—crammed with intellectuals, the Old School Tie brigade, long-haired experts and the people-who-know-the-best-people—have taken a mighty drop in the estimation of the very ordinary men and women of Britain who are armed with just a little bit of commonsense and caution."[94]

This recalibration of class politics culminated in Margaret Thatcher's emergence in the 1970s as the head of a transformed Conservative party identified more with the nonconformist petty bourgeoisie than with the aristocratic or upper-middle-class Anglican establishment. (Though

Oxford educated, Thatcher was, famously, the daughter of a grocer, and a devout Methodist.) When, immediately on the heels of her accession to power, she denounced Anthony Blunt in Parliament, the revived scandal became a cause célèbre for this "New Right," consolidating the various interests the Tories now represented in their hostility toward the intellectual elites:

> For the Right in Britain, invigorated by Mrs Thatcher's victory in the general election of May 1979, Blunt was the apotheosis of a particular species of privileged, ungrateful, over-educated, unpatriotic, left-wing intellectual—and homosexual to boot. He embodied the hypocrisy of a liberal class which gave thanks for its inherited freedoms by betraying them. The press harped on about the naturally lax, relativistic morals of intellectuals and their automatic assumption that they were better than anyone else; these were the obvious reasons for Blunt's misdeeds. [...] Blunt became defined as a caricature of his class (privileged, therefore overindulged), his calling (academic, therefore elitist and snobbish) and his sexual orientation (homosexual, therefore predatory and wedded to secrets).[95]

Mutatis mutandis, Blunt is also emblematic of the internal American enemy as imagined by McCarthyism, targeted by Goldwater conservatives, and resurrected during the culture wars of the Reagan years—an enemy comprising, in Richard Hofstadter's words, "'striped-pants diplomats,' Ivy League graduates, high-ranking generals, college presidents, intellectuals, the Eastern upper classes, Harvard professors, and members of Phi Beta Kappa."[96] Indeed, the anti-intellectual, conservative populism that was so successfully mobilized by McCarthy, and which has played a prominent role in U.S. politics ever since, closely resembles its British counterpart—with the obvious difference that in the American version of the phenomenon England and Englishness per se are themselves strongly implicated in the image of the elite object of contempt. Even pseudo-Englishness is suspect; one of the accusations frequently lobbed at Dean Acheson was that his patrician New England accent sounded British. In the 1954 essay "McCarthy and the Intellectuals" Leslie Fiedler identified the birth of a new kind of Republican Party populism that "opposed to the People the Intellectuals rather than 'the Economic Royalists,'"[97] demonstrating the way McCarthyite binarisms, while ultimately relying on class grievances, construct class identity in terms of a profoundly gendered sense of moral righteousness rather than economic interests:

> McCarthy discovered a symbolic butt in the State Department "Red," the "Park Avenue Pinko," capable of welding together the fractured Populist image of the Enemy. [. . .] With something like genius, McCarthy touched up the villain he had half-found, half-composed, adding the connotations of wealth and effete culture to treachery, and topping all off with the suggestion of homosexuality. McCarthy's constant sneering references to "State Department perverts" are not explained by his official contention that such unfortunates are subject to blackmail, but represent his sure sense of the only other unforgivable sin besides being a Communist. The definition of the Enemy is complete—opposite in all respects to the American Ideal, simple, straightforward, ungrammatical, loyal, and one-hundred-percent male. Such an Enemy need not be *proven* guilty; he is guilty by definition.[98]

As Fiedler noted, this caricature was (as it has continued to be) a singularly potent and effective means for Republicans to alienate voters from a Democratic Party otherwise more responsive to their economic concerns: "The Enemy for McCarthy is not only a dandy, a queer, an intellectual, and a Communist; he is (or was, at least, in the beginning) a Democrat or a Democrat's friend."[99] Thus, in the climate of the 1950s the Democratic presidential candidate would in all probability have been denounced as an egg-headed homosexual Communist sympathizer even if he had not been the urbane intellectual Adlai Stevenson, so relentlessly red- and lavender-baited throughout his unsuccessful contests against Eisenhower. True, since Stevenson's second defeat in 1956, Democrats have occasionally succeeded during national campaigns in representing their nominee as more down-to-earth, patriotic, and virile than the Republican candidate. But it is nonetheless equally true that the Democrats have been persistently dogged by the legacy of McCarthy's image of theirs as "the party of treason."

At the time that Fiedler published his essay in August of 1954, however, Senator McCarthy himself had recently ventured into the attack on the army that effectively ended his career, and he would be censured by his Senate colleagues just a few months later. The decline in his political fortunes is an object lesson not just in choosing your enemies carefully but also in the probable trajectory of a quest for traitors who are both believed to be ubiquitous and feared to be invisible. In the effort to establish a Ganelon type the McCarthyite inquisitions and purges had turned their attention from Communists to homosexuals, to intellectuals, to Democrats in general, and for a while to adulterers. And then they began to implicate Republicans. After Eisenhower took office McCarthy amended his war cry, "twenty years of treason"—with which he had indicted the administrations of Roosevelt and Truman—to "twenty-one years of treason."[100] Since the United States has only two major political parties, at that point it was no longer a doctrine, minority group, or party being called into question as the Other of national identity, as Hofstadter points out, but "the legitimacy of the political order itself."[101] The concept of treason relies on meaningful definitions of *them* and *us*, inside and outside, *ceux qui en sont* and *ceux qui n'en sont pas*. Once the definitions have become so expansive and imprecise that there is only an omnipresent and indistinct "them," the logic of the purge collapses. Before that happened to McCarthyism, though, the trial of Julius and Ethel Rosenberg had distilled all the hostilities and fears of the Cold War into one espionage scandal, creating lethally intense divisions across the nation and, in particular, among American Jews.

6

STRICTLY A JEWISH SHOW

Playwrights and movie script writers could do a lot with a case like this.

—Emanuel H. Bloch

Plays and legal trials are so closely related generically that the phrase *courtroom drama* might almost be said to be a redundancy. Courtroom trials offer many of the same features as an ensemble theater piece: a fixed cast of characters, some central and some minor; set pieces of oratory delivered by trained speakers; an audience; and a narrative arc that is supposed to end in dramatic resolution, with a verdict and sentencing. Trial transcripts read very much like scripts, with dialogue and limited stage directions, and demand a similar interpretive effort from readers who have only the written text to enable them to reconstruct the live performance. In addition, both public trials and theatrical productions are sites of communally produced, and communally contested, meanings in a way that other genres often are not; these are forms not simply capable of being publicly performed and interpreted but destined to be.

It is perhaps not surprising, then, that the highly publicized 1951 atomic espionage trial of Julius and Ethel Rosenberg, and their codefendants Morton Sobell and Ethel's brother David Greenglass, has spawned multiple filmic and theatrical reinterpretations of the case. The Rosenbergs' defense attorney Emanuel "Manny" Bloch seemed to anticipate as much when he said to the jurors: "You have been fortunate because you have seen unfolded before you one of the most moving dramas that any human being could concoct. You have seen a brother testify against his sister, in a case where her life might be at stake. You have seen issues dealing with the atomic bomb, the most terrible and destructive weapon yet invented by man. This case is packed with drama. Playwrights and movie script writers could do a lot with a case like this. You have been fortunate. You had a front seat."[1] Forty years later Tony Kushner would become the latest in that succession of "playwrights and movie script writers" when he made Roy Cohn, assistant U.S. attorney during the Rosenbergs' trial, a central character in *Angels in America* (1992–1994) and resurrected the ghost of Ethel Rosenberg to haunt him. Kushner also wrote the screenplay for the HBO movie of *Angels* that aired in 2003, reinterpreting his own material and the elements he took from the Rosenberg case yet again.[a]

Secrecy, deception, and concealed identities play a part in *Angels* and also, according to Kushner, helped spark his original interest in theater more generally. "I grew up very, very closeted, and I'm sure that the disguise of theatre, the doubleness, and all that slightly tawdry stuff interested me,"[2] he has said, suggesting the relationship of drama, as a creative way of leading a double life, to both homosexuality and espionage. But unlike Auden and Proust, Kushner does not seem drawn to spies and spying because he is particularly interested in the figure of the spy as a literary device or in the theme of espionage per se. *Angels* does not dwell on the particulars of the Rosenberg case; the play never even offers an opinion about whether Ethel Rosenberg was guilty of espionage. Instead, it is the questions of loyalty, betrayal, belonging, and identity raised by the affair and concretized in the characters of Roy and Ethel that make the case such crucial backstory for the confrontations Kushner stages among Jews and queers, conservatives and progressives, the living and the dead.

After revisiting and expanding on the previous chapter's discussion of Cold War rhetoric in order to illuminate the ways in which it both implicated Jewishness and loosened the ties binding Jews to Communism, I will look at the Rosenberg trial more closely, particularly as it is preserved in the transcript of the court proceedings. Given how much has been written about the Rosenbergs and the likelihood that readers will be familiar with their story, I spend less time on the case than on the other two espionage scandals investigated in this volume. It is nonetheless important for my study because of the way it highlights postwar struggles over the meaning of Jewish American identity. The conviction and eventual execution of a

---

a. My own analysis draws not only on the printed text of *Angels* (of which there have been two different editions) but also on the three very different productions of the play that I have seen and on the HBO movie, treating all of these experiences collectively as "the text."

Jewish couple for spying and the responses of other American Jews to the affair illuminate the limits of and tensions within any ideological position staked on a concept of group identity, the evolving relationship of minority groups to citizenship in the West, and the multiple, conflicting valences of the concept of loyalty. Tony Kushner picks up and restages these dramatic topoi in *Angels in America* as he tries to work through the fraught relations between identity and politics. In *Angels*, I will argue, Kushner uses the public, ritual, and communal space/event of the play to provide both a forum for and an example of the messy, ongoing processes of democracy and enfranchisement. He thus enables us to imagine renewed forms of queer, Jewish Being that resist and transcend the deception and secrecy historically attached to those identities.

SAVE YOUR HATE FOR WHAT COUNTS: COLD WAR ANTI-COMMUNISM

The Rosenberg affair and *Angels in America* can both be read as elements in a continuing dialogue about the nature of American Jewish identity and its relation to American politics. In order to approach that topic I will need to return to the postwar political landscape and to a point skirted in the previous chapter, namely, the comparative paucity of allusions to Jews or Jewishness in Cold War antihomosexual, anti-Communist discourses, whether British or American. Considering the prominence and power that narratives associating Jews with espionage, sexual deviance, and subversion had in earlier decades—indeed, centuries—the omission is striking. If the logic of those narratives had been sustained, the immediate postwar period should have been an exceptionally hazardous time for American Jewry. By the late 1940s many second- and third-generation Jews were assimilated enough to be indistinguishable from non-Jews, whereas the first Red Scare, after World War I, targeted radicals whose class or ethnic difference was often perceptible. Thus, we would expect assimilated American Jews in the postwar period to fulfill the role of double agents better than their parents had and to be more easily associated with the threatening invisibility of Communists and homosexuals.

Furthermore, after 1948 there was, for the first time, a Jewish nation-state to which Jews might reasonably be expected to be loyal, not just a hypothetical homeland to which they could be accused of belonging in an abstract sense. And as we witnessed in the exchange between Jacob

Blaustein and David Ben-Gurion cited in chapter 1, American Jews were indeed concerned that Israel's efforts to encourage Jewish immigration might raise doubts about their own patriotism. Finally, the postwar Communist spy scandals in Britain, Canada, and the United States actually did involve numerous Jews. Bruno Pontecorvo was Jewish, as were many of the Comintern agents in Britain who recruited, trained, or handled the Cambridge spies. Victor Rothschild, scion of the banking family, was friendly with Burgess and Blunt and suspected by some of being a member of their spy ring. A number of the Canadians named as Soviet agents by Russian defector Igor Gouzenko in 1945 were Jewish, as well as most of the scientists at Berkeley Radiation Laboratory investigated by HUAC in 1949.

And yet, while these facts were occasionally noted in the press, outside of far-Right realms of hysterical conspiracy theorizing they seem to have had far less purchase on the interest of the public, the media, or the governments involved than one would predict and certainly less than the issue of homosexuality. In an article on postwar anti-Communism and homophobia Barbara Epstein observes that when studying the 1950s American press she failed to find the anti-Semitism she had, implicitly, anticipated—and failed to find it not only in mainstream media outlets but even in scandal rags like *Whisper* and *Dare*: "Articles dealt with threats from many quarters: homosexuals, sex perverts and criminals, Communists, spies and foreign agents, dishonest politicians, corrupt trade union officials, blacks, Asians. In reading these magazines I was struck by the absence of anti-Semitism or of any mention of Jews."[3]

But Epstein also notes that Cold War rhetoric is framed in terms quite familiar from anti-Semitic discourses. As we saw in chapter 5, the anti-Communist and antihomosexual ideologies of the Cold War repeatedly line up terms historically identified with Jews, in a version of the kind of syzygy that Proust uses to teach his readers to associate Jews first with inverts, then with Germans, and so on, until by invoking any part of the constellation the writer can instantly recall all its other constituents. Secretive, conspiratorial, physically and psychically unhealthy, exotic, intellectual and well-educated, urban, individually weak but collectively powerful, alien, deviant and treacherous: this is the idiom of several centuries' worth of anti-Semitism, operating in the 1950s to "Jewify" Communists and homosexuals while largely ignoring, or even explicitly exempting, Jews themselves.

Indeed it seems, when we consider Cold War discourse, that the Red and Lavender Scares represent a kind of fossilized anti-Semitism, in which the original organic matter, Jews, has been replaced with a different sub-stance but the shape of the original preserved. Or perhaps a more accurate metaphor—since fossils are static whereas discourses change—would describe the ideological situation after World War II as a relay race in which the Communist functions as a transitional figure passing the baton from the Jew to the homosexual. Jews *can*, in this metaphorical construction, be perceived as maintaining a connection to both Communism and homosex-uality, but they can also, under certain conditions, successfully hand off the baton and drop out of the race altogether.

So the years after World War II, when the events and rhetoric of the Cold War might have been expected to occasion an upsurge of anti-Semitism in the United States, turned out to be instead what historian Arthur Goren has called a "Golden Decade" for American Jews.[4] Political scientists, sociologists, and cultural observers have, ever since the 1950s, been investigating the apparent redirection of anti-Semitic tropes away from Jews and toward non-Jewish objects during this period. One espe-cially well-known early analysis is outlined in David Riesman and Nathan Glazer's 1955 article "The Intellectuals and the Discontented Classes," in which they hypothesize that in an era of general financial prosperity and increasing sexual emancipation, stereotypes about the alleged wealth of Jews and virility of African American men had less visceral appeal than formerly, allowing a new emblem of unearned privilege and unrestrained sexual deviance to emerge in their place: "How powerful, then, is the politi-cal consequence of combining the image of the homosexual with the image of the intellectual—the State Department cooky-pusher Harvard-trained sissy thus becomes the focus of social hatred and the Jew becomes merely one variant of the intellectual sissy."[5]

Less psychoanalytic explanations for the sudden and steep postwar decline in explicitly anti-Semitic views, rhetoric, and political movements include the revelations of the extent of Nazi genocide, hostility to Hitler, greater militancy and activism on the part of Jewish organizations, and increased prosperity and optimism among many classes of Americans, reducing the tendency toward scapegoating. Above all, the fact that anti-Communism trumped all other ideological considerations during this period, although it presented American Jews with a number of significant challenges—a point to which we will return momentarily—also offered more expansive possibilities for Jewish inclusion in the polity than at per-haps any time since the nation's founding.

For example, to revisit the question of why U.S. Jews were able to express support for Israel without jeopardizing their standing as loyal Americans, a simple though not sufficient explanation is that by the early 1950s the Soviet Union had begun to back Israel's Arab enemies in the Middle Eastern conflict, while the United States adopted Israel as a democratic ally in the region; thus, loyalty to Israel became, in the context of the superpower face-off, consistent with loyalty to America. Of even broader significance were the widespread social changes of the postwar period, assisted and often deliberately created by federal policies that attempted to defuse domestic Communism by favoring the embourgeoisement of working-class ethnics—not only Jews, but also Italians, Poles, and others. Housing policies relocated them to the suburbs, moving them out of urban neighborhoods that promoted labor activism,[6] and the provisions of the GI Bill encouraged advances in their education and professional status. Hence, Jews became increasingly suburbanized, professionalized, and deradicalized members of a newly consolidated "white" middle class.

Another notable result of the "Cold War consensus" against Communism is that after the war some of the rhetorical glue historically binding Jews to deicide and the devil started to come unstuck, creating a space in which Judaism might become aligned with Christianity in what began to be widely referred to as a "Judeo-Christian" (or sometimes "Hebraic-Christian" or "Judaic-Christian") tradition. The term *Judeo-Christian* originated in the late nineteenth century but was not much used in its current sense, implying a unity of tradition and belief between the two religions, until the 1930s. By the late 1940s the term was ubiquitous and had come to designate a specifically American religious consensus that united Protestants, Catholics, and Jews against Communism, which was itself often cast as a satanic "religion of atheism" rather than a political ideology. "As of 1952," writes one historian of religion, "good Americans were supposed to be, in some sense, committed Judeo-Christians. It was a recent addition to the national creed."[7]

Historian Deborah Dash Moore attributes the widespread promotion of a Judeo-Christian synthesis especially to military policies during World War II that encouraged and enforced this new "tradition" by offering ecumenical religious services, stocking lifeboats with copies of scriptures from each of the three faiths, and housing Jewish, Protestant, and Catholic military chaplains together.[8] Once the nondemocratic enemy became Communism rather than Nazism, invoking this Judeo-Christian tradition as the foundation of egalitarianism, rights-based democracy, and universal ethics provided a powerful narrative about America's national identity and moral superiority over the Soviet Union. In 1952 Eisenhower gave a speech in which, after referring to an argument he had had with Soviet marshal Georgy Zhukov, he cited the Declaration of Independence and then paraphrased it, saying, "In other words, our form of Government has no sense unless it is founded in a deeply felt religious faith, and I don't care what it is. With us of course it is the Judeo-Christian concept but it must be a religion that all men are created equal."[9]

The postwar promotion of "Judeo-Christianity" as a religious culture of democracy helps to explain what seems an extraordinary lacuna: the absence of anti-Semitism in Joe McCarthy's campaign against Communists. It is a speaking silence, and one that struck observers at the time. Leslie Fiedler commented that McCarthy "has left behind the backwoods doctrine which identifies the Elders of Zion with the International Bankers, and the Bankers with the Bolsheviks";[10] clearly, this was surprising to Fiedler, a departure from script. Furthermore, in addition to abandoning anti-Semitic rhetoric and attacks on Jewish individuals *as* Jews—Seymour Lipset and Earl Raab note that a "singular difference between McCarthy and earlier extreme right-wing anti-Communists was his lack of interest in investigating or publicizing the activities of men who belonged to minority ethnic groups"[11]—McCarthy leaned heavily on Jewish advisors, most notoriously his right-hand man, Roy Cohn.

This is interesting less for what it indicates about McCarthy's personal feelings about Jews than because of the consequences it had for his larger campaign and ideological legacy. In the 1930s right-wing demagoguery had been ethnically fractured: Father Coughlin's supporters were largely Catholic, Gerald Winrod's and William Pelley's were conservative Protestants, all of them were anti-Semites, and so on. But McCarthy, although Irish Catholic himself, was able to pull together an ecumenical coalition of anti-Communists that included a sizable number of evangelicals as well as some Jews.[12] His supporters, if not philo-Semites, "were not any more anti-Semitic than his opponents," according to polls analyzed by Lipset and Raab.[13] And while his principal support came from segments of the Republican Party and elements to the right of the GOP, survey data indicate that he did attract some percentage of Democrats as well.[14] Despite his extremism, McCarthy had hit on an excellent strategy for building a mass movement in a multiethnic society: he targeted a single un-American enemy defined by ideology rather than race or religion and created a capacious tent for its opponents. Theoretically, such a movement could attract any American regardless of religion, race, or class, provided he was anti-Communist. True, the enemy ultimately became too broadly defined, as we saw in the previous chapter, and so the ideological boundaries between inside and outside eventually collapsed. But arguably, McCarthy's coalition survived his self-immolation in 1954, bringing together the factions that—united by opposition to Communism and support for what they defined as "Judeo-Christian values"—eventually launched the Reagan revolution. (Without McCarthyism, it would surely have been harder for a non-church-going divorcé of Irish descent to win the 1980 presidential race with fervent support from conservative Protestants who saw *him*, rather than the pious Southern Baptist Jimmy Carter, as a defender of their own religious values.)

Neither McCarthy nor more centrist Republicans succeeded in attracting large numbers of Jews to their campaigns or causes; Jewish Americans remained, in the 1950s as they are today, overwhelmingly Left-liberal in their politics and institutionally affiliated with the Democratic Party. (Even Roy Cohn was a registered Democrat all his life.)[15] But presumably that was not the point, any more than defining America as a "Judeo-Christian" nation was primarily an effort to woo a minority comprising only about 2 percent of the population. Rather, the rhetorical shift away from both anti-Semitism and anti-Catholicism helped to consolidate the Cold War consensus against Communism, with potential benefits for any politician or political movement willing to dispense with ethnicity-based politicking to focus instead on the broader support available for anti-Communist campaigns. As Tony Kushner's fictional Roy Cohn would say decades later in explaining to the play's one African American character why, despite his long history of reactionary agitation, he has never had much time for racists: "You want to keep your eye on where the most powerful enemy really is. I save my hate for what counts."[16]

ANTI-SEMITISM AND THE RIGHT

I do not intend to suggest that American anti-Semitism simply vanished after World War II. The ranks of prominent anti-Communists still included a few dyed-in-the-wool anti-Semites, not all of them in fringe groups. Popular prewar rabble-rousers like Coughlin, Winrod, and Pelley had been more or less suppressed, but John Rankin still raged on the floor of the House of Representatives that

[Jews] whine about discrimination. Do you know who is being discriminated against? The white Christian people of America, the ones who created this nation. [...] A racial minority seized control in Russia and in all her satellite countries, such as Poland, Czechoslovakia, and many other countries I could name. They have been run out of practically every country in Europe in the years gone by, and if they keep stirring race trouble in this country and trying to force their communistic program on the Christian people of America, there is no telling what will happen to them here.[17]

In a more sophisticated idiom we find George Kennan writing in a 1949 memo that it is, essentially, only *ceux qui ne se nationalisent pas* who are attracted to Communism: "'Unsuccessful and untalented' intellectuals as well as other 'maladjusted groups in our country—Jews, Negroes, immigrants—all those who feel handicapped in the framework of a national society' made up the ranks of communists, Kennan asserted."[18] More common, and ambiguous, are attacks on Communists that apparently implicate Jews or stereotypes of Jewishness without explicitly connecting them. In a *Reader's Digest* article on the Rosenbergs, J. Edgar Hoover first mentions that Harry Gold, an American courier for Soviet agents, was born Henrich Golodnitsky to Russian parents and then claims that when Gold attended parties with Marxists discussing Russia, he found that the name of his parents' "native land" had for him "an odd appeal."[19] Hoover never refers specifically to Gold's Jewishness, letting his name and Russian origin signify whatever the reader chooses. Thus, the atavistic loyalties of Jews are not so much implied here as waved at in a gesture so ambiguous it could plausibly mean something else, or nothing.

Anti-Semitism—explicit, implicit, or vaguely intimated—was not, then, absent from the anti-Communist rhetoric of the postwar period. But it ceased to be a commonplace to be routinely invoked whenever Jews and Communism appeared in any kind of apposition. And at the same time, avowals of philo-Semitism became more common in public discourse—in the appeals to the Judeo-Christian tradition mentioned earlier, for instance, and even in popular films. The immediate postwar period saw the production of a number of well-received "social issues" films including Edward Dmytryk's *Crossfire* and Elia Kazan's *Gentleman's Agreement*, both about anti-Semitism and both popular and critical successes that were nominated for multiple Academy Awards. *Gentleman's Agreement*, which won the Oscar for Best Picture in 1947, attacked social discrimination against Jews as unpatriotic, saying of anti-Semites that they are "persistent little traitors to everything that this country stands for and stands on and you have to fight 'em. Not just for the poor, poor Jews [. . .] but for everything this country stands for."

Gentleman's Agreement had a Jewish screenwriter and was based on a novel by a Jewish author, and although its star, like *Crossfire*'s, was a gentile, the two films featured Jewish actors in supporting roles. Neither Dmytryk nor Kazan was Jewish, but both were former Communists and within months of the films' premieres would be called before HUAC to testify about their leftist connections. It might be possible, then, to read the films as interventions by Jews or members of the far Left, attempting to influence mainstream gentile public opinion, rather than as barometers of that opinion. Even from that perspective it seems significant that after the war Jewish or left-wing writers and directors were able and motivated to make movies about anti-Semitism that they had not, after all, been making before the war. But let us take, as additional evidence of a change in the postwar climate, the example of a very different film that appeared a decade later.

In 1959 *The FBI Story* appeared, a puff piece starring Jimmy Stewart and portraying the FBI as a defender of civil liberties and minority rights. In one scene the film describes the Ku Klux Klan's members as "terrorists," and then—while saying nothing about the Klan's violence toward African Americans—shows hooded men vandalizing an elegant house in which the table is set for Shabbat dinner and a picture of a rabbi reading scripture hangs over the fireplace. As the Klansmen smash the place up, Stewart says in an indignant voiceover, "They ransacked homes, and defiled ancient devotions." *The FBI Story* did have a Jewish director. But like the two earlier films, it also featured a non-Jewish star—and if Gregory Peck, who played the protagonist of *Gentleman's Agreement,* was famously liberal, Jimmy Stewart was equally well known for his conservatism. In addition, Hoover, who exercised tight control over representations of the bureau, personally approved *The FBI Story.*

I am not contending that after World War II conservatives rushed en masse to embrace Jews or that the FBI suddenly became a progressive institution, any more than the French Army and the Catholic Church did under the Third Republic. The objects of conservative reaction, though, were shifting. As in fin-de-siècle France, public advocacy of social and religious tolerance for Jews was becoming an increasingly important feature of American national ideology even on the political Right, while Jewishness per se seemed to carry less and less ideological freight.

THE PRICE OF ADMISSION

This new ideological climate, along with improved social and economic status, appeared to hold out the promise to Jewish Americans not just of formal citizenship, not special privileges reserved for a tiny elite among them, not a begrudged assimilation, but full inclusion *as Jews* in the life of the nation in which they lived, for one of the first times in the history of the Diaspora. As Goren writes, the idea that Protestantism, Catholicism, and Judaism were "the religions of democracy" placed "Judaism and its bearers in the mainstream of the nation's cultural and spiritual tradition."[20] This was a potent lure to Jews to join in the postwar consensus.

Of course, such unprecedented integration required Jews, like other minorities, to accommodate and conform to a specific set of national values and identifications. They were enjoined to reject the Communist Party and popular front groups, to denounce the Soviet Union, to embrace a concept of religious piety that was often implicitly or explicitly Protestant, and to adhere to prevailing norms of gender and sexual behavior. And all of these were potentially more problematic for Jews than for Christian minority groups. For instance, if anti-Communism was, as Stephen Whitfield has written, a singularly effective way for a historically suspect religious minority to "[take] out final citizenship papers,"[21] that tactic was nevertheless much easier for Roman Catholics, who had traditionally been fiercely anti-Communist on religious grounds, making them "almost automatically charter members of the anti-Communist crusade."[22] In contrast, before the war Jews were heavily represented in Left movements and groups including the Communist Party. Even the majority of American Jews who were not party members often admired the Soviets' opposition to Fascism and apparent commitment to combating anti-Semitism. When, after the war, the Soviet Union went with whiplash-inducing speed from being treated as America's respected ally to being described as her mortal enemy, it was a difficult adjustment for many leftists but especially for those who had believed—however mistakenly—that the Soviet Union was a staunch defender of, and safe haven for, Jews.

In place of their former political loyalties and affiliations, American Jews were asked to substitute a purely religious identity grounded in a concept of Judaism compatible with Protestant norms. The concept of observance, for example, was refocused on attendance at weekly services rather than on daily prayer or keeping kosher. The argument that Jewishness should be defined entirely in terms of religion, and the effort to accommodate Protestant mores and styles of worship, was not new and indeed had been essential to the development of Reform Judaism in the nineteenth century. But the ideological context of the 1950s differed from that of the nineteenth century in its sharp bifurcation between a religious Judaism embraced as an integral component of American democracy and a secular Jewishness viewed as dangerously proximate to godless Communism. The case for Jewish citizenship thus became predicated not on a First Amendment distinction between the claims of religion and those of the state but instead on the fitness of Jews to participate in a religiously defined nation.

In 1949 Fiedler could still argue that Jewish integration was, or ought to be, advanced on the terrain of secularism: "We were invited in" to Western culture, Fiedler writes, "precisely on the terms of being 'free-thinkers'; we sang the 'Marseillaise' as loud as any of them."[23] As Fiedler acknowledges in the article, however, this classic liberal position was already eroding, and within a few years it would be very difficult to find prominent Americans claiming that Jews ought to be admitted to citizenship on the grounds of their freethinking. According to Moore, this trend was spurred in large part by the wartime military policies that promoted exclusively religious definitions of Jewish identity among the troops. Religious services provided the only military forum for Jewish social life, and Jewish troops were expected to join in religious rituals whether or not they had any religious training or background. That such an environment might at first have been unfamiliar or even alienating to many Jewish soldiers is suggested by the fact that a survey of American Jewish men carried out just before the war had showed that "72 percent of youth aged sixteen to twenty-four had not spent any time in religious services during the year but identified as Jews nonetheless."[24]

What was imposed by the military during the war, then, and became more generally accepted afterward was a Jewishness collapsed entirely into Judaism: "For American Jews, Judaism and Jewishness became identical only during the decade beginning in 1945."[25] To return to two of the films I have placed as bookends to this period, it is telling that in 1947 in *Gentleman's Agreement* the main character argues vigorously that it is possible to be Jewish and yet have "no religion." In the later *The FBI Story*, in contrast, the Klan attacks a home whose Jewishness is indicated exclusively by religious artifacts and symbols. There aren't even any Jewish people in the scene; what is assaulted, and what the FBI purportedly defends, is not Jews but Judaism.

Another World War II–era film, *Guadalcanal Diary* (1943), underlines how Protestantized this Judaism was. The first scene of the film shows a Protestant service on a ship's deck crowded with uniformed Marines, and the camera zooms in on two men enthusiastically singing the Christian hymn "Rock of Ages." Then one, Sammy, jokingly reveals that he sings so well because his "father was a cantor in a synagogue"—the last three words clearly added for the benefit of viewers who would not know what a cantor was. The punch line, obviously, is that Jewish soldiers fit into both the military and, by implication, America because of their readiness to embrace Protestant traditions. A 1953 article by Michael Blankfort called "The Education of a Jew," published in the ultraconservative periodical *American Mercury*, makes a similar point more seriously. Blankfort's apologia describes his return to the Orthodox Judaism in which he was raised after a period of being tempted by Communism and atheism. He insists that there is no genuinely secular form of Jewishness, "so interwoven are the semi-secular writings with our religious writings."[26] Crucially, in Blankfort's description his adult relationship to Judaism differs sharply from his experience as a child, when he was strictly observant but could not actually understand the Hebrew he read fluently, and says that he feared God without loving Him. Early in his life he is thus a stereotypically legalistic Jew, without personal faith, feeling constrained "to continue with the observances of the Jewish laws long after they had lost meaning for me."[27] As he abandons Communism in later years, though, he comes to love God and develops an emotional rather than intellectual response to his religion, finding in it "peace of the spirit."[28] These are not exclusively Protestant conceptions of the nature of faith, but Blankfort's description of religious conversion as a personal, affective commitment to a benevolent deity is one that Protestants would immediately recognize and approve. Especially given the forum in which the article appeared, it appears to function, like the scene in *Guadalcanal Diary*, to reassure Protestants that religious Jews can be absorbed into a Christian nation because their beliefs and practices dovetail with Christian ones.

In addition to espousing anti-Communism and adopting a religiously based identity, Jewish Americans were also expected to hew to the exceptionally rigid gender binaries and family structure promoted during the postwar period. For men this could be facilitated by participation in the war effort. As has long been true in the West, military service was an expedient way for male Jews to assume normative masculinity, and the mass mobilization during World War II did more than any previous American war to "fulfill a long-standing dream of Jewish radical movements to transform Jews into warriors," enabling young Jewish men to "forge new Jewish identities based on American military norms of virility, cooperation, and initiative."[29] The importance of military service to Jewish claims on citizenship is prominently flagged in all the 1940s movies I have discussed. The hymn-singing marine of *Guadalcanal Diary*, Sammy Klein, is a minor character but the very first one introduced by name, so that Jewish participation in the armed forces is highlighted within the first minute of the film. In *Gentleman's Agreement* the protagonist's Jewish best friend is a veteran, still in uniform and depicted as an all-American, masculine family man whose recent service to his country points up the injustice of the social discrimination he suffers. And in *Crossfire* discrimination escalates to violence when an innocent Jewish man is murdered by a rabidly anti-Semitic soldier who assumes his victim "played it safe" and sat out the war in comfort; later we learn that the murder victim was in fact honorably discharged from the army after being wounded at Okinawa.[b]

This vision of Jewish men as honorable and patriotic warriors was in many ways attractive and strategically useful, but it nevertheless tended to foreclose other kinds of masculine identity: the gentle Talmudist whom Daniel Boyarin invokes or Paul Breines's "scholars, saints, socialists, and schlemiels."[30] And adapting to postwar gender roles was even more difficult for Jewish women; they had long been subject to criticism that they were loud, domineering, vulgar, or unfeminine, but these stereotypes were especially hard to counter during a period when all women were supposed to be home-focused and dependent on men. As we will see below, the Rosenberg case shows clearly how anxious Jewish men *and* women were in the early

---

b. *Crossfire* demonstrates another way in which Cold War animus was redirected from Jews to homosexuals. The novel on which the film is based, *The Brick Foxhole*, is about the murder of a homosexual Marine. RKO agreed to buy the rights to the novel only under the condition that the subject of the movie would be changed to anti-Semitism rather than homophobia (*Crossfire*, DVD "Extras"). Once again "Jew" stands in for "homosexual," but now it is because the former has become an acceptable object of identification and sympathy for a mass audience, while its historical doppelgänger is still, emphatically, not.

1950s to demonstrate their compliance with dominant gender standards—and equally, how vulnerable they were to accusations that they had failed.

CONFLICTING LOYALTIES

In sum, after World War II American Jews confronted a situation in which they appeared, rather suddenly, to have a chance of being treated as full citizens on every level—formally, culturally, socially—without having to convert, which had previously been the only path to total integration in most Western societies, and not always a permitted or successful one at that. This situation created an exceptionally strong incentive to suppress, both figuratively and literally, any remaining elements within Jewish-American communities that could be associated with subversion, heresy, or sex/gender deviance. The Rosenbergs' trial—which pitted Jewish defendants and defense attorneys against Jewish witnesses, two Jewish prosecutors, and a Jewish judge—offered a miniaturized dramatization of a national struggle over the future shape of Jewish American identity.

At the heart of the case were the issues of treason and loyalty, not only in the legal charges against the Rosenbergs, but embedded in the family and communal struggles during and after the trial, which often set personal, racial, and national loyalties against each other. From the outset of the trial the prosecution attempted to demonstrate that, as Representative Martin Dies had once said, "communism is nothing more nor less than organized treason and those who abet it run grave risks of being *particeps criminis*."[31] Prosecutors claimed in their opening statement that "the evidence will show that the loyalty and the allegiance of the Rosenbergs and Sobell were not to our country, but that it was [*sic*] to Communism, Communism in this country and Communism throughout the world" (*RRS*, 180). Though the Rosenbergs were formally charged with "conspiracy to commit espionage," which is not nearly so difficult to prove under U.S. law as treason, the argument that they were actually unfairly tried and sentenced for treason has been made frequently. During the trial the prosecutors described the defendants as "traitorous Americans," said that David Greenglass had played "the treacherous role of a modern Benedict Arnold," and made frequent references to the Rosenbergs' "treasonable acts" (*RRS*, 182, 184, 2284, 2313).

In short, prosecutors knew they could not possibly convict the Rosenbergs of treason, but they tried very hard to ensure that the jury and the judge thought of their crimes in those terms. And in fact, in Judge Kaufman's sentencing statement he called the Rosenbergs "these traitors in our midst" and then, blaming them for the Korean War, said "who knows but that millions more of innocent people may pay the price of your treason" (*RRS*, 2450–52). At least one of the jurors seems to have interpreted the charges the same way; in an interview he said he felt the death sentence passed on the Rosenbergs was merited because "conspiracy and treason were the same thing."[32] That the point is legally untenable makes it no less indicative of the centrality that the idea of treason, in multiple forms, assumed during the trial.

Most intimately, treason was implicated in the dysfunctional Rosenberg-Greenglass family romance, which set David, his wife Ruth, and the rest of Ethel's family viciously against Ethel and Julius in a fight literally to the death. In Cold War rhetoric, affectively healthy, normatively gendered families were supposed to reinforce national values and national security, yet the privacy meant to shield and nurture familial relations could also conceal pathologies disordering both the family and the nation. Because privacy coincides with secrecy, the sacrosanct family home can easily be read as the site of conspiracy: "The trial of Julius and Ethel Rosenberg for passing atomic secrets to the Soviet Union [. . .] suggested that individual behaviour in sensitive places might have extreme international consequences: what transpired behind closed doors between consenting adults, even between husband and wife and the extended family, could undermine the nation's safety."[33] Indeed, in the absence of any substantive physical evidence of the conspiracy in which the Rosenbergs and Greenglasses had allegedly been involved, the jury's decision rested chiefly on the testimony of the two couples against each other about events that had taken place in their homes "behind closed doors," so that the international espionage case was wholly contained within and dependent on the domestic drama. With virtually no outside referents to rely on, jurors had to settle a question of state security by choosing sides in a family quarrel.

The prosecutors undoubtedly realized that the prospect of David and Ruth Greenglass sending their own kin to the electric chair might be disturbing to the jury. Ruth had already grappled publicly with the unpleasant ramifications of their decision to cooperate with the government in the months before the trial. After first David and then—on the basis of his accusations— the Rosenbergs were arrested in the summer of 1950, Ruth was interviewed in the *Jewish Daily Forward*. The interviewer asked why she and her husband hadn't confessed to the FBI in 1945 if, as she claimed, that was when they first realized they were doing something wrong in passing secrets about the atomic bomb to Harry Gold. Ruth's self-justificatory response describes the tension she felt between her family, ethnic, and national loyalties and takes care to suggest to the *Forward*'s Jewish readership that it was only with difficulty that she had put her national allegiance first: "'That is the tragedy,' Ruth lamented. 'That is what troubled us. David realized that he took a false step in giving Gold information, but you must bear in mind that David's sister and her husband, Julius Rosenberg, were involved. In general it is very difficult to be a stool-pigeon, particularly for a Jew. And when it concerns your own family the problem is even more difficult.'"[34]

During the trial, attorneys on both sides worked to simplify and contain the ramifications of Ruth's statement by amalgamating all loyalty with national loyalty. Defense attorney Manny Bloch tried to reinforce in the jury's mind a connection between David's treachery toward his sister and his betrayal of his country, reminding them first that David was a confessed spy and then immediately adding, "Any man who will testify against his own blood and flesh, his own sister, is repulsive, is revolting, who [*sic*] violates every code that any civilization has ever lived by" (*RRS*, 2193). Prosecutors countered by rhetorically recasting the familial betrayal as the Rosenbergs' and emphasizing David's wartime military service as a factor that heightened *their* treacherousness rather than his: in his summation Saypol said to the jury that "the issue in this case, we are all agreed, transcends any family consideration; but clearly the breach of family loyalty is that of an older sister and brother-in-law dragging an American soldier into the sordid business of betraying his country for the benefit of the Soviet Union" (*RRS*, 2286). Saypol thus deftly produces a streamlined account of treason in which the Rosenbergs' betrayal of Ethel's brother aligns neatly with their betrayal of the United States. But he suppresses the messier possibility evoked by Ruth's confession to the *Forward*: that there might be irreducible conflicts, not only between the loyalties individuals feel to their countries, their families, their religious or political ideals, their communities of birth or choice, and so on, but also between any individual's personal definition of loyalty and the specific—yet also labile and sometimes arbitrary—ways in which national governments define it for their own security purposes.

DOUBLE AGENCY: THE BEGINNING OF THE END

Both sides, then, attempted to bring the case in line with a narrative that foregrounded the national loyalty of Jewish Americans, while disagreeing about the nature of Jewishness and its appropriate relationship to national identity. On one side were Judge Irving Kaufman, lead prosecutor Irving Saypol, and Saypol's confidential assistant Roy Cohn, representing the bourgeois Jews to whom full enfranchisement appeared to be available under the Cold War dispensation—successful professionals living on Park Avenue, ferociously anti-Communist, religiously observant, involved with mainstream Jewish organizations such as the ADL, graduates of prestigious schools like Fordham (Kaufman) and Columbia (Cohn). Additionally, Kaufman, Saypol, and Cohn all emerge from the printed text of the transcript as articulate, confident, and even witty orators. In contrast, the defendants, and the witnesses from their social circle, represented a community with close ties to an older immigrant culture: they were Communists or former Communists, still residing on the Lower East Side, with either no college education or degrees from the less prestigious, more ethnic CCNY;[35] they spoke less grammatical English than the prosecutors and with less assurance. The Rosenbergs remained invested in the CPUSA's wartime doctrine that "Communism is Twentieth Century Americanism," whereas to Kaufman the couple, like all Communists, "represented an awful aberration" from his ideal of American Jewishness.[36]

Although nearly all the major players involved were Jewish, the seated jury was entirely gentile.[c] When Bloch told the jurors that they had had "a front seat" at the trial he was casting them as the audience of a spectacle staged by Jews. Years later the jury foreman made explicit the jurors' own awareness of themselves as spectators of an essentially Jewish performance, recalling "that when the death sentence was given to the Rosenbergs, 'I felt good that this [...] was strictly a Jewish show. It was Jew against Jew. It wasn't the Christians hanging the Jews.'"[37] Moore contends that "Jews were less pleased with this arrangement" than the gentile foreman because "playing a Jewish drama before a Christian America" highlighted Jewish difference at a time when Jews were striving to assimilate and

---

c. This has been offered by the Rosenbergs' supporters as evidence that the government must have rigged the jury, but the pattern of dismissals during the voir dire proceedings does not substantiate the charge.

demonstrate that they were just like other Americans.[38] As I have argued above, however, the kind of integration on offer during the Cold War required conformity in specific aspects of behavior and ideology but not the complete eradication of ethnic and religious difference, and in fact the trial transcript suggests that the Jewish lawyers and judge were quite comfortable acknowledging that difference.

At one point, for instance, Manny Bloch described his client, Julius, as a "schnook," and then had an exchange with Kaufman about the correct way to translate the word:

> MR. E. H. BLOCH: And when Davey came around and said he was in trouble, like a schnook—that is a Jewish word; it means this— I am trying to get the exact translation—well, a very easygoing fool—[Julius] goes to his doctor to try to get a false certificate for Davey.
>
> THE COURT: Is the word stooge what you are looking for?
>
> MR. E. H. BLOCH: Stooge? Stooge. (*RRS*, 2213)

If Bloch wanted to downplay his own or his clients' Jewishness, it was hardly necessary for him to use Yiddish slang in the courtroom. Kaufman's intervention is equally supererogatory, as Bloch has already explained his meaning; it serves only to draw attention to the ethnicity Kaufman shares with Bloch—while also, perhaps, signaling the judge's superior ability to navigate between linguistic and cultural contexts by substituting his translation for Bloch's. The whole exchange conveys a sense of charade, since the two men both know that they, and the other Jews in the room, are perfectly familiar with the meaning of *schnook*. Their conversation is purely for the benefit of the gentile jury before whom they thus enact their Jewishness, in a way that emphasizes that it is the jurors who are alien visitors to this scene, not they. Compare the tenor of this incident to the embarrassment experienced by that other Bloch, in Proust, when his uncle uses Yiddish in front of gentiles and thus "over-expos[es] his oriental side";[39] the gulf between the two performances of Jewishness, one inadvertent and awkward and the other self-assured and deliberate, is a measure of how differently Jewishness had come to signify in 1950s America.

Unapologetically Jewish, the principals in the case also were emphatic about the Americanness of everyone involved. Even while enacting a stark and largely class-based antagonism, the two sides seemed to be operating on an understanding that their argument was not about whether Jews could be Americans but only about what Jewish Americans ought to look like. Moore maintains that Jewish Americans in the 1950s were angry at the Rosenbergs for, among other things, "showing the reality of Jewish second-class citizenship."[40] I would say that on the contrary, the case and public response to it demonstrated just how close to first-class citizenship American Jews had come. In the nineteenth century French Jews fell somewhere in the middle of a spectrum from alien to citizen, making it possible for the charge of treason against Dreyfus to be meaningful while also allowing mass reaction to crystallize around the image of the Jew as foreigner. Mid-twentieth-century American Jews were that much farther along the spectrum toward citizenship, and so the full fury of national, and Jewish, opinion fell on the Rosenbergs not as aliens or even as double agents but as American traitors. Antagonism to the Rosenbergs was, thus, provoked in part by their betrayal of an American filiation that they, both legal teams, and indeed most of the mainstream press took for granted.

During the trial Manny Bloch repeatedly stressed the distinctively American qualities of both his clients and his opponents. In his summation, for instance, he referred to the jury as "American jurors" and said to them, "You are going to show to the world that in America a man can get a fair trial" (RRS, 2238-A). He told Kaufman, "We feel that the trial has been conducted and we hope that we have contributed our share with that dignity and that decorum that befits an American trial" (RRS, 2167). And then, after the jury returned its verdict and Kaufman pronounced the sentence of death, Bloch said to him, "I know that the Court conducted itself as an American judge" (RRS, 2433). Bloch's gratitude for the Americanness even of his adversaries seems to have been motivated by an overriding desire to maintain himself and his clients within a sphere of national identity and values he was anxious to claim they shared with the judge.

Kaufman fully concurred, but this did not work in the Rosenbergs' favor. In his sentencing statement Kaufman framed the couple's crime in terms emphasizing their American citizenship and deliberate malevolence toward their own nation, saying that "our national well-being requires that we guard against spying on the secrets of our defense, whether such spying is carried on through agents of foreign powers or through *our own nationals* who prefer to help a foreign power. [. . .] The thought that *citizens of our country* would lend themselves to the destruction of *their own country* by the most destructive weapon known to man is so shocking that

I can't find words to describe this loathsome offense" (*RRS*, 2337a, 2390; emphasis added). Similarly, an editorial in the *Los Angeles Times* published the day after the sentencing specifically describes the defendants as Americans. The editorial does make note of the Rosenbergs' Russian ancestry, as Hoover had commented on Gold's—again, Russian, and so associated with Communism, but not specifically Jewish. But as we saw, in Hoover's piece he alluded to the "odd appeal" that the word *Russia* held for Gold and wrote that "father and mother had fled from their native land, yet the name vaguely stirred their son," invoking an irrational response to the ancestral homeland as one explanation for Gold's treachery.[41] In contrast, the *Los Angeles Times* mentions the Rosenbergs' immigrant background only in order to condemn them for abandoning the classic trajectory of the upwardly mobile immigrant in favor of something that here is explicitly named as foreign *to them*, as well as to the writer: "They will take full advantage of American judicial procedure, as they took full advantage of American educational and social conditions which enabled them, children of Russian immigrants, to rise from New York City's tenement district to a position of substance. But they preferred to give their loyalty to Communist, alien Russia. So much for the Rosenbergs. [. . .] Rosenberg and Greenglass were respected, trusted Americans."[42]

What we are witnessing here is, I want to suggest, the beginning of the end of the trope of double agency as it applied to American Jews. For Kaufman, Saypol, and Cohn; for the numerous Jewish intellectuals, writers, reporters, and organization leaders who denounced the Rosenbergs; and for a large swath of the American media and public, the Rosenbergs were not racially predestined to split their loyalties between the nation of their birth and their international tribe, and their crime was not evidence of an atavistic reversion to type. It was simply an act of conscious wrongdoing by American citizens whose Jewishness was incidental to their deliberate decision to betray "their own country" to a foreign nation.

GOD AND MONSTERS

With this understanding of the framework within which the antagonists in the Rosenberg case approached their contest, let us now look in more detail at the way the trial and its aftermath responded to the Cold War consensus and contributed to the formation of Cold War Jewish American identity. Both sides in the trial evinced a keen awareness of the salient points on which Jewish normalization was premised in the 1950s: patriotism, religious piety, and sexual and gendered normativity. And so in the course of the trial the prosecution and defense teams laid out the ways in which they themselves, their clients, or the witnesses they called fulfilled the requirements of Cold War citizenship, while endeavoring to demonstrate that those on the other side failed to do so. After the trial those who either supported or opposed the Rosenbergs took up the same project. The result was a communal shaping of "American Jewishness" that ultimately ratified the expulsion from that identity category of Communism, atheism, and sex/gender deviance.

During the trial the Rosenbergs and their counsel attempted to dodge the issue of Communism altogether, proclaiming its irrelevance and, in the case of the Rosenbergs when they were on the witness stand, taking the Fifth every time the prosecution mentioned the subject during cross-examination. Instead, they emphasized their Americanness. During the two years of appeals that followed sentencing they also affirmed their commitment to American ideals of justice and to Jewish values and practices, through publications like the Rosenbergs' *Death House Letters*, statements to the press, and legal briefs. But by then it was too late to counter the much more successful narrative elaborated by the prosecutors and judge, who particularly stressed the Rosenbergs' deviations from (Jewish) American norms during the trial. Although Kaufman had reminded the jury throughout the trial, somewhat unpersuasively, that the Rosenbergs' Communist affiliations were not the basis for the charges against them, he himself more or less accepted the equivalence of Communism and sedition, saying, "I additionally must assume that the basic Marxist goal of world revolution and the destruction of capitalism was well known to the defendants, if in fact not subscribed to by them, when they passed what they knew was this nation's most deadly and closely guarded secret weapon to Soviet agents" (*RRS*, 2452). Kaufman further accepted the presumption that, as Communists, the Rosenbergs must be atheists when he claimed that they "made a choice of devoting themselves to the Russian ideology of denial of God" and alluded to them as "the principals in this diabolical conspiracy to destroy a God-fearing nation" (*RRS*, 2451, 2453).

Earlier in the trial Cohn and Saypol had also promulgated the idea that the Soviet Union was a religion or deity that the Rosenbergs, like other Communists, worshiped. In his opening remarks Saypol told the jury that "the evidence will show their loyalty to and worship of the Soviet Union"

(*RRS*, 181). At another point Cohn mentioned "Soviet Russia" and Saypol promptly chimed in, "That is the God that they direct themselves to, both of them" (*RRS*, 221) As a counterexample, Kaufman and Saypol made sure the media knew that they themselves were religiously observant; *Time* magazine reported that Kaufman "had spent long hours in prayer at his synagogue" while the *New York Times* wrote that both he and Saypol had sought "spiritual guidance" at their respective temples during the last week of the trial.[43] These public professions of piety clearly illustrate how normalized a specific kind of observant Judaism had become as an adjunct to political and moral rectitude in the early 1950s, fully able to function as a marker of a Jew's inclusion in the national consensus over and against the presumable godlessness of any Communist, whether Jew or gentile.

Above all, both sides in the case deployed gender stereotypes and proscriptions about normative sexuality to anathematize the other side's witnesses and defend their own. In 1992 legal scholar Sheila Brennan published the first feminist analysis of the gender dynamics of the case, arguing that "Ethel Rosenberg's status as Julius's wife, and as a woman who did not fit stereotypical gender-role expectations during the ultraconservative Cold War era of the 1950's, were critical factors in her conviction and execution";[44] since Brennan's piece appeared numerous others have elaborated on this thesis. The question of *Julius*'s gender and sexual positioning has barely been glossed in this work, however. Furthermore, most analyses of the gender politics of the trial have neglected to comment on the way the defense, as well as the prosecutors, leaned on prevailing notions of sexual normalcy and appropriate gender behavior in making their case.

Within moments of opening his defense Manny Bloch had characterized Julius as "an American citizen" in asking the jury to treat him fairly (*RRS*, 188). In comparison, his father and cocounsel, Alexander Bloch, said in his opening statement in defense of Ethel that "she did not transmit or conspire to transmit any information to any government. She was a housewife, basically a housewife and nothing more" (*RRS*, 190). He went on to ask the jurors to reserve their judgment until hearing all the evidence, adding, "I am quite sure if you do that you will find that Mrs. Rosenberg has committed no crime, and instead of being punished here, she should be sent back to her family to take care of her children" (*RRS*, 190). Hence, the Rosenbergs are immediately presented by their attorneys in terms of his citizenship and her domesticity, each defined by gender-appropriate status and each recommended to the jury's consideration on sharply different terms.

Even before Ethel was taken into custody she was trying to demonstrate her own gender conformity to the public. The day after Julius's arrest, photographers took a number of staged pictures of Ethel in the kitchen of the couple's apartment showing her pretending to wash dishes and prepare a meal; clearly, at that early stage in the case asserting gender orthodoxy already seemed essential to the Rosenbergs' self-defense. When Alexander Bloch put Ethel on the stand he had her confirm that she had been responsible for all the Rosenbergs' household chores, asking her, "Did you do all the chores of a housewife? [. . .] Cooking, washing, cleaning, darning, scrubbing?" thereby prompting her reiterated affirmations of domestic competence (*RRS*, 1928). Finally, in a clemency petition Ethel wrote to President Truman in January 1953, when she was pleading for her life, she said to him that "upon the birth of our two sons, I ceased my outside employment, and discharged the responsibility of mother and housewife."[45] The ostensible context for this information is to show that the Rosenbergs were too poor to afford household help and thus couldn't have been receiving payment from the Russians, but the petition also intervenes in what had become, by 1953, a strident campaign to depict Ethel as a monstrously masculinized woman and unnatural mother.

That campaign had begun during the trial. When the case first began in 1950 the government was much more interested in Julius and, as we now know from files released in the 1970s, not even persuaded of Ethel's involvement in the conspiracy. At trial, prosecutors nonetheless set out to make her seem sufficiently powerful to merit conviction and punishment along with her husband. From the outset they reinforced, as frequently as they could, the fact that Ethel was older than both David and Julius, stretching the age difference between her and her brother from six to "almost seven" years and bringing the issue of her age up in contexts where it had no relevance except to position the diminutive woman (she was barely five feet tall) as a more dominant figure than she might otherwise have seemed. In response, Manny Bloch attempted to frame her relationship to David as one of appropriate maternal solicitude, referring to him repeatedly as her "baby brother" and prompting Ethel to admit on the stand that she "loved him very much" (*RRS*, 1968).

The prosecution, however, was able to repurpose even Ethel's conventionally feminine characteristics or conduct as further evidence of her treachery. At one point David testified that Ethel had told Ruth that between childcare and "staying up late at night [. . .] typing over notes that Julius brought her," she was very tired. But, David added, "she also stated that she didn't mind it so long as Julius was doing what he wanted to do,"

FIGURE 6.1   Ethel Rosenberg washing dishes. (Copyright © Corbis)

that is, spying for the Soviets (*RRS*, 632). Caring for children, supporting her husband emotionally, sacrificing herself, and typing all seem like appropriate feminine behaviors, except that the Communist cause they serve inverts them instead into signs of Ethel's unnatural motherhood and masculinized criminality. In Saypol's reformulation secretarial activity, for instance, is refigured as an attack with a blunt instrument: "Just so had she on countless other occasions sat at that typewriter and struck the keys, blow by blow, against her country in the interests of the Soviets" (*RRS*, 2291).[d]

d. Despite Saypol's dramatic "countless other occasions," one incident of typing notes was the only active contribution Ethel was accused of making to the conspiracy, and we now know that David Greenglass did not "remember" this event—about which he later said he had lied—until immediately before the trial began (see Roberts, *Brother*, 483).

Bloch retaliated by painting Ruth Greenglass as unnaturally dominant over her husband, depicting her as the kind of hard-edged, duplicitous femme fatale eminently familiar to audiences of film noir. Sarcastically referring to Ethel as a "terrible spy"—and since the transcript specifies that he was pointing at her, we can assume that tiny Ethel did not look very terrible at that moment—he contrasts her with the woman he is trying to portray as the mastermind of the conspiracy, whose testimony, he insists, was carefully rehearsed:

> And so Greenglass—and entre nous, I submit that it wasn't Dave Greenglass; I think this part was hatched primarily by Mrs. Ruth Greenglass. I think you can ascertain people; I think she is the smarter of the two—and this is the perfect target (pointing to defendant Julius Rosenberg). [. . .] Now, look at that terrible spy (pointing to the defendant Ethel Rosenberg). Look at that ter-rible spy and compare her to Ruthie Greenglass, who came here all dolled up, arrogant, smart, cute, eager-beaver, like a phonograph record. [. . .] And she wants you to believe that she didn't rehearse this story with Dave and Dave Greenglass didn't rehearse this story with her. Cute, cute. Maybe some of you are more acute in sizing up women than others, but if Ruth Greenglass is not the embodi-ment of evil, I would like to know what person is? (*RRS*, 2208–10)

Bloch's gambit obviously failed, and his image of Ruth as a malevolently clever, domineering woman instead became almost precisely the image of Ethel that was promulgated in the following years. In Kaufman's sentenc-ing statement, carefully formulated to justify his imposition of the death penalty on both members of the couple, Ethel still appears as a second-ary figure in the conspiracy yet is already becoming, by virtue of her age, an equal partner in the crime: "The evidence indicated quite clearly that Julius Rosenberg was the prime mover in this conspiracy. However, let no mistake be made about the role which his wife, Ethel Rosenberg, played in this conspiracy. Instead of deterring him from pursuing his ignoble cause, she encouraged and assisted the cause. She was a mature woman—almost three years older than her husband and almost seven years older than her younger brother. She was a full-fledged partner in this crime" (*RRS*, 2453).

After the sentencing, in a very short space of time, the "full-fledged partner" morphed into the "mastermind" in the view of government

officials and the press. The speed with which Ethel was labeled the archi-
tect of the espionage conspiracy has been attributed both to Ethel's own
unemotional conduct on the witness stand and to the public's uneasiness
about executing the mother of two small children;[46] to justify the death
sentence Ethel had to be made to seem both unnaturally potent and insuf-
ficiently maternal. "Ethel's quick denials and repeated reliance on the Fifth
Amendment created the image of a cold, well-composed woman lack-
ing 'normal' feminine characteristics. Ethel further defied convention by
remaining calm even when questioned about her brother's incriminating
testimony. This unexpected behavior from a woman, and the media reaction to it, has been suggested as the beginning of the theory that it was
Ethel, not Julius, who was the actual force behind the spy ring."[47]

In an interview in the 1970s the jury foreman described Ethel, in a
much-quoted line, as "a steely, stony, tight-lipped woman," adding that
"she was the mastermind. Julius would have spoken if she had permitted
him. He was more human. She was more disciplined."[48] Whether this was
really his impression of the Rosenbergs at the time of the trial or whether
he absorbed it from the media afterward, it certainly became a widespread
view in the two years between the sentencing and the execution. During
that period the Rosenbergs' *Death House Letters* were published; Ethel's
letters, in particular, were perceived as "strident and vindictive," and her
"desire for retribution [. . .] did not meet societal gender expectations."[49]
At the same time, Morris Ernst, a lawyer with the ACLU and Hoover's close
friend, was promoting the theory that sexual and gender deviance characterized most Communists and especially marriages between Communists, including the Rosenbergs'. In 1952 Ernst coauthored a *Report on the
American Communist* describing the gender inversion that was, the writers
stated, typical of Communists, along with both homosexuality and impo-
tence: "Citing the Kinsey report as a standard by which to measure, the
authors also claimed that there is 'a reasonable . . . quota of homosexual
or suppressed homosexual tendencies' in the party. They pointed out that
(unnamed) psychoanalysts see common psychological traits in the Communist and the homosexual. [. . .] Moreover, Ernst and Loth observed a
gender role reversal in the Communist marriage: 'the tendency seems to
be that in Communist marriages the wife is the more dominant partner.' "[50]

Ernst offered the FBI his opinion that the Rosenbergs, whom he never
met, fit this pattern and that "Julius is the slave and his wife, Ethel, is the
master."[51] His report circulated through government offices and may have

influenced both Hoover and Eisenhower to recommend against clemency. Hoover had initially opposed killing Ethel because she was a mother and also was "presumed to be acting under the influence of her husband,"[52] but he apparently changed his mind as the image of Ethel as a domineering wife and bad mother became more prevalent. For his part Eisenhower wrote a letter to his son David explaining why he had refused to grant clemency to Ethel: "It goes against the grain to avoid interfering in the case where a woman is to receive capital punishment. Over against this, however, must be placed one of two [sic] facts that have greater significance. The first of these is that in this instance it is the woman who is the strong and recalcitrant character, the man is the weak one. She has obviously been the leader in everything they did in the spy ring."[53]

In later years no one was more vitriolic about this subject than Roy Cohn. In his ghostwritten "autobiography" Cohn boasts that he argued in favor of executing Ethel during one of several illegal conversations he claims to have had with Kaufman ex parte; in his description, Ethel emerges as a virilized crime lord:

> It turned out that [David] resented [Ethel] terribly. That she was the one who wore the pants in the family, she had recruited him into the spy ring. [. . .] So the business about the typing was minimal next to what we now knew Ethel was in this espionage ring. And if we didn't know it after talking to David, Ruth, and the mother [Tessie Greenglass], we certainly would have known it by watching Ethel Rosenberg in court. She was pulling defense attorney Manny Bloch's coat, sending messages all over the place, she was the whole show, and there's nothing more conclusive in a courtroom than the demeanor of the witness. Anybody in that room had to know who was the power in the Rosenberg family— and I use "family" as in Corleone. [. . .] "The way I see it," I said [to Kaufman], "is that she's worse than Julius. She's the older one, she's the one with the brains, she recruited her younger brother into the Young Communist League and into the spy ring, she's the one who typed the atomic bomb documents, she engineered this whole thing, she was the mastermind of this conspiracy. So unless you're willing to say that a woman is immune from the death penalty, I don't see how you can justify sparing her."[54]

Cohn's biographer also cites his "ferocious" hatred of Ethel, quoting him saying that "I think she was the stronger of the two. [. . .] Ethel was the strong one, not the weak one. [. . .] I never had any doubt, not only about her guilt, but I feel she was the strong one among the two of them and belonged in that case as much as [Julius] did, if not more."[55]

What is easily overlooked in these so evidently misogynist reactions to the Rosenbergs is that the inalienable correspondent of Ethel's gender deviance is Julius's, and that overt hostility toward her as "the stronger of the two" must entail a less explicit but perhaps equally clamant antagonism toward him as the "slave." If Ethel was what Lait and Mortimer liked to call a "he-woman," Julius must be a "she-man." His aberrant gender was emphasized less than hers by prosecutors and the press; perhaps, since the preponderance of the evidence presented at trial already incriminated him and executing men is generally less controversial than executing women, there was less need to play explicitly on images of masculine deviance in order to prosecute the case against Julius successfully or justify his death sentence. And yet lurking in the background of the affair, sometimes concealed behind a masculinized wife or sister but always threatening to emerge, we can make out a shadowy but quite recognizable figure: the queer Jewish man.

The prosecution moved quickly to establish the normative masculinity of its key witnesses, frequently alluding to David's military role and describing him as "an American soldier." The Rosenbergs' counsel also referred to David's wartime service, but in order to amplify the magnitude of his crime, saying that "he disgraced the uniform of every soldier in the United States by his actions" (RRS, 2192–93). Their references to him as a soldier, though, failed to counteract, and may even have contributed to, the picture the prosecution drew of an essentially normal American man. The prosecution also successfully recuperated the image of their very first witness, Max Elitcher, from the defense's attempt to cast doubt on his mental stability. Early in the trial Bloch drew from Elitcher an admission that he had seen a psychiatrist, a potentially damning confession in an era when therapy was not yet routine among the middle classes. But Saypol was then able to redirect the subject to the benefits of counseling for the Elitchers' marriage, so that rather than sounding unbalanced Elitcher is able to present himself as competently heterosexual and consequently stable and reliable:

SAYPOL: What was it that made you go or caused you to go to a psychiatrist, to a doctor?

ELITCHER: Well, after our marriage we found that we had domestic difficulties and we found it difficult to live with each other. We found that I had personality problems and she had personality problems which prevented a happy existence together. [. . .] It was only after I had gone [to a psychiatrist] and had been able to recognize some of my problems, that our married life did adjust itself, and I will say right now that it couldn't be much happier as married life goes. (RRS, 52728)

The defense clearly understood the prosecution's strategy, jumping in to object when prosecutors asked one of their own witnesses whether he was a World War II veteran and of what service—a question that was, as Bloch immediately pointed out, immaterial to the witness's testimony and posed only in order to "build up" his image (RRS, 1141). Bloch must have known that by comparison Julius's masculinity seemed precarious, as did Morton Sobell's. Saypol made sure to remind jurors that Sobell had never served in the military and "was afraid of the draft" (RRS, 2310–11). Julius also had not enlisted during the war, instead taking a civilian position with the Army Signal Corps; thus he could not be represented by his attorneys as a warrior, not even a treacherous one. Furthermore, his nickname, often used during the trial rather than his full name, was the feminine "Julie." Media reports created an image of a physically unimpressive, even feeble, man with adjectives like "puffy," "sallow," and "bespectacled"; at one point *Time* magazine referred to him as "the mousy little engineer."[56] (Julius was 5′9″, the average height for an American man; but of course that is not really what *Time* meant.) After the trial, as we have seen, he was routinely emasculated in narratives about Ethel's dominance. And Julius's involvement of his younger brother-in-law in Communism, which began when David was only a teenager, was referred to several times as a "seduction," throwing over Julius's actions a faint tinge not only of conspiracy but also of homoerotic pedophilia.

At the same time, seemingly in contradiction, Julius was also portrayed as cunning and sinister, a figure so potent that he could plausibly be blamed for the potential annihilation of millions of people. An early journalistic defender of the Rosenbergs complained that during the trial Julius's image had been distorted into the caricature of a man so powerful he belonged to the realm of fiction: "His wife's brother and sister-in-law, David and Ruth Greenglass, had portrayed Julius as a master spy—a man of intrigue,

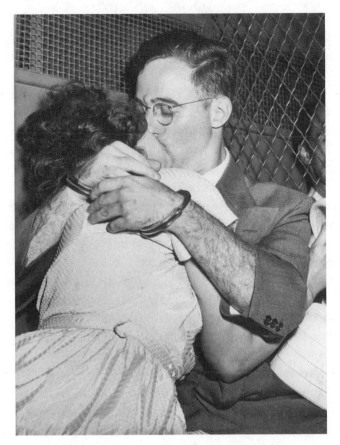

FIGURE 6.2   Ethel and Julius Rosenberg. (Copyright © Corbis)

mystery, cunning and ubiquitous wisdom such as moves in the pages of
E. Phillips Oppenheim."[57] It also seems at odds with their emphasis on
Julius's physical inadequacy that the media simultaneously remarked on
the Rosenbergs' physically passionate relationship; news reports referred
to the frequency with which the two embraced and published photos of
them kissing furiously, reinforcing Julius's heterosexuality. But the dual
valences of Julius's public portrayal—his effeminacy on the one hand and
his malevolent power and hypersexuality on the other—are completely
consonant with the lecherous, yet neurasthenic, Jew who was a staple of
fin-de-siècle anti-Semitic rhetoric.

In a broader sense, the double-edged representation of Julius also reflects
a more general uncertainty about how to place the Communist, whether Jewish or gentile, in the lexicon of masculinity. Breines is unsure, for example,

where Jewish Communists fit into the opposition he describes between "tough Jews" and Jewish "scholars, saints, socialists, and schlemiels." "The notion of tough Jews would surely be too loose were Karl Marx squeezed into it," Breines writes, while conceding that Trotsky might make the grade.[58] If Jewish Communists do not fit a neat binary paradigm between toughness and softness, it may be because American discourses about Communists, particularly during the Cold War, evinced a certain schizophrenia in accounting for the nature of Communist power. As we saw in the previous chapter, there were two dominant representations of Communists from the early 1920s onward: the violent Bolshevik and the sneaky Red spy, with the first image gradually giving way to the second by the 1950s in depictions of the domestic Communist. But there had to be a way of accounting for the acute danger allegedly posed by a figure so unmanly. This could be supplied, as it was in the case of the homosexual, by the threat that these she-men might join in a politico-erotic coupling with the slavering Bolshevik thug—the Soviet Union, armed with an atom bomb. Alternatively, the requisite sense of horror could be provoked by bringing effeminacy and power together under what Freedman terms "the sign of monstrosity."[59]

Freedman uses that phrase when discussing Tony Kushner's association of his character Roy Cohn with a highly overdetermined symbol of both Communist and Jewish monstrosity: the octopus. In 2009 Kushner told me in conversation that he was not "consciously aware" when he wrote *Angels in America* that Saypol and Kaufman applied the same image to Julius Rosenberg during the trial. Confecting a vivid picture of the operation of a conspiracy for the jurors, Saypol said to them, "Imagine a wheel. In the center of the wheel, Rosenberg, reaching out like the tentacles of an octopus. [...] Rosenberg, Sobell, Elitcher—always the objective in the center coming from all the legs, all the tentacles going to the one center" (*RRS*, 2275). Later, Kaufman said again that the spy ring had "tentacles which reach into the most vital places" (*RRS*, 2448). When John Rankin proclaimed in the House in 1947 that "all these racial disturbances you have seen in the South have been inspired by the tentacles of this great octopus, communism,"[60] he was probably well aware that Nazi and earlier anti-Semitic propaganda frequently depicted Jews as octopi encircling the globe with their tentacles.[e] Whether or not Saypol and Kaufman also knew this—and it is hard to see how, just a few years after the end of the Third

---

e. Googling "Jews" and "octopus" will produce dozens of such images, both from the Nazi era and on contemporary anti-Semitic or anti-Israel Web sites.

Reich, they could have failed to know—there is no doubt that their simile mobilizes all the revulsion, fear, and panicked energies of anti-Semitism and hurls them at Julius Rosenberg.

It would be easy to interpret this maneuver as evidence of Saypol and Kaufman's "Jewish self-hatred," a term that tends to surface frequently in criticism of their conduct during the trial. But I would suggest that it is important to distinguish among several different strategies by which members of a subaltern group may respond to hostile stereotypes about the group. Let us say that the purest expression of self-hatred is the syllogism "Jews are detestable; I am a Jew; therefore I am detestable." At one remove from that might be the self-justifying statement, "Jews are detestable; I am a Jew; but I am not like other Jews, therefore I am not detestable." It is possible to argue that this was Saypol and Kaufman's attitude in employing the octopus image. In my view, however, there is a third distancing strategy far more in evidence in the Rosenberg case, which could be summarized in the syllogism "Jews like us are admirable; those Jews are not like us; therefore they are not really Jewish." This approach assumes that it is some Other within the group who is the outlier, not the self. Saypol and Kaufman could wield the octopus imagery with impunity because the work of presenting themselves as normative examples of American Jewry, and of excising Communists like the Rosenbergs from that communal body, was already so far advanced. The tactic conveys, rather than the timidity some have ascribed to American Jews during this period, a self-confidence robust enough to insist on the value and legitimacy of a particular kind of Jewish-American identity.

ANATHEMATIZING THE ROSENBERGS

On the other hand, Saypol and Kaufman's use of this traditionally anti-Semitic image also demonstrates how intense was the struggle to eradicate difference within the Jewish American community. In the Manichaean context of the Cold War it did not appear to be possible to acknowledge a diversity of political opinion within American Judaism.[f] And so the

f. Nor did it seem possible to admit that anti-Semitism might be operating, in very different ways, both in the United States and in the Soviet bloc. Opponents of the Rosenbergs often pointed out, with considerable justification, that most of the people anxious to highlight potential prejudice in the Rosenberg case and to accuse the U.S. government of protofascism—including the Rosenbergs themselves—were completely silent about the 1952 purge of the Russian Jews accused in the "Doctor's Plot," the show trials and executions of Rudolf Slansky and other Czech Jews, and other manifestations of Stalin's murderous anti-Semitism.

quasi-inevitable outcome of the confrontation between pro- and anti-
Rosenberg Jews was for each side to deny the authentic Jewishness of the
other side. Defenders of the Rosenbergs condemned Kaufman and the
Jewish prosecutors as race traitors; enemies of the Rosenbergs not only
similarly accused the couple of betraying Jewry but went to some lengths
to demonstrate that they, and in many instances their supporters, were not
really Jews.

Leslie Fiedler offered the most extended and eloquent articulation of
this strategy in "Afterthoughts on the Rosenbergs," published in Stephen
Spender's journal, *Encounter*, a few months after the Rosenbergs' execu-
tion. Fiedler responds resentfully to the "moral blackmail" exercised by the
Rosenbergs' supporters, who demanded that liberals should "[revivify] the
battered belief that [. . .] the Jew (but in what sense were the Rosenbergs
Jews?) is always framed."[61] Having asked in what sense the Rosenbergs were
Jews, Fiedler goes on to show that the correct answer is: not in any sense.

Appalled by the passionate triteness of the Rosenbergs' *Death House
Letters*—he very nearly implies that they deserved execution for bad writing—Fiedler claims that in those letters the couple draws on their Jewish
heritage only where it can be falsified in the service of a bogus, and vulgar,
political agenda: "They neither know nor care what Judaism actually is
about; they will use as much of it as they need, defining it as they go. [. . .]
Thrilled by the sound of the shofar, [Ethel] thinks of the Jews everywhere
hastening to the synagogues to pray for a Happy New Year, but hastens to
remind them via her husband that 'we must not use prayer to the Almighty
as an excuse for avoiding our responsibilities to our neighbors . . . the daily
struggle for social justice.' [. . .] It is like the curtain line of an *agit-prop*
choral production at the combined celebration of *Rosh Hashanah* and the
anniversary of the Russian Revolution."[62] Fiedler characterizes even the
Rosenbergs' Jewish funeral as an "absurd masquerade," the tallis-draped
coffins, Jewish hymns, and Jewish prayers offered by a rabbi all part of a
Communist-orchestrated "hoax."[63] The American Jewish Committee's
Solomon Andhil Fineberg, too, wrote sarcastically that during the funeral
"Rabbi Abraham Cronbach and a cantor provided the religious note."[64] So
the rabbi and the cantor, while they escape being labeled non-Jewish themselves, are reduced to props, their Jewishness neutralized by the inauthen-
ticity of the occasion on which they exercise it.

Fiedler does not explain what "Judaism actually is about," but clearly
whatever it is, *he* represents its correct instantiation. Equally clearly, it

cannot be about left-wing politics, earnest rhetoric about social justice, or tacky public spectacles that marry Jewish liturgy to the themes and symbols of the popular front. As David Suchoff writes, Fiedler "condemned the Rosenbergs as specters of the working-class, immigrant Jewish past,"[65] but in fact his reasoning goes further, severing his own kind of Jewishness so entirely from the Rosenbergs' kind that they no longer qualify as Jewish at all. More than condemned or even disowned, they are *exorcised* from the body of American Jewry by the force of Fiedler's repudiation.

RESTAGING THE 1950S

The Rosenbergs' trial and its aftermath played a critical part in defining Jewish American identity in the 1950s and in precipitating "the decline of a viable Jewish left in the United States. [. . .] The Rosenberg case hastened and legitimated the purge of the Jewish left from the organized Jewish community."[66] This is not to say, of course, that every Jew in America accepted that model of identity or the terms of anti-Communist ideology without complaint. Even as mainstream a figure as Supreme Court justice Felix Frankfurter was put off by Irving Kaufman's public display of religiosity during the trial; in 1958 Frankfurter wrote to Judge Learned Hand that "'I despise a Judge who feels God told him to impose a death sentence,' and he vowed 'I am mean enough to try to stay here [on the Supreme Court] long enough so that K will be too old to succeed me.'"[67] Nor did the Cold War consensus hold firmly once Jewish America moved, along with the rest of the country, into the turbulent waters of the 1960s. But the effects of the case, like the debates it provoked, lingered for decades.

These were then brought back to vivid life in *Angels in America*, in which Kushner restages the intracommunity conflicts the case dramatized and, arguably, tries to bring Jews back within a framework of consensus—one in which, we would assume, the terms are now set by the political Left with which Kushner identifies. Having been formally exorcised from the Jewish community in the 1950s, the ghost of Ethel Rosenberg is invited back by Kushner to haunt Roy Cohn and the reflections he inspires on the possibilities and limits of the politics of identity. The characters of Ethel and Roy obviously work to provide historical depth and resonance to Kushner's investigation of Reaganism; in particular, as one critic notes, "as a 'Saint of the Right' [. . .] Cohn represents a point of continuity between the anticommunism of the 1950s and the Republican ascendancy of the

Reagan 1980s,"[68] as does Ronald Reagan himself, never seen but often referenced in the play. But even more importantly, Kushner's Roy Cohn serves both to focus and to problematize the text's efforts to resolve the ideological and spiritual rifts it portrays within its multiple, overlapping, combative communities.

After all, within a group cohering around the presumption of a shared identity, ontology is frequently (if only delusionally) supposed to yield consensus. By reinvoking the Rosenberg trial and Cohn's role in it, Kushner recalls the collapse of that supposition into charges and countercharges of treason among Jews during the 1950s. Roy proclaims that he values loyalty above all else and says he was proud to help execute the Rosenbergs "because I fucking hate traitors."[69] But the play allows us to ask whether it was not Roy Cohn who was the archtraitor, a man whose loyalty to his vision of a conservative America entailed multiple betrayals of both Jews and homosexuals.

In numerous interviews Kushner has located the genesis of the play in Cohn's 1986 death from AIDS and the reluctant sense of identification it provoked among gay people generally and in Kushner specifically, saying that "in a certain sense, his dying of this disease made him a part of the gay and lesbian community even if we don't really want him to be a part of our community";[70] elsewhere Kushner asks, "How broad, how embracing was our sense of community? Did it encompass an implacable foe like Roy? Was he one of us?"[71] *Est-ce qu'il en était?* Did Roy Cohn's ethnicity, religion, and sexual practices place him inside the communities marked "Jews" and "gay people" whether or not he, or they, liked it? Or did his role in the conviction and execution of the Rosenbergs, his assistance to Joe McCarthy, his lengthy legal career "as a savvy practitioner of situational immorality,"[72] and his attacks on gay rights place him beyond the pale, constituting unforgivable treachery to those communities? And did it matter whether he chose to be identified with them?

Such questions recall Proust and his project of incessantly demarcating, and then displacing, the horizons of personal and communal identities—and, as in *À la recherche*, any apparent answers that the play provides to those questions are at best provisional. Kushner also follows Proust in positing an analogy between the collective and the self, although he does not destabilize the notion of the self as Proust does but only bifurcates it psychologically. Viewing Cohn not just as a member of the same collectivity to which Kushner belongs, that of gay Jewish men, but as a hated part of himself, Kushner has called the man "a maliciously exuberant expression for my own dark side. [. . .] I think I have a great deal of self-hatred, a profound feeling of fraudulence, of being detestable and evil."[73] Kushner's analogy confirms that if identity groups are thought of as constituting unitary selves, then antagonism within the group will necessarily be viewed as self-hatred. And it prepares us to understand why, if American Jews in the 1950s tried to settle that psychic division by killing the Rosenbergs, an American Jew in the 1990s might attempt to accomplish the same thing by killing Roy Cohn.

ISAAC AND JACOB

Any discussion of the relationship between identity politics and Roy Cohn must take into account the ways that he negotiated his own relationship to the identity categories "Jew" and "homosexual"—or perhaps negotiates, for we are dealing here less with the historical figure of Cohn than with his fictional incarnation, whom I will henceforth call "Roy," a distinction many critics do not make and one it is admittedly difficult to sustain at times. Both Cohn and Roy have been, almost invariably, described as self-loathing queers in denial about their sexuality and also, occasionally, as self-hating Jews. Daniel Kiefer, for example, writes that "in the character of Roy Cohn Kushner brings to life the great American traitor in matters sexual, racial, and political. The Roy Cohn of history was the perfect example of the closeted homosexual who reviles homosexuals, the Jew who hates Jews, and the patriot who scorns the law of the land."[74] Unraveling the psychological complexities of the historical Roy Cohn would be well beyond my own capacities and the parameters of this study. I would argue, though, that Kushner's Roy is something much more complicated, and more interesting, than a self-loathing closet case. It is, indeed, quite difficult to reconcile the character's expansive, energetic arrogance, his sheer brio, with the idea of self-hatred. If we take him on his own terms, then he is not in denial and does not hate himself at all but instead takes pride and pleasure in being both "a heterosexual man who fucks around with guys" (*MA*, 46) and "the tough Jew par excellence,"[75] a man who opposes toughness, muscularity, and the exercise of power to the spectres of effeminate homosexuals and weak Jewish "scholars, saints, socialists, and schlemiels."

Among many critical responses to the lengthy speech in *Millennium Approaches* in which Roy categorizes sexualities according to their degree of "clout," I am most persuaded by that of Ross Posnock, who contends that Roy should be taken at his word when he tells his doctor that it is neither "sophistry" nor "hypocrisy" for him to claim heterosexual status regardless of his sexual conduct: "This self-invention is Kushner's Cohn at his most Nietzschean, as he transvalues sexuality by equating it with power rather than with identity. [. . .] Kushner's Cohn forces us to be skeptical about assuming that a hidden reality of agonizing sexual self-hatred rages inside him. Such an assumption is derived from the modern therapeutic regime that constructs sexuality itself as a constitutive truth of identity. In short, Kushner's Cohn asks us to entertain the possibility that Cohn was neither out nor closeted."[76] If, therefore, I still refer to Roy occasionally as "homosexual" or "gay," it is not in defiance of the text but solely because our "modern therapeutic regime" provides no precise, and concise, term for the liminal sexual territory he claims.

Roy's Jewishness occupies a less ambiguous zone than his sexuality—as was true of Cohn—but is also expressed in terms of clout, or toughness. However, rather than associating Jewishness in general with effeminacy and presenting himself as an exception, as he does with homosexuality, Roy defines toughness as the ur-Jewish identity and valorizes it over Jewish victimization. Musing about the Hebrew patriarchs, he refers to Isaac as "the sacrifice. That jerk"; Jacob, however, who becomes Israel and thus avatar and progenitor of the whole Jewish people, Roy admires as "a ruthless motherfucker" (P, 81). Hence, both Jewishness and sexuality are valued in accordance with their functions and potentials within matrices of power; both can be used, and are used by Roy, strategically to further political ends. One critic points out that Roy includes, among his questionable "litigation strategies," both "schtupping" judges and getting theater tickets for them,[77] in lines foregrounding his Jewishness and his relationship to gay sexuality and culture. Indeed, Roy's speech through the play is markedly inflected with both Yiddishisms and flamboyantly camp expressions and intonations, and he repeatedly reveals his familiarity with Jewish and gay cultural practices: he eats liver sandwiches, swaps lines in Yiddish with Ethel, and shows off his insider's expertise about gay-themed Broadway musicals: "No you wouldn't like La Cage, trust me, I know" (MA, 12). His character can therefore hardly be characterized as closeted or passing; if he is in vociferous agreement with the gender norms and political imperatives of the Cold War period and their renaissance under Reagan, that does not signify denial of his subaltern identities but rather the refusal to inhabit them as positions of subalternity.

The text opposes to Roy a series of "negations," people who nominally share one or more identity categories with him but who derive from those identities entirely different ontologies or politics. Belize, the African American nurse who does drag and hates America, explicitly calls himself Roy's negation (P, 77), but there are at least two others, Louis Ironson and Ethel Rosenberg. Ethel is his nemesis, forever joined to him by their shared Ashkenazi heritage, their place in history, and their positions on opposing sides of the Cold War. Louis, a liberal gay Jew and son of "New Deal Pinko Parents" (P, 122), never meets Roy alive, but their inverted mirror images touch at several points: they both have sex with men, they are perhaps equally selfish, they both seduce the Mormon Joe Pitt—Roy politically, Louis sexually. And they are both sexualized via their noses, that traditional sign of Jewish difference and metaphor for the Jewishly different phallus: Louis initiates Joe into homosex through an appeal to his olfactory sense, while Roy boasts about the childhood nose operation, a "symbolic circumcision," his mother insisted he have "to toughen me up" (P, 81).

That the two men can be read as doubles is underscored by the fact that the actor Ben Shenkman played both Roy and Louis in stage productions before being cast as Louis in the HBO movie version of *Angels*. That they are also antitheses is clear, not only because Roy's conservatism could eat Louis's ambivalent liberalism for lunch, but because—particularly in Shenkman's interpretation of the role—Louis is so whiney, constructing his own Jewishness only in reference to the prejudice he believes it provokes in others rather than through a genealogy of ruthlessness. Referring to Roy's nose operation, Alisa Solomon writes that "this symbolic circumcision simultaneously marks Roy's Jewishness and his refusal to participate in stereotypical Jewish victimhood," an attitude she contrasts with that of Louis, who "clings for moral legitimacy to his histrionic suffering."[78]

Roy also contrasts his own toughness with Irving Kaufman's, claiming that he had to pressure Kaufman to convict the Rosenbergs and give Ethel the death sentence and referring to the judge, who is not named, only as "that timid Yid nebbish on the bench" (MA, 108). In reality, of course, Kaufman was quite a tough Jew himself, albeit of a more refined ilk than Cohn. But in the play Roy's goal in thus apostrophizing Kaufman is to emphasize his own antinebbishness, his toughness as a model Jew—one with sufficient virility to act as an antidote to Julius Rosenberg, the even more offensively effeminized, deviant Jew hovering invisibly at the margins of the play.

For what has happened to Julius? He is almost entirely erased from the play's historical memory, alluded to briefly only once, when Ethel gives "his regards" to Roy (*MA*, 111). Critics have offered various explanations of Ethel's presence in the play, most of which point to the largely extinct cultural and political tradition she represents as the Communist child of immigrants. But this cannot be the only explanation for her solo appearance, since that role could equally well be performed by Julius. Two obvious reasons for Kushner to focus on Ethel instead of Julius are that her gender difference accents her political differences from both Roy and Louis[79] and, more importantly, that it draws out the misogyny informing Roy's hatred of her, of homosexuals, and of un-tough Jewish men. What Julius represented in the 1950s is then split up among other Jewish men in the play: his monstrosity is assigned to Roy, leaving Louis (whose name might be homophonically related to a truncated "Julius") as a shell of the formerly threatening figure of the Jewish/ Communist male—still on the left, a deviant, and a sneak, but too ineffective and isolated to be a serious threat to anyone. Roy, though, becomes the octopus in Julius's place, imbuing that symbol not only with the ominous voracity traditionally invested in it by anti-Semites but also, as Freedman points out, with connotations of both phallic and oral sexuality:

> An octopus [. . .] has "eight loving arms," but it also has "all those suckers": the multiplication of phalli suggested by the arms is reoriented by the trope of the suckers, which unites implications of cheating, vampirism, and fellatio in a vivid image of monstrosity that is both recognizably Jewish and demonstrably queer. The figure of Cohn thus represents an audacious attempt to think through to the center of anti-Semitic imagery, to the cultural queering of the Jew, and finally to the representation of the Jew as at once monstrous, empowered, and perverse—an image Kushner then installs at the center of the play's most malignant icon of queer/Jewish identity.[80]

Splitting Jewish monstrosity, and Jewish power, from Left politics in this way may be Kushner's commentary on the transfer of power in American politics more generally from the New Deal Left to the reinvigorated Right of the 1980s. It also enables Kushner to distinguish genres of Jewish masculinity and Jewish queerness from one another—perhaps, as some have suggested, so as to revive a "gentle" Jewish manliness, or *menschlichkeit*, in the person of Louis, at the play's end while suppressing the violence

Roy represents.[81] "Thinking through" anti-Semitic imagery seems, however, to imply a more complicated undertaking than simply projecting that imagery onto a hated antagonist so as to valorize his inverse, and so that is a reading I will question later in this chapter when I consider the implications of *Perestroika*'s conclusion.

WRESTLING WITH BELIZE

Before we address the role of Jewishness at the play's end, though, we should look at the model of Jewishness Roy represents as he moves toward his final, metaphorical confrontation with his Jewish antitheses in *Perestroika*'s fifth act, when Louis joins Ethel in saying the Mourner's Kaddish over Roy's corpse. I will approach that scene by detouring through four earlier moments in *Perestroika* in which Roy, while still living, interacts with Belize, "the Negro night nurse, my negation" (*P*, 75). In dialogue with Belize, Roy articulates his understanding of his identities as a Jew and a man, an understanding that clearly reflects the norms consecrated in the 1950s by the Cold War in general and the Rosenberg case in particular. Belize and Roy's relationship takes the form of a series of jousts in which each tries to maneuver the other onto his own terrain, Belize stipulating terms of engagement that depend on biopolitics—the status of bodies, their acts, and the identities they can generate—while Roy insists on a conservative vision of a world premised on aggressive individualism and structured through relations of economic power.

Roy's first encounter with Belize, immediately after he is admitted to the hospital in the last stages of AIDS, begins with Roy demanding a white nurse as his "constitutional right" and Belize informing him that as a hospital patient, "you don't have any constitutional rights" (*P*, 23). Roy is thus immediately stripped not just of clout but of citizenship, moved out of the polis and into a realm where for the moment only his materiality as a sick person is relevant to his status; later he will even admit his own disenfranchisement, telling Ethel that America is "just no country for the infirm" (*P*, 58). So Belize is able to gain the upper hand with his opening gambit, despite his class and race, simply by virtue of being a healthy person armed with professional authority and a sharp needle. Roy counters with a mocking invocation of the "historical liberal coalition" between Jews and African Americans, which he characteristically defines in terms of capitalist relations: "Jews and coloreds, historical liberal coalition, right? My people being the first to sell retail to your people, your people being the first people my people could afford to hire to sweep out the store Saturday mornings, and then we all held hands and rode the bus to Selma. Not me of course, I don't ride buses, I take cabs. But the thing about the American Negro is, he never went Communist. Loser Jews did. But you people had Jesus so the reds never got to you" (P, 24). Here Roy, who really wants Belize to keep him company, affirms that they have a connection but then defines it as one rooted in the economic superiority of Jews to African Americans. After emphasizing the financial basis of Jewish-black "solidarity," Roy then exempts himself, by virtue of his class status, even from that kind of economic coalition: "I don't ride buses, I take cabs." He also classifies himself as a Jew—they are "my people" to him—while distinguishing the kind of Jew he is from "Loser," Communist Jews, repeating the gesture of disavowal he and other anti-Communist Jews made in the 1950s and also, not coincidentally, affirming the crucial role of religious belief as a prophylactic against Communism.

Belize responds to Roy's attempt to control the terms of their connection by giving Roy vital information about AIDS treatments and then—after Roy calls him a "butterfingers spook faggot nurse" and asks why Belize would help him—saying he does so in an act of "solidarity. One faggot to another" (P, 27). Belize verbally drags Roy into an identification he wants to refuse and, simultaneously, demonstrates that contrary to what Roy has said earlier in the play, homosexuals do not have to lack "clout." Daryl Ogden observes that Belize's specialized knowledge comes not from his medical training but from gay community groups like ACT UP, which challenged the medical establishment's approach to AIDS, attacking, for example, the double-blind testing protocols against which Belize warns Roy.[82] Used as the basis for communal action, homosexuality can "actually be a politically powerful identity,"[83] the point on which Belize is able to end discussion; by the time Roy responds with another jab at Belize's economic powerlessness by threatening to demote him to "flipping Big Macs," Belize has left the room and is out of earshot (P, 27).

At their second meeting Belize and Roy move from a contest over the terms on which they will establish their relationship to openly venomous conflict. In doing so, they seem to reenact the period in the late 1960s when Jewish and black Americans, who had temporarily united in the struggle for civil rights, began to turn against each other as each group started to assert more aggressive political claims and tactics.[84] Warren Rosenberg writes that in American literature of the period, "the African American male is seen as a competitive threat to Jewish masculinity." He offers the example of Bernard Malamud's 1971 novel *The Tenants*, which features a violent fight between a Jew and a black man in which they exchange racial insults while castrating and finally killing each other, and compares it to the fight between Belize and Roy in act 3 scene 2.[85]

The parallel is in fact close enough that one suspects Kushner had Malamud's novel in mind when writing the scene. Malamud's combatants call each other "Bloodsuckin Jew Niggerhater" and "Anti-Semitic Ape."[86] In *Perestroika* Roy and Belize hurl comparable racial slurs at each other after Belize asks for some of Roy's precious stash of AZT and Roy refuses to give it to him because, characteristically, he is "not moved by an unequal distribution of goods on this earth" and is not interested in helping redistribute his own wealth (*P*, 55). During their foul-mouthed fusillade, Roy defines Belize in terms of both racial abjection ("nigger," "spade," "lackey," "slave," and "ape") and homosexual effeminacy ("cunt" and "faggot"). Belize retaliates with "cocksucking," also defining Roy as a passive homosexual, and follows up with a volley of anti-Semitic abuse: "cloven-hoofed," associating the Jew with Satan; "pig," designating Roy as *treyf*, abhorrent to other Jews; and finally, "kike," to which Roy responds, "*Now* you're talking" (*P*, 56–57). Now, indeed, Belize is talking in terms Roy considers meaningful, using speech as a vehicle for the aggressive assertion of dominance, and he is rewarded for having achieved fluency in Roy's language by getting several bottles of the AZT. So if Belize "won" their first bout by forcing Roy into an identification with him as a fellow homosexual ("solidarity. One faggot to another"), Roy wins the second round by forcing Belize onto the ground of racial antagonism and obliging him to name Roy as Other to himself in an act of both violence and recognition.

A few scenes later in act 3 Roy and Belize have their most intimate encounter, in which each is most pointedly defined as the other's inversion or negation at the moment when they are also moving toward sexual union or death—or perhaps toward death *as* sexual union, for every opposition in the scene dissolves into likeness, an effect reflecting Roy's morphine-induced haziness in this encounter, as well as the dialectical movement of the play as a whole. Roy associates Belize with darkness, monstrosity, and death, calling him a "bogeyman," a "schvartze toytenmann," and "the Negro night nurse, my negation," who has "come to escort me to the underworld"; ultimately, he names him "nothing." Belize concurs, identifying himself as "your negation," and finally, "just the shadow on your grave"

(*P*, 74–77). They have inverted concepts of the afterlife, too; Roy takes Belize's description of Heaven, a place "like San Francisco [...] full of music and lights and racial impurity and gender confusion," to be a depiction of Hell (*P*, 76). While confirming Belize's absolute otherness, though, Roy's language simultaneously evokes both erotic desire and identification. He propositions Belize in terms that stress their racial difference while aligning lovemaking with death: "You wrap your arms around me now. Squeeze the bloody life from me. [...] Dark strong arms, take me like that" (*P*, 75). In calling Belize the "bogeyman," Roy conjures earlier images of his own monstrosity, reminding us that Belize initially metaphorized Roy as a vampire (*P*, 22). And in naming him a "toytenmann" Roy recalls his own self-description in act 3 scene 2 as "a goddam dead man" (*P*, 56).

Several pages later Roy—no longer stoned on morphine—and Belize retreat momentarily from this movement toward synthesis in their last scene together before Roy's death, returning instead to their tussle over status. When Roy complains that "every goddam thing I ever wanted they have taken from me. Mocked and reviled, all my life," Belize responds dryly, "Join the club." Roy snaps back, "I don't belong to any club you could get through the front door of," again emphasizing his social and economic power and Belize's subaltern status (*P*, 87). And he ends their conversation by saying to Belize, "You. Me. No. Connection. Nobody . . . with me now. But the dead" (*P*, 88). Significantly, in the lines immediately before this, Roy has been talking to Ethel Rosenberg's ghost, invisible to Belize; she is "the dead" whom Roy has with him. Roy's overt purpose in this passage is to affirm that his class, race, and social status override the identification Belize makes between the two of them as homosexuals. But it is revealing that, as in their first scene together, when Roy discusses the relationship between "your people" and "my people," Kushner now has Roy demarcate his difference from Belize by identifying himself as a Jew. In that first scene, as we saw, Roy's kind of Jew—affluent, conservative, emphatically white— was implicitly differentiated from "Loser Jews," the ones who went Communist. But now, as he slides toward death himself, he announces his *connection* to those other Jews he had previously cast as his antitheses. As the real Cohn's death from AIDS "made him a part of the gay and lesbian community even if we don't really want him to be a part of our community," Roy's physical disintegration and confrontation with his own mortality increasingly bring him into proximity with the treasonous, radical, gender-deviant, dead Rosenbergs.

THE KADDISH: RECONCILIATION AND RETALIATION

The movement toward identification and connection between conflicting archetypes of Jewish identity seems to reach its apotheosis in the scene where Belize calls Louis to Roy's hospital room to say the Kaddish over the corpse. Louis, "an intensely secular Jew," does not remember the prayer and fumbles for words until Ethel appears and begins to recite it with him. At first he merely repeats what she says, but then begins to retrieve the words himself from some store of either individual or collective memory, and the two complete the prayer together (*P*, 122–23). This scene is usually read as a gesture toward reconciliation—what one critic calls a "movement toward a new community based on a solidarity across both new and old lines of group identification."[87] In this reading, Belize's ethic of "softness, compliance, forgiveness, grace," triumphs, allowing "love and justice" to meet (*MA*, 100; *P*, 122). Kushner himself has confirmed that the scene is about forgiveness, saying that when the image of Ethel Rosenberg first popped into his head as he was writing the play, he "didn't know why she had come," and he "finally figured it out that she had been trying to find some way to forgive [Roy]. Because the play is very much [. . .] concerned with questions of forgiveness and the possibility of forgiveness."[88] Others have asserted that it is not only Ethel who needs to forgive Roy but also Louis, Belize, Kushner himself, and the audience, "as if our humanity depended on our mourning for the most vicious, hateful, reactionary American ever to deny his queerness."[89]

I do not doubt that on one level, and a very important one, *Angels* is indeed about forgiveness, and that for Ethel and Louis to say the Kaddish is a gesture of reconciliation. But it is simultaneously an act of mastery and revenge, and not simply because of the innovative ending they add to the prayer: "You sonofabitch" (*P*, 123). Louis and Ethel are able to join in Jewish community with Roy but only, quite literally, over his dead body. To insist on asserting their commonality with their archenemy is a curiously double gesture of reconciliation and retaliation; they forgive Cohn his treason against "his people" while simultaneously punishing him for it by confirming that left-wing, "cloutless," sex/gender-deviant Jews—"Loser Jews"—*are* his people.

If we apply this analysis of the Kaddish scene to its political implications, reading it as Kushner's intervention into the intracommunal antagonisms of the 1950s, we can also see it as an attempt both to heal a breach and to eliminate the opposition. The surrealist or supernatural elements of *Angels* allow Kushner to tamper with the historical narrative, to stage what one critic calls "breaks with history," for instance, by letting Ethel Rosenberg triumph over Roy Cohn[90] and so reversing the outcome of that period in the 1950s when Jewish Americans disavowed the radical Left and affirmed the conservative, homophobic, gender-normative values of Cold War culture in exchange for citizenship—one kind of citizenship, at any rate. The effort of Cohn and the Rosenbergs' other Jewish adversaries to expunge what the couple represented from the community of American Jews would thus be countered and redressed by Roy's textual death and posthumous reconciliation with his enemies and victims.

From this perspective Kushner can, certainly, be seen as staging a reconciliation within American Jewry, imagining that Right and Left, the "tough cookies" and the "socialists and schlemiels," can be brought back together. But reconciliation and forgiveness are themselves the values of the schlemiels, not of the tough cookies, and so the rift between Jewish Left and Right—and the psychic rupture between Kushner and his "own dark side"— would be not so much mended as overcome by suppressing one term. When we consider, in addition, that it is Belize who orchestrates the Kaddish, and that Belize and Roy have been struggling throughout *Perestroika* to impose antithetical definitions of identity and community on each other, it is hard not to wonder if Belize is simply trying to ensure that he has the last word. Let us keep in mind that Roy expires after a final scene with Ethel in which he tricks her into betraying sympathy for him and then triumphantly shouts, "I WIN!" before collapsing (*P*, 114). The fact that the lone representative of the Jewish political Right in the play has to *die* before he can be welcomed into the community composed of Ethel, Louis, and Belize suggests that the Kaddish could be a way of saying, "No, Roy—*we* win."

ROY COHN THE REVENANT: DEAD DOESN'T MATTER

The interpretation of the Kaddish scene I have just offered is not where my reading of the play ends, however, for three reasons. The first is that the play as a whole, and indeed Kushner's dialectical imagination in all his work, encourages us to think in terms of ongoing movement forward rather than final resolutions. The second is that Roy refuses to stay dead. And the last is that Ethel makes her final appearance in *Angels* not spe-cifically to engage with Louis's politics but rather to remind him how to pray. All of these points, it seems to me, need to be taken into consideration in any account of the text's political functions both conscious and, perhaps, unconscious.

If Ethel, Louis, and Belize are Roy's antitheses, then one outcome of their confrontation with Roy should be synthesis or, at any rate, the generation of something new and revolutionary.[g] Catherine Stevenson asserts that in much of Kushner's work, "mothers and their relationships to the next generation of children serve as important loci for dramatizing the operation of the dialectic" and that *Perestroika* specifically "casts mother figures as catalysts whose actions release new creative energy that empowers children to rewrite individual and social history."[91] Stevenson focuses particularly on the figure of Hannah yet never mentions Ethel, who is played by the same actor who plays Hannah, and of whom Roy says that she "reminded us all of our little Jewish mamas" (*MA*, 108). As mother/catalyst in the Kaddish scene Ethel might provide a way of, as it were, sublating Roy and producing, in Louis or even Belize, a newly energized progressivism that moves beyond the calcified Cold War dichotomy represented by reactionary Roy and the Stalinist Rosenbergs. And there are, indeed, indications that Louis and Belize take from this encounter with Roy something they will carry out with them into the gay community and AIDS activism, concretized in the AZT they spirit out of Roy's hospital room. In *Millennium* Louis says to Belize that "*power* is the object, not being tolerated" (*MA*, 90), and taking the AZT—which Roy acquired illicitly by pulling some of the many strings he controlled within the Reagan administration—is "a tacit acknowledgment of the lessons in power that Cohn might have to teach the gay community."[92] Furthermore, that they thank Roy for the drugs by saying the Kaddish, essentially paying with the prayer for the goods they are going to redistribute, suggests acquiescence with Roy's view that the social sphere is organized by relations of exchange—and of course, it is Ethel who makes the exchange possible, engendering it with Roy. The interactions between the characters do not, then, stop at the terminus of either revenge *or* reconciliation but instead produce effects, symbolized by the AZT, that reverberate in the wider community and into the future.

The second reason that the Kaddish scene cannot signify only the suppression, or even the sublation, of Roy and what he embodies (political

g. On Kushner's use of dialectical oppositions to produce oxymorons rather than synthesis, see Savran, "Ambivalence."

reaction, monstrosity, misogyny, treason . . .) is the curious way that "Cohn keeps rising from the dead, like a zombie or golem"[93]—or like the vampire to which Belize initially compared him. First Roy feigns death in order to taunt Ethel. Then, after he "really" dies and has had the Kaddish said over him, he reappears in act 5 scene 4, "dressed in a fabulous floor-length black velvet robe de chambre," in order to haunt a terrified Joe, to whom he explains, "Dead [. . .] doesn't matter" (P, 124). Finally, in act 5 scene 9—a scene described in the directions as "optional" and rarely included in productions of the play—Roy shows up "in Heaven, or Hell or Purgatory" agreeing to act as God's defense attorney in the lawsuit with which the angels are threatening Him (P, 140).

Despite these repeated postmortem appearances by Roy, his absence from the epilogue to *Perestroika*—in which a multicultural little group of the leading characters assembles in Central Park—is often taken to mean that for better or for worse, he has finally been expunged from the universe of the play. But I am not convinced that Roy's absence from the final scene fully cancels out the implications either of his dynamism throughout the play or of his uncanny textual afterlives. In the last pages of *Perestroika* Roy, though dead, is definitely not gone, and his apparition in act 5 scene 9 conveys no sense of finality, only an eager anticipation of his next court battle. Furthermore, Kushner grants Roy an afterlife one imagines he will thoroughly enjoy: still a lawyer despite his earthly disbarment, wearing a robe that simultaneously connotes opulent wealth, outré fabulousness, and judicial power. (And he is counsel to the Aleph Glyph yet, the origin of all language—a gratifying eternal reward indeed for a character whose political and theatrical power derives from his dazzlingly energetic speech.) Kushner has also, it appears, tried to squelch his own generosity toward Roy by making the ninth scene optional. Yet there the scene, and Roy, remain, on the printed page if not in performance. Freedman acknowledges that Roy's repeated revivals are an "endeavor to bring Cohn's uncanny power under authorial control. [. . .] The energies gathered in Cohn exceed his author's attempts to order and organize them. The persistence of these efforts to kill Cohn, mourn him, revive him, then kill him again attests to the power he continues to exert over his author."[94]

The two most recent major productions of the play, the HBO movie and the 2010 off-Broadway revival, demonstrate both that Roy continues to exert that power and that Kushner remains ambivalent toward his character. In the film Roy is played by Al Pacino—physically attractive, notably heterosexual, and a member of the American ethnic minority most frequently stereotyped as hypervirile—imbuing the character with precisely the kind of charismatic masculinity to which he aspires (as did the real Cohn, who would probably have been delighted by the casting choice). It is also a kind of masculinity that presumably remains seductive to many queer Jewish boys growing up in America, however progressive their politics, suggesting that the author's will to suppress Roy could be counterbalanced by desire for him, as well as identification with him. Louis's confession to Joe that "the more appalling I find your politics the more I want to hump you" (P, 71) might well be Kushner, or at least his play, speaking to Roy. Rosenberg writes that "Kushner knows quite well that he is seduced by Cohn" but contends that in making that seduction manifest he succeeds in overcoming it,[95] a reading with which I cannot fully agree. Not that Kushner does not keep trying: he rewrote *Perestroika* yet again for the 2010 revival in order "to prevent Roy from having a final laugh. The devil no longer steals the show."[96]

One effect of this obsessive textual game of fort-da is to call into question the premise that Jewish American identity has been successfully reclaimed for a progressive politics by the play's end. Roy, as an exemplar of aggressive Jewish conservatism, simply will not go away, even if we—and his author—want him to. It is true that there are no conservatives in the pluralist community Kushner presents in the epilogue (that we know of— Hannah remains a political cipher), and that the only Jew in that scene is the liberal Louis. But the end of the play does not represent the end of history, and there is a reason that Prior's pronouncement "We will be citizens" is in the future tense. For enfranchisement is not only a set of formal rights and responsibilities but also always a work in progress, as we are reminded by Louis's reference to "another national entity that does not yet exist, the state of Palestine."[97] At the conclusion of *Angels*, I would argue, Roy has not actually been eliminated; although he is not part of the "ideal body politic," he still haunts the play, which implies at the very least that America, and American Jews in particular, will have to continue to reckon with the political forces Roy represents. Even if such a politics can and should be contested, the pattern of the text argues against the hope that it can be expunged.

It also becomes plain that the central ideological disputes of the 1950s were not truly settled, either by the execution of the Rosenbergs in that decade or after the Reagan years, when we look at the way they have continued to replay themselves in reactions to *Angels*. The hostility of some conservative reviewers has inspired misreadings that clearly respond not to the actual text of the play but to the Cold War arguments it references. Probably the most frequently quoted of these hostile reviews appeared first in the right-wing *Washington Times* in April 1993 and then was expanded into a *National Review* article published two months later. In these pieces columnist Richard Grenier seems particularly indignant that Kushner has made Ethel Rosenberg a nice person and contemptuously accuses him of thinking the traitorous Rosenbergs were idealistic "saints and martyrs."[98] The point was taken up in a *Wall Street Journal* review of the 2010 revival that deplores the way the play "implicitly proclaims the innocence of Julius and Ethel Rosenberg."[99] These accusations correspond precisely to the terms of reproach the Rosenbergs' adversaries used against their supporters but hardly at all to the text—for while it is true that as written, Ethel can be played as a sympathetic character, affability is no guarantee of innocence, and Kushner never claims it is. Similarly, Grenier appears convinced that because Kushner is both gay and a dialectical materialist he is also a secularist; as Anthony Lioi writes, "It is particularly important to Richard Grenier's analysis of *Millennium Approaches* that Kushner's Marxism be taken as a dogmatic statement of atheism."[100] This too, of course, reflects the dominant consensus of the Cold War but is otherwise a bizarre interpretation of a play so replete with religious themes, imagery, language, and characters.

Grenier's investment in Cold War ideology is most apparent in his uneasy treatment of Jewishness in the play. The first version of his review is candidly uncomfortable with the work's *Yiddishkeit*; Grenier opens with the line, "If you notice a hint of Yiddish in my voice, it's because I've just survived the first Broadway preview of 'Angels in America, Millennium Approaches,'" and then complains that during the show he had to ask Rona Jaffe the meaning of the word *feh*. He also notes that Roy Cohn was a personal acquaintance of his and "nothing like" Kushner's character Roy, who is "very Jewish."[101] In the second version of the review, however, Grenier—like conservatives in the 1950s—retreats from overt anti-Semitism into a vaguely philo-Semitic affirmation of Judeo-Christianity, now directing his animosity toward homosexuality and *secular* Judaism. Grenier has apparently realized, in the interval between the publication of the two versions of the piece, that he is the "son of a Jewish mother," and he uses this newly revealed insider status (he now explains the meaning of *feh* to his readers without mentioning that two months earlier he didn't know the word himself) to inveigh against those other, agnostic Jews who condone homosexuality only because "they have become alienated from their own traditional beliefs" and "have become a paradigm of the thoroughly secularized world, with its repudiation of moral prohibitions as expressed by the great Western religions, Christianity as well as Judaism."[102] Grenier's reviews demonstrate that just as was true forty years earlier, anti-Semitism often hovers in the background of homophobia and anti-Left politics, and he clearly thinks that executing the Rosenbergs didn't kill Jewish radicalism nearly dead enough. But he also illustrates that, as in the 1950s, Jews can be readily absorbed into conservative narratives provided they are anti-Communist, homophobic, religious, and not "very Jewish."

Reviewers like Grenier are arguing with a straw man, however, for *Angels in America* dispenses with the Cold War binarism between Jewish secularism and a religious orthodoxy modeled on Protestantism, in the same way that, politically, it seeks a way out of the Cold War's ideological impasses. Roy's reincarnations dispel the idea that Jewish American identity can be counted on to yield political consensus. If there is any such thing as Jewishness at all—any way to account for Kushner's sense that Roy Cohn was his "dark side"—it obviously does not ground itself in the political in this play. Kushner has wrestled with the question of how else Jewishness might be constituted. In a 1994 interview he bemoaned the fact that "Jewish culture" has been driven "from its progressive basis," and said of Jews, "I don't know what to call us at this point. I mean we're not a religion, it makes everyone uneasy to think of us as a race, including Jews, it's very odd; we've wound up being the oddest phenomena in modern history."[103] In the light of Kushner's contention that "we're not a religion," it may seem strange for me to argue that in *Angels* Jewishness is, finally, constructed on the terrain of the religious. And in view of the numerous critical readings of the play launched from the Left that complain, precisely for that reason, that Kushner eventually abandons real political engagement for mushy spirituality, it may be even more perverse to insist that in *Angels* the religious is the requisite foundation of any subsequent engagement with the political, certainly for Jews and perhaps for everyone. Yet that is the conclusion to which my reading of *Perestroika*, and specifically of Ethel's role in the Kaddish scene, tends.

LEARNING TO DAVEN

As we saw earlier, most analyses of Ethel's role in the play focus, with evident reason, on her embodiment of radical immigrant political culture. Yet in the Kaddish scene, her final appearance (apparition?) in the play, Ethel coaches Louis in religious observance—a peculiar role for Kushner to assign to a woman much better known for her politics than for her piety. After all, if her primary purpose were to infuse Louis's pallid liberalism with revolutionary enthusiasm, leading him through a reading of the *Communist Manifesto* would seem more to the point than helping him recite the Kaddish. Apparently, with Roy dead she no longer has a political function, nor can she still be explained as Roy's psychic projection, a piece of unfinished political business. Instead, she is called up to remind Louis of something about Judaism that, on some level, he already knows, since after she begins prompting him he is able to recite the prayer independently. But what is it that she enables him to remember?

It may be that Ethel recalls Louis to a tradition of Jewish ethics that he strayed from when he decided to leave Prior. When struggling with that decision Louis consulted the rabbi Chemelwitz—played by the same actor who plays Ethel—asking him, "What does the Holy Writ say about someone who abandons someone he loves at a time of great need?" The rabbi's response—"The Holy Scriptures have nothing to say about such a person"—suggests that in deserting his sick lover, Louis is putting himself entirely outside the realm of human behavior encompassed by Jewish moral teaching (*MA*, 25). When he reencounters the rabbi/Ethel in *Perestroika*, Louis, reciting a prayer integral to the Jewish liturgy, signals his return to the fold.[h]

Louis's nostotic trajectory is also evident in his move, after he abandons Prior, to the Lower East Side, "where the Jews lived when they first arrived. And now, a hundred years later, the place to which their more seriously fucked-up grandchildren repair" (*P*, 28). He lives there for a while with Joe, but it is also where he eventually realizes what damage Joe's conservative

---

h. Not all the characters played by a single actor are simply doubles of each other, and even the rabbi and Ethel represent significantly different generations and cultural traditions within American Judaism. Nonetheless, given that these are the only two scenes in which this actor engages with Louis, it is plausible that there is some important parallel between the two characters in relation to *him*.

legal decisions have done in the world and so is able to leave him and try to return to Prior, possessing slightly greater moral clarity than he had at the play's beginning and a little better prepared to act like a human, a mensch. His stay in Alphabetland connects him to his immigrant grandmother and the tradition she, along with the rabbi, represents; it is the two of them who, from Heaven, send Louis the message that he should struggle with the Almighty because "it's the Jewish way." (The literal meaning of Sarah Ironson's Yiddish is "Thusly acts a Jew" or perhaps "It's what a Jew does" [*P*, 135].) Here, too, the encounter with Jews of earlier generations yields theological or moral insights rather than political ones, perhaps suggesting that Louis's politics can do little real good until he backs them up with a robust, and ultimately religiously grounded, ethics of personal conduct.

Up to this point it might appear that I am proposing a reading of *Angels* in which, in the matter of religion, Kushner comes down firmly on the side of the Cold Warriors for whom Jewishness was equivalent to a modernized Judaism and religious piety was a prerequisite of inclusion in the American polity. The Judaism of this play is both older and newer than the 1950s model, however, and not nearly so Protestantized. This Judaism is open to agnostic uncertainties and informed by mysticism; it emphasizes communal ritual and tradition more than personal, individual belief. That is why, in the Kaddish scene, Ethel can reasonably stand in as one of its representatives. Kushner told me that he had "no idea if Ethel Rosenberg actually knew the Kaddish or not," but that it seemed "plausible" that she would as a member of the second generation and so that much closer to Orthodox tradition than the deracinated third generation. This is not religion as private internal experience but rather religion as ritualized public performance. It is religion expressed in a language that is not the vernacular and is perhaps not even understood by worshipers who are nonetheless familiar with and capable of being moved by the incantatory power of its cadences—a form of devotion largely alien to Protestants.

It is religion, in fact, as theater. Kushner has attested to the (for him deeply cathected) relationship between the religious and the theatrical, explaining that "since I was a very little kid, I've always had an affinity for the supernatural. That's the side of me that's attracted to the theater."[104] And referring specifically to the Kaddish scene, Kushner says,

> I've always been very moved by Jewish prayer. I think the most moving scene in both parts of *Angels in America* is when Ethel

> Rosenberg says the Kaddish for Roy Cohn. And the Kaddish has
> always been a prayer that . . . I mean, I think it's a sort of a genetic
> thing. It's almost worked into the gene structure at this point. It
> has tremendous resonance for me. So does the Sh'ma. And I do
> believe—I wouldn't be in theater if I didn't believe this—that cer-
> tain forms of ritual practice can transform one's consciousness
> through gesture and through design and through ritual.[105]

Kushner's belief that ritual practice can transform consciousness moti-
vates my earlier claim that in *Angels* religion becomes the medium through
which social and political change can be achieved. The parallel he draws
between religion and theater also recalls, but transfigures, the relationship between homosexuality and theater I pointed to at the beginning of
this chapter. There Kushner attributed his interest in "the disguise of theatre, the doubleness," to his "closeted" youth.[106] How do we account for the
connections Kushner makes between theater as a forum for public ritual,
on one hand, and as a disguise for private desires and double identities, on
the other?

The key, I think, is that the theater allows the private and secretive to
be made productively public and communal; the mise-en-scène of doubleness or passing alchemizes disguise into spectacle. Kushner takes Jewishness and queerness, identities with profound historical relationships to
secrecy, and, by associating them with the communal enactment of Jewishness in the form of traditional ritual, de-privatizes them, makes them
machines for altering consciousness on a mass scale. "We won't die secret
deaths anymore," proclaims Prior at the play's end. The Judaism of *Angels*
is, as many critics have observed, thoroughly queered, but so too are its
queerness and its queers "Jewified" in a process that undoes the demono-
logical work of McCarthyite/Reaganite ideologies: "Kushner rebukes and
reverses the contemporary right wing's use of anti-Semitic iconography to
demonize lesbians and gay men."[107] Instead, Kushner endows homosexuality with the vatic dignity of Judaism's "ancient devotions." In Prior, the play
trades in the figure of the spy for that of the prophet.

Prior thus imitates Swann, turning, like him, "from a witty, ironic man-
about-town into something of a prophet."[108] Both of them embrace their
status as pariahs and in doing so become "the depository of a special kind
of knowledge."[109] Swann's transformation is enabled by his disease and his
Jewishness, Prior's by his disease and his homosexuality—and perhaps also

by his Jewishness. For Alisa Solomon proposes that as Prior learns to "do what a Jew does" and grapple with the Almighty, and in his dual status as victim and prophet, he becomes a "metaphorical Jew."[110] He even develops a limp, as Jacob does after wrestling with a divine figure who may be either an angel or God. So Prior, like Roy, is identified with the biblical patriarch, father of the whole nation of Israel.

I would, in fact, enlarge the scope of the play's "Jewifying" operation beyond Prior or even queers to include every character with a relationship to the spiritual or supernatural, and even the audience. Now, Freedman maintains that "the disappointment of the play" is that in the end it abandons Jewish difference and accedes to supersessionism.[111] There is no doubt, certainly, that Prior is powerfully connected to Christian traditions and iconographies as well as Jewish ones, and we should bear firmly in mind that the Christian millenarian thought woven through the play, and elaborated in the final recounting of the story of the Angel of Bethesda, has always included fantasies about the conversion of the Jews. But it is possible to argue that *Angels* instead, or also, enacts a sweeping conversion of the gentiles that is inaugurated in the first scene of *Millennium*, at Sarah Ironson's funeral. In this scene Rabbi Chemelwitz informs the assembled mourners that all of them are Ironson's descendants, charged with continuing the journey of the eastern European Jewish immigrants she represented. In some productions of the play the rabbi faces and speaks past the other actors to the audience, so that the theater becomes an extension of the synagogue and the audience becomes part of the congregation, receiving the rabbi's admonition that "in you that journey is" along with those on stage (*MA*, 11). In these productions the audience is thus interpellated into an Ashkenazic historical and religious tradition within minutes of the play's beginning.[i] In addition, brushes with the supernatural in *Angels* almost always entail Jewish languages or rituals, even when there are no Jews present. The ghost of Prior Walter 1 chants a mystical mixture of English and Hebrew phrases that are references to Kabbalistic concepts (*MA*, 88). At another point Emily, a gentile nurse who does not speak Hebrew, suddenly erupts into recitation of "El Male Rachamim" as the angel approaches, apparently pushing a kind of spiritual storm front ahead of her that Emily can sense (*MA*, 98).

---

i. A potent effect that is unhappily lost in the movie version of *Angels*.

Most significantly, the trope of the *brokhe*, or blessing, creates an intricate figurative chain running between and around Roy, Joe, Ethel, Prior, and, ultimately, out to the audience. Earlier I touched on the scene where Roy contrasts the hapless victim Isaac with the "ruthless motherfucker" with whom he himself identifies, Jacob/Israel. That scene, though, actually places Roy in the position of *Isaac*, while it is Joe who takes the role of Jacob, kneeling at his metaphorical father's feet to receive his blessing. "A *Brokhe*," says Roy. "You don't even have to trick it out of me, like what's-his-name in the Bible" (*P*, 80). Despite his conscious identification with the tough Jew Jacob, Roy is also, even against his own will, the Loser Jew, the victim, the sacrifice, recalling the words embroidered on Cohn's panel on the AIDS quilt: "Bully. Coward. Victim." Then the opposition between Jacob and Isaac is realigned and broken down again in the Kaddish scene in which Roy's own victim, Ethel, becomes Isaac and blesses her treacherous, wayward, ruthless son, the "motherfucker" who has indeed fucked over the mother.[112]

Finally, Prior—another victim—wrestles with the Angel of America, goes on to receive a blessing from the angels in Heaven, and then in turn pronounces that blessing, "*More Life*," on us, the audience (*P*, 146). First he becomes Jacob; then he assumes the role of Isaac and makes all of us Jacob. Jacob, who becomes Israel; who wrestles with the divine, which is "the Jewish way." Hence every member of the audience is, ultimately, placed under the sign of the Jew, gathered into Israel and charged with the moral responsibility of living a Jewish life—making *Angels*, truly, a strictly Jewish show. Lioi writes that the end of the play provides "a sense of transformative ritual that offers the audience the New Heaven and New Earth in their own lives. Thus, when Prior speaks the Blessing, he pours out the action of the play past the proscenium arch and into the messiness of history. In this sense, *Angels* has more in common with the medieval passion plays and the Eleusinian Mysteries than with other Broadway shows: it is sacramental, it enacts the secrets it narrates, and effects real change in the willing participant."[113]

Let us remember, though, the provenance of that "Blessing" and ask what kinds of change accepting it might require us to countenance. For its bestowal inscribes us in a tradition that includes both willing sacrifices and ruthless motherfuckers. *Angels* has been accused of being idealistic in the sense of being immaterial, "u-topian," and the political and theological ends toward which the play encourages us are unquestionably those of pluralism, ecumenicism, civic engagement, communitarianism, and an ever-expanding enfranchisement of the dispossessed. But as Kushner has said elsewhere, sounding oddly like his character Roy, "here's the thing about politics: It's not an expression of your moral purity and your ethics and your probity and your fond dreams of some utopian future. Progressive people constantly fail to get this."[114] Roy's example—in acquiring the AZT he needs, for instance—presents progressives with the uncomfortable possibility that the price of achieving political efficacy might sometimes be to lay claim to his monstrous empowerment and accept the "messiness" of politics as a struggle to change the nation and not merely reimagine it. In these pages I have taken issue with readings of *Angels* that propose that, for better or for worse, Roy and his tough Jewishness have been eradicated by the end of the play. On the contrary, the final blessing that Prior transmits to the audience makes us inheritors of a legacy of both Jewish gentleness and Jewish clout, asking us to remember that as spiritual *and* political animals we may require both, and that we are all, indeed, the heirs not only of Sarah Ironson but also of Roy Cohn.

CONCLUSION

JACK DONAGHY: The television audience doesn't want your elitist
    East Coast alternative intellectual left-wing...
LIZ LEMON: Jack, just say "Jewish." This is taking forever.
                    —"Stone Mountain," *30 Rock*

Throughout this book I have been advancing three interrelated arguments. The first is that in the modern West—specifically in France, Great
Britain, and the United States, although my analysis should apply to other
developed nation-states as well—a distinct and peculiar position has been
assigned to people considered to be marginal to the nation by virtue of
some critical, but obscured, difference from "normal" citizens. The invisibly different are not necessarily more threatened, subjugated, or discriminated against than those who are identifiably Other; in many cases they are
much less so. But because such people occupy a liminal space between the
wholly alien and the fully normative, they evoke acute anxieties about the
cohesion and security of the nation-state that are apt to be expressed in
representations of members of these groups as traitors and spies, double
agents whose loyalties are never certain.

The second argument concerns actual espionage cases involving Jews,
homosexuals, or Communists in which, as is true of the Dreyfus Affair
and the Burgess-Maclean scandal, efforts to explain and contain treason
focused obsessively on the perceived racial or sexual difference of the
accused. That this did not happen during the Rosenberg case seems to
have resulted from the successful civic integration of enough American
Jews that the Rosenbergs could be constructed as marginal to their own
ethnic group rather than to their nation, and the treachery of which they
were accused could be attributed solely to their Communism rather than
to their Jewishness. Finally, I have suggested that in the twentieth century
bourgeois white gay men writers evinced a particular interest in spies,

espionage, and treason as literary figures and themes, reflecting the imbrication of homosexuality with these tropes in dominant discourses.

In concluding this book I want to speculate about the relevance of my
observations to the current state of politics and literature, in an era when
nation-states are ceding political, legal, and economic power to para- or
suprastate entities like international corporations and tribunals; when
espionage has become the province of enormous bureaucracies and state
surveillance of the citizenry is an established, if contested, fact in Western
democracies; and when both conventional large-scale military conflicts
and the Cold War have given way, in the priorities of the West, to the so-
called war on terror. The comments that follow are necessarily not only
speculative but highly provisional, as the parameters of the discourses
about citizenship, nationhood, race, religion, and sexuality with which
this book is concerned shift almost daily. The earliest stages of this project
were undertaken in the late 1990s; since then we have witnessed—among
many other events pertinent to my themes here—the terrorist attacks on
September 11, 2001, the wars in Iraq and Afghanistan, the establishment
of marriage or marriage equivalents for same-sex couples in several countries, the collapse of financial markets worldwide, the election of the first
African American president of the United States, raging controversy over
the position of Muslims in the West, and the repeal of the ban on openly
gay people serving in the U.S. military. Any of these could provoke endless
elaborations on and emendations to my thesis; I will confine myself to brief
remarks on a few points of particular interest to me.

One of these is the question of the current status of anti-Semitism, and
of Jews and homosexuals, particularly in the United States. As Jonathan
Freedman has suggested, historically the confluence of Jewishness with
perversion reinforced, and was reinforced by, the belief in Jewish conspiracy; Jewish deviance became a way of describing and accounting for the
"unnatural" and fearsome political and economic power ascribed to Jews.
Thus, the anti-Semitic slurs in currency through the first half of the twentieth century "sutured the Jew both to sociopolitical power and to nonproc-
reative sexual practices. It was as if the perverse political power of the Jew
could be expressed only by that figure's indulgence in deviant forms of sexuality."[1] For more than a hundred years a parallel trope of unnatural homosexual power—perhaps first distinctly articulated by Chancellor von Bismarck, with his fear that homosexuality posed a danger to the state—has
been accumulating force, until today conservative politicians and cultural

warriors can get hordes of voters to the polls and generate millions of dollars in donations by invoking "the gay Mafia" and its sinister "homosexual agenda" of undermining national values.

In view of the pronounced, profound historic relation between the figurations of homosexuals and Jews in the Western imagination, scholars of Jewish and queer studies have argued that as the perverse power of the Jew can be expressed only by reference to deviance, the perverse power of the deviant is still, in some transmuted yet recognizable form, referable to Jewishness. In a 1993 piece in the *Village Voice* Alisa Solomon laid out the way antigay organizations in the United States not only have borrowed the themes and strategies of anti-Semitic propaganda but have even literally reproduced Nazi cartoons about Jews in their campaigns, modifying them only by changing Jews to gay men.[2] The rhetoric of such campaigns has changed very little in the years since Solomon wrote that article. (If some religious Right groups have softened their rhetoric and now emphasize their loving motives for wanting to help homosexuals, we should remember that there is a long history of philo-Semites who advocated embracing Jews in order to speed their conversion to Christianity and so help them to blot out the stain of their race; it is a very particular kind of love whose aim is to eliminate its object.) The assimilation of homosexuals to Jewishness can also be found in the rhetoric of the highest political and judicial bodies, for instance in Justice Antonin Scalia's 1996 dissent in *Romer v. Evans*, which, Janet Jakobsen writes, "sounds as if it comes directly from *The Protocols of the Elders of Zion*. Scalia portrays homosexuals, like Jews, as a small but overprivileged minority with both financial capital and political influence well in excess of either numbers or justified expectation."[3] We might easily conclude with Solomon that "these days, the target of anti-Semitism is queers."[4]

But it must be stressed that these days the target of anti-Semitism is also, still, Jews, and this is perhaps even truer now—after the 2008 economic crisis drew attention to the involvement of Jewish financiers in many of the financial scandals and collapsed institutions[a]—than it was in

---

a. Shortly after the economic meltdown began I heard a bus driver in San Francisco volubly explaining to nearby passengers that the recession had been deliberately engineered by the Rothschilds. To be fair, he later implicated the Rockefellers as well, and it was not even clear that he knew the Rothschilds are Jewish. The incident nonetheless demonstrates the extraordinary endurance of one specific anti-Semitic trope dating back to the early nineteenth century, the belief that this single Jewish family controls the global economy.

the 1990s, when Solomon wrote that line. Furthermore, the intercalation of homosexuals and Jews remains a standard feature of both anti-Semitic and homophobic discourses in the United States, whether in the claim of radical schismatic Catholics that a "Jewish-homosexual alliance" is undermining the priesthood, Aryan Nation founder Richard Butler's contention that "homosexuality is financed by the Jews,"[5] or simply in reiterated characterizations of the members of both groups as wealthy, conspiratorial elitists—representations that have changed very little since the 1890s. It is not surprising that virtually all the classic canards of anti-Semitism, including even the blood libel and accusations of involvement with freemasonry, can be found today circulating widely among hate groups and on the Internet. But they are also quite current in more legitimate forums. As the exchange from 30 Rock quoted at the beginning of this chapter sardonically illustrates, Jewish remains instantly recognizable shorthand today for an ideational complex also comprising (though not reducible to) homosexuality, and often discursively contrasted with a normalized body politic—Jack Donaghy's "television audience"—variously imagined as "the heartland," "working families," Peoria, or "the little people," but always constituting the "Real America."

Witness the statements journalist Rick Sanchez made about Daily Show host Jon Stewart in the autumn of 2010, when he accused "left-wing elite northeast establishment guys" like Stewart of bigotry, economic privilege, and inability "to relate to a guy like me." Sanchez also suggested that Jews control the media and scoffed derisively at the idea that they are "an oppressed minority."[6] For that matter, consider the response that this book project provoked from an external reviewer for the National Humanities Center when I applied for a fellowship there some years ago. The anonymous reviewer complained that I describe "Jews, homosexuals (male), and Communists as being (equally) outsiders," and asked, "Has she forgotten the notably caressing relation between the USA (Clinton and his predecessors) and Israel, a relation that puts Arafat and the Palestinians at an acute disadvantage in every bout of diplomacy? Jews as outsiders? Not at all. Homosexuals? Has she ever been in New York, where it's a disability for a man to be known to be involved with a woman (and vice versa)? [...] There is no possibility that such flimsy documentation will produce conclusions of any merit." Setting aside the question of the merit of this book, which I must leave to my readers to decide, what is striking about this review is the unselfconsciousness with which it recapitulates, as if they were reasonable scholarly arguments, so many elements of the very discourses *Double Agents* endeavors to interrogate: the sinister political influence of Jews, the unjust cultural dominance of homosexuals, the locus classicus of New York as the seat of the cabal—and, crucially, the insistence that given their power, it is impermissible to describe either Jews or gay men as victims of prejudice. That the administrators of the National Humanities Center accepted this review and passed it on to me without comment also suggests that such assumptions are so deeply engrained in American culture as to appear unproblematic even to well-informed and, one hopes, thoughtful academics.

Contemporary gay rights politics would be well served by further reflection on this imbrication of Jewishness and homosexuality. The fight to extend full formal civic equality to so-called sexual minorities should perhaps lean more heavily on the ways in which sexuality resembles the ambiguous status of Jewishness in its multiple valences as ethnicity, culture, and faith—and somewhat less heavily on the analogies between sexuality and race as "immutable characteristics" that currently dominate the discourse of mainstream gay rights organizations. Homosexuality can constitute a voluntary affinity or culture as well as a fixed status. Furthermore, erotic desire more closely resembles religious faith than it does race—a matter of what Enlightenment thinkers termed *conscience*, a passionately felt impulse that can scarcely be considered immutable and yet is so profoundly central to identity and integrity that the form of its expression was the first of the liberties to be protected by an amendment to the U.S. Constitution. Analogizing queerness to Jewishness allows us to embrace a wide range of possible etiologies for and identifications with sexuality, a range within which some elements of sexual Being might be considered "innate" or determined—as rabbinic law affirms, for instance, that Jewishness is transmitted through maternal inheritance—but the ways to express and name that inheritance are even more protean than the examples of Bloch and Swann would suggest. Such an analogy would answer Jakobsen's call to "resist the constitution of" the relationship between queerness and Jewishness "within a negative discourse"[7] by emphasizing not their shared historical abjection but instead their ludic volatility as loci of identity, community, pleasure, and meaning.

For much of the twentieth century, the intercalation of Jews and homosexuals was, within that "negative discourse," processed through their mutual relationship to Communism. Now that the Cold War has given way to the confrontation with Islamic fundamentalism, what analogies, if any, might we draw between the two, or to the cases investigated here? What relevance, for instance, does the Dreyfus case have to the treatment of other accused traitors? After the Rosenbergs were convicted in 1951 comparisons between their situation and that of Alfred Dreyfus began to be drawn, first in a series of articles in the *National Guardian* that asked, "Is this the Dreyfus Case of cold-war America?"[8] As the uproar over the case spread to Europe the example of Dreyfus was invoked more frequently, and eventually Dreyfus's daughter Jeanne would be one of the tens of thousands who sent telegrams to the White House pleading, in her father's name, for clemency for the Rosenbergs.[9] Those hostile to the couple denied any parallel between the two cases on the grounds that Dreyfus was innocent and the Rosenbergs were guilty, or that the Rosenbergs' trial was fair and Dreyfus's was not—forgetting that Dreyfus's innocence was hardly obvious in the mid-1890s, nor was it generally known at first that his trial had been irregular, and if his had been a capital offense, he would have been dead long before he could have been exonerated.

If we should take anything from the Dreyfus Affair, it is not that France convicted an innocent man or even that prejudice should not be allowed to sway the outcome of trials. It is that the conviction of the innocent is always a possibility whenever prosecutors rely on closed tribunals, ex parte submissions to the court, or the invocation of state secrets as grounds for the refusal to present the case against a defendant fully and transparently. Concerns about security and the desire to protect classified information are understandable in the attempt to prosecute acts of terrorism, but they were warranted in France in the 1890s, too. When we judge the circumstances of Dreyfus's conviction, we would do well to remember that a mere two decades earlier France had lost a bloody war and considerable territory to a formidable power with which it shared a border, that Dreyfus had familial and linguistic ties to that nation, and that the espionage he was accused of really was taking place. Furthermore, in the ten-month period before Dreyfus was arrested, anarchists had bombed the French Parliament and, in a separate incident, assassinated President Sadi Carnot. If the United States faced similar conditions today, a modern Dreyfus might think himself very lucky to get off with a sentence of permanent exile.

In the context of this discussion we could also ask whether the situation of Western Muslims today is analogous to that of Jews in nineteenth-century

France or to Communists in the 1950s, and whether, as some have suggested, the war on terror is simply the Cold War redux. Here I think the parallel is imperfect, though nonetheless relevant; to be concise I will confine my explanation to the United States, even though the status of Muslims and the problem of terrorism are also of urgent concern in France and Britain. In general, I would argue, Muslims do not at this point quite occupy the position of the invisible Other in the American imaginary, because their difference is still popularly construed as both perceptible and obviously foreign. This construction relies on orientalizing fantasies like those that motivated attacks on turbaned Sikhs after September 11, paired with a failure to recognize many Muslim Americans as such at all (witness the fact that people of Middle Eastern descent are categorized as "white" on census forms). We have not yet seen posters and articles indicating how to identify a Muslim as we once saw them explain how to recognize a Jew or spot a homosexual; the assumption seems to be that "we" know what "they" look like. In October 2010 reporter Juan Williams controversially confessed that he was made nervous by seeing "people who are in Muslim garb" on airplanes.[10] But if the logic of nineteenth-century anti-Semitism or the Red Scare currently prevailed, it would be the Muslim wearing a suit and tie who would cause alarm, not the one in tunic and skullcap. Finally, there have not yet been extensive, sustained accusations that the U.S. government has been massively infiltrated by Al Qaeda or its affiliates, comparable to the charge by cold warriors that state institutions were riddled with Communists.

The obvious counterexample is the claim that Barack Obama is a secret Muslim, which polls have shown about 20 percent of Americans believe. Whether that is more or fewer people than believed that Franklin D. Roosevelt was a Jew is impossible to say, but certainly in both cases the attribution of an occult identity to the president has helped to delegitimize his authority. Nonetheless, I would argue that panic about Obama's putative Islamism is still more a way of indirectly naming his visible racial difference—as suggested by the morphing of the dap into a "terrorist fist jab"—than it is about the sincere belief that he spearheads a widespread Islamic conspiracy.

As I write this conclusion there are signs that this is beginning to change, and that American Muslims are starting to move out of the category of the recognizably foreign and closer to the uncanny inside/outside status accorded to Jews during the Dreyfus Affair and Communists during the Cold War. If this is indeed happening, we should expect to see increased anxiety about how to identify Muslims and accusations of conspiracy and espionage directed against native-born American citizens. In the immediate aftermath of September 11 attention was focused on external threats and foreign enemies, but very quickly cases arose of American-born or naturalized citizens accused of supporting or fighting alongside Islamic terrorists, including John Walker Lindh (the "American Taliban"), José Padilla, and Adam Gadahn, the first U.S. citizen to be charged with treason since just after World War II. In 2003 came the first case of alleged espionage, when Muslim military chaplain James Yee was arrested for sedition and spying (charges that were later dismissed). In 2009 there was a flurry of media attention to Colleen LaRose, or "Jihad Jane," a white American-born woman accused of conspiracy and support of terrorists. Finally, in 2011 a group of House Republicans launched investigations into Muslim American groups they accused of, among other things, planting spies in the U.S. government.

The war on terror could still take many different courses. It could be that terrorism and/or Islamism will continue to be imagined primarily as external and alien forces, a perception that could motivate either a renewed isolationism and anxiety about border security or overseas military interventions, or both simultaneously. Or perhaps the inquiry that the House Republicans conducted will in years to come be remembered as the equivalent of the postwar HUAC hearings, the period that instigated wholesale public hysteria, the anathematization of ever-expanding groups of potential internal enemies, mass firings of government employees for suspected terrorist sympathies, the explosion of domestic surveillance, and an aggressively conservative counterreaction by American Muslims to distance themselves from radical Islam. At the moment, all of these things appear to be going on at once, and it is hard to know which tendencies will prevail. It is also possible to imagine that, given both the conservative terms on which the United States tends to extend citizenship privileges (think of the centrality that access to military service and marriage have assumed in the gay rights movement) and the deep historical and theological connections between the Abrahamic religions, a sufficiently pious, sexually normative, and patriotic American Muslim population could, a few years hence, be as integrated as American Jews are now. Depending on how the kaleidoscope shifts, within decades we may find conservatives reflexively paying lip service to America's Judeo-Christian-Islamic heritage.

Finally, if subversion itself is bound to remain a concern to the modern nation-state, we should ask whether the figures of the spy and the traitor, or the themes of espionage and treason, are likely to continue to be of literary interest, and if so, what kind of writer is likely to find them useful. I have suggested in this book that loyalty, like faith and desire, is perforce an interior and affective orientation; centuries of efforts to establish irrefutable proofs of religious, sexual, or political orthodoxy—from the tortures of the Inquisition to modern polygraphs—have failed. Loyalty is, in short, a matter of the imagination, and maybe that is why imaginative texts have dealt with it so much more satisfactorily than white papers and congressional committees. It is probable that they will continue to do so—but the kinds of demands made on people's loyalties, the forms disloyalty takes, and the cultural value assigned to loyalty are certain to change. If the power of nation-states should decline, for example, then literature about corporate espionage or the pressures of allegiance to international movements like pan-Arabism might take the place of texts focusing on national identity.

For Proust, Auden, and Kushner tropes of espionage and treason were useful ways to illuminate the status of subalterns in relationship to the nation. They all assign a privileged epistemological position to homosexual men as "the depository of a special kind of knowledge," a status Proust and Kushner also attribute to Jews. Pariahs, spying on a social realm to which they are not fully loyal, know things that the more fully enfranchised do not; if, like Swann and Prior, they choose to become prophets, they can make that knowledge a public good. All three of these writers envision possibilities for the transformation of the nation incubating in the experiences of their pariahs, and all of them eventually move beyond the paradigm of treason or the figure of the spy to imagine new forms of citizenship. Proust, most radically of the three, suggests that the complex affiliations of *ceux qui ne se nationalisent pas* might become a model allowing us to think past the confines of national boundaries altogether. Auden proposes that the function of gay men as the "loyal opposition" to the state can "serve as a paradigm / now of what a plausible Future might be" in a transfigured polity. And Kushner imagines an America in which racial, sexual, and religious minorities "will be citizens" at last, fulfilling what Louis calls the "prospect of some sort of radical democracy spreading outward and growing up."[11]

What are the constraints on and challenges of citizenship in Western democracies in the twenty-first century, and what kind of writer might wish to refract them through the image of the spy or the theme of treason? One grim contemporary example appears to undercut any possibility that the spy will continue to be a useful vantage point from which to think the reinvention of the nation-state, at least in an affirmative sense. The wildly popular Jason Bourne movies, like the Robert Ludlum novels on which they are based, feature an American spy on the run from his own government, a notable evolution in the representation of the secret agent. James Bond had his conflicts with his superiors at MI6, but they were not out to kill him. Ludlum's *Bourne Trilogy*, set in the waning years of the Cold War, appeared after Vietnam and Watergate had provoked increased public skepticism about the value and legitimacy of state surveillance both abroad and domestically, a skepticism that in the film adaptations becomes open criticism of the sinister machinations of U.S. intelligence. The writers I investigate in this book used spies as figures for ethnic or sexual marginality; the fact that Jason Bourne is a heterosexual white man (in the films, a blue-eyed blond from Missouri) may suggest that the paranoia and alienation Auden ascribed to the homosexual have now—in the age of warrantless wiretapping in the United States, security cameras on every street corner in England, and full-body scanners in airports—become the normative psychological stance of even the most "average" citizen.

Of course, spy thrillers as a genre are supposed to provoke pleasurable tension and fear. This is not to say that the specific historical forms of that fear are not symptomatic, but only that the genre probably does not exhaust everything there is to say about modern nations and citizens. Even if nation-states are transferring power to corporations, or if citizenship confers less protection from state surveillance and violence than someone like Auden might have hoped, full civic enfranchisement remains a goal for many subalterns. Writers occupying a suitably liminal space between subordination and privilege—those representing what Pierre Bourdieu would call a "dominated fraction of the dominant class"—might well still find that espionage and treason are the most adequate objective correlatives for their relationship to social or state power. If so, the next writer to make espionage one of the governing metaphors of his fiction, or the spy a master trope of his poetry, might be Jewish, or gay, or just conceivably she might be a woman of exceptional social privilege. Surely, though, among writers of the future to make full use of the theme of double agency, at least one will be a bourgeois Muslim man, born in the West, socially assimilated, and formally a citizen but liable at any moment to be moved abruptly into the category of the alien. If nations are to be anything other than apparatuses of surveillance and repression—if they are to be useful, as well as necessary, fictions—then we will have to hope for such writers: men and women with, in Rebecca West's words, a drop of treason in their veins.

ABBREVIATIONS

PROUST'S IN SEARCH OF LOST TIME

WBG Vol. 2, *Within a Budding Grove*
GW   Vol. 3, *The Guermantes Way*
SG   Vol. 4, *Sodom and Gomorrah*
C   Vol. 5, *The Captive*
F   Vol. 6, *The Fugitive*
TR   Vol. 7, *Time Regained*

OTHER ABBREVIATIONS

EA   Auden. *The English Auden.*
MA   Kushner. *Angels in America.* Part 1, *Millennium Approaches.*
P   Kushner. *Angels in America.* Part 2, *Perestroika.*
RRS Committee to Secure Justice. Rosenberg, Julius, Ethel Rosen-
     berg, and Morton Sobell.

NOTES

INTRODUCTION

1. U.S. Constitution, article III, section 3.
2. West, *The Meaning of Treason*, 276.
3. Brown, *Loyalty and Security*, 4–5.
4. Ibid., 5.
5. Bell, "Treason, Technology, and Freedom of Expression," 1033.
6. Kaplan, "Refiguring the Jewish Question," 116.
7. Auden, *English Auden*, 386.

1. CITIZENS, ALIENS, AND TRAITORS

1. Sedgwick, *Epistemology*, 75.
2. Itzkovitz, "Secret Temples," 193.
3. Diamant, "Judaism, Homosexuality and Other Sign Systems," 179.
4. See Cheyette and Valman, "Introduction," 15.
5. See Rosenstock, "Messianism, Machismo and 'Marranism,'" 203.
6. "Virginia Statute for Religious Freedom," 74–75.
7. Washington, "Reply to the Hebrew Congregation in Newport, Rhode Island," 91–92.
8. Quoted in Mendes-Flohr and Reinharz, *Jew in the Modern World*, 114–15.
9. Quoted in ibid., 115.
10. Quoted in Hyman "French Jewish Community from Emancipation to the Dreyfus Affair," 26.
11. Macaulay, "Civil Disabilities of the Jews," 226.
12. Cheyette, *Constructions of "the Jew" in English Literature and Society*, 17.
13. See J. Berman, *Modernist Fiction, Cosmopolitanism, and the Politics of Community*, 77.

14. Quoted in Burns, *France and the Dreyfus Affair*, 5.
15. Marrus, *Politics of Assimilation*, 108.
16. Ibid., 91.
17. Noah, "Proclamation to the Jews," 107.
18. Friedländer, "Present Crisis of American Jewry," 342.
19. Holmes, *Anti-Semitism in British Society*, 19.
20. Ibid., 104.
21. Fredrickson, *Racism*, 94–95.
22. See Itzkovitz, "Secret Temples," 177.
23. Brandeis, "The Jewish Problem," 496.
24. Cheyette and Valman, "Introduction," 2.
25. See P. Lewis, *Modernism, Nationalism, and the Novel*, 215.
26. Mendes-Flohr and Reinharz, *Jew in the Modern World*, 302.
27. Quoted in Selzer, *Kike!* 57.
28. P. Lewis, *Modernism, Nationalism, and the Novel*, 95.
29. Endelman, *Jews of Britain*, 67–68.
30. Holmes, *Anti-Semitism in British Society*, 17.
31. Kaplan, "Refiguring the Jewish Question," 114.
32. See Holmes, *Anti-Semitism in British Society*, 151.
33. Bredin, *Affair*, 26.
34. Fredrickson, *Racism*, 68.
35. Kleeblatt, "Body of Alfred Dreyfus," 77.
36. Kaplan, "Refiguring the Jewish Question," 113, 124. Cf. Arendt, *Origins of Totalitarianism*, 84.
37. Quoted in E. Crémieu-Foa, *La campagne antisémitique*, 24.
38. Marrus, *Politics of Assimilation*, 25.
39. Holmes, *Anti-Semitism in British Society*, 36–42.
40. Castelin, *Revue antisémite*, 1.
41. Saurel, "Nouvelles chansons antijuives."
42. Kaplan, "Refiguring the Jewish Question," 124.
43. P. Lewis, *Modernism, Nationalism, and the Novel*, 37.
44. Marrus, *Politics of Assimilation*, 12–13.
45. Quoted in Halasz, *Captain Dreyfus*, 123.
46. Drumont, *La France juive*, 48–49.
47. Ibid., 49.
48. Quoted in D. L. Lewis, *Prisoners of Honor*, 52.
49. Drumont, *La France juive*, 273–74.
50. Holmes, *Anti-Semitism in British Society*, 80.
51. Drumont, *La France juive*, 25.
52. Lipset and Raab, *Politics of Unreason*, 183.
53. Selzer, *Kike!* 2; Dinnerstein, *Anti-Semitism in America*, 48.
54. Freedman, *Klezmer*, 45.
55. See Lipset and Raab, *Politics of Unreason*, 99.
56. Ibid., 139.

57. Ford, *International Jew*, 21–22.
58. Itzkovitz, "Secret Temples," 178.
59. Rosenstock, "Messianism, Machismo and 'Marranism,'" 207.
60. Frantzen, *Before the Closet*, 232.
61. Ibid., 236.
62. Archer, *Sovereignty and Intelligence*, 14.
63. Edelman, "Homographesis," 191–92.
64. Bray, *Homosexuality in Renaissance England*, 20.
65. Kiernan, *Duel in European History*, 93.
66. Pepys, *Diary of Samuel Pepys*, 210.
67. Trumbach, "London's Sodomites," 11.
68. Courouve, *Vocabulaire de l'homosexualité masculine*, 25.
69. Ibid., 27.
70. Ibid., 96.
71. See Raffalovich, *Uranisme et unisexualité*; and Weindel and Fischer, *L'homosexualité en Allemagne*.
72. Dubarry, *Les invertis*, 142.
73. Ibid., 128–29.
74. McFarlane, *Sodomite*, 51.
75. See Grand-Carteret, *Derrière "lui*," 4.
76. Dobelbower, "Petits bleus," 137.
77. Kettle, *Salome's Last Veil*, 2.
78. White, "Efficiency and Vice," 451–52.
79. Bland, "Trial by Sexology?" 185–86; Kettle, *Salome's Last Veil*, 4, 11.
80. Quoted in Kettle, *Salome's Last Veil*, 21.
81. Quoted in ibid., 245.
82. Bland, "Trial by Sexology?" 195.
83. McFarlane, *Sodomite*, 32.
84. Freedman, *Klezmer*, 40.
85. Gilman, *Jewish Self-Hatred*, 74–75; W. Johnson, "The Myth of Jewish Male Menses," 293.
86. Boyarin, *Unheroic Conduct*, 4.
87. Reizbaum, *James Joyce's Judaic Other*, 91.
88. Kaplan, "Refiguring the Jewish Question," 124–25.
89. Drumont, *La France juive*, 25n1.
90. Weininger, *Sex and Character*, 307–8.
91. Pellegrini, "Whiteface Performances," 109. See also Kaplan, "Refiguring the Jewish Question," 124.
92. See Drumont, *La France juive*, 64–65; and Evans-Gordon, *Alien Immigrant*, 263, 302.
93. Arendt, *Origins of Totalitarianism*, 83.
94. Kaplan, "Refiguring the Jewish Question," 125.
95. Dubarry, *Les invertis*, 93, 106.
96. Saint-Paul, *L'homosexualité et les types homosexuels*, 105–6n1.
97. Timayenis, *American Jew*, 87.

98. Mayne, *Intersexes*, 76.

99. Gilman, *Jewish Self-Hatred*, 250.

100. Franklin, "Jew Boys, Queer Boys," 137.

101. See Kaplan, "Refiguring the Jewish Question," 124–25.

102. Bredin, *Affair*, 38.

103. Gide, *Corydon*, 107.

104. Carlier, *La prostitution antiphysique*, 92–93.

105. Dean, *Imperial Brotherhood*, 68.

106. Dubarry, *Les invertis*, 150.

107. Quoted in Fernandez, "Sous l'œil de la police et de la médecine," iv.

108. Carlier, *La prostitution antiphysique*, 214.

109. Weininger, *Sex and Character*, 306–7, 311.

110. Symonds, *Letters of John Addington Symonds*, 808.

111. D. Berman, *Gaiety Transfigured*, 41.

112. Quoted in Cheyette, *Constructions of "the Jew" in English Literature and Society*, 90.

113. Holmes, *Anti-Semitism in British Society*, 142–43; "Bolshevist Portraits," *Times* (London).

114. H.R. Rep. No. 1109, at 10.

115. Ford, *International Jew*, 217.

116. Churchill, "Zionism Versus Bolshevism," 5.

117. Quoted in Marrus, *Politics of Assimilation*, 261n4.

118. Ben-Gurion and Blaustein, "An Exchange of Views," 567.

2. THE DREYFUS AFFAIR

1. See Peter, "Dimensions de l'affaire Dreyfus," 1156–58.

2. *Calendrier des Youtres*, 14.

3. Quoted in Bredin, *Affair*, 326, 79.

4. Halasz, *Captain Dreyfus*, 93.

5. Zola, *J'accuse*, 47.

6. Halasz, *Captain Dreyfus*, 192; Mayeur, "Les catholiques français," 330–34.

7. Dreyfus, *Le procès Dreyfus*, 79.

8. Dreyfus, *La révision du procès Dreyfus: Enquête*, 249.

9. Quoted in Nordau and Nordau, *Max Nordau*, 141.

10. Proust, *In Search of Lost Time*, Vol. 3, *Guermantes Way*, 390; hereafter cited in text as *GW*.

11. Chapman, *Dreyfus Case*, 16.

12. Ibid., 49.

13. Bredin, *Affair*, 43.

14. Service historique de la Défense, 4J 118½, items 288, 291.

15. Quoted in D. L. Lewis, *Prisoners of Honor*, 21.

16. Bredin, *Affair*, 533.

17. Quoted in Grousset, *L'affaire Dreyfus et ses ressorts secrets*, 45.

18. Barrès, *Scènes et doctrines du nationalisme*, 111–12.

19. Paléologue, *Journal de l'affaire Dreyfus*, 21, 53.

20. D'Ormescheville, "Rapport sur l'affaire de M. Dreyfus," item 10.

21. Ibid., item 4.

22. Zola, *J'accuse*, 101.

23. Kleeblatt, "Body of Alfred Dreyfus," 85.

24. Barrès, *Scènes et doctrines du nationalisme*, 100.

25. Quoted in Peter, "Dimensions de l'affaire Dreyfus," 1156.

26. Kleeblatt, "Body of Alfred Dreyfus," 78.

27. Burns, *France*, ix. See also Marrus, *Politics of Assimilation*, 201–2; and Peter, "Dimensions de l'affaire Dreyfus," 1167.

28. Steiner, "Totem and Taboo," 386–87.

29. Ibid., 387.

30. Marrus, *Politics of Assimilation*, 201.

31. Quoted in Bredin, *Affair*, 353.

32. Quoted in Halasz, *Captain Dreyfus*, 123.

33. P. Lewis, *Modernism, Nationalism, and the Novel*, 77.

34. Barrès, *Scènes et doctrines du nationalisme*, 97.

35. Bredin, *Affair*, 252.

36. Zola, *J'accuse*, 92.

37. Ibid., 125.

38. Quoted in Bredin, *Affair*, 272.

39. D. L. Lewis, *Prisoners of Honor*, 209.

40. See Chapman, *Dreyfus Case*, 301.

41. See Grand-Carteret, *L'affaire Dreyfus et l'image*.

42. Chapman, *Dreyfus Case*, 242.

43. Peter, "Dimensions de l'affaire Dreyfus," 1163–64.

44. Quoted in Chapman, *Dreyfus Case*, 284.

45. Marrus, *Politics of Assimilation*, 284.

46. Ibid., 25.

47. Hyman, "Dreyfus Affair," 89.

48. Marrus, *Politics of Assimilation*, 228.

49. Quoted in D. L. Lewis, *Prisoners of Honor*, 165.

50. Marrus, *Politics of Assimilation*, 227.

51. Ibid., 226.

52. Ibid., 24, 99.

53. Reinach, *L'affaire Dreyfus*, 5.

54. Quoted in Chapman, *Dreyfus Case*, 143.

55. See Marrus, *Politics of Assimilation*, 221.

56. Proust, *In Search of Lost Time*, vol. 5, *The Captive*, 46.

57. Boyarin, *Unheroic Conduct*, 47.

58. Marrus, *Politics of Assimilation*, 197.

59. Ibid., 153.

60. Kiernan, *Duel in European History*, 41.

61. Ibid., 62, 99.

62. Quoted in Crémieu-Foa, *La campagne antisémitique*, 27; hereafter cited in text.

63. Quoted in Compagnon, "Notice," 103.

64. Kleeblatt, "Body of Alfred Dreyfus," 88.

65. Ibid., 87–88.

66. Dobelbower, "Petits bleus," 131.

67. Ibid., 133, 137.

68. Ibid., 133–34.

69. Service historique de la Défense, 4J 118½; quoted in Gervais, Huret, and Peretz, "Une relecture du 'dossier secret,'" 149.

70. Quoted in Thomas, *L'affaire sans Dreyfus*, 276.

71. Zola, *J'accuse*, 102.

72. Zola, *L'affaire Dreyfus*, 218.

73. Ibid., 202–3.

74. Ibid., 176, 241.

75. Guyot, *La révision du procès Dreyfus*, 22.

76. Dreyfus, *La révision du procès Dreyfus: Débats*, 66; and *Le procès Dreyfus*, 81–82.

77. Dreyfus, *Le procès Dreyfus*, 179.

78. Halasz, *Captain Dreyfus*, 69.

79. Dreyfus, *La révision du procès Dreyfus: Enquête*, 137.

80. Quoted in Paléologue, *Journal de l'affaire Dreyfus*, 16.

81. Ibid., 18.

82. Quoted in D. L. Lewis, *Prisoners of Honor*, 93.

83. Archives nationales, BB19 84.

84. Gervais, Huret, and Peretz, "Une relecture du 'dossier secret,'" 131.

85. Archives nationales, BB19 108.

86. Maguire, "Oscar Wilde and the Dreyfus Affair," 11.

87. Ibid., 12.

88. Dreyfus, *La révision du procès Dreyfus: Enquête*, 598–99.

89. Dardenne-Cavaignac, *L'affaire Dreyfus*, 150.

90. Quoted in Gervais, Huret, and Peretz, "Une relecture du 'dossier secret,'" 141.

91. Musée d'art et d'histoire du Judaïsme.

92. Quoted in Burns, *France*, 116.

93. See Dreyfus, *La révision du procès Dreyfus: Enquête* 213; and Burns, *France*, 24.

94. Chapman, *Dreyfus Case*, 166; and Bredin, *Affair*, 219.

95. Bredin, *Affair*, 369.

96. D'Ormescheville, "Rapport sur l'affaire de M. Dreyfus," item 8. See also Dreyfus, *Le procès Dreyfus*, 16–17.

97. D. L. Lewis, *Prisoners of Honor*, 223.

98. Paléologue, *Journal de l'affaire Dreyfus*, 138.

99. Courouve, *Vocabulaire de l'homosexualité masculine*, 79.

100. Dardenne-Cavaignac, *L'affaire Dreyfus*, 57.

101. Quoted in ibid., 300.

102. Quoted in ibid., 300.

103. D. L. Lewis, *Prisoners of Honor*, 222.

104. Thomas, *L'affaire sans Dreyfus*, 55.
105. D. L. Lewis, *Prisoners of Honor*, 81.
106. Thomas, *L'affaire sans Dreyfus*, 45.
107. Ibid., 44.

3. SECRET DOSSIERS

1. Sedgwick, *Epistemology*, 177.
2. Proust, *In Search of Lost Time*, vol. 3, *The Guermantes Way*, 320–21; hereafter cited in text as *GW*.
3. Ibid., vol. 4, *Sodom and Gomorrah*, 146; hereafter cited in text as *SG*.
4. Ibid., vol. 2, *Within a Budding Grove*, 452; hereafter cited in text as *WBG*.
5. Shattuck, *Proust's Way*, 42.
6. Ibid.
7. J. Berman, *Modernist Fiction, Cosmopolitanism, and the Politics of Community*, 88.
8. McDonald, *Proustian Fabric*, 70.
9. Proust, *In Search of Lost Time*, vol. 7, *Time Regained* , 327–28; hereafter cited in text as *TR*.
10. Woods, "High Culture and High Camp," 127.
11. Arendt, *Origins of Totalitarianism*, 80.
12. Proust, *In Search of Lost Time*, vol. 5, *The Captive*, 536; hereafter cited in text as *C*.
13. Bersani, *Marcel Proust*, 61.
14. Genette, *Figures of Literary Discourse*, 256.
15. Courouve, *Vocabulaire de l'homosexualité masculine*, 102.
16. Genette, *Figures of Literary Discourse*, 216.
17. Ibid.
18. Proust, *In Search of Lost Time*, vol. 6, *The Fugitive*, 710; hereafter cited in text as *F*.
19. Ladenson, *Proust's Lesbianism*, 73–75.
20. Genette, *Figures of Literary Discourse*, 234.
21. P. Lewis, *Modernism, Nationalism, and the Novel*, 10.
22. Ibid., 153–55, 160.
23. Delhorbe, *L'affaire Dreyfus et les écrivains français*, 227.
24. J. Berman, *Modernist Fiction, Cosmopolitanism, and the Politics of Community*, 91.
25. Kaplan, "Refiguring the Jewish Question," 121.
26. P. Lewis, *Modernism, Nationalism, and the Novel*, 163.
27. Freedman, "Coming Out of the Jewish Closet with Marcel Proust," 537.
28. J. Berman, *Modernist Fiction, Cosmopolitanism, and the Politics of Community*, 91.
29. Bem, "Le juif et l'homosexuel," 103.
30. Ibid., 107.
31. Diamant, "Judaism, Homosexuality and Other Sign Systems," 180.
32. Sedgwick, *Epistemology*, 75
33. Kristeva, *Time and Sense*, 157.

34. Girard, *Deceit, Desire, and the Novel*, 224–25.

35. Rivers, "The Myth and Science of Homosexuality," 133–34.

36. Kristeva, *Time and Sense*, 98.

37. Girard, *Deceit, Desire, and the Novel*, 225.

38. Sprinker, *History and Ideology in Proust*, 114.

39. Girard, *Deceit, Desire, and the Novel*, 205.

40. J. Berman, *Modernist Fiction, Cosmopolitanism, and the Politics of Community*, 111–12.

41. Ibid., 112–13.

42. Ibid., 91.

43. Sedgwick, *Between Men*, 88–89.

44. Bem, "Le juif et l'homosexuel," 109.

45. J. Berman, *Modernist Fiction, Cosmopolitanism, and the Politics of Community*, 111.

46. Bredin, *Affair*, 529.

47. P. Lewis, *Modernism, Nationalism, and the Novel*, 150.

48. Bersani, *Homos*, 149; and P. Lewis, *Modernism, Nationalism, and the Novel*, 166.

49. P. Lewis, *Modernism, Nationalism, and the Novel*, 166.

50. Rivers, "The Myth and Science of Homosexuality," 224.

51. J. Berman, *Modernist Fiction, Cosmopolitanism, and the Politics of Community*, 74.

4. TRUTH BREATHING DOWN THE NECK OF FICTION

1. Maugham, *Escape from the Shadows*, 203.

2. Spears, *Poetry of W. H. Auden*, 34.

3. Auden, *English Auden*, 156; hereafter cited in text as *EA*.

4. James, "Auden's Achievement," 56.

5. Cunningham, *British Writers of the 1930s*, 2.

6. Bergonzi, *Reading the Thirties*, 138.

7. Cunningham, *British Writers of the 1930s*, 2.

8. Lehmann, *I Am My Brother*, 226.

9. Pudney, *Thank Goodness for Cake*, 45.

10. Davenport-Hines, *Auden*, 16.

11. Connolly, "Spy-mania," 748.

12. Quoted in Furbank, *E. M. Forster*, 237, 238.

13. Quoted in Carpenter, *W. H. Auden*, 291.

14. Lehmann, *I Am My Brother*, 30–31.

15. Davenport-Hines, *Auden*, 206.

16. Penrose and Freeman, *Conspiracy of Silence*, 115, fourth image following 296.

17. Connolly, *Enemies of Promise*, 214.

18. MacNeice, *Strings Are False*, 103–4.

19. Connolly, *Enemies of Promise*, 162.

20. Isherwood, *Lions and Shadows*, 75–76.

21. Bozorth, *Auden's Games of Knowledge*, 77.

22. Gardiner, "Auden," 16.

23. Isherwood, *Lions and Shadows*, 76.

24. Skelton, *Poetry of the Thirties*, 18.
25. Quoted in Spencer, "Sixteen Comments on Auden," 25.
26. Cunningham, *British Writers of the 1930s*, 208.
27. Ibid., 152.
28. Ibid., 153.
29. Ibid., 150–51.
30. Quoted in Spencer, "Sixteen Comments on Auden," 26–27.
31. Beach, *Making of the Auden Canon*, 16.
32. Blunt, "From Bloomsbury to Marxism," 164–65.
33. MacNeice, *Strings Are False*, 97.
34. Isherwood, *Kathleen and Frank*, 502.
35. Quoted in Carpenter, *W. H. Auden*, 243.
36. Orwell, *Inside the Whale*, 36.
37. Isherwood, *Lions and Shadows*, 43.
38. C. D. Lewis, *Buried Day*, 96.
39. Quoted in Carpenter, *W. H. Auden*, 308.
40. Auden, "Children of Abraham," 224–25.
41. Isherwood, *Lions and Shadows*, 23, 24.
42. Quoted in Cunningham, *British Writers of the 1930s*, 149.
43. Hoggart, *Auden*, 20.
44. Isherwood, *Lions and Shadows*, 248.
45. Spender, *Vienna*, 42.
46. Spears, *Poetry of W. H. Auden*, 15.
47. Cunningham, *British Writers of the 1930s*, 260.
48. Isherwood, *Christopher and His Kind*, 12.
49. Quoted in Mendelson, *Early Auden*, 59.
50. Southworth, *Sowing the Spring*, 147.
51. James, "Auden's Achievement," 54.
52. Connolly, *Enemies of Promise*, 219.
53. Pudney, *Thank Goodness for Cake*, 53.
54. MacNeice, *Strings Are False*, 103.
55. Auden, "How Not to Be a Genius," 348.
56. Connolly, *Enemies of Promise*, 253.
57. Bozorth, "'Whatever You Do Don't Go to the Wood,'" 114.
58. Spears, *Poetry of W. H. Auden*, 26.
59. See Fuller, *Reader's Guide to W. H. Auden*, 34.
60. Bozorth, *Auden's Games of Knowledge*, 34.
61. Auden, *Juvenilia*, 239.
62. O'Neill and Reeves, *Auden, MacNeice, Spender*, 9.
63. Bozorth, *Auden's Games of Knowledge*, 34.
64. Freud, "Psychoanalytic Notes on an Account of a Case of Paranoia," 43.
65. See Spears, *Poetry of W. H. Auden*, 34.
66. Ibid.
67. Callan, *Auden*, 80.

68. O'Neill and Reeves, *Auden, MacNeice, Spender*, 10–11.

69. Callan, *Auden*, 80.

70. See Davenport-Hines, *Auden*, 60; and Bozorth, *Auden's Games of Knowledge*, 110.

71. Bozorth, *Auden's Games of Knowledge*, 127.

72. Auden, *Collected Poems*, 123.

73. See Bozorth, *Auden's Games of Knowledge*, 51.

74. O'Neill and Reeves, *Auden, MacNeice, Spender*, 164.

75. Carpenter, *W. H. Auden*, 126.

76. Auden, *Forewords and Afterwords*, 294.

77. Isherwood to Forster, April 29, 1939. Christopher Isherwood Papers, box 121, folder 17.

78. Isherwood to Forster, September 27, 1939. Christopher Isherwood Papers, box 121, folder 17.

79. Richards, *Selected Letters*, 105.

80. Carpenter, *W. H. Auden*, 324.

81. Davenport-Hines, *Auden*, 221.

82. Auden to Isherwood, April 5, 1944. Christopher Isherwood Papers, 2996.

83. See Spears, *Poetry of W. H. Auden*, 63n13; and Spender, *W. H. Auden*, 151.

84. Gardiner, "Auden," 16.

85. Isherwood to Lehmann, October 31, 1940. Christopher Isherwood Papers, box 121, folder 20.

86. Isherwood to Spender, November 23, 1946. Christopher Isherwood Papers, box 122, folder 14.

87. Isherwood to Lehmann. December 26, 1940. Christopher Isherwood Papers, box 121, folder 20.

88. Quoted in Caserio, "Auden's New Citizenship," 93.

89. Ibid., 91.

90. Bozorth, *Auden's Games of Knowledge*, 208, 246.

91. Auden, *Collected Poems*, 845.

92. Auden to Isherwood, March 2, 1945. Christopher Isherwood Papers, 3002.

93. Spender, *W. H. Auden*, 131.

5. THE GANELON TYPE

1. Penrose and Freeman, *Conspiracy of Silence*, 237–38.

2. Boyle, *Fourth Man*, 174.

3. West and Tsarev, *Crown Jewels*, 128.

4. Boyle, *Fourth Man*, 304.

5. Sinclair, *Red and the Blue*, 88.

6. Sutherland, *Great Betrayal*, 59.

7. Quoted in Sinclair, *Red and the Blue*, 88.

8. FBI, *Philby/MacLean/Burgess*, 1b:168.

9. Ibid., 2a:5.

10. Ibid., 1c:35.

11. "Squalid Truth," *Sunday Pictorial*, 1.

12. Boyle, *Fourth Man*, 84.

13. Quoted in Carter, *Anthony Blunt*, 475.

14. Blunt, "Anthony Blunt."

15. Penrose and Freeman, *Conspiracy of Silence*, 364.

16. Ibid., 409.

17. Cecil, *Divided Life*, 110–11.

18. Sutherland, *Great Betrayal*, 49.

19. "Comment," *Observer*, 8.

20. Connolly, *Missing Diplomats*, 15.

21. Denby, "Another Country," 99.

22. Mouffe, "Hegemony and New Political Subjects," 94.

23. Banville, *Untouchable*, 287.

24. Quoted in Penrose and Freeman, *Conspiracy of Silence*, 205.

25. Quennell, foreword, 9.

26. Carter, *Anthony Blunt*, 58–59.

27. See Cunningham, *British Writers of the 1930s*, 348; Davenport-Hines, *Auden*, 276; and Carter, *Anthony Blunt*, 167.

28. FBI, *Philby/MacLean/Burgess*, 1b:189.

29. United Kingdom, National Archives, file 5:4.

30. FBI, *Philby/MacLean/Burgess*, 1b:103.

31. "Mr Auden's Statement," *Manchester Guardian*, 5.

32. Carpenter, *W. H. Auden*, 369.

33. Steiner, "The Cleric of Treason," 192.

34. Milmo, "Poet WH Auden Suspect in Soviet Spy Ring."

35. U.S. Congress, Cong. Rec. 10806 (1950).

36. D. Johnson, *Lavender Scare*, 7.

37. U.S. Congress, Cong. Rec. 1961 (1950); and D. Johnson, *Lavender Scare*, 16.

38. S. Doc. No. 4178, at 3.

39. Lerner, "Scandal in the State Department," part 1, 24.

40. See Dean, *Imperial Brotherhood*; and D. Johnson, *Lavender Scare*.

41. D'Emilio, *Sexual Politics, Sexual Communities*, 48–49.

42. Dean, *Imperial Brotherhood*, 68.

43. Waldeck, "Homosexual International," 137; hereafter cited in text.

44. U.S. Congress, Cong. Rec. A2652 (1950).

45. Lait and Mortimer, *Washington Confidential*, 95.

46. Schlesinger, *Vital Center*, 127.

47. S. Doc. No. 241, at 3.

48. U.S. Congress, Joint Committee on Atomic Energy, *Soviet Atomic Espionage*, 12.

49. U.S. Congress, Cong. Rec. 2900 (1947).

50. Towne, "Homosexuality in American Culture," 9.

51. Towne, "Sexual Gentlemen's Agreement," 28.

52. Towne, "Homosexuality in American Culture," 8.

53. Ibid., 9.

54. U.S. Congress, Cong. Rec. A3661 (1950).

55. Lait and Mortimer, *U.S.A. Confidential*, 43.

56. "Reds Plot D.C. Disaster?" *Washington Daily News*, 4.

57. Lerner, "Scandal in the State Department," part 4: 2, 26.

58. Quoted in S. Doc. No. 4179, at 7.

59. Dean, *Imperial Brotherhood*, 65.

60. Ibid., 265–66n37.

61. See Ross, *No Respect*, 46.

62. Nadel, *Containment Culture*, 16.

63. Dean, *Imperial Brotherhood*, 67.

64. Schlesinger, *Vital Center*, 126.

65. Lerner, "Scandal in the State Department," part 6, 7.

66. O'Donnell, "Capitol Stuff," C4.

67. S. Doc. No. 4178, at 1.

68. Quoted in Whitfield, *Culture of the Cold War*, 186.

69. Lerner, "Scandal in the State Department," part 2, 5; part 3, 34.

70. Corber, *Homosexuality in Cold War America*, 11.

71. Ibid., 63.

72. Lait and Mortimer, *U.S.A. Confidential*, 44, 45.

73. Brown, *Loyalty and Security*, 259.

74. D. Johnson, *Lavender Scare*, 119–21.

75. S. Doc. No. 241, at 2.

76. Fletcher to Boykin, "Proposed New Manual for Special Agents," 7–8.

77. S. Doc. No. 241, at 4.

78. U.S. Congress, Investigations Subcommittee, box 7, 2256.

79. Ibid., 2299–300.

80. S. Doc. No. 241, at 12.

81. U.S. Congress, Investigations Subcommittee, box 7, 2300.

82. Ibid., 2259.

83. Cherne, "How to Spot a Communist," 24–25.

84. West, *New Meaning of Treason*, 312.

85. Fiedler, *End to Innocence*, 18.

86. "Inexplicable Explanation," *Daily Telegraph*, 6.

87. "Kind of Folly," *Spectator*, 406.

88. Greene, *Confidential Agent*, 81–82.

89. Davenport-Hines, *Sex, Death and Punishment*, 300–301.

90. Ibid., 302; and Carter, *Anthony Blunt*, 355–56.

91. Boyle, *Fourth Man*, 404.

92. Carter, *Anthony Blunt*, 349.

93. "Theydunit," *Newsweek*, 22.

94. "Foreign Office Scandal," *Daily Mirror*, 1.

95. Carter, *Anthony Blunt*, xiv–xv.

96. Hofstadter, *Paranoid Style in American Politics*, 84.

97. Fiedler, *End to Innocence*, 81.

98. Ibid., 77.

99. Ibid., 78.

100. Hofstadter, *Paranoid Style in American Politics*, 97.

101. Ibid., 100.

6. STRICTLY A JEWISH SHOW

1. Committee to Secure Justice, *Rosenberg, Rosenberg, and Sobell*, 2172–73; hereafter cited in text as *RRS*.

2. Savran, "Theatre of the Fabulous," 133.

3. Epstein, "Anti-Communism, Homophobia, and Masculinity in the Postwar U.S.," 23.

4. Goren, *Politics and Public Culture of American Jews*, 186.

5. Riesman and Glazer, "Intellectuals and the Discontented Classes," 58.

6. See May, *Homeward Bound*, 9–11, 161.

7. Silk, "Notes on the Judeo-Christian Tradition in America," 65.

8. Moore, *GI Jews*, 121–23.

9. Quoted in Henry, "'And I Don't Care What It Is,'" 41.

10. Fiedler, *End to Innocence*, 59.

11. Lipset and Raab, *Politics of Unreason*, 240.

12. Hofstadter, *Paranoid Style in American Politics*, 70.

13. Lipset and Raab, *Politics of Unreason*, 240.

14. Plotke, "Introduction to the Transaction Edition," xxi.

15. Von Hoffman, *Citizen Cohn*, 175.

16. Kushner, *Angels in America*, part 2, *Perestroika*, 26; hereafter cited in text as *P*.

17. U.S. Congress, Cong. Rec. 4320 (1952).

18. Dean, *Imperial Brotherhood*, 262n14.

19. Hoover, "Crime of the Century," 151.

20. Goren, *Politics and Public Culture of American Jews*, 193.

21. Whitfield, *Culture of the Cold War*, 92.

22. Riesman and Glazer, "Intellectuals and the Discontented Classes," 67.

23. Fiedler, "What Can We Do About Fagin?" 412.

24. Moore, *GI Jews*, 272n52.

25. Goren, *Politics and Public Culture of American Jews*, 193.

26. Blankfort, "Education of a Jew," 40.

27. Ibid., 36–37.

28. Ibid., 40.

29. Moore, *GI Jews*, 9.

30. Breines, *Tough Jews*, 116.

31. Quoted in Robins, *Alien Ink*, 79.

32. Quoted in Morgan, "Rosenberg Jury," 132.

33. Smith, "National Security and Personal Isolation," 315.

34. Roberts, *Brother*, 274.

35. See Moore, "Reconsidering the Rosenbergs," 22, 32.

36. Ibid., 32.
37. Morgan, "Rosenberg Jury," 124.
38. Moore, "Reconsidering the Rosenbergs," 28.
39. Proust, *In Search of Lost Time*, vol. 2, *Within a Budding Grove*, 484.
40. Moore, "Reconsidering the Rosenbergs," 35.
41. Hoover, "Crime of the Century," 151.
42. "Death for the Atom Spies," *Los Angeles Times*, A4.
43. "Worse Than Murder," *Time*, 22; and Conklin, "Atom Spy Couple Sentenced to Die," 11.
44. Brennan, "Popular Images of American Women," 44.
45. Quoted in Schneir and Schneir, *Invitation to an Inquest*, 186.
46. See Brennan, "Popular Images of American Women," 62–63.
47. Ibid., 56.
48. Quoted in Morgan, "Rosenberg Jury," 127.
49. Brennan, "Popular Images of American Women," 59.
50. Cuordileone, *Manhood*, 78.
51. Quoted in Meeropol, "Rosenberg Realities," 241.
52. Philipson, *Ethel Rosenberg*, 302.
53. Meeropol, "Rosenberg Realities," 241.
54. Zion, *Autobiography of Roy Cohn*, 72, 77.
55. Von Hoffman, *Citizen Cohn*, 103.
56. "Last Appeal," *Time*, 7.
57. Reuben, "Not One Shred of Evidence," 4.
58. Breines, *Tough Jews*, 102–3.
59. Freedman, *Klezmer America*, 54.
60. U.S. Congress, Cong. Rec. 551 (1947).
61. Fiedler, *End to Innocence*, 25, 28.
62. Ibid., 42.
63. Ibid., 37.
64. Fineberg, *Rosenberg Case*, 121.
65. Suchoff, "The Rosenberg Case and the New York Intellectuals," 157.
66. Moore, "Reconsidering the Rosenbergs," 25–26.
67. Radosh and Milton, *Rosenberg File*, 411.
68. Garner, "*Angels in America*," 180.
69. Kushner, *Angels in America*, part 1, *Millennium Approaches*, 108; hereafter cited in text as *MA*.
70. Quoted in Rose, "Tony, Tonys, and Television," 46.
71. Quoted in Cadden, "Strange Angel," 83.
72. Roberts, *Brother*, 310.
73. Quoted in Lubow, "Tony Kushner's Paradise Lost," 60.
74. Kiefer, "*Angels in America* and the Failure of Revelation," 24.
75. Freedman, *Klezmer America*, 102.
76. Posnock, "Roy Cohn in America," 75.
77. Quinn, "Corpus Juris Tertium," 82.

78. Solomon, "Wrestling with *Angels*," 120.
79. Ibid., 129.
80. Freedman, *Klezmer America*, 49–50.
81. See Rosenberg, *Legacy of Rage*, 283.
82. Ogden, "Cold War Science and the Body Politic," 255–56.
83. Ibid., 255.
84. Breines, *Tough Jews*, 68–69.
85. Rosenberg, *Legacy of Rage*, 168, 184.
86. Malamud, *Tenants*, 229.
87. Cadden, "Strange Angel," 87.
88. Kushner, "Interview."
89. Kiefer, "*Angels in America* and the Failure of Revelation," 32.
90. Vorlicky, "Blood Relations," 46.
91. Stevenson, "'Seek for Something New,'" 759, 764.
92. Cadden, "Strange Angel," 87.
93. Freedman, "Angels, Monsters, and Jews," 97.
94. Ibid.
95. Rosenberg, *Legacy of Rage*, 273n5.
96. McNulty, "*Angels* Grounded," D1.
97. Savran, "Queering the Nation," 222.
98. Grenier, "With Roy, Ethel, and 'Angels,'" B3; and "Homosexual Millennium," 54–55.
99. Teachout, "Seven Ways of Looking at '*Angels*,'" D11.
100. Lioi, "Great Work Begins," 115n9.
101. Grenier, "With Roy, Ethel, and 'Angels,'" B3.
102. Grenier, "Homosexual Millennium," 56.
103. McLeod, "Oddest Phenomena in Modern History," 82–83.
104. Lioi, "Great Work Begins," 97.
105. Cohen, "Wrestling with Angels," 228.
106. Savran, "Theatre of the Fabulous," 133.
107. Solomon, "Wrestling with *Angels*," 120.
108. Freedman, *Klezmer America*, 43.
109. Savran, "Ambivalence, Utopia, and a Queer Sort of Materialism," 36.
110. Solomon, "Wrestling with *Angels*," 120.
111. Freedman, *Klezmer America*, 41.
112. See Lioi, "Great Work Begins," 110.
113. Ibid., 112.
114. Greenman, "Tony Kushner, Radical Pragmatist," 93.

CONCLUSION

1. Freedman, "Angels, Monsters, and Jews," 93.
2. Solomon, "Eternal Queer," 29.
3. Jakobsen, "Queers Are Like Jews, Aren't They?" 65.

4. Solomon, "Wrestling with *Angels*," 127.

5. Beirich, "New Crusaders," 20; and quoted in Solomon, "Wrestling with *Angels*," 122.

6. Walker, "CNN Fires Rick Sanchez."

7. Jakobsen, "Queers Are Like Jews, Aren't They?" 73.

8. Reuben, "Rosenberg Case," 1.

9. Schneir and Schneir, *Invitation to an Inquest*, 241.

10. Folkenflik, "NPR Ends Williams' Contract."

11. Kushner, *Angels in America*, part 1, *Millennium Approaches*, 89.

BIBLIOGRAPHY

Except where textual irregularities are significant, I have silently emended minor spelling and punctuation errors in quotations from unpublished letters and manuscripts. Where not otherwise indicated, translations are my own.

Archer, John Michael. *Sovereignty and Intelligence: Spying and Court Culture in the English Renaissance*. Stanford: Stanford University Press, 1993.

Archives nationales. Dossier de procédure de l'affaire Dreyfus (1875–1906). BB 19. Edited by H. Patry and J. Chaumié. Paris.

Arendt, Hannah. *The Origins of Totalitarianism: Antisemitism, Imperialism, Totalitarianism*. New York: Harcourt Brace Jovanovich, 1979.

Auden, W. H. "Children of Abraham." 1944. *Prose*, Vol. 2, *1939–1948*. Edited by Edward Mendelson. Princeton: Princeton University Pres, 2002.

——. *Collected Poems*. Edited by Edward Mendelson. New York: Vintage, 1991.

——. *The English Auden: Poems, Essays and Dramatic Writings, 1927–1939*. Edited by Edward Mendelson. London: Faber and Faber, 1977.

——. *Forewords and Afterwords*. Selected by Edward Mendelson. New York: Random House, 1973.

——. "How Not to Be a Genius." *New Republic*. April 26, 1939, 348, 350.

——. *Juvenilia: Poems, 1922–1928*. Edited by Katherine Bucknell. Princeton: Princeton University Press, 1994.

Banville, John. *The Untouchable*. New York: Knopf, 1997.

Barrès, Maurice. *Scènes et doctrines du nationalisme*. 1925. Paris: Trident, 1987.

Baumont, Maurice. *Aux sources de l'affaire*. Paris: Productions de Paris, 1959.

Beach, Joseph Warren. *The Making of the Auden Canon*. Minneapolis: University of Minnesota Press, 1957.

Beirich, Heidi. "The New Crusaders." *Intelligence Report* (Winter 2006): 18–27.

Bell, Tom W. "Treason, Technology, and Freedom of Expression." *Arizona State Law Journal* 37 (2005): 999–1045.

Bem, Jeanne. "Le juif et l'homosexuel dans À *la recherche du temps perdu.*" *Littérature* 37 (February 1980): 100–112.

Ben-Gurion, David and Jacob Blaustein. "An Exchange of Views." *American Jewish Year Book* 53 (1952): 564–68.

Bergonzi, Bernard. *Reading the Thirties: Texts and Contexts.* London: Macmillan, 1978.

Berman, David. *Gaiety Transfigured: Gay Self-Representation in American Literature.* Madison: University of Wisconsin Press, 1991.

Berman, Jessica. *Modernist Fiction, Cosmopolitanism, and the Politics of Community.* Cambridge: Cambridge University Press, 2001.

Bersani, Leo. *Homos.* Cambridge, Mass.: Harvard University Press, 1995.

——. *Marcel Proust: The Fictions of Life and of Art.* New York: Oxford University Press, 1965.

Billy, Robert de. *Marcel Proust: Lettres et conversations.* Paris: Portiques, 1930.

Bland, Lucy. "Trial by Sexology? Maud Allen, Salome and the Cult of the Clitoris Case." In *Sexology in Culture: Labelling Bodies and Desires.* Edited by Lucy Bland and Laura Doan. 183–98. Chicago: University of Chicago Press, 1998.

Blankfort, Michael. "The Education of a Jew." *American Mercury.* July 1953, 35–40.

Blunt, Anthony. "From Bloomsbury to Marxism." *Studio International* 186, no. 960 (November 1973): 164–68.

——. "Anthony Blunt: A Spy Case Package." First aired November 20, 1979. *The Cambridge Spies.* Directed by Tim Fywell. BBC Video, 2003. DVD.

Boyarin, Daniel. *Unheroic Conduct: The Rise of Heterosexuality and the Invention of the Jewish Man.* Berkeley: University of California Press, 1997.

Boyarin, Daniel, Daniel Itzkovitz, and Ann Pellegrini, eds. *Queer Theory and the Jewish Question.* New York: Columbia University Press, 2003.

Boyarin, Jonathan and Daniel Boyarin, eds. *Jews and Other Differences: The New Jewish Cultural Studies.* Minneapolis: University of Minnesota Press, 1997.

Boyle, Andrew. *The Fourth Man.* Original title *The Climate of Treason.* New York: Dial Press, 1979.

Bozorth, Richard. "'Whatever You Do Don't Go to the Wood': Joking, Rhetoric, and Homosexuality in *The Orators.*" In *W. H. Auden: "The Language of Learning and the Language of Love." Uncollected Writing, New Interpretations.* Edited by Katherine Bucknell and Nicholas Jenkins. 113–36. Oxford: Clarendon, 1994.

——. *Auden's Games of Knowledge: Poetry and the Meanings of Homosexuality.* New York: Columbia University Press, 2001.

Brandeis, Louis D. "The Jewish Problem: How to Solve It." 1915. In Mendes-Flohr and Reinharz, *The Jew in the Modern World,* 496–97.

Bray, Alan. *Homosexuality in Renaissance England.* London: Gay Men's Press, 1982.

Bredin, Jean-Denis. *The Affair: The Case of Alfred Dreyfus.* New York: Braziller, 1986.

Breines, Paul. *Tough Jews: Political Fantasies and the Moral Dilemma of American Jewry.* New York: Basic Books, 1990.

Brennan, Sheila M. "Popular Images of American Women in the 1950's and Their Impact on Ethel Rosenberg's Trial and Conviction." *Women's Rights Law Reporter* 14, no. 1 (Winter 1992): 43–63.

Brown, Ralph S. *Loyalty and Security: Employment Tests in the United States*. New Haven: Yale University Press, 1958.

Bunzl, Matti. "Book Review: Jews, Queers, and Other Symptoms: Recent Work in Jewish Cultural Studies." *GLQ* 6, no. 2 (2000): 321–41.

Burns, Michael. *France and the Dreyfus Affair: A Documentary History*. Boston: Bedford, 1999.

Cadden, Michael. "Strange Angel: The Pinklisting of Roy Cohn." In Geis and Kruger, *Approaching the Millennium*, 78–89.

Calendrier des Youtres. Paris: Librairie parisienne, 1899.

Callan, Edward. *Auden: A Carnival of Intellect*. New York: Oxford University Press, 1983.

Carlier, François. *La prostitution antiphysique*. 1887. Paris: Sycomore, 1981.

Carpenter, Humphrey. *W. H. Auden: A Biography*. London: George Allen and Unwin, 1981.

Carter, Miranda. *Anthony Blunt: His Lives*. New York: Farrar, Straus and Giroux, 2001.

Caserio, Robert. "Auden's New Citizenship." *Raritan* 17 (1997): 90–103.

Castelin, André-Louis. *Revue antisémite*. February 1, 1897. Paris: Parti français.

Cecil, Robert. *A Divided Life: A Biography of Donald Maclean*. London: Bodley Head, 1988.

Chapman, Guy. *The Dreyfus Case: A Reassessment*. London: Hart-Davis, 1955.

Cherne, Leo. "How to Spot a Communist." *Look*. March 4, 1947, 21–25.

Cheyette, Bryan. *Constructions of "the Jew" in English Literature and Society*. Cambridge: Cambridge University Press, 1993.

Cheyette, Bryan and Nadia Valman. "Introduction: Liberalism and Anti-Semitism." *The Image of the Jew in European Liberal Culture, 1789–1914*. Edited by Bryan Cheyette and Nadia Valman. 1–26. London: Vallentine Mitchell, 2004.

Churchill, Winston S. "Zionism Versus Bolshevism. A Struggle for the Soul of the Jewish People." *Illustrated Sunday Herald*. February 8, 1920, 5.

Cohen, Norman J. "Wrestling with Angels." In Vorlicky, *Tony Kushner in Conversation*, 217–30.

Committee to Secure Justice for Morton Sobell. *Rosenberg, Julius, Ethel Rosenberg, and Morton Sobell. Transcript of record. Supreme Court of the United States, October term, 1951. No. 111. Julius Rosenberg and Ethel Rosenberg, petitioners, v. the United States of America. No. 112. Morton Sobell, petitioner, v. the United States of America.* New York: Committee to Secure Justice for Morton Sobell, 1952.

Compagnon, Antoine. "Notice." In *À la recherche du temps perdu*. By Marcel Proust. Edited by Jean-Yves Tadié. 3:1185–261. Paris: Gallimard, 1988.

Conklin, William R. "Atom Spy Couple Sentenced To Die; Aide Gets 30 Years." *New York Times*. April 6, 1951, 1, 11.

Connolly, Cyril. *Enemies of Promise*. 1938. New York: Macmillan, 1948.

——. *The Missing Diplomats*. London: Queen Anne Press, 1952.

——. "Spy-Mania." *The New Statesman and Nation*. June 15, 1940, 748.

Corber, Robert J. *Homosexuality in Cold War America: Resistance and the Crisis of Masculinity*. Durham: Duke University Press, 1997.

Courouve, Claude. *Vocabulaire de l'homosexualité masculine*. Paris: Payot, 1985.

Crémieu-Foa, Ernest. *La campagne antisémitique: Les duels, les responsabilités*. Paris: Alcan-Lévy, 1892.

Crossfire. Directed by Edward Dmytryk. 1947. Turner Home Entertainment, 2005. DVD.

Cunningham, Valentine. *British Writers of the 1930s*. Oxford: Oxford University Press, 1988.

Cuordileone, K. A. *Manhood and American Political Culture in the Cold War*. New York: Routledge, 2005.

Daily Mirror. "Foreign Office Scandal." September 20, 1955, 1.

Daily Telegraph. "The Inexplicable Explanation." September 24, 1955, 6.

Dardenne-Cavaignac, Cécile. *L'affaire Dreyfus: Crise de conscience nationale*. Vol. 7. Unpublished manuscript. Paris: Bibliothèque Nationale, NAF 13499, n.d.

Davenport-Hines, Richard. *Sex, Death and Punishment: Attitudes to Sex and Sexuality in Britain since the Renaissance*. London: Collins, 1990.

——. *Auden*. New York: Pantheon, 1995.

Day Lewis, Cecil. *The Buried Day*. 1960. London: Chatto and Windus, 1969.

Dean, Robert D. *Imperial Brotherhood: Gender and the Making of Cold War Foreign Policy*. Amherst: University of Massachusetts Press, 2001.

Delhorbe, Cécile. *L'affaire Dreyfus et les écrivains français*. Neuchâtel, France: Victor Attinger, 1932.

Delrouze, Guy. "Le préjugé contre les moeurs: Son origine, sa valeur, ses dangers." *Akademos* 7–9 (July 15, 1909): 1–24.

D'Emilio, John. *Sexual Politics, Sexual Communities: The Making of a Homosexual Minority in the United States, 1940–1970*. Chicago: University of Chicago Press, 1983.

Denby, David. "Another Country." July 16, 1984. In *Film Review Annual, 1985*. Edited by Jerome S. Ozer. 98–99. Englewood, N.J.: Ozer, 1985.

Diamant, Naomi. "Judaism, Homosexuality and Other Sign Systems in *À la recherche du temps perdu*." *Romanic Review* 82, no. 2 (1991): 179–92.

Dinnerstein, Leonard. *Anti-Semitism in America*. New York: Oxford University Press, 1994.

Dobelbower, Nicholas. "Petits bleus et billets doux: Dangerous Correspondence(s) of the Dreyfus Affair." In *Intolerance and Indignation: L'affaire Dreyfus*. Edited by Jean-Max Guieu. 130–40. Paris: Fischbacher, 1999.

D'Ormescheville, Bexon. "Rapport sur l'affaire de M. Dreyfus (Alfred), capitaine breveté au 14ᵉ régiment d'artillerie, (etc. etc.)." November 3, 1894. *The Dreyfus Affair in the Making of Modern France: Rare Books and Pamphlets from the Dreyfus Collection of the Harvard College Library*. Edited by L. Scott Lerner. Cambridge, Mass.: Houghton Library, Harvard University, 1996.

Dreyfus, Alfred, defendant. *La révision du procès Dreyfus: Enquête de la Cour de cassation*. 2 vols. Paris: Stock, 1899.

——. *La révision du procès Dreyfus: Débats de la Cour de cassation*. Paris: Stock, 1899.

——. *Le procès Dreyfus devant le Conseil de guerre de Rennes (7 août–9 septembre 1899).* Compte rendu sténographique "in extenso" [Verbatim record "in full"]. 3 vols. Paris: Stock, 1900.

Drumont, Edouard. *La France juive: Essai d'histoire contemporarine.* 1886. Beirut: Éditions Charlemagne, 1994.

Dubarry, Armand. *Les invertis (Le vice allemand).* Paris: Chamuel, 1896.

Ebert, Isabelle. "'Le premier Dreyfusard': Jewishness in Marcel Proust." *French Review* 67, no. 2 (December 1993): 196–217.

Edelman, Lee. "Homographesis." *Yale Journal of Criticism* 3, no. 1 (Fall 1989): 189–207.

Endelman, Todd M. *The Jews of Britain, 1656 to 2000.* Berkeley: University of California Press, 2002.

Epstein, Barbara. "Anti-Communism, Homophobia, and the Construction of Masculinity in the Postwar U.S." *Critical Sociology* 20, no. 3 (1994): 21–44.

Evans-Gordon, William Eden. *The Alien Immigrant.* London: Heinemann, 1903.

The FBI Story. Directed by Mervyn LeRoy. 1959. Warner Home Video, 2006. DVD.

Federal Bureau of Investigation. *Philby, Kim/MacLean, Donald/Burgess, Guy (Cambridge Spy Ring).* Files 1a–9c. FBI Electronic Reading Room. Washington, D.C.

Fernandez, Dominique. "Sous l'œil de la police et de la médecine: L'homosexualité au XIXᵉ siècle." In *La prostitution antiphysique.* By François Carlier. i–ix. Paris: Sycomore, 1981.

Fiedler, Leslie. *An End to Innocence.* Boston: Beacon Press, 1955.

——. "What Can We Do About Fagin? The Jew-Villain in Western Tradition." *Commentary.* May 1949, 411–18.

Fineberg, Solomon Andhil. *The Rosenberg Case: Fact and Fiction.* New York: Oceana, 1953.

Fletcher, Travis L. to S. D. Boykin. "Proposed New Manual for Special Agents." February 29, 1952. SY-General 1952 folder, box 1, Security Division subject files, lot 53-D-233, BSCA, RG 59. National Archives and Records Administration. College Park, MD.

Folkenflik, David. "NPR Ends Williams' Contract After Muslim Remarks." NPR, October 21, 2010. http://www.npr.org/templates/story/story.php?storyId=130712737.

Ford, Henry. *The International Jew: The World's Foremost Problem: Being a Reprint of a Series of Articles Appearing in the "Dearborn Independent" from May 22 to October 2, 1920.* Dearborn, Mich.: Dearborn Publishing, 1920.

Franklin, Paul B. "Jew Boys, Queer Boys: Rhetorics of Antisemitism and Homophobia in the Trial of Nathan 'Babe' Leopold Jr. and Richard 'Dickie' Loeb." In Boyarin, Itzkovitz and Pellegrini, *Queer Theory and the Jewish Question,* 121–48.

Frantzen, Allen J. *Before the Closet: Same-Sex Love from "Beowulf" to "Angels in America."* Chicago: University of Chicago Press, 1998.

Fredrickson, George M. *Racism: A Short History.* Princeton: Princeton University Press, 2002.

Freedman, Jonathan. "Angels, Monsters, and Jews: Intersections of Queer and Jewish Identity in Kushner's *Angels in America.*" *PMLA* 113, no. 1 (January 1998): 90–102.

——. "Coming Out of the Jewish Closet with Marcel Proust." In Boyarin, Itzkovitz and Pellegrini, *Queer Theory and the Jewish Question,* 334–64.

——. *Klezmer America: Jewishness, Ethnicity, Modernity.* New York: Columbia University Press, 2008.

Freud, Sigmund. "Psychoanalytic Notes on an Autobiographical Account of a Case of Paranoia (Dementia Paranoides)." Translated by James Strachey. In *The Standard Edition of the Complete Psychological Works of Sigmund Freud.* 12:9–82. London: Hogarth Press, 1999.

Friedländer, Israel. "The Present Crisis of American Jewry." 1915. *Past and Present: Collected Essays.* Cincinnati: Ark, 1919. 341–3.

Fuller, John. *A Reader's Guide to W. H. Auden.* New York: Farrar, Straus and Giroux, 1970.

Furbank, P. N. *E. M. Forster: A Life.* New York: Harcourt Brace Jovanovich, 1977.

Garber, Marjorie and Rebecca L. Walkowitz, eds. *Secret Agents: The Rosenberg Case, McCarthyism, and Fifties America.* New York: Routledge, 1995.

Gardiner, Margaret. "Auden: A Memoir." *New Review* 3, no. 28 (July 1976): 9–19.

Garner, Stanton B., Jr. "*Angels in America*: The Millennium and Postmodern Memory." In Geis and Kruger, *Approaching the Millennium*, 173–84.

Geis, Deborah R. and Steven F. Kruger, eds. *Approaching the Millennium: Essays on "Angels in America."* Ann Arbor: University of Michigan Press, 1997.

Genette, Gérard. *Figures of Literary Discourse.* Translated by Alan Sheridan. New York: Columbia University Press, 1982.

Gentleman's Agreement. Directed by Elia Kazan. 1947. 20th Century Fox, 2003. DVD.

Gervais, Pierre, Romain Huret, and Pauline Peretz. "Une relecture du 'dossier secret': Homosexualité et antisémitisme dans l'affaire Dreyfus." *Revue d'histoire moderne et contemporaine* 55, no. 1 (January-March 2008): 125–60.

Gide, André. *Corydon.* 1924. Translated by Richard Howard. New York: Farrar, Straus and Giroux, 1983.

Gilman, Sander L. *Jewish Self-Hatred: Anti-Semitism and the Hidden Language of the Jews.* Baltimore: Johns Hopkins University Press, 1986.

Girard, René. *Deceit, Desire, and the Novel: Self and Other in Literary Structure.* 1961. Translated by Yvonne Freccero. Baltimore: Johns Hopkins University Press, 1965.

Goren, Arthur A. *The Politics and Public Culture of American Jews.* Bloomington: Indiana University Press, 1999.

Grand-Carteret, John. *L'affaire Dreyfus et l'image: 266 caricatures françaises et étrangères.* Paris: Flammarion, 1898.

——. *Derriére "lui" (L'homosexualité en Allemagne).* 1908. Lille, France: Cahiers Gai-Kitsch-Camp, 1992.

Greene, Graham. *The Confidential Agent.* 1939. London: Heinemann, 1971.

Greenman, Ben. "Tony Kushner, Radical Pragmatist." *Mother Jones.* November/December 2003, 92–3, 98.

Grenier, Richard. "The Homosexual Millennium: Is It Here? Is It Approaching?" *National Review.* June 7, 1993, 52–6.

——. "With Roy, Ethel, and 'Angels.'" *Washington Times.* April 18, 1993, B3.

Grousset, Pascal. *L'affaire Dreyfus et ses ressorts secrets: Précis historique.* Paris: Godet, 1899.

Guadalcanal Diary. Directed by Lewis Seiler. 1943. 20th Century Fox, 2002. DVD.

Guyot, Yves. *La révision du procès Dreyfus: Faits et documents juridiques*. Paris: Stock, 1898.

Halasz, Nicholas. *Captain Dreyfus: The Story of a Mass Hysteria*. New York: Simon and Schuster, 1955.

Henry, Patrick. "'And I Don't Care What It Is': The Tradition-History of a Civil Religion Proof-Text." *Journal of the American Academy of Religion* 49, no. 1 (March 1981): 35–49.

Hichens, Mark. *Oscar Wilde's Last Chance—The Dreyfus Connection*. Edinburgh: Pentland, 1999.

Hofstadter, Richard. *The Paranoid Style in American Politics and Other Essays*. New York: Knopf, 1966.

Hoggart, Richard. *Auden: An Introductory Essay*. New Haven: Yale University Press, 1951.

Holmes, Colin. *Anti-Semitism in British Society, 1876–1939*. London: Edward Arnold, 1979.

Hoover, J. Edgar. "The Crime of the Century." *Reader's Digest*. May 1951, 149–68.

Hyman, Paula E. "The Dreyfus Affair: The Visual and the Historical." *Journal of Modern History* 61, no. 1 (March 1989): 88–109.

——. "The French Jewish Community from Emancipation to the Dreyfus Affair." In *The Dreyfus Affair: Art, Truth, and Justice*. Edited by Norman Kleeblatt. 25–36. Berkeley: University of California Press, 1987.

Isherwood, Christopher. *Christopher and His Kind, 1929–1939*. New York: Farrar, Straus and Giroux, 1976.

——. *Kathleen and Frank*. New York: Simon and Schuster, 1971.

——. *Lions and Shadows: An Education in the Twenties*. Norfolk, Conn.: New Directions, 1947.

——. Papers. Huntington Library. San Marino, California.

Itzkovitz, Daniel. "Secret Temples." In Boyarin and Boyarin, *Jews and Other Differences*, 176–202.

Jakobsen, Janet R. "Queers Are Like Jews, Aren't They? Analogy and Alliance Politics." In Boyarin, Itzkovitz and Pellegrini, *Queer Theory and the Jewish Question*, 64–89.

James, Clive. "Auden's Achievement." *Commentary*. December 1973, 53–8.

Johnson, David K. *The Lavender Scare: The Cold War Persecution of Gays and Lesbians in the Federal Government*. Chicago: University of Chicago Press, 2004.

Johnson, Willis. "The Myth of Jewish Male Menses." *Journal of Medieval History* 24, no. 3 (1998): 273–95.

Kaplan, Morris B. "Refiguring the Jewish Question: Arendt, Proust, and the Politics of Sexuality." In *Feminist Interpretations of Hannah Arendt*. Edited by Bonnie Honig. 105–33. University Park: Pennsylvania State University Press, 1995.

Kettle, Michael. *Salome's Last Veil: The Libel Case of the Century*. London: Granada, 1977.

Kiefer, Daniel. "*Angels in America* and the Failure of Revelation." *American Drama* 4, no. 1 (Fall 1994): 21–38.

Kiernan, Victor Gordon. *The Duel in European History: Honour and the Reign of Aristocracy*. Oxford: Oxford University Press, 1988.

Kleeblatt, Norman L. "The Body of Alfred Dreyfus: A Site for France's Displaced Anxieties of Masculinity, Homosexuality and Power." In *Diaspora and Visual Culture*:

Representing Africans and Jews. 76–91. Edited by Nicholas Mirzoeff. London: Routledge, 2000.

Kristeva, Julia. *Time and Sense: Proust and the Experience of Literature*. Translated by Ross Guberman. New York: Columbia University Press, 1996.

Kushner, Tony. *Angels in America: A Gay Fantasia on National Themes*. 2 parts. New York: Theatre Communications Group, 1992–1994.

——. "Interview." *Heir to an Execution: A Granddaughter's Story*. Directed by Ivy Meeropol. HBO Home Video, 2004. DVD.

Ladenson, Elisabeth. *Proust's Lesbianism*. Ithaca: Cornell University Press, 1999.

Lait, Jack and Lee Mortimer. *U.S.A. Confidential*. New York: Crown, 1952.

——. *Washington Confidential*. New York: Crown, 1951.

Landy, Joshua. "Proust, His Narrator, and the Importance of the Distinction." *Poetics Today* 25, no. 1 (Spring 2004): 91–135.

Langlade, Jacques de. *La mésentente cordiale: Wilde-Dreyfus*. Paris: Éditions Julliard, 1994.

Lehmann, John. *I Am My Brother*. New York: Reynal, 1960.

Lerner, Max. "Scandal in the State Department." Twelve-part series. *New York Post*. July 10–22, 1950.

Levine, Wally. "Ten Ways to Spot a Homosexual." *Whisper*. August 1956, 24–25, 59–60.

Lewis, David Levering. *Prisoners of Honor: The Dreyfus Affair*. 1973. 2nd edition. New York: Holt, 1994.

Lewis, Pericles. *Modernism, Nationalism, and the Novel*. Cambridge: Cambridge University Press, 2000.

Lioi, Anthony. "The Great Work Begins: Theater as Theurgy in *Angels in America*." *Cross Currents* 54, no, 3 (Fall 2004) 96–117.

Lipset, Seymour Martin and Earl Raab. *The Politics of Unreason: Right-Wing Extremism in America, 1790–1977*. 2nd edition. Chicago: University of Chicago Press, 1978.

Los Angeles Times. "Death for the Atom Spies." April 6, 1951, A4.

Lubow, Arthur. "Tony Kushner's Paradise Lost." *New Yorker*. November 30, 1992, 59–64.

Macaulay, Thomas Babington. "Civil Disabilities of the Jews." *Critical and Historical Essays*. 2:225–36. London: Dent, 1907.

MacNeice, Louis. *The Strings Are False: An Unfinished Autobiography*. 1941. New York: Oxford University Press, 1966.

Maguire, J. Robert. "Oscar Wilde and the Dreyfus Affair." *Victorian Studies* 41, no. 1 (Autumn 1997): 1–30.

Malamud, Bernard. *The Tenants*. New York: Farrar, Straus and Giroux, 1971.

Manchester Guardian. "Mr Auden's Statement." June 11, 1951, 5.

Marrus, Michael R. *The Politics of Assimilation*. Oxford: Clarendon, 1971.

Maugham, Robin. *Escape from the Shadows*. London: Hodder and Stoughton, 1972.

May, Elaine Tyler. *Homeward Bound: American Families in the Cold War Era*. 1988. Twentieth-anniversary edition. New York: Basic Books, 2008.

Mayeur, Jean-Marie. "Les catholiques français." In *L'affaire Dreyfus de A à Z*. Edited by Michel Drouin. 330–41. Paris: Flammarion, 1994.

Mayne, Xavier [Edward Irenaeus Prime Stevenson]. *The Intersexes: A History of Similisexualism as a Problem in Social Life*. 1908. New York: Arno, 1975.

McDonald, Christie. *The Proustian Fabric: Associations of Memory*. Lincoln: University of Nebraska Press, 1991.

McFarlane, Cameron. *The Sodomite in Fiction and Satire, 1660–1750*. New York: Columbia University Press, 1997.

McLeod, Bruce. "The Oddest Phenomena in Modern History." In Vorlicky, *Tony Kushner in Conversation*, 77–84.

McNulty, Charles. "*Angels* Grounded." *Los Angeles Times*. October 29, 2010, D1.

Meeropol, Robert. "Rosenberg Realities." In Garber and Walkowitz, *Secret Agents*, 235–51.

Mendelson, Edward. *Early Auden*. New York: Viking, 1981.

Mendes-Flohr, Paul and Jehuda Reinharz, eds. *The Jew in the Modern World*. 2nd edition. New York: Oxford University Press, 1995.

Milmo, Cahal. "Poet WH Auden Suspect in Soviet Spy Ring, Documents Reveal." *New Zealand Herald*. March 2, 2007.

Moore, Deborah Dash. *GI Jews: How World War II Changed a Generation*. Cambridge, Mass.: Belknap, 2004.

——. "Reconsidering the Rosenbergs: Symbol and Substance in Second Generation American Jewish Consciousness." *Journal of American Ethnic History* 8, no. 1 (Fall 1988) 21–37.

Morgan, Ted. "The Rosenberg Jury." *Esquire*. May 1975, 105–32.

Mouffe, Chantal. "Hegemony and New Political Subjects: Toward a New Concept of Democracy." Translated by Stanley Gray. In *Marxism and the Interpretation of Culture*. Edited by Cary Nelson and Lawrence Grossberg. 89–104. Urbana: University of Illinois Press, 1988.

Musée d'art et d'histoire du Judaïsme. Dreyfus Collection. Paris.

Nadel, Alan. *Containment Culture: American Narratives, Postmodernism, and the Atomic Age*. Durham: Duke University Press, 1995.

Newsweek. "Theydunit." July 15, 1963, 22, 25.

Noah, Mordecai Manuel. "Proclamation to the Jews." September 15, 1825. In "Some Early American Zionist Projects." By Max J. Kohler. *Publications of the American Jewish Historical Society* 8 (1900): 106–13.

Nordau, Anna and Max Nordau. *Max Nordau: A Biography*. New York: Nordau Committee, 1943.

Observer. "Comment." September 25, 1955, 8.

O'Donnell, John. "Capitol Stuff." *Daily News*. March 27, 1950, C4.

Ogden, Daryl. "Cold War Science and the Body Politic: An Immuno/Virological Approach to *Angels in America*." *Literature and Medicine* 19, no. 2 (Fall 2000) 241–61.

O'Neill, Michael and Gareth Reeves. *Auden, MacNeice, Spender: The Thirties Poetry*. New York: St. Martin's Press, 1992.

Orwell, George. *Inside the Whale and Other Essays*. Harmondsworth: Penguin, 1957.

Paléologue, Maurice. *Journal de l'affaire Dreyfus*. Paris: Plon, 1955.

Pearson, Drew. "Here Wilson Sides with Labor." *Washington Post*. July 17, 1951, B13.

Pellegrini, Ann. "Whiteface Performances: 'Race,' Gender, and Jewish Bodies." In Boyarin and Boyarin, *Jews and Other Differences*, 108–49.

Penrose, Barrie and Simon Freeman. *Conspiracy of Silence: The Secret Life of Anthony Blunt*. London: Grafton, 1986.

Pepys, Samuel. *The Diary of Samuel Pepys*. Edited by Robert Latham and William Matthews. Vol. 4. Berkeley: University of California Press, 1983.

Peter, Jean-Pierre. "Dimensions de l'affaire Dreyfus." *Annales economie sociétés civilisations* 6 (November-December 1961): 1141–67.

Philipson, Ilene. *Ethel Rosenberg: Beyond the Myths*. New York: Franklin Watts, 1988.

Plotke, David. "Introduction to the Transaction Edition (2001): The Success and Anger of the Modern American Right." In *The Radical Right*. Edited by Daniel Bell. 3rd edition. xi–lxxix. New Brunswick: Transaction, 2002.

Posnock, Ross. "Roy Cohn in America." *Raritan* 13, no. 3 (Winter 1994): 64–77.

Press, Jacob. "You Go, Figure; or, the Rape of a Trope in the 'Prioress's Tale.'" In Boyarin, Itzkovitz, and Pellegrini, *Queer Theory and the Jewish Question*, 285–310.

Proust, Marcel. *À la recherche du temps perdu*. Edited by Jean-Yves Tadié. Vol. 2. *Le côté de Guermantes I*. Paris: Gallimard, 1988.

——. *In Search of Lost Time*. 1913–1927. Translated by C. K. Scott Moncrieff and Terence Kilmartin. Revised by D. J. Enright. 6 vols. New York: Modern Library, 1992–1993.

Pudney, John. *Thank Goodness for Cake*. London: Michael Joseph, 1978.

Quennell, Peter. Foreword to *The Missing Diplomats*. By Cyril Connolly. 5–10. London: Queen Anne Press, 1952.

Quinn, John R. "Corpus Juris Tertium: Redemptive Jurisprudence in *Angels in America*." *Theatre Journal* 48, no. 1 (March 1996): 79–90.

Radosh, Ronald and Joyce Milton. *The Rosenberg File*. 2nd edition. New Haven: Yale University Press, 1997.

Raffalovich, Marc-André. *Uranisme et unisexualité: Étude sur différentes manifestations de l'instinct sexuel*. Lyon: Storck, 1896.

Reinach, Joseph. *L'affaire Dreyfus*. Vol. 1, *Vers la justice par la vérité*. Paris: Stock, 1898.

Reinach, Salomon. "La prétendue race juive." *Revue des études juives* 47 (December 6, 1903): 1–14.

Reizbaum, Marilyn. *James Joyce's Judaic Other*. Stanford: Stanford University Press, 1999.

Reuben, William A. "Not One Shred of Evidence Presented by U.S. to Back Up Its Charges." *National Guardian*. September 19, 1951, 4–5.

——. "The Rosenberg Case: These Are the Facts." *National Guardian*. August 22, 1951, 1, 3.

Rey, Michel. "Parisian Homosexuals Create a Lifestyle, 1700–1740: The Police Archives." Translated by Robert A. Day and Robert Welch. In *'Tis Nature's Fault: Unauthorized Sexuality During the Enlightenment*. Edited by Robert P. Maccubbin. 179–91. Cambridge: Cambridge University Press, 1987.

Richards, I. A. *Selected Letters of I.A. Richards*. Edited by John Constable. Oxford: Clarendon, 1990.

Riesman, David and Nathan Glazer. "The Intellectuals and the Discontented Classes." *Partisan Review* (Winter 1955): 47–72.

Riggi, John. "Stone Mountain." *30 Rock*. Season 4, episode 3. Directed by John Scardino. Aired October 29, 2009. NBC.

Rivers, J. E. "The Myth and Science of Homosexuality in *À la recherche du temps perdu*." In *Homosexualities and French Literature*. Edited by George Stambolian and Elaine Marks. 262–78. Ithaca: Cornell University Press, 1979.

Roberts, Sam. *The Brother*. New York: Random House, 2001.

Robins, Natalie. *Alien Ink: The FBI's War on Freedom of Expression*. New York: William Morrow, 1992.

Rose, Charlie. "Tony, Tonys, and Television." In Vorlicky, *Tony Kushner in Conversation*, 44–50.

Rosenberg, Warren. *Legacy of Rage: Jewish Masculinity, Violence, and Culture*. Amherst: University of Massachusetts Press, 2001.

Rosenstock, Bruce. "Messianism, Machismo and 'Marranism': The Case of Abraham Miguel Cardoso." In Boyarin, Itzkovitz, and Pellegrini, *Queer Theory and the Jewish Question*, 199–227.

Ross, Andrew. *No Respect: Intellectuals and Popular Culture*. New York: Routledge, 1989.

Saint-Paul, Georges [Dr. Laupts]. *L'homosexualité et les types homosexuels*. Paris: Vigot Frères, 1910.

Saurel, Elie-Noël. "Nouvelles chansons antijuives." Paris: Le Forgeron patriote, 1899. FC9 D8262 Zzx2, Houghton Library, Harvard University.

Savran, David. "Ambivalence, Utopia, and a Queer Sort of Materialism: How *Angels in America* Reconstructs the Nation." In Geis and Kruger, *Approaching the Millennium*, 13–39.

——. "Queering the Nation." *Performing America: Cultural Nationalism in American Theater*. Edited by Jeffrey D. Mason and Ellen J. Gainor. 210–29. Ann Arbor: University of Michigan Press, 1999.

——. "The Theatre of the Fabulous." In *Essays on Kushner's "Angels."* Edited by Per Brask. 129–54. Winnipeg: Blizzard, 1995.

Schlesinger, Arthur M., Jr. *The Vital Center: The Politics of Freedom*. Boston: Houghton Mifflin, 1949.

Schneir, Walter and Miriam Schneir. *Invitation to an Inquest*. Garden City, N.Y.: Doubleday, 1965.

Sedgwick, Eve Kosofsky. *Between Men: English Literature and Male Homosocial Desire*. New York: Columbia University Press, 1985.

——. *Epistemology of the Closet*. Berkeley: University of California Press, 1990.

Selzer, Michael, ed. *Kike! A Documentary History of Anti-Semitism in America*. New York: Meridian, 1972.

Service historique de la Défense, département de l'armée de Terre. Dossier affaire Dreyfus. Microfilm 5ye59615. Vincennes, France.

Shattuck, Roger. *Proust's Way: A Field Guide to "In Search of Lost Time."* New York: Norton, 2000.

Silk, Mark. "Notes on the Judeo-Christian Tradition in America." *American Quarterly* 36, no. 1 (Spring 1984): 65–85.

Sinclair, Andrew. *The Red and the Blue: Cambridge, Treason, and Intelligence.* Boston: Little, Brown, 1986.

Skelton, Robin, ed. *Poetry of the Thirties.* Harmondsworth: Penguin, 1964.

Smith, Geoffrey. "National Security and Personal Isolation: Sex, Gender, and Disease in the Cold-War United States." *International History Review* 14, no. 2 (May 1992): 307–37.

Solomon, Alisa. "The Eternal Queer." *Village Voice*, April 27, 1993, 29, 34.

——. "Wrestling with *Angels*: A Jewish Fantasia." In Geis and Kruger, *Approaching the Millennium,* 118–33.

Southworth, James G. *Sowing the Spring: Studies in British Poets from Hopkins to MacNeice.* Oxford: Blackwell, 1940.

Spears, Monroe K. *The Poetry of W. H. Auden: The Disenchanted Island.* New York: Oxford University Press, 1963.

Spectator. "A Kind of Folly." September 30, 1955, 406.

Spencer, Bernard. "Sixteen Comments on Auden." *New Verse* 26–27 (November 1937): 23–31.

Spender, Stephen. *Journals, 1939–1983.* Edited by John Goldsmith. London: Faber and Faber, 1985.

——. *Vienna.* London: Faber and Faber, 1934.

——, ed. *W. H. Auden: A Tribute.* New York: Macmillan, 1975.

Sprinker, Michael. *History and Ideology in Proust: "À la recherche du temps perdu" and the Third French Republic.* Cambridge: Cambridge University Press, 1994.

Steiner, George. "The Cleric of Treason." *New Yorker,* December 8, 1980, 158–95.

——. "Totem and Taboo." *Salmagundi* 88, no. 89 (Fall 1990–Winter 1991): 385–98.

Stevenson, Catherine. " 'Seek for Something New': Mothers, Change, and Creativity in Tony Kushner's *Angels in America, Homebody/Kabul,* and *Caroline, or Change.*" *Modern Drama* 48, no. 4 (Winter 2005): 758–76.

Suchoff, David. "The Rosenberg Case and the New York Intellectuals." In Garber and Walkowitz, *Secret Agents,* 155–69.

Sunday Pictorial. "The Squalid Truth." September 25, 1955, 1.

Sutherland, Douglas. *The Great Betrayal: The Definitive Story of Blunt, Philby, Burgess, and Maclean.* New York: Times Books, 1980.

Symonds, John Addington. *The Letters of John Addington Symonds, 1885–1893.* Edited by Herbert M. Schueller and Robert L. Peters. Vol. 3. Detroit: Wayne State University Press, 1969.

Teachout, Terry. "Seven Ways of Looking at 'Angels.' " *Wall Street Journal.* October 29, 2010, D11.

Thoinot, Léon-Henri. *Attentats aux moeurs et perversion du sens génital.* 1898. Translated and enlarged as *Medicolegal Aspects of Moral Offenses* by Arthur W. Weysse. Philadelphia: Davis, 1923.

Thomas, Marcel. *L'affaire sans Dreyfus.* Paris: Librairie Arthème Fayard, 1971.

Timayenis, Telemachos Thomas. *The American Jew: An Exposé of His Career.* New York: Minerva, 1888.

Time. "The Last Appeal." June 29, 1953, 7–10.

——. "Worse Than Murder." April 16, 1951, 22–23.

Times (London). "Bolshevist Portraits." March 29, 1919, 10.

Towne, Alfred. "Homosexuality in American Culture: The New Taste in Literature." *American Mercury*. August 1951, 3–9.

——. "Sexual Gentlemen's Agreement." *Neurotica* 6 (Spring 1950): 23–8.

Trumbach, Randolph. "London's Sodomites: Homosexual Behavior and Western Culture in the Eighteenth Century." *Journal of Social History* 11, no. 1 (1977): 1–33.

United Kingdom, National Archives. "Auden, Wystan." KV/2/2588, files 1–16.

U.S. Congress. *Congressional Record*. 80th Cong., 1st sess. 1947. Vol. 93, parts 1, 3.

——. *Congressional Record*. 81st Cong., 2nd sess. 1950. Vol. 96, parts 2, 8, 15.

——. *Congressional Record*. 82th Cong., 2nd sess. 1952. Vol. 98, parts 4, 10.

U.S. Congress. Investigations Subcommittee, Committee on Expenditures in the Executive Departments. Permanent Subcommittee on Investigations. Executive Hearings (14 July 1950–26 July 1950). Boxes 6 and 7. Washington, D.C.: National Archives and Records Administration.

U.S. Congress. Joint Committee on Atomic Energy. *Soviet Atomic Espionage*. 82nd Cong., 1st sess. Washington, D.C.: Government Printing Office, 1951.

"Virginia Statute for Religious Freedom." 1786. In *Documents of American Constitutional and Legal History*. Vol. 1, *From the Founding Through the Age of Industrialization*. Edited by Melvin I. Urofsky and Paul Finkelman. 2nd edition. 73–75. New York: Oxford University Press, 2002.

Von Hoffman, Nicholas. *Citizen Cohn*. New York: Doubleday, 1988.

Vorlicky, Robert. "Blood Relations: Adrienne Kennedy and Tony Kushner." In *Tony Kushner: New Essays on the Art and Politics of the Plays*. Edited by James Fisher. 41–55. Jefferson, N.C.: McFarland, 2006.

——, ed. *Tony Kushner in Conversation*. Ann Arbor: University of Michigan Press, 1998.

Waldeck, Rosa Goldschmidt. "Homosexual International." *Human Events* 9, no. 16 (April 16, 1952): 137–40.

Walker, Hunter. "CNN Fires Rick Sanchez After His Radio Meltdown." *TheWrap* .*com*. October 1, 2010. http://www.thewrap.com/tv/column-post/breaking-cnn-fires-rick-sanchez-21390.

Washington Daily News. "Reds Plot D.C. Disaster?" May 20, 1950, 4.

Washington, George. "Reply to the Hebrew Congregation in Newport, Rhode Island." August 17, 1790. In Lewis Abraham, "Correspondence Between Washington and Jewish Citizens." *Proceedings of the American Jewish Historical Society* 3 (1894): 91–92.

Weindel, Henri de and F.-P. Fischer. *L'homosexualité en Allemagne*. Paris: Félix Juven, 1908.

Weininger, Otto. *Sex and Character*. 1902. 6th edition. London: Heinemann, 1906.

West, Nigel and Oleg Tsarev. *The Crown Jewels: The British Secrets at the Heart of the KGB Archives*. New Haven: Yale University Press, 1999.

West, Rebecca. *The Meaning of Treason*. New York: Viking, 1947.

——. *The New Meaning of Treason*. New York: Viking, 1964.

White, Arnold. "Efficiency and Vice." *English Review* 22 (June 1918): 446–52.

Whitfield, Stephen J. *The Culture of the Cold War*. Baltimore: Johns Hopkins University Press, 1991.

Wilkinson, Lynn R. "Proust and the Dreyfus Affair." *MLN* 107, no. 5 (December 1992): 976–99.

Woods, Gregory. *Articulate Flesh: Male Homo-Eroticism and Modern Poetry*. New Haven: Yale University Press, 1987.

——. "High Culture and High Camp: The Case of Marcel Proust." In *Camp Grounds: Style and Homosexuality*. Edited by David Bergman. 121–33. Amherst: University of Massachusetts Press, 1993.

Zion, Sidney. *The Autobiography of Roy Cohn*. Secaucus, N.J.: Lyle Stuart, 1988.

Zola, Emile. *J'accuse . . . ! La vérité en marche*. 1898. Brussels: Complexe, 1988.

——, defendant. *L'affaire Dreyfus. Le procès Zola devant la Cour d'assises de la Seine (7 février–23 février 1898)*. Compte rendu sténographique "in extenso" [Verbatim record "in full"]. Paris: Éditions du siècle, 1898.

INDEX

Page numbers in boldface indicate photographs, and the designation "n" after a page number indicates footnotes.